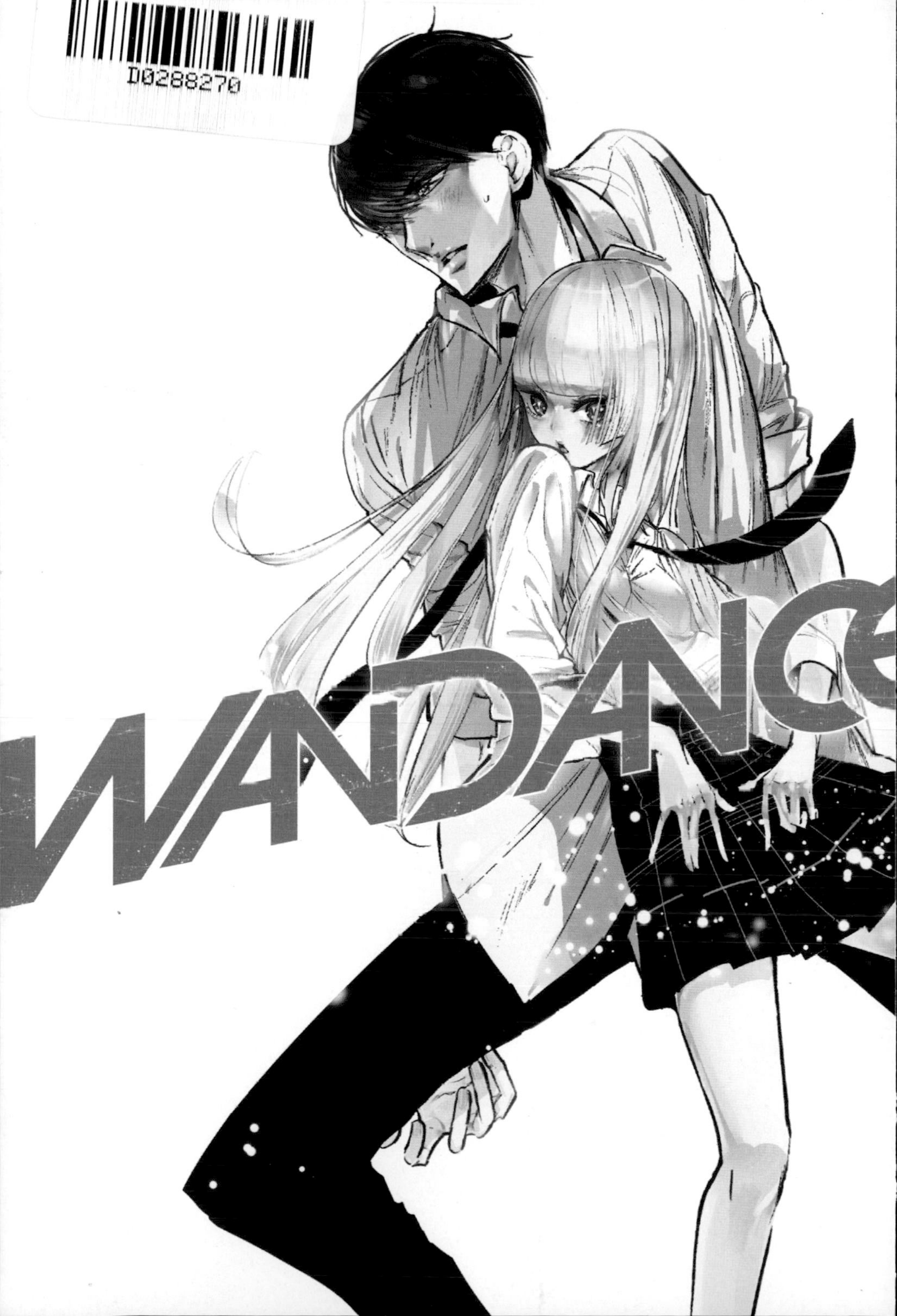
WANDANC

CONTENTS

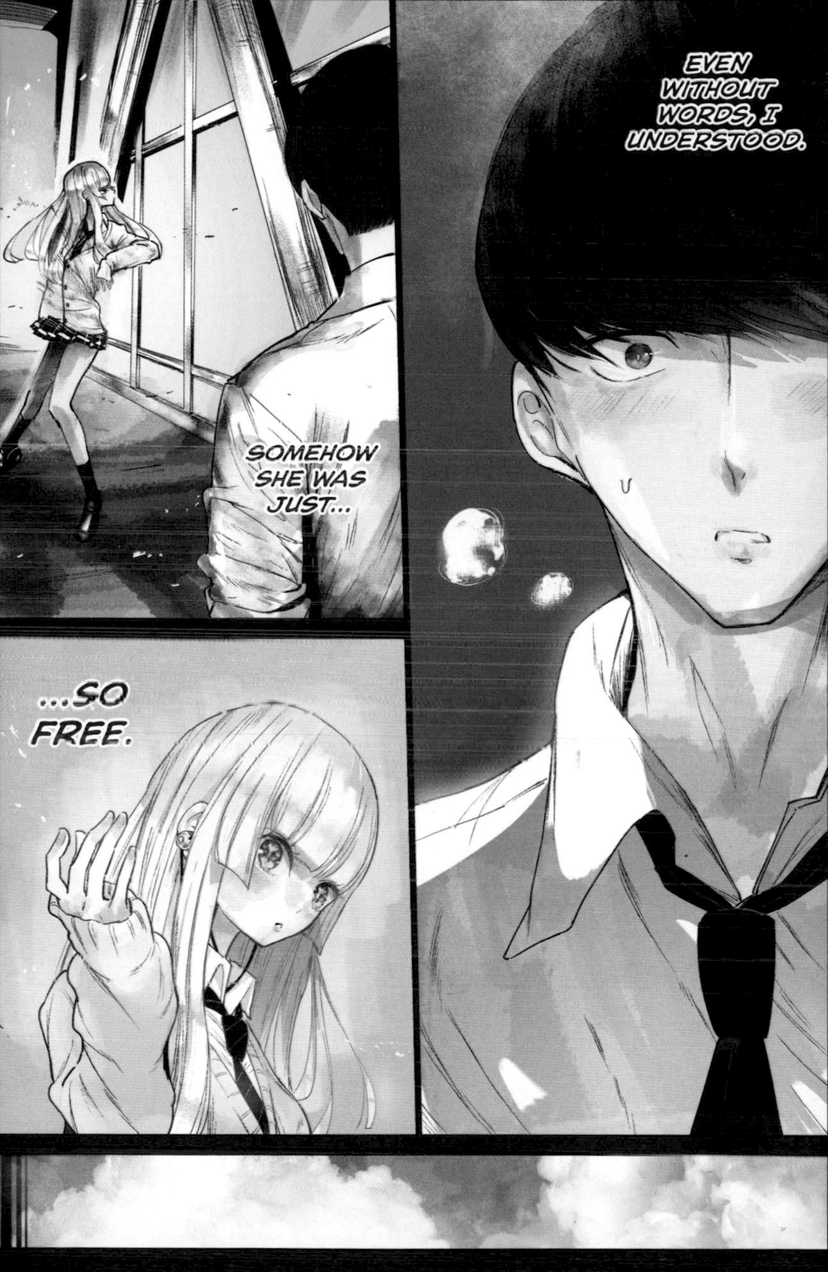

EVEN WITHOUT WORDS, I UNDERSTOOD.
SOMEHOW SHE WAS JUST...
...SO FREE.

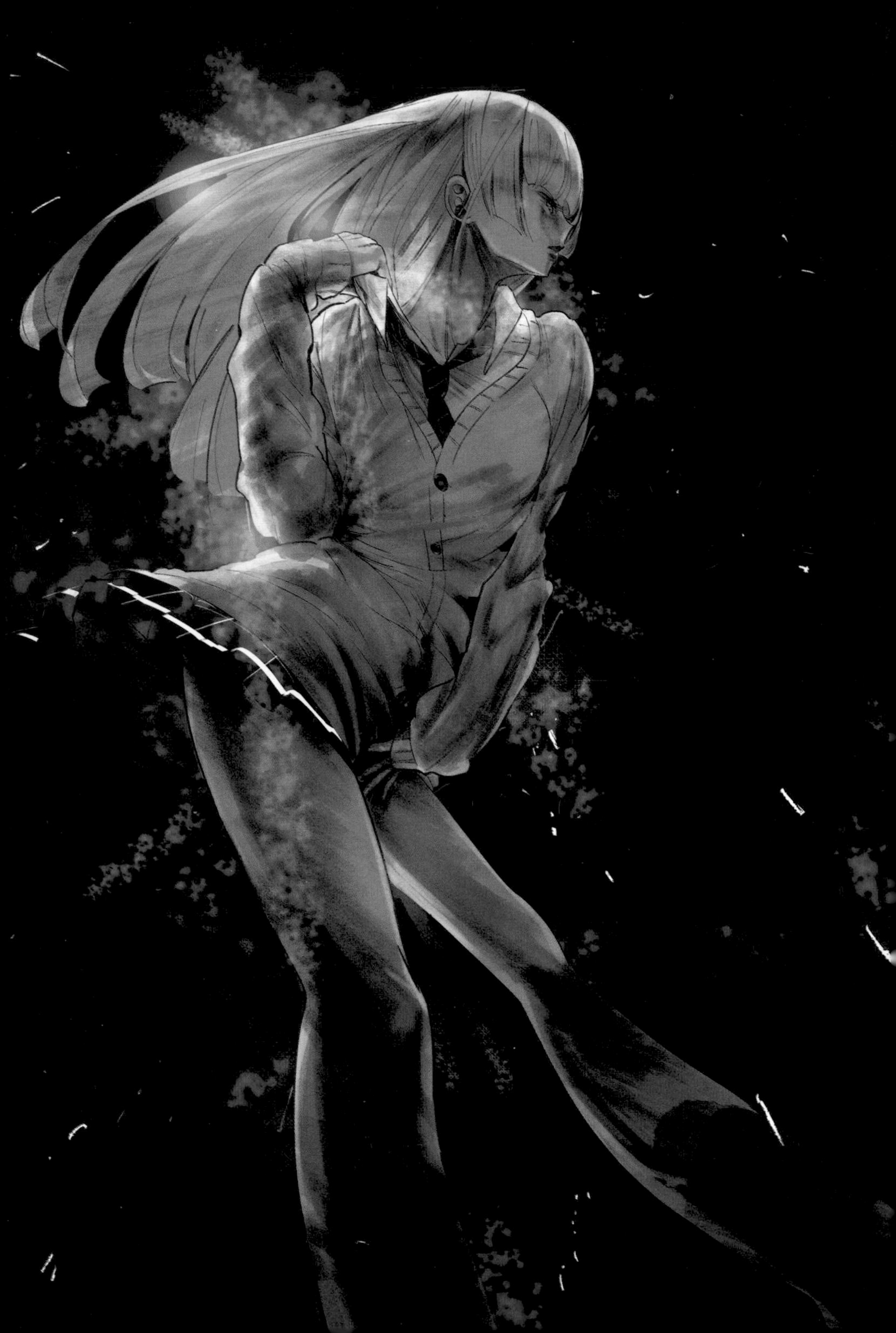

Ch. 1: How Wanda-san Dances

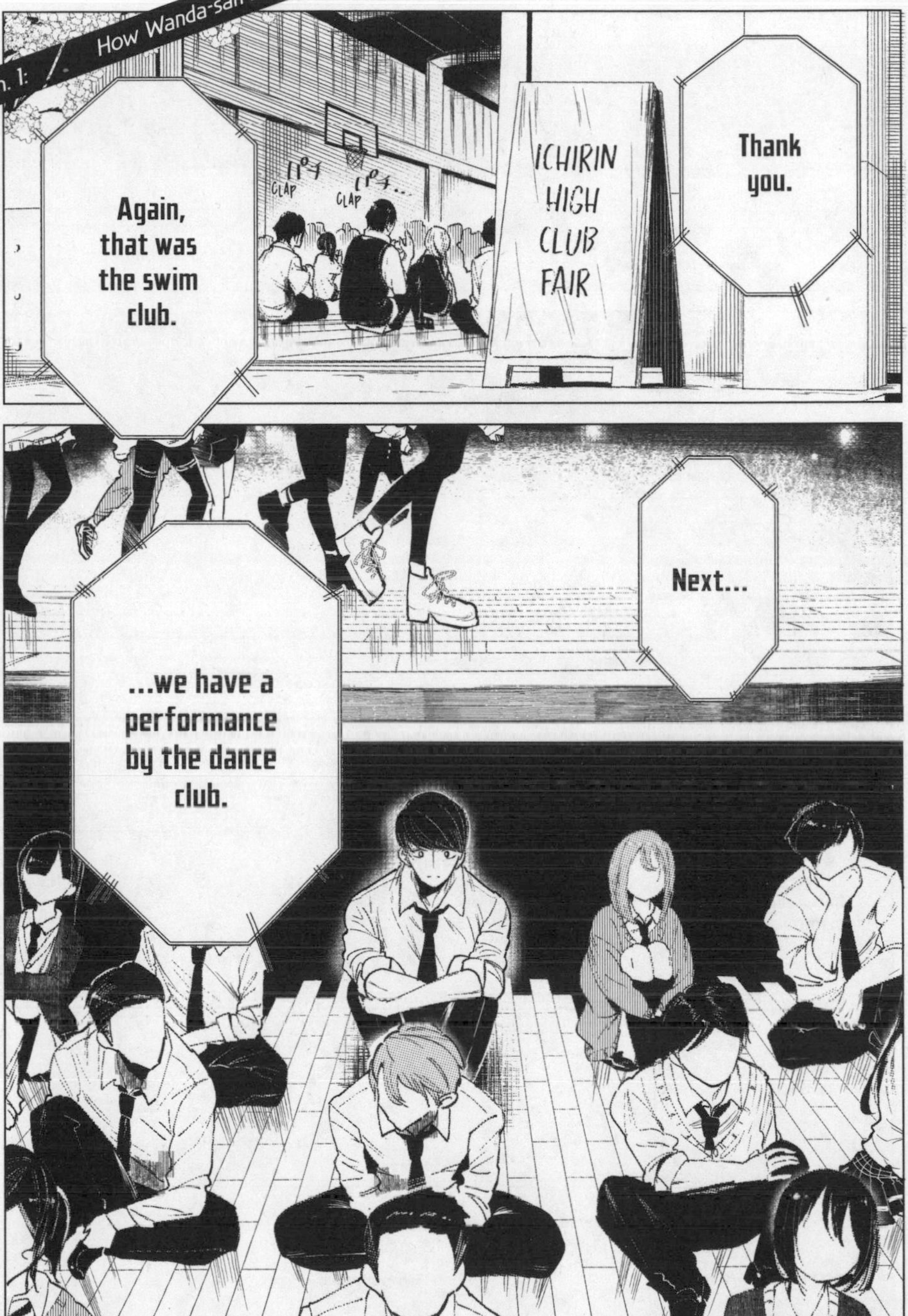
Thank you.
ICHIRIN HIGH CLUB FAIR
CLAP
CLAP
Again, that was the swim club.
Next...
...we have a performance by the dance club.

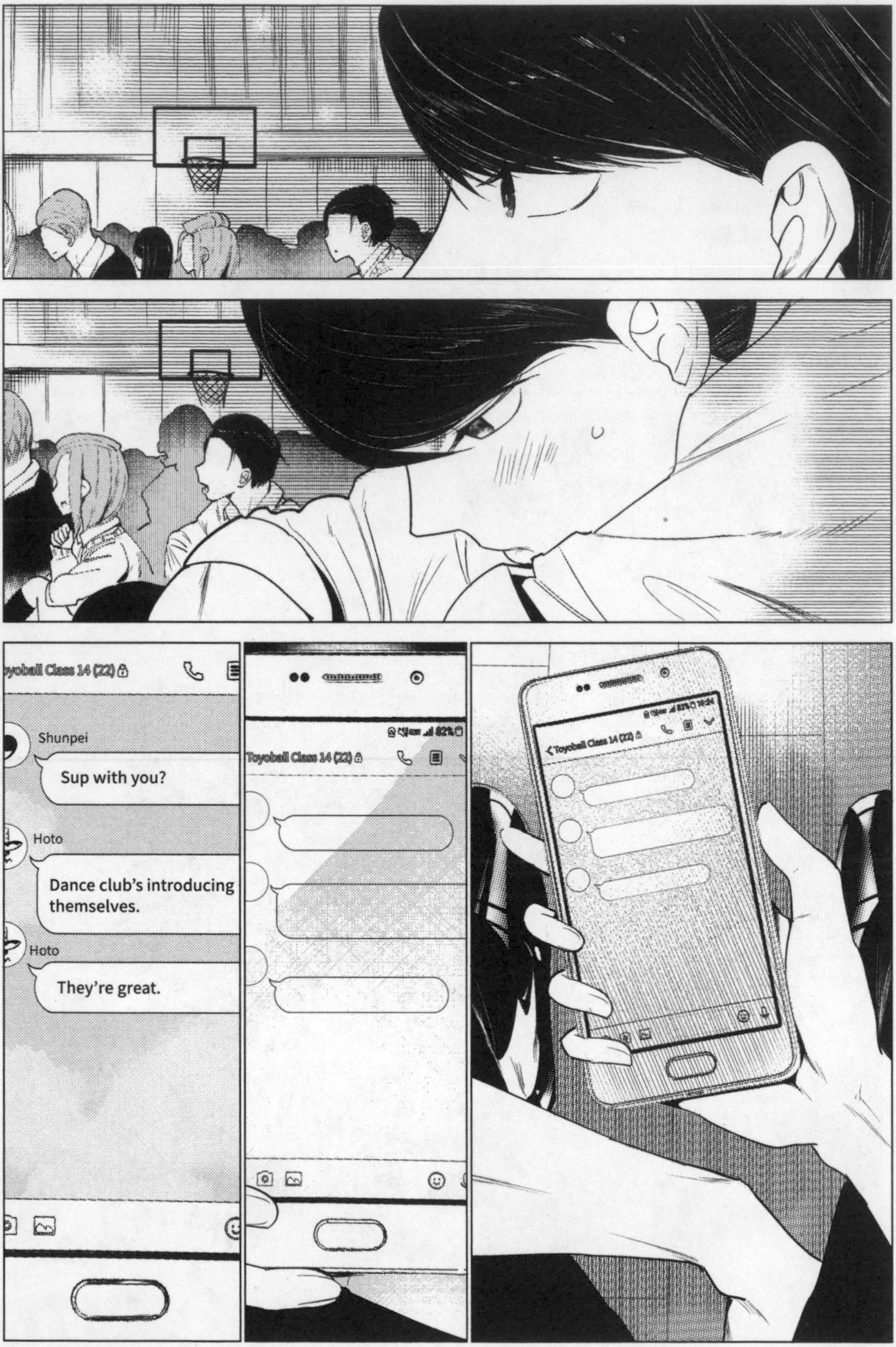
Toyoball Class 14 (22)
Toyoball Class 14 (22)
Shunpei
Sup with you?
Hoto
Dance club's introducing themselves.
Hoto
They're great.

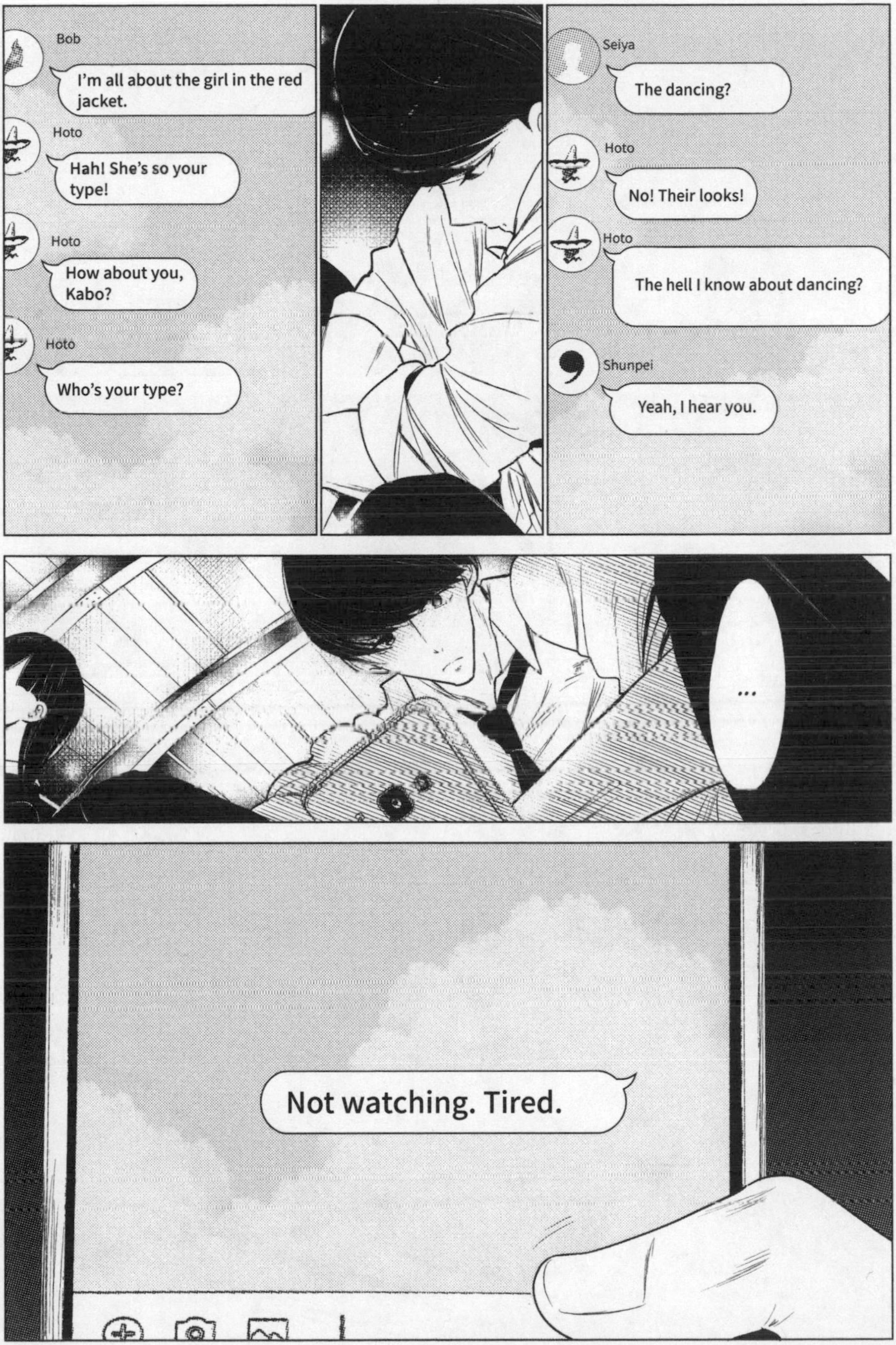
Seiya
The dancing?
Hoto
No! Their looks!
Hoto
The hell I know about dancing?
Shunpei
Yeah, I hear you.
Bob
I'm all about the girl in the red jacket.
Hoto
Hah! She's so your type!
Hoto
How about you, Kabo?
Hoto
Who's your type?
...
Not watching. Tired.

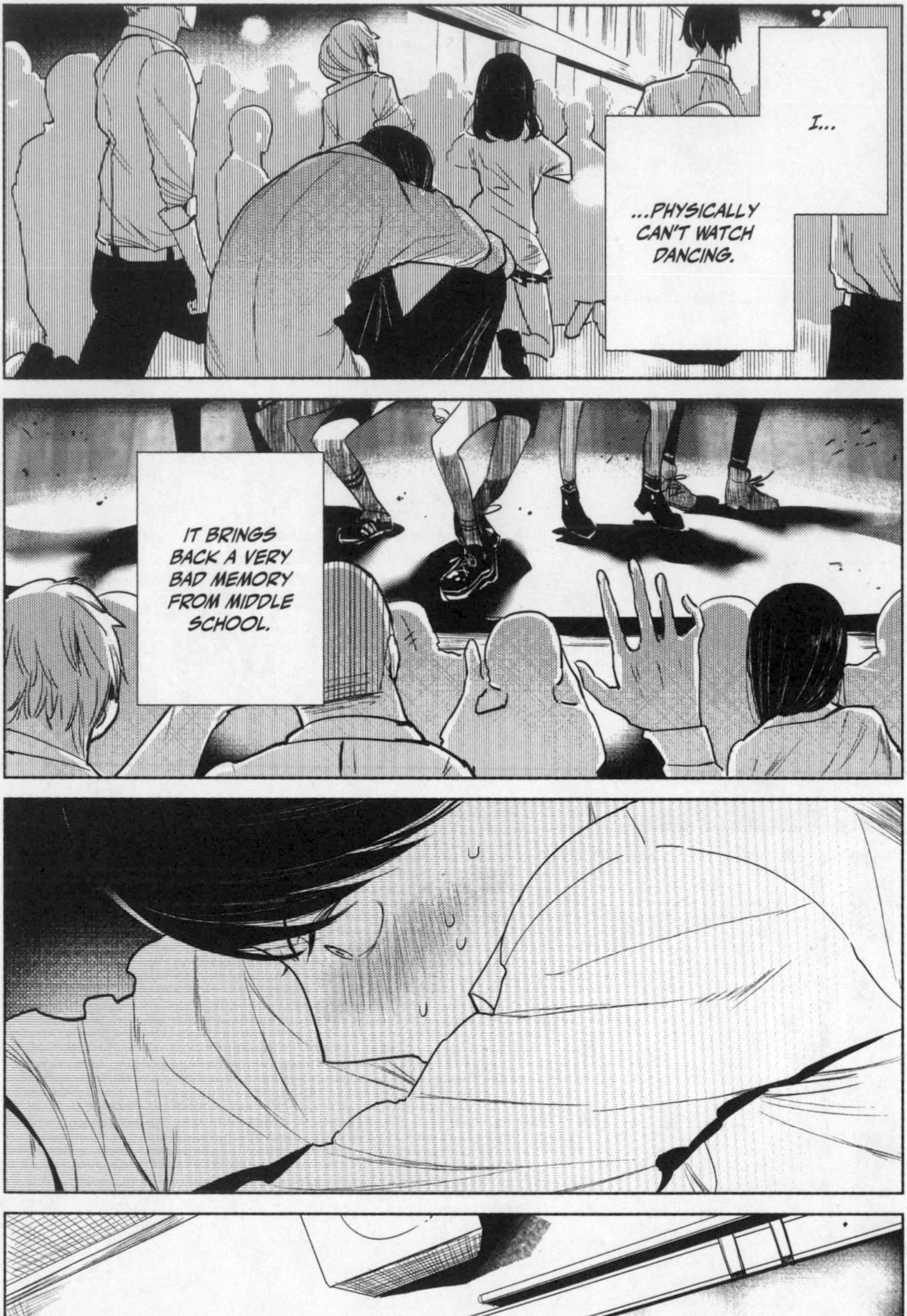
I...
...PHYSICALLY CAN'T WATCH DANCING.
IT BRINGS BACK A VERY BAD MEMORY FROM MIDDLE SCHOOL.

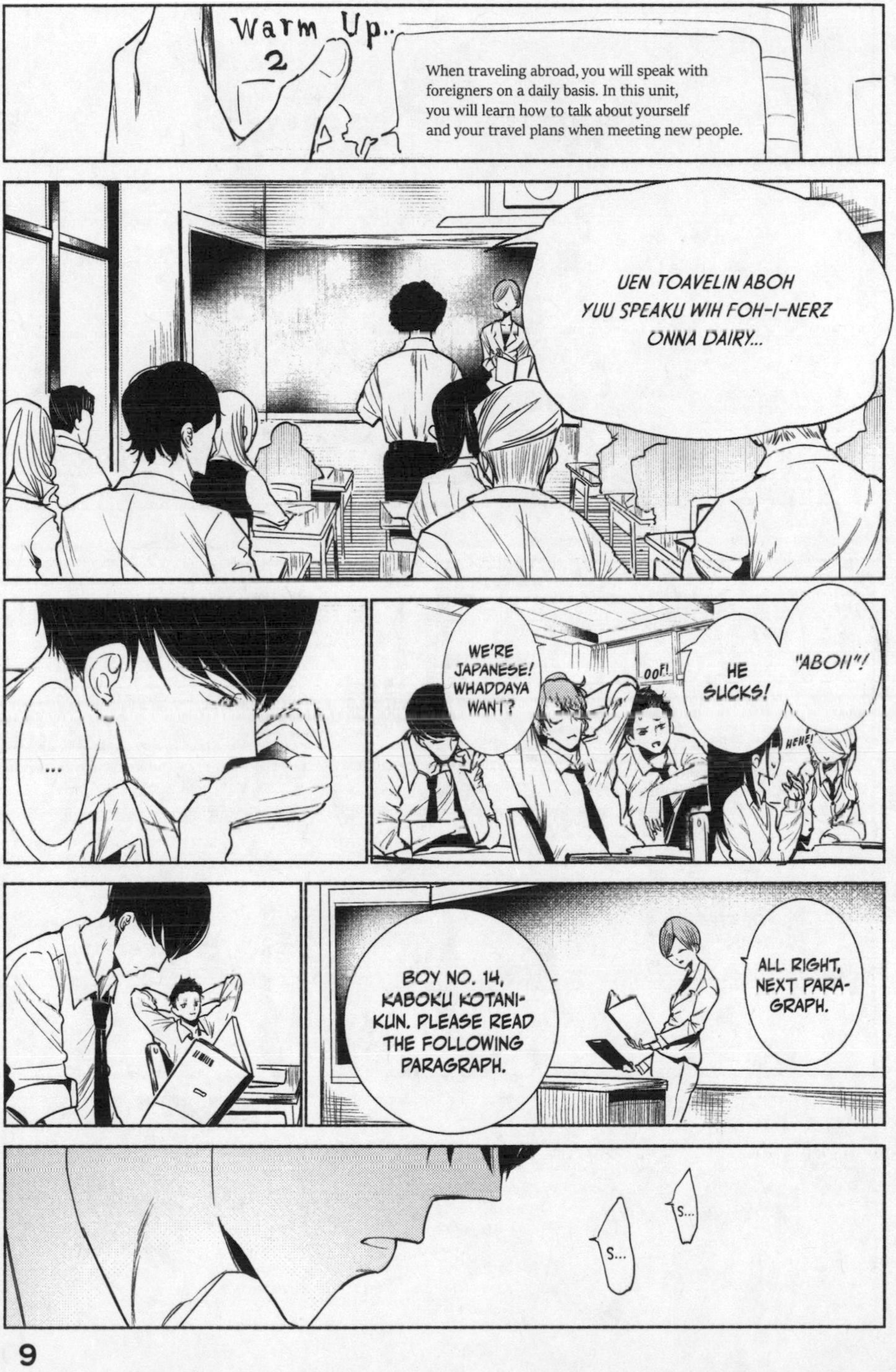
Warm Up..
2
When traveling abroad, you will speak with foreigners on a daily basis. In this unit, you will learn how to talk about yourself and your travel plans when meeting new people.
UEN TOAVELIN ABOH YUU SPEAKU WIH FOH-I-NERZ ONNA DAIRY...
"ABOH"!
HE SUCKS!
OOF!
WE'RE JAPANESE! WHADDAYA WANT?
HEHE!
...
ALL RIGHT, NEXT PARA-GRAPH.
BOY NO. 14, KABOKU KOTANI-KUN. PLEASE READ THE FOLLOWING PARAGRAPH.
S...
S...

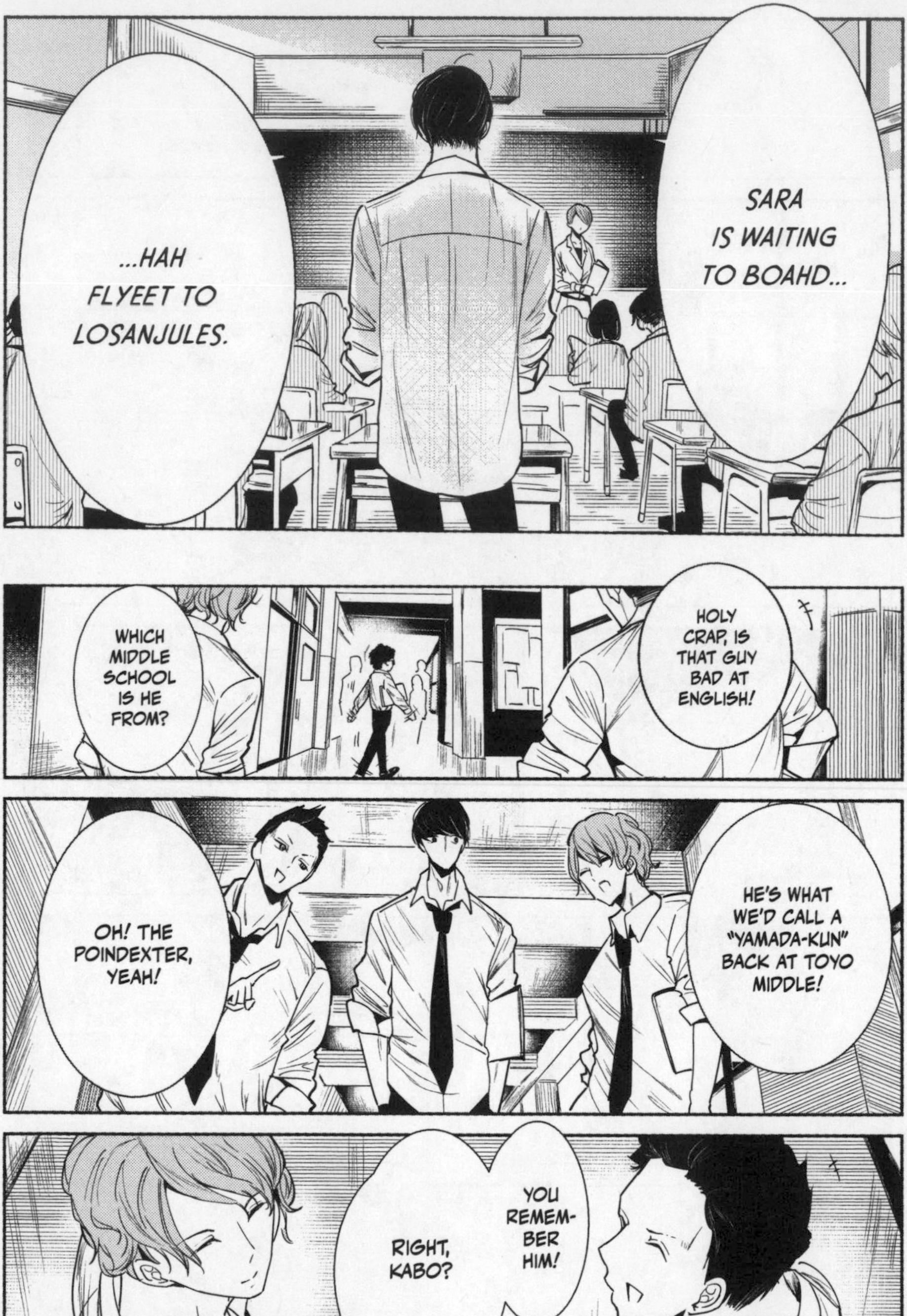
SARA IS WAITING TO BOAHD...
...HAH FLYEET TO LOSANJULES.
HOLY CRAP, IS THAT GUY BAD AT ENGLISH!
WHICH MIDDLE SCHOOL IS HE FROM?
HE'S WHAT WE'D CALL A "YAMADA-KUN" BACK AT TOYO MIDDLE!
OH! THE POINDEXTER, YEAH!
YOU REMEMBER HIM!
RIGHT, KABO?

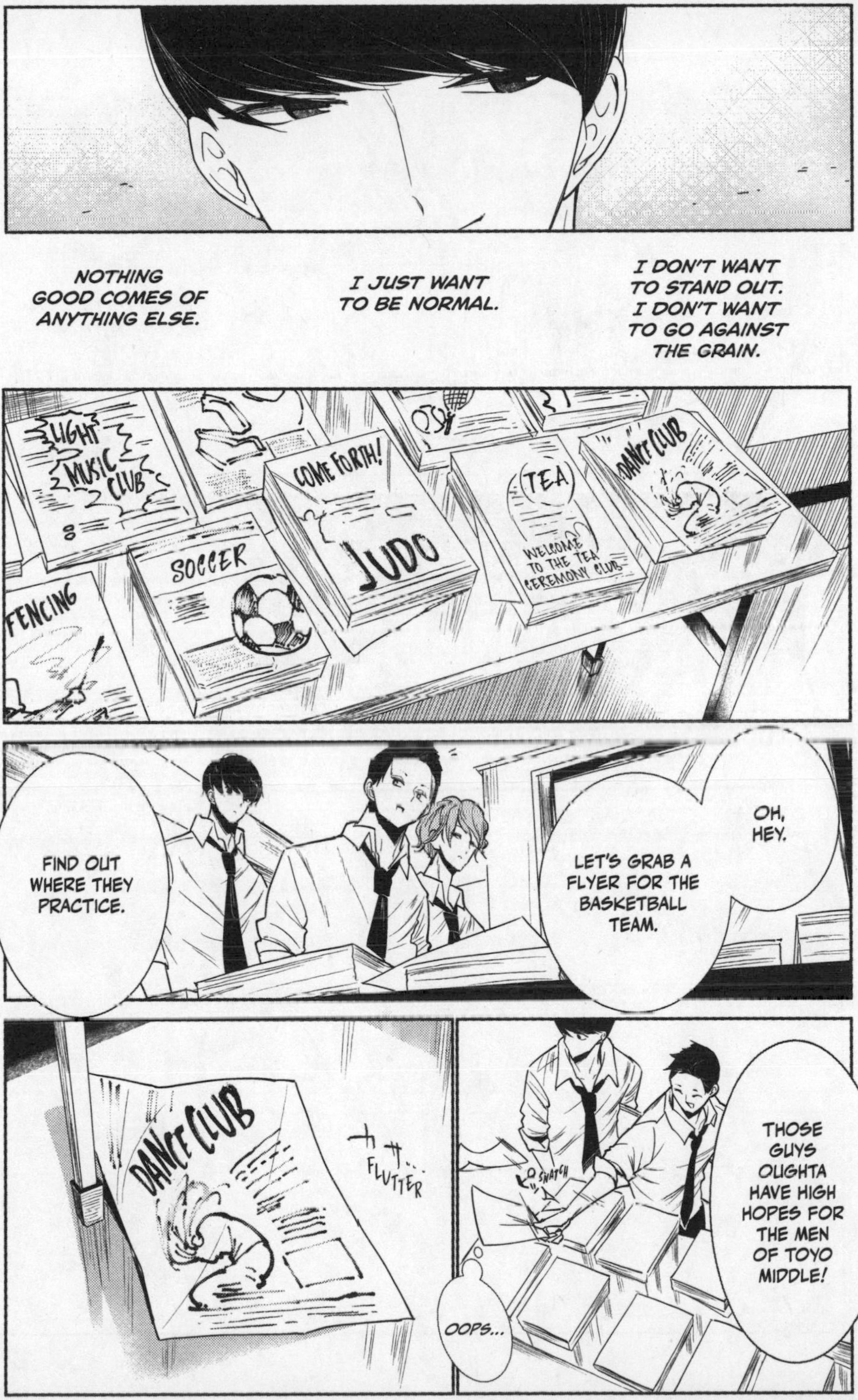
I DON'T WANT TO STAND OUT. I DON'T WANT TO GO AGAINST THE GRAIN.
I JUST WANT TO BE NORMAL.
NOTHING GOOD COMES OF ANYTHING ELSE.
DANCE CLUB
TEA
WELCOME TO THE TEA CEREMONY CLUB
COME FORTH!
JUDO
LIGHT MUSIC CLUB
SOCCER
FENCING
OH, HEY.
LET'S GRAB A FLYER FOR THE BASKETBALL TEAM.
FIND OUT WHERE THEY PRACTICE.
THOSE GUYS OUGHTA HAVE HIGH HOPES FOR THE MEN OF TOYO MIDDLE!
SNATCH
OOPS...
FLUTTER...
DANCE CLUB

SHOULD I PICK THAT UP...?
Bit of a neat freak

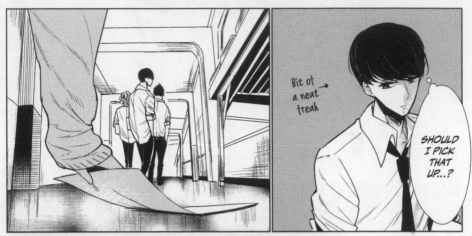

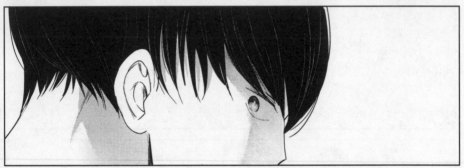

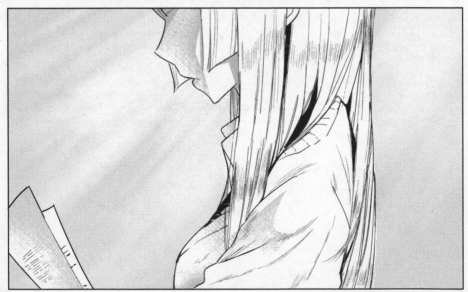

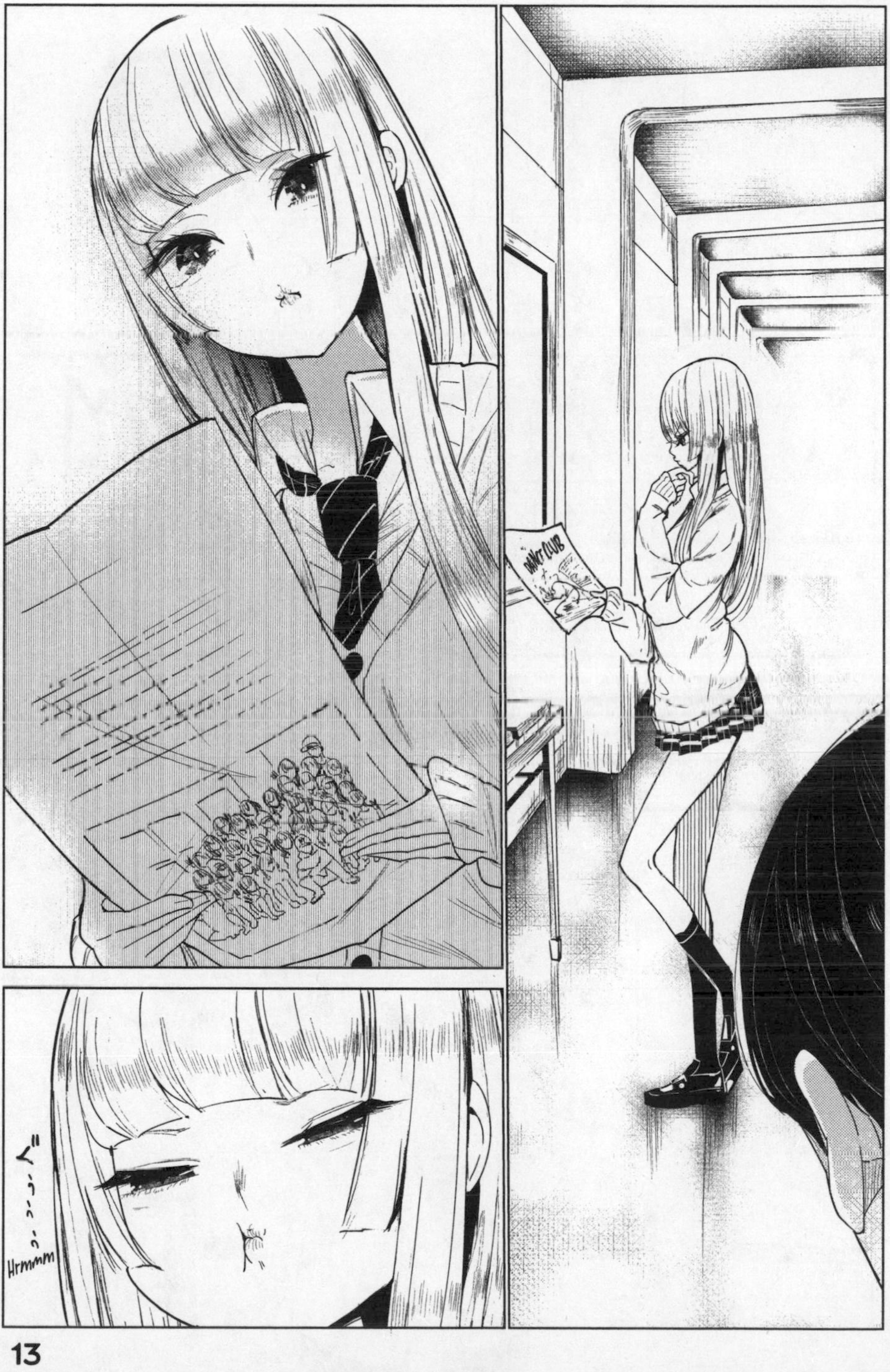
DANCE CLUB
Hrmmm

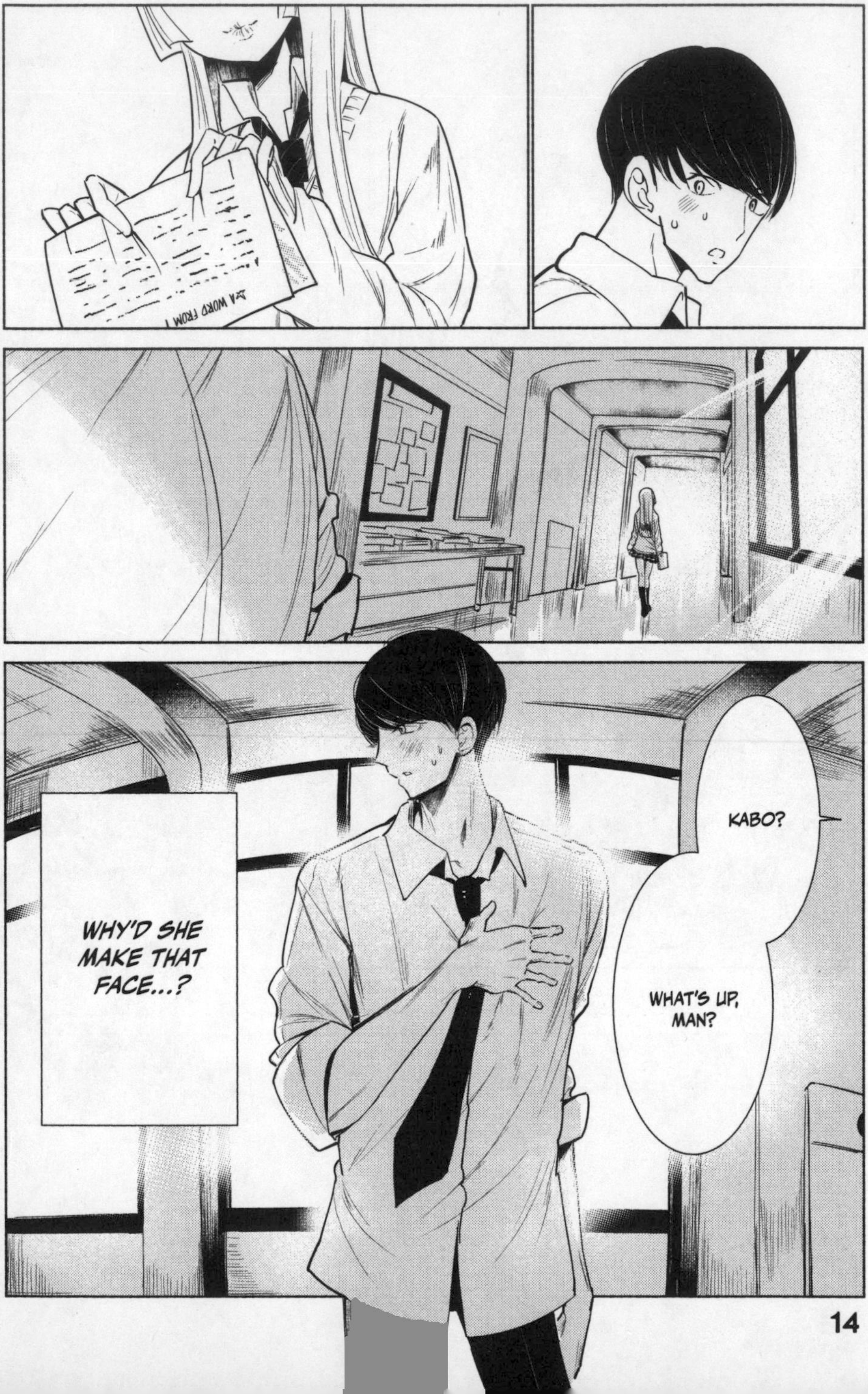
KABO?
WHAT'S UP, MAN?
WHY'D SHE MAKE THAT FACE...?

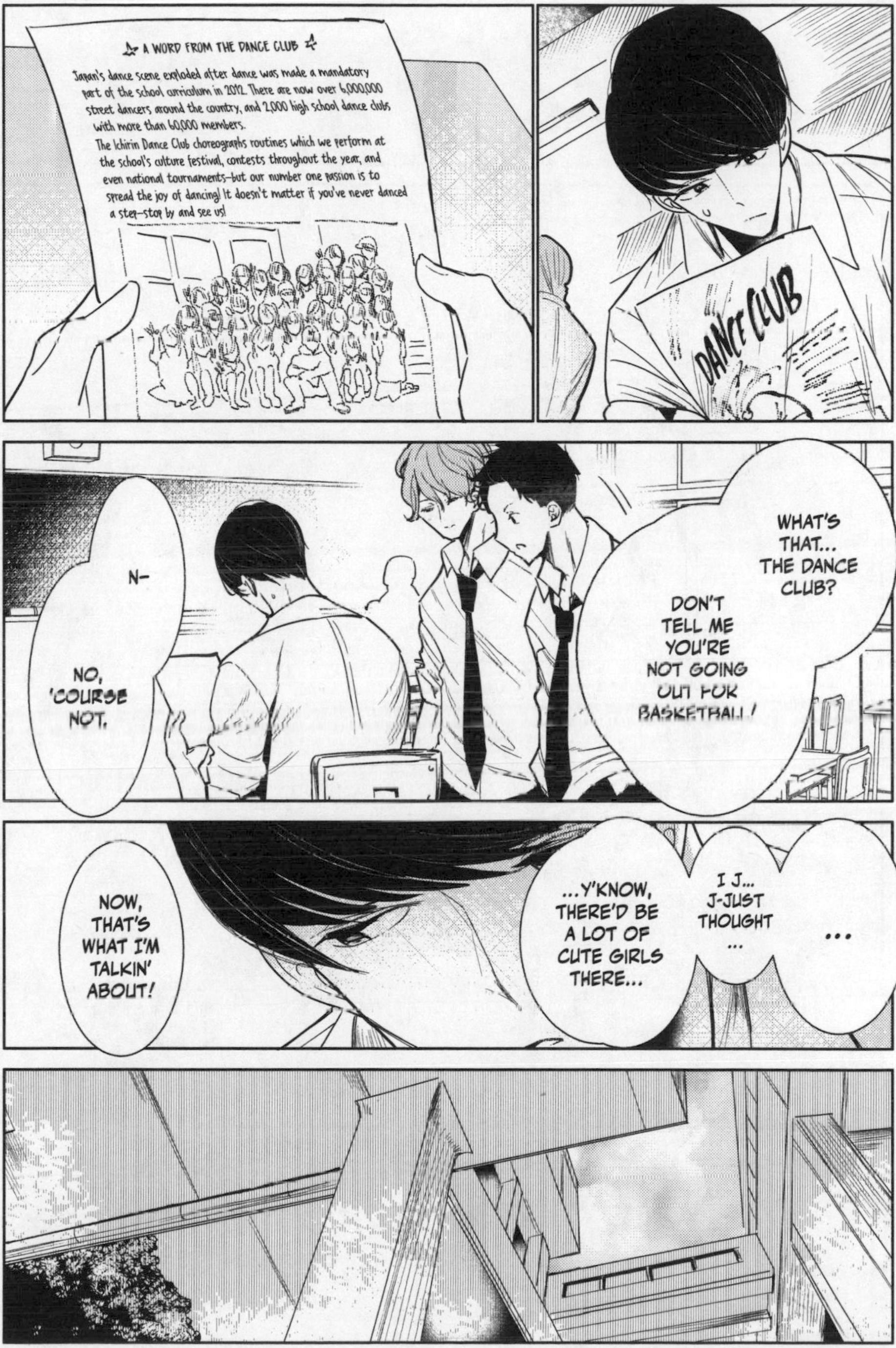
DANCE CLUB
A WORD FROM THE DANCE CLUB
Japan's dance scene exploded after dance was made a mandatory part of the school curriculum in 2012. There are now over 6,000,000 street dancers around the country, and 2,000 high school dance clubs with more than 60,000 members.
The Ichirin Dance Club choreographs routines which we perform at the school's culture festival, contests throughout the year, and even national tournaments—but our number one passion is to spread the joy of dancing! It doesn't matter if you've never danced a step—stop by and see us!
WHAT'S THAT... THE DANCE CLUB?
DON'T TELL ME YOU'RE NOT GOING OUT FOR BASKETBALL!
N–
NO, 'COURSE NOT.
...
I J... J-JUST THOUGHT ...
...Y'KNOW, THERE'D BE A LOT OF CUTE GIRLS THERE...
NOW, THAT'S WHAT I'M TALKIN' ABOUT!

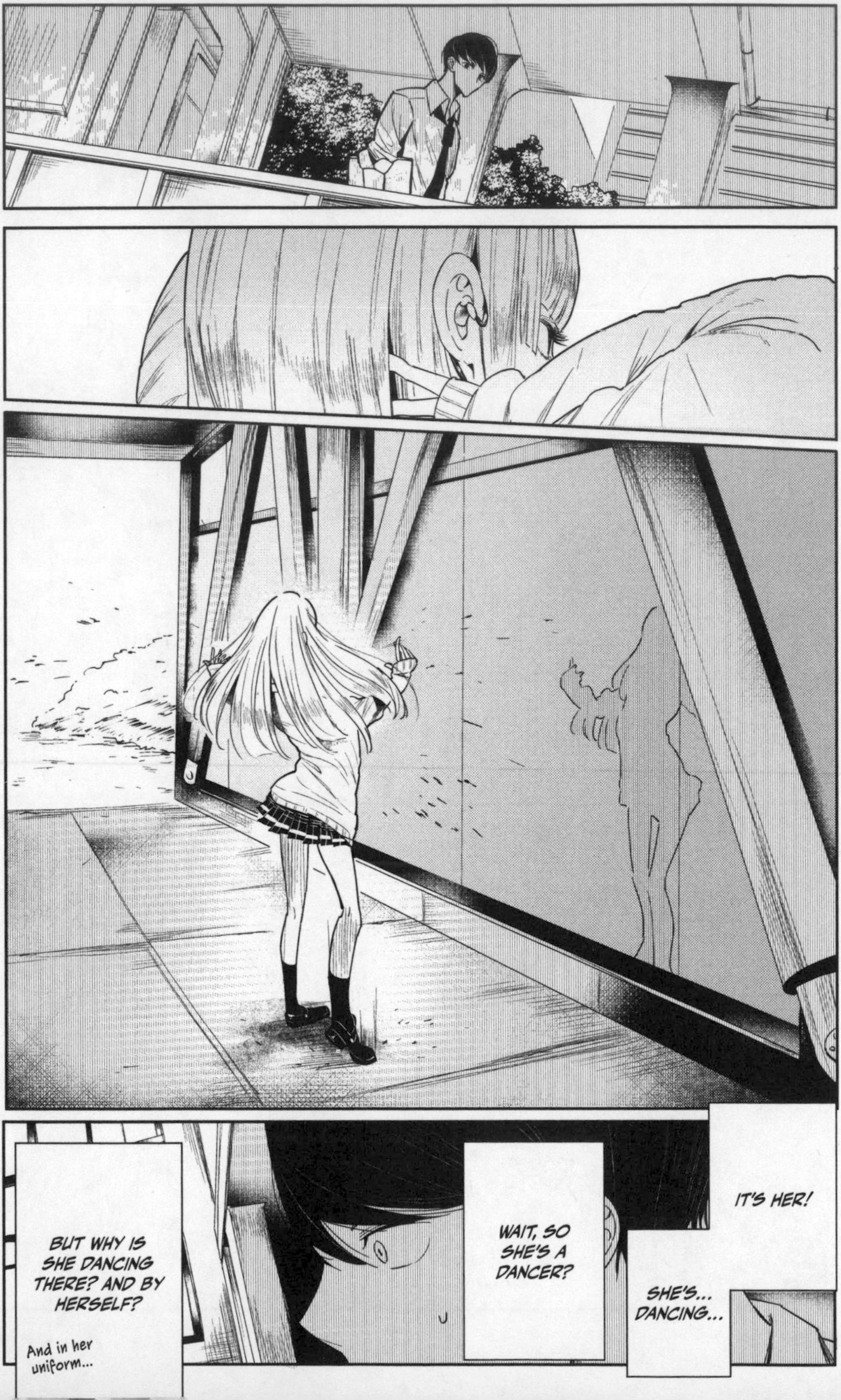
IT'S HER!
SHE'S... DANCING...
WAIT, SO SHE'S A DANCER?
BUT WHY IS SHE DANCING THERE? AND BY HERSELF?
And in her uniform...

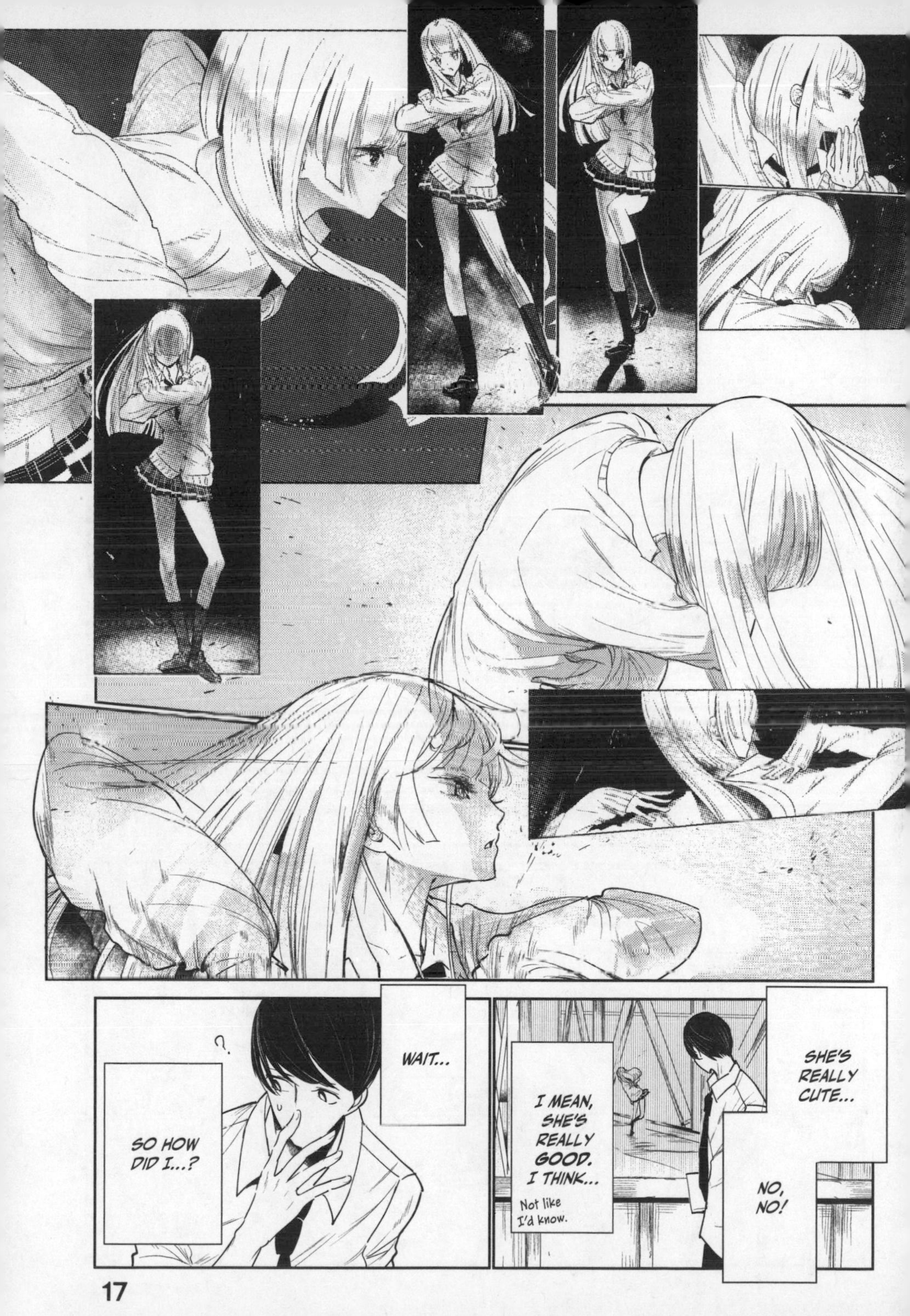
SHE'S REALLY CUTE...
I MEAN, SHE'S REALLY GOOD. I THINK...
Not like I'd know.
NO, NO!
WAIT...
?
SO HOW DID I...?

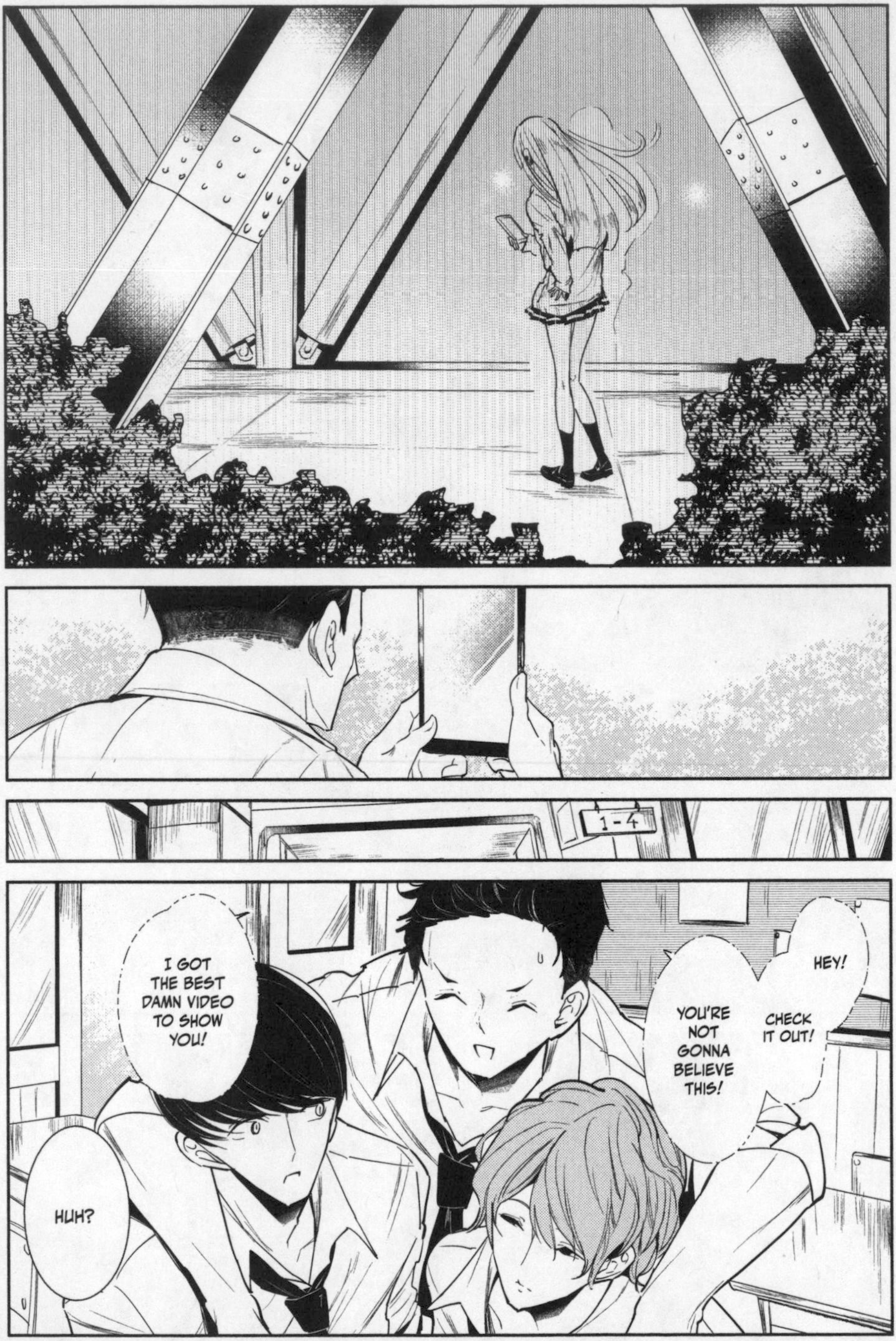
1-4
HEY!
CHECK IT OUT!
YOU'RE NOT GONNA BELIEVE THIS!
I GOT THE BEST DAMN VIDEO TO SHOW YOU!
HUH?

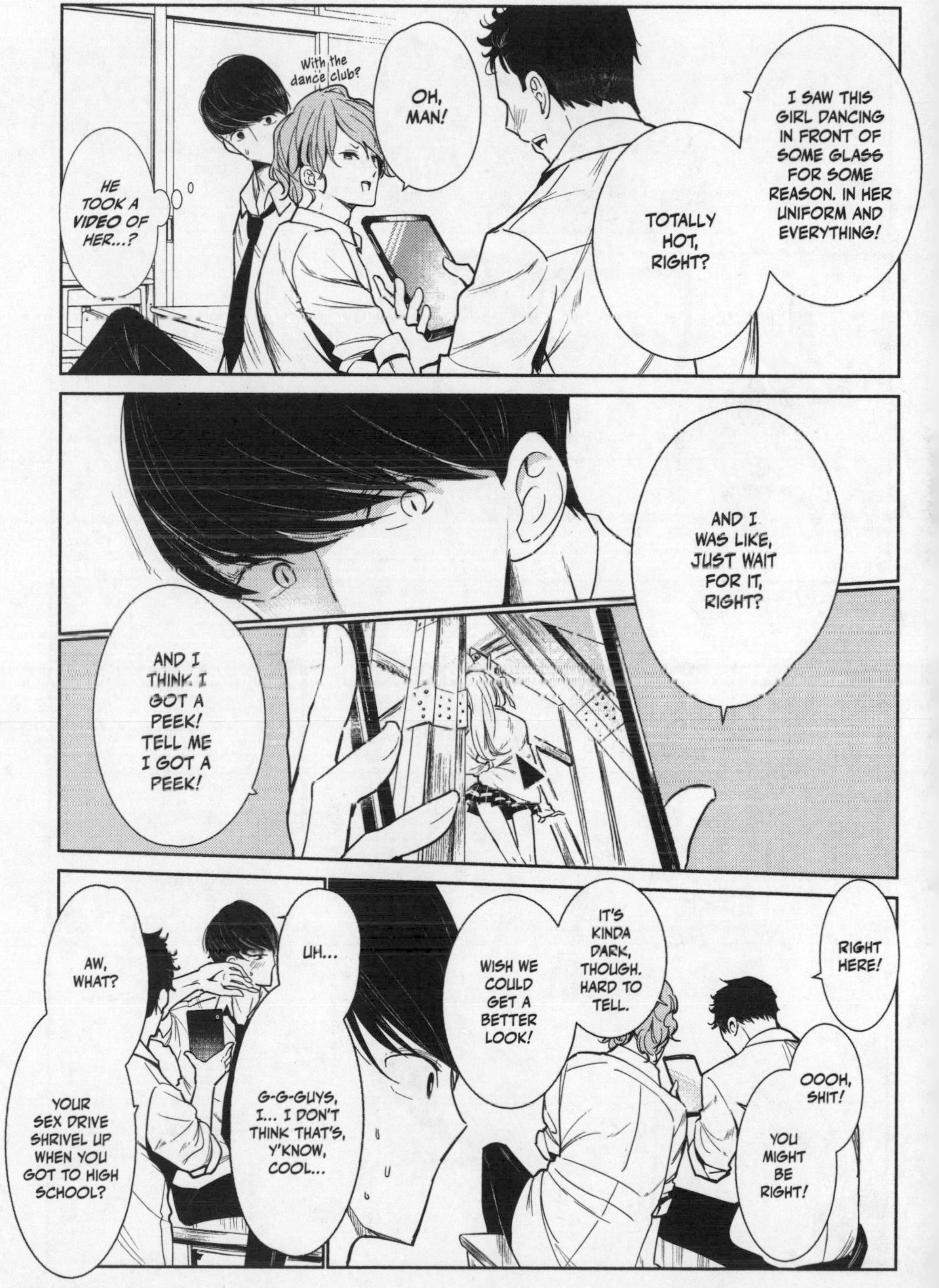
I SAW THIS GIRL DANCING IN FRONT OF SOME GLASS FOR SOME REASON. IN HER UNIFORM AND EVERYTHING!
TOTALLY HOT, RIGHT?
OH, MAN!
With the dance club?
HE TOOK A VIDEO OF HER...?
AND I WAS LIKE, JUST WAIT FOR IT, RIGHT?
AND I THINK I GOT A PEEK! TELL ME I GOT A PEEK!
RIGHT HERE!
OOOH, SHIT!
YOU MIGHT BE RIGHT!
IT'S KINDA DARK, THOUGH. HARD TO TELL.
WISH WE COULD GET A BETTER LOOK!
UH...
G-G-GUYS, I... I DON'T THINK THAT'S, Y'KNOW, COOL...
AW, WHAT?
YOUR SEX DRIVE SHRIVEL UP WHEN YOU GOT TO HIGH SCHOOL?

AHEM!
THIS SUBJECT WILL BE A COMBINED LECTURE OF CLASSES 3 AND 4.
Japanese Class
Quiz -10.45
YOU'LL NOW CHECK EACH OTHER'S ANSWERS.
TRADE YOUR QUIZ WITH THE PERSON SITTING NEXT TO YOU.
HERE YOU GO.

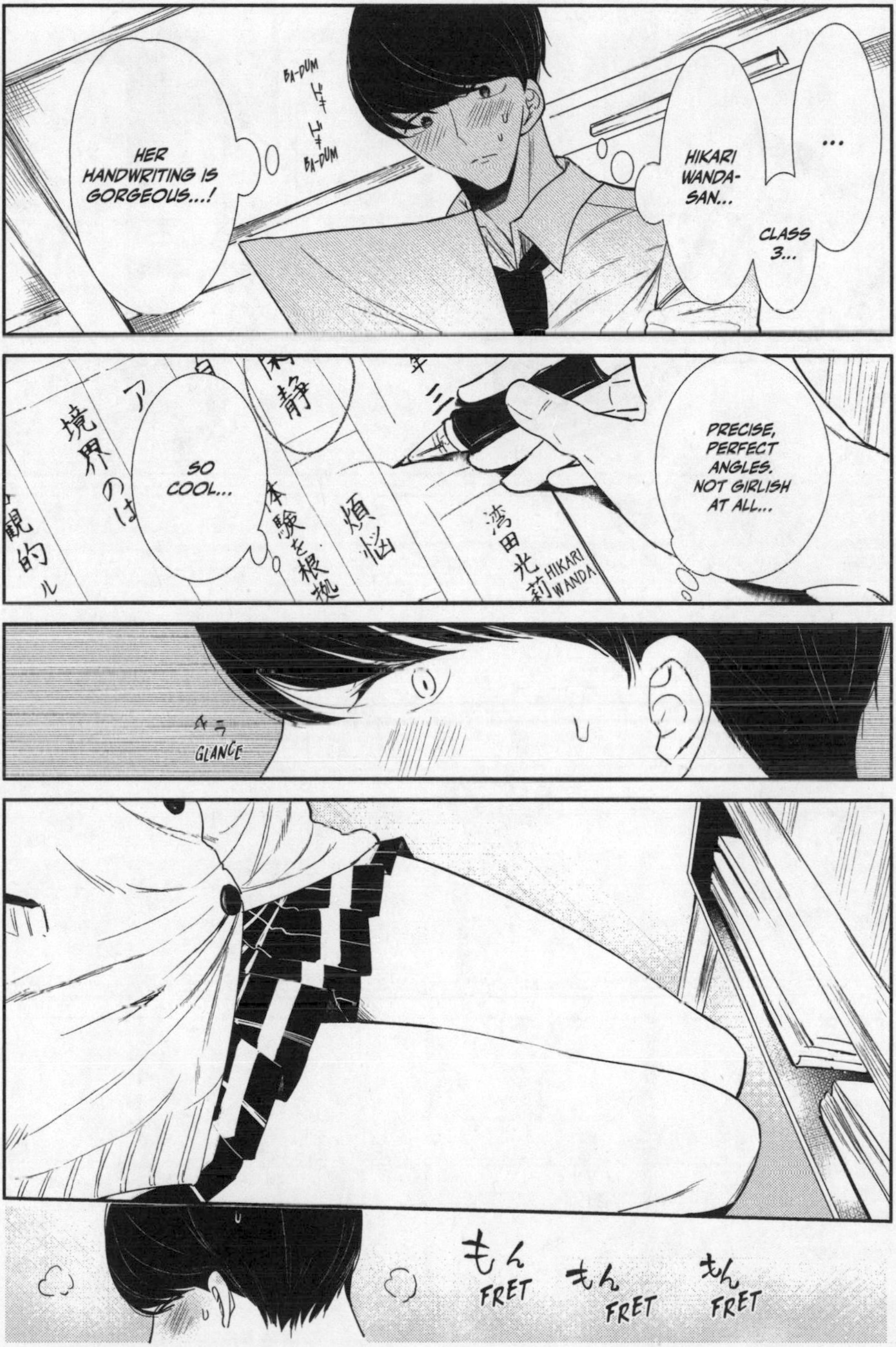
...
HIKARI WANDA-SAN...
CLASS 3...
ドキ BA-DUM
ドキ BA-DUM
HER HANDWRITING IS GORGEOUS...!
PRECISE, PERFECT ANGLES. NOT GIRLISH AT ALL...
湾田光莉 HIKARI WANDA
SO COOL...
チラ GLANCE
もん FRET
もん FRET
もん FRET

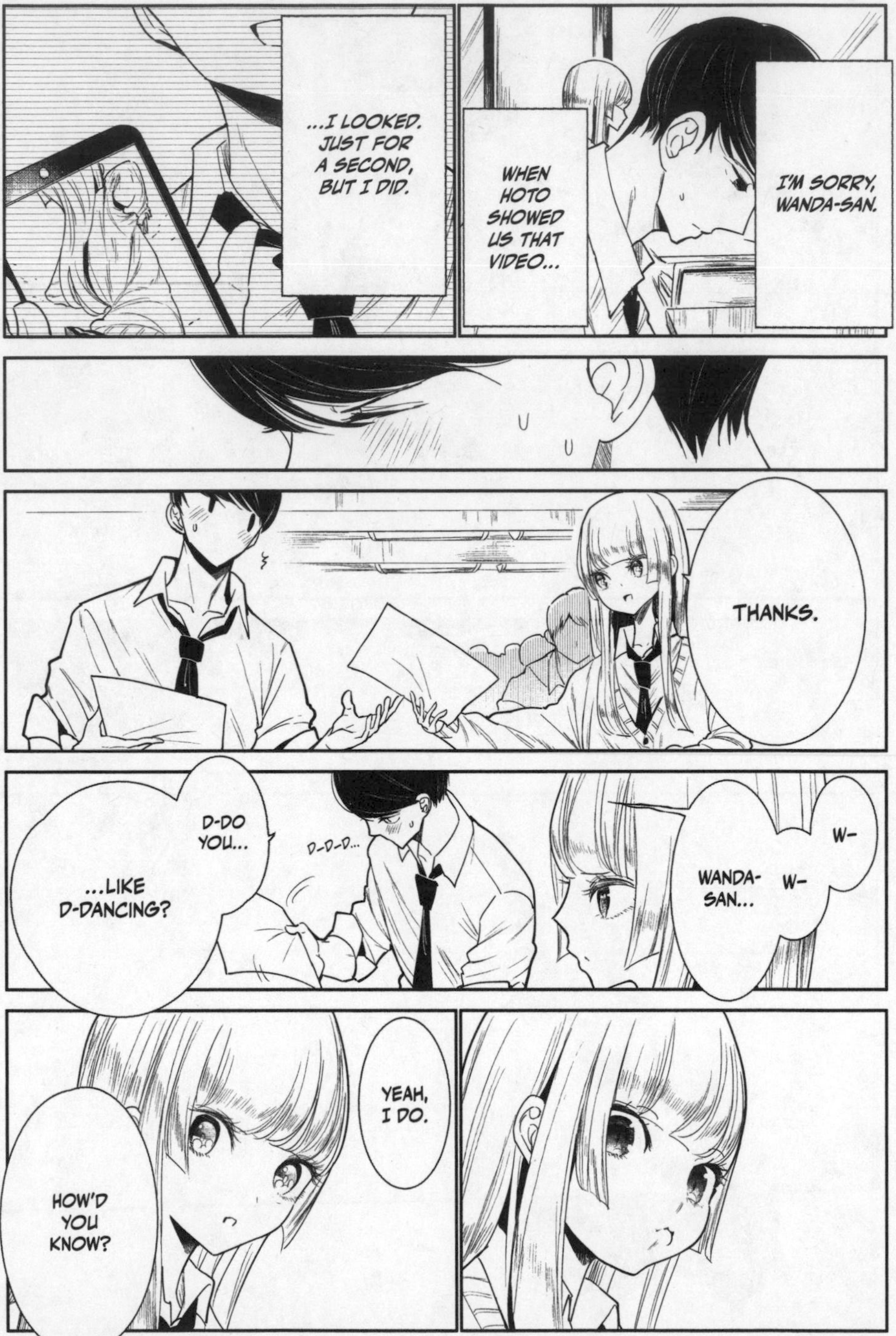
I'M SORRY, WANDA-SAN.
WHEN HOTO SHOWED US THAT VIDEO...
...I LOOKED. JUST FOR A SECOND, BUT I DID.
THANKS.
W- W- WANDA-SAN...
D-D-D...
D-DO YOU...
...LIKE D-DANCING?
YEAH, I DO.
HOW'D YOU KNOW?

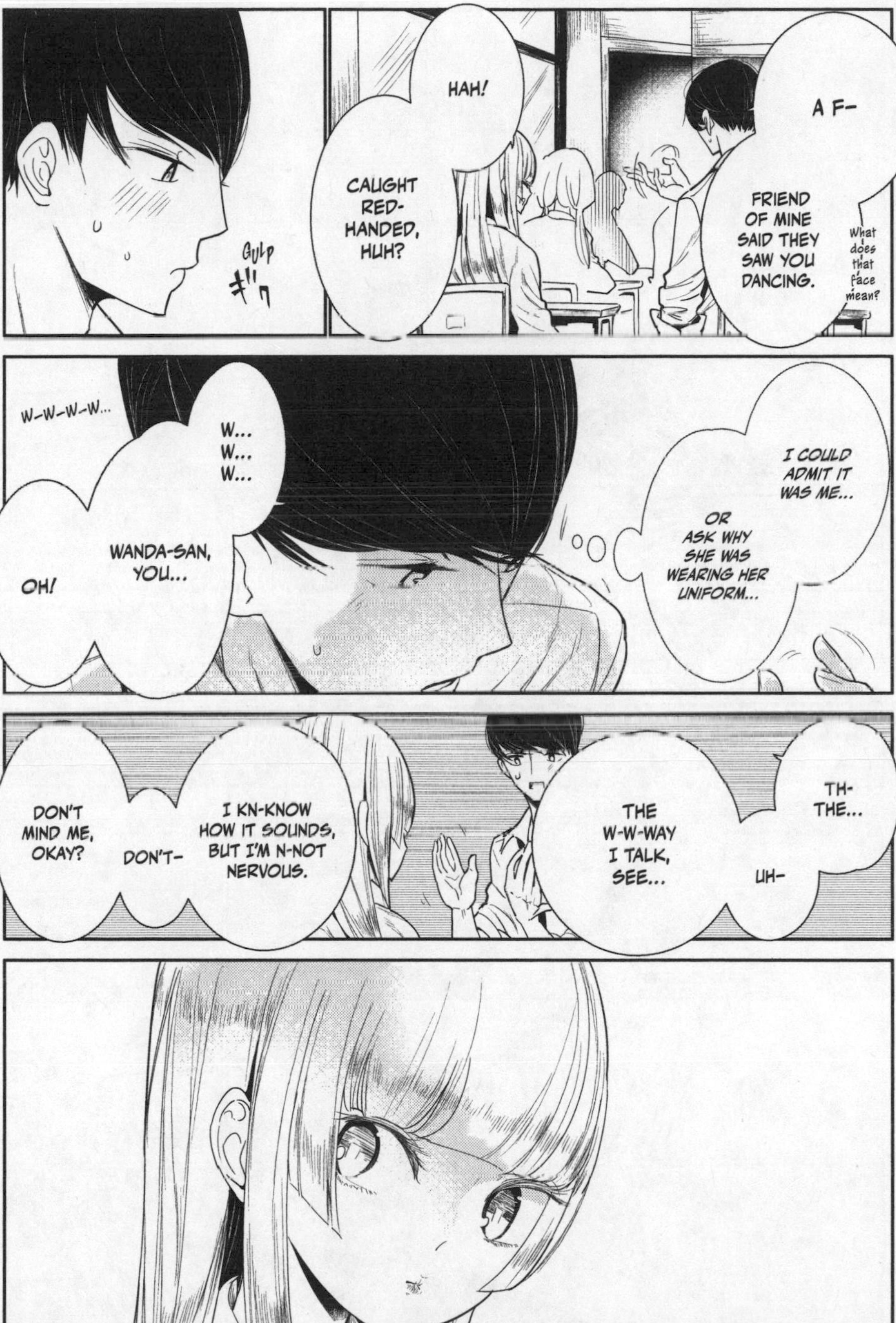
A F-
FRIEND OF MINE SAID THEY SAW YOU DANCING.
What does that face mean?
HAH!
CAUGHT RED-HANDED, HUH?
Gulp
ギク
I COULD ADMIT IT WAS ME...
OR ASK WHY SHE WAS WEARING HER UNIFORM...
W... W... W...
W-W-W-W...
WANDA-SAN, YOU...
OH!
TH- THE...
UH-
THE W-W-WAY I TALK, SEE...
I KN-KNOW HOW IT SOUNDS, BUT I'M N-NOT NERVOUS.
DON'T-
DON'T MIND ME, OKAY?

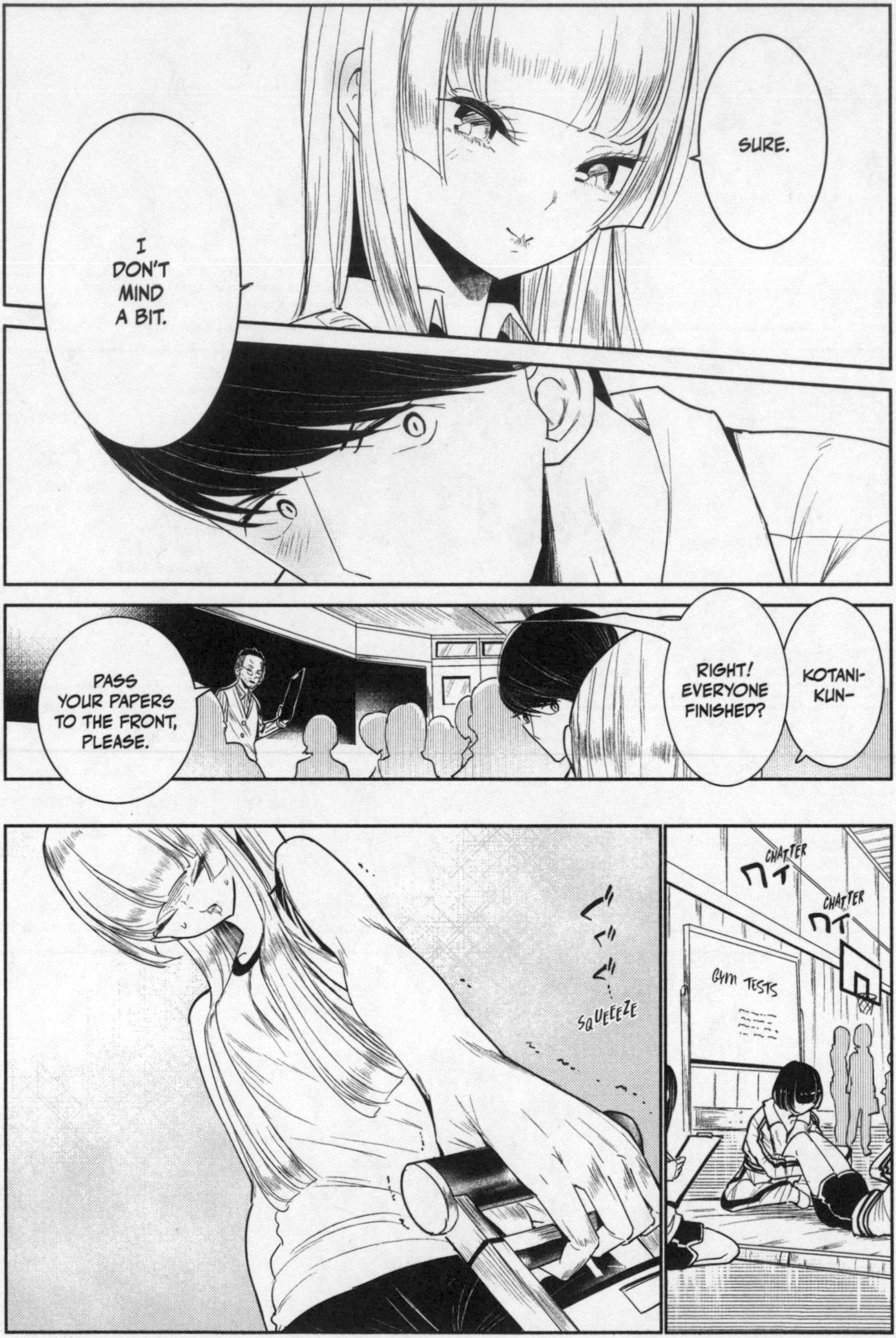
SURE.
I DON'T MIND A BIT.
KOTANI-KUN-
RIGHT! EVERYONE FINISHED?
PASS YOUR PAPERS TO THE FRONT, PLEASE.
CHATTER
CHATTER
GYM TESTS
SQUEEEZE

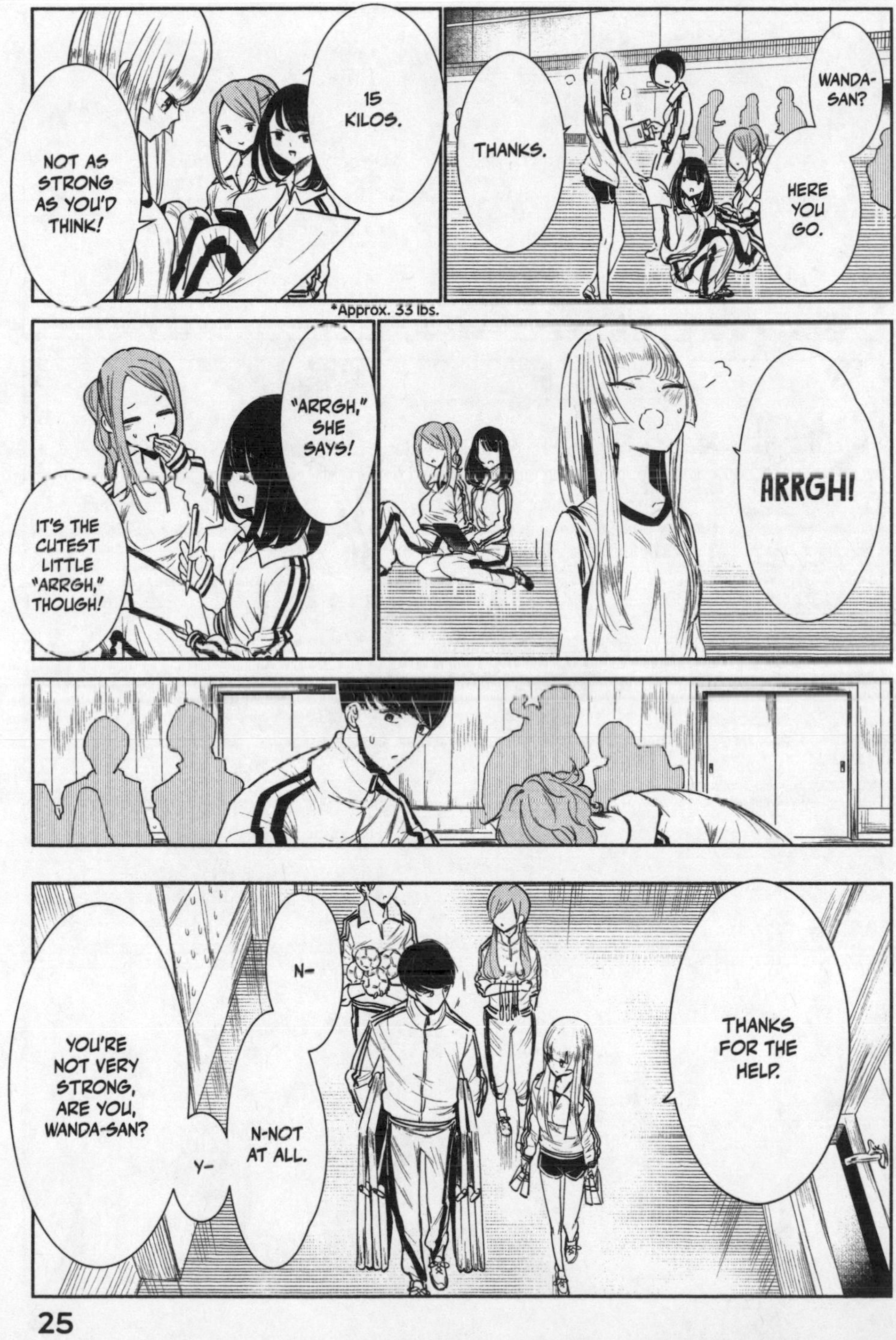
WANDA-SAN?
HERE YOU GO.
THANKS.
15 KILOS.
NOT AS STRONG AS YOU'D THINK!
ARRGH!
"ARRGH," SHE SAYS!
IT'S THE CUTEST LITTLE "ARRGH," THOUGH!
THANKS FOR THE HELP.
N-
N-NOT AT ALL.
Y-
YOU'RE NOT VERY STRONG, ARE YOU, WANDA-SAN?
*Approx. 33 lbs.

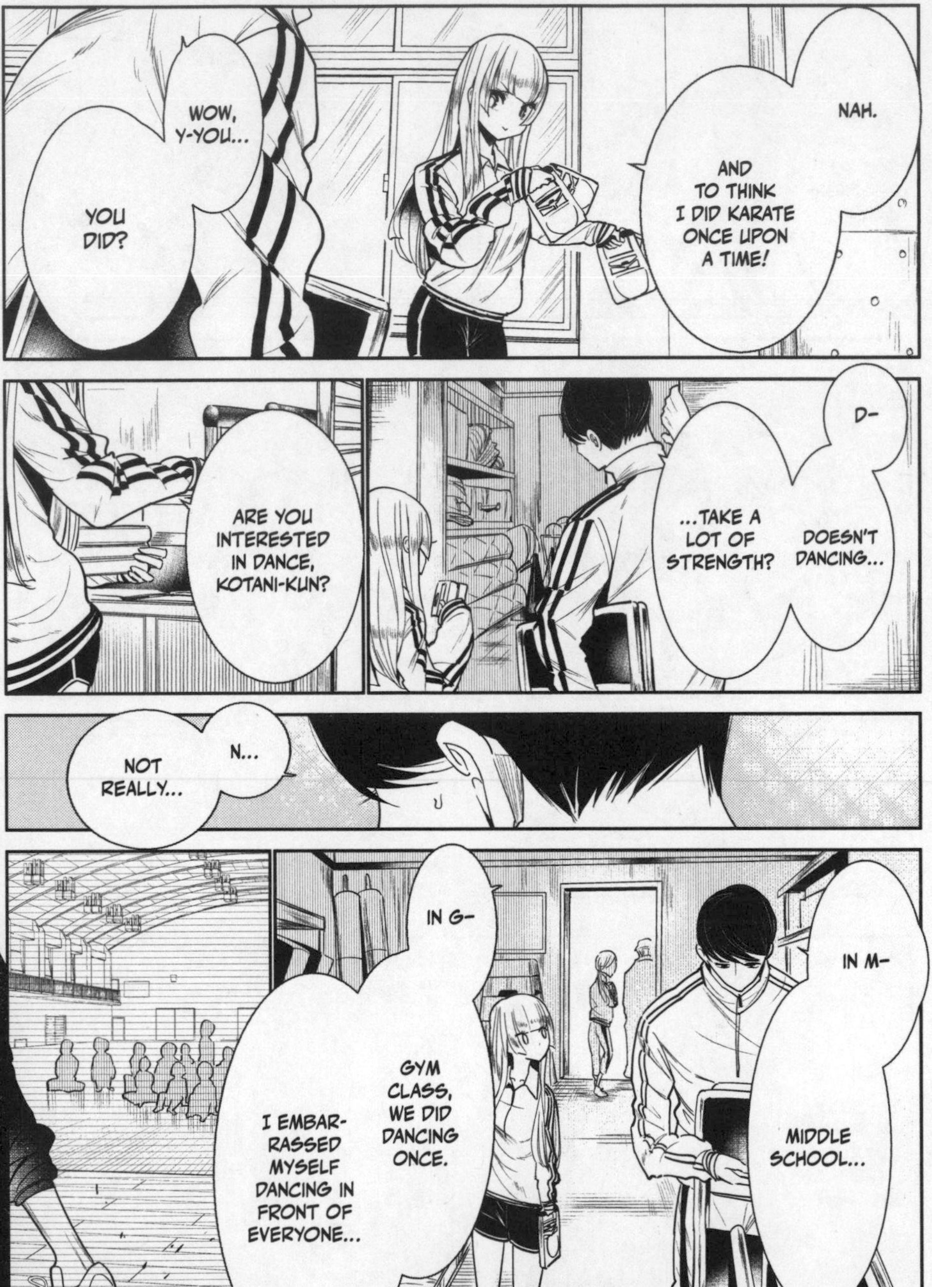
NAH.
AND TO THINK I DID KARATE ONCE UPON A TIME!
WOW, Y-YOU...
YOU DID?
D-
DOESN'T DANCING...
...TAKE A LOT OF STRENGTH?
ARE YOU INTERESTED IN DANCE, KOTANI-KUN?
N...
NOT REALLY...
IN M-
MIDDLE SCHOOL...
IN G-
GYM CLASS, WE DID DANCING ONCE.
I EMBARRASSED MYSELF DANCING IN FRONT OF EVERYONE...

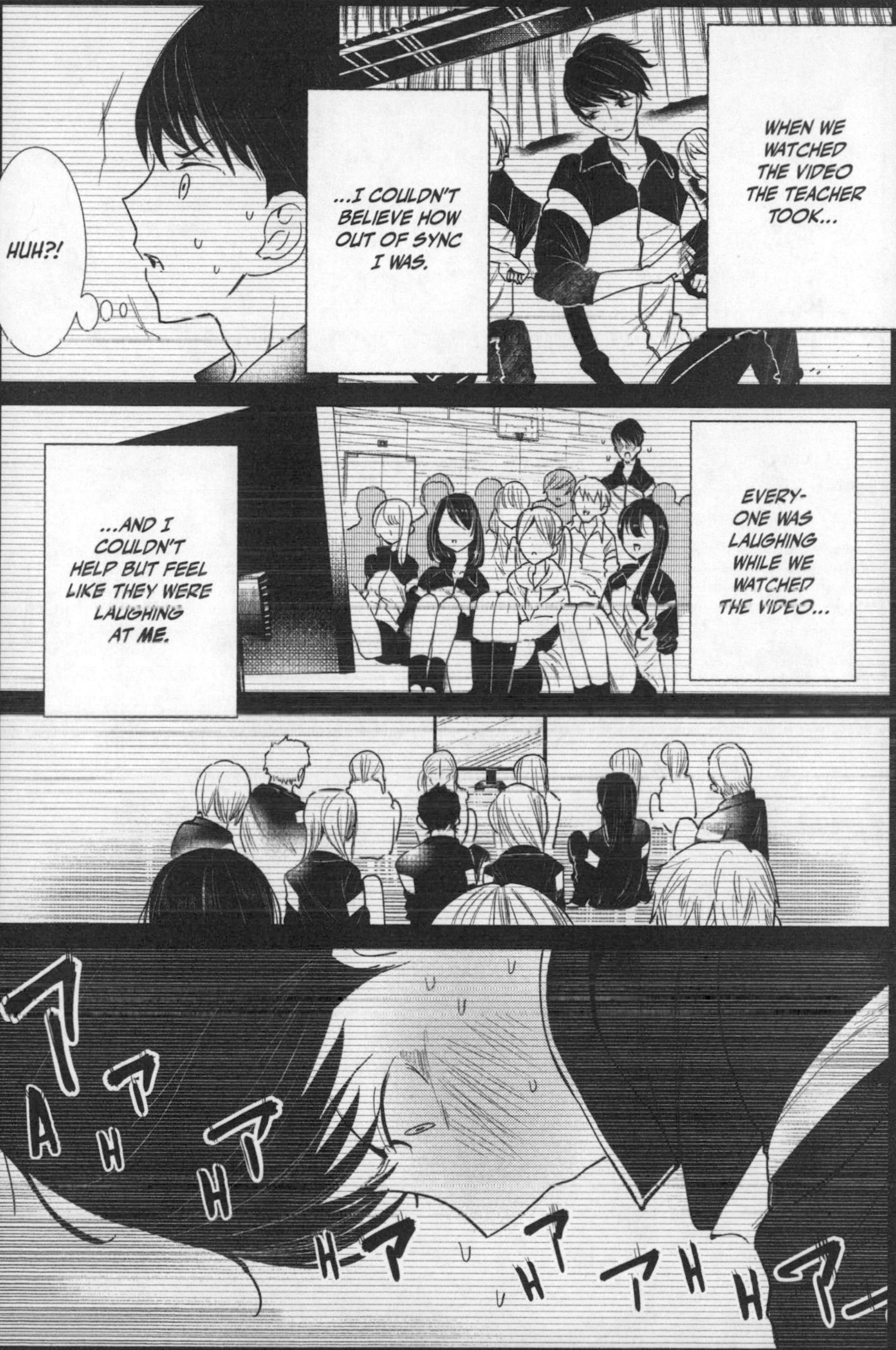
WHEN WE WATCHED THE VIDEO THE TEACHER TOOK...
...I COULDN'T BELIEVE HOW OUT OF SYNC I WAS.
HUH?!
EVERY-ONE WAS LAUGHING WHILE WE WATCHED THE VIDEO...
...AND I COULDN'T HELP BUT FEEL LIKE THEY WERE LAUGHING AT ME.
AHHHHHH

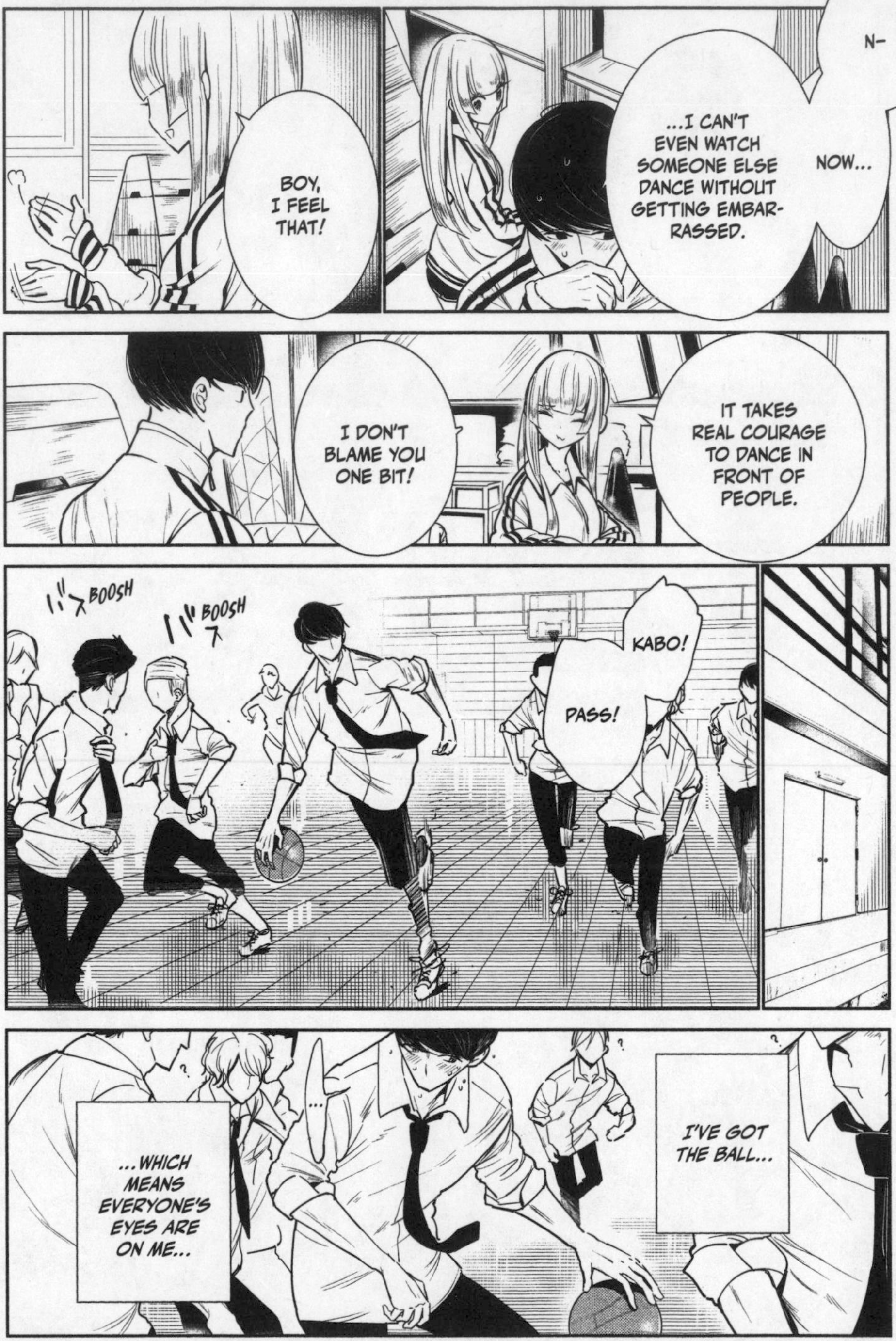
N–
NOW...
...I CAN'T EVEN WATCH SOMEONE ELSE DANCE WITHOUT GETTING EMBAR-RASSED.
BOY, I FEEL THAT!
IT TAKES REAL COURAGE TO DANCE IN FRONT OF PEOPLE.
I DON'T BLAME YOU ONE BIT!
KABO!
PASS!
BOOSH
BOOSH
I'VE GOT THE BALL...
...
...WHICH MEANS EVERYONE'S EYES ARE ON ME...

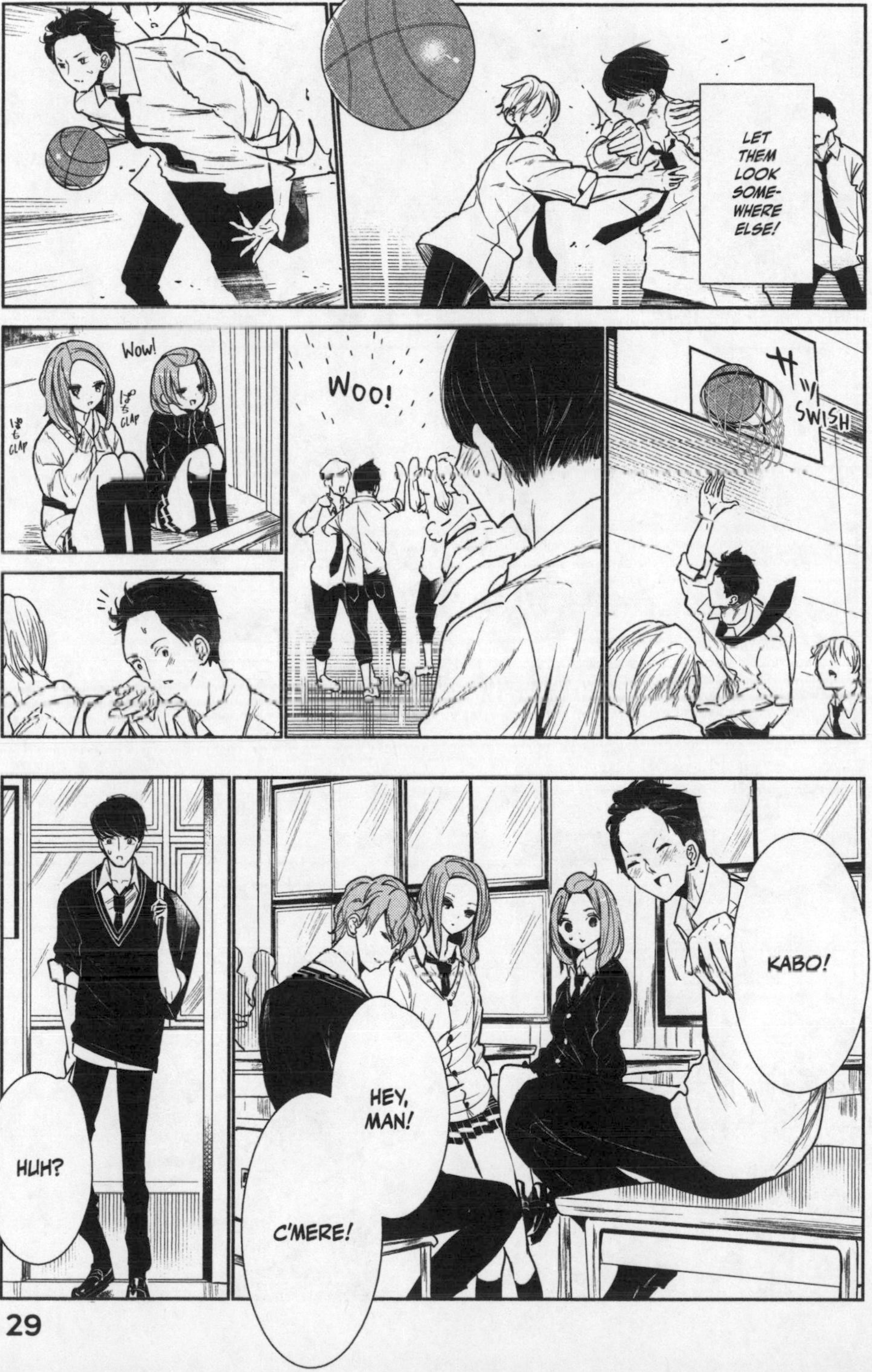
LET THEM LOOK SOMEWHERE-ELSE!
サッ
SWISH
WOO!
WOW!
ぱち CLAP
ぱち CLAP
KABO!
HEY, MAN!
C'MERE!
HUH?

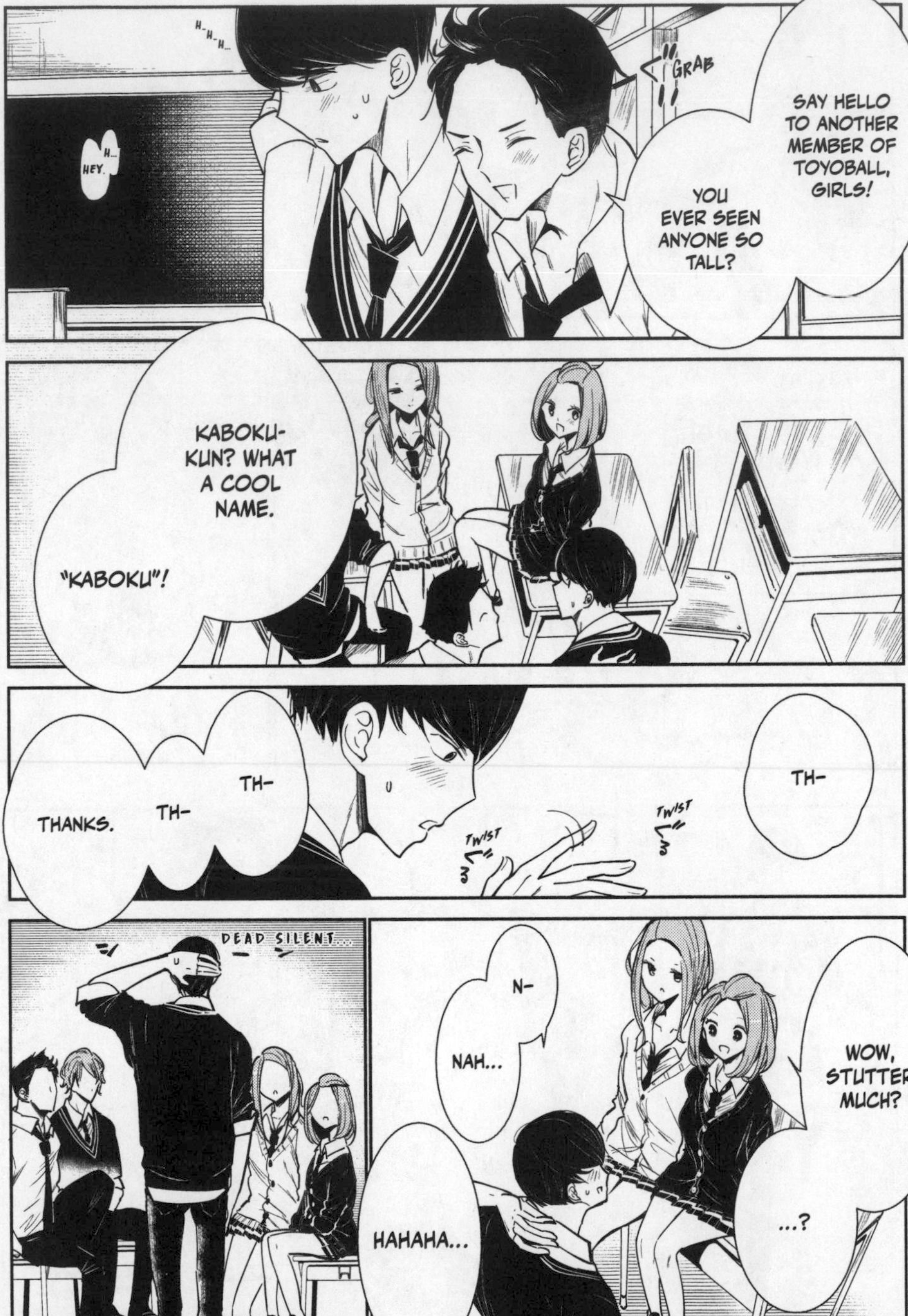

SAY HELLO TO ANOTHER MEMBER OF TOYOBALL, GIRLS!
YOU EVER SEEN ANYONE SO TALL?
GRAB
H-H-H...
H... HEY.
KABOKU-KUN? WHAT A COOL NAME.
"KABOKU"!
TH-
TWIST
TWIST
TH-
TH-
THANKS.
WOW, STUTTER MUCH?
...?
N-
NAH...
HAHAHA...
DEAD SILENT...

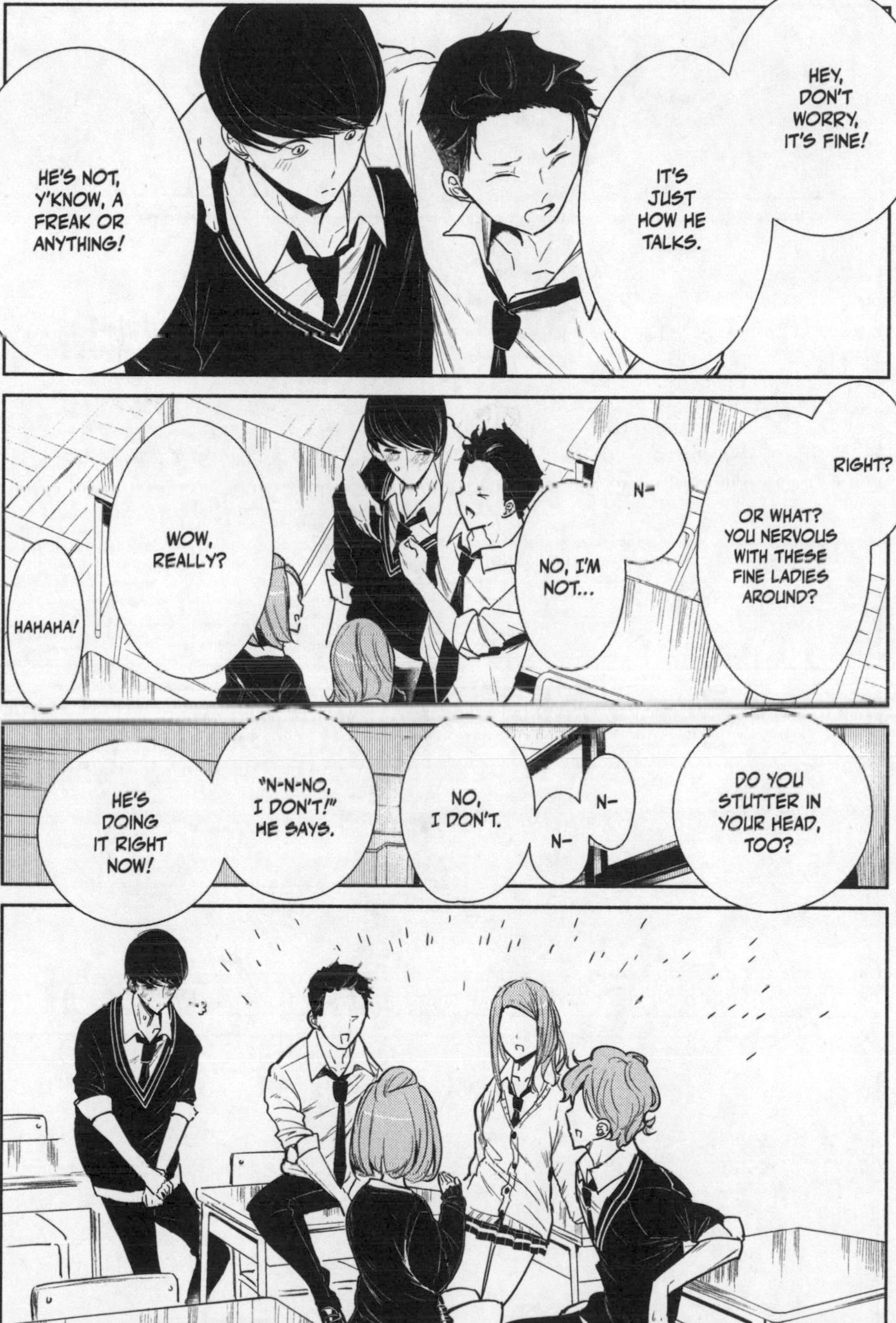
HEY, DON'T WORRY, IT'S FINE!
IT'S JUST HOW HE TALKS.
HE'S NOT, Y'KNOW, A FREAK OR ANYTHING!
RIGHT?
OR WHAT? YOU NERVOUS WITH THESE FINE LADIES AROUND?
N-
NO, I'M NOT...
WOW, REALLY?
HAHAHA!
DO YOU STUTTER IN YOUR HEAD, TOO?
N-
N-
NO, I DON'T.
"N-N-NO, I DON'T!" HE SAYS.
HE'S DOING IT RIGHT NOW!

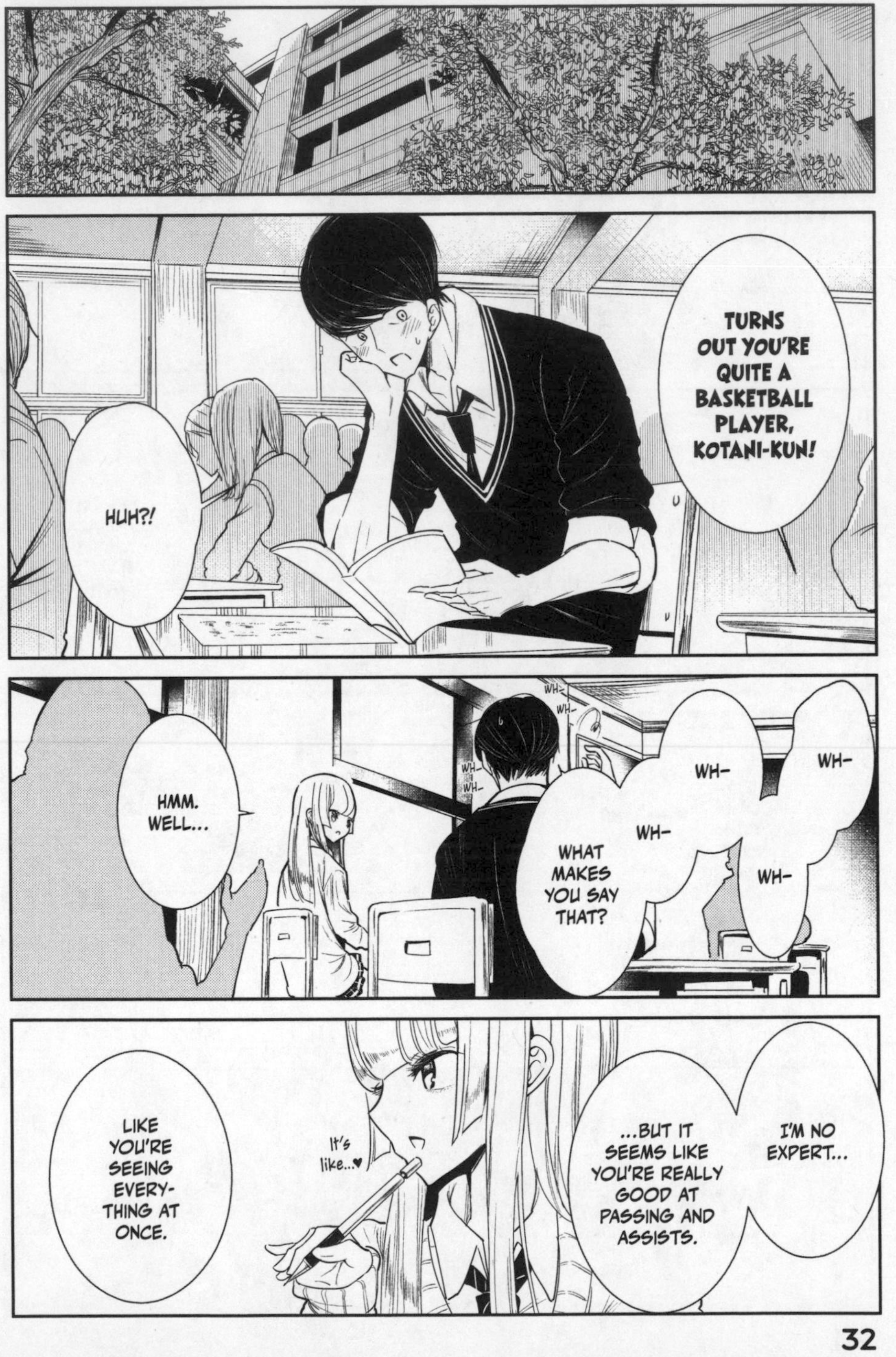
TURNS OUT YOU'RE QUITE A BASKETBALL PLAYER, KOTANI-KUN!
HUH?!
WH- WH-
WH- WH-
WH- WH- WH- WH- WH-
WHAT MAKES YOU SAY THAT?
HMM. WELL...
I'M NO EXPERT...
...BUT IT SEEMS LIKE YOU'RE REALLY GOOD AT PASSING AND ASSISTS.
It's like...♥
LIKE YOU'RE SEEING EVERY-THING AT ONCE.

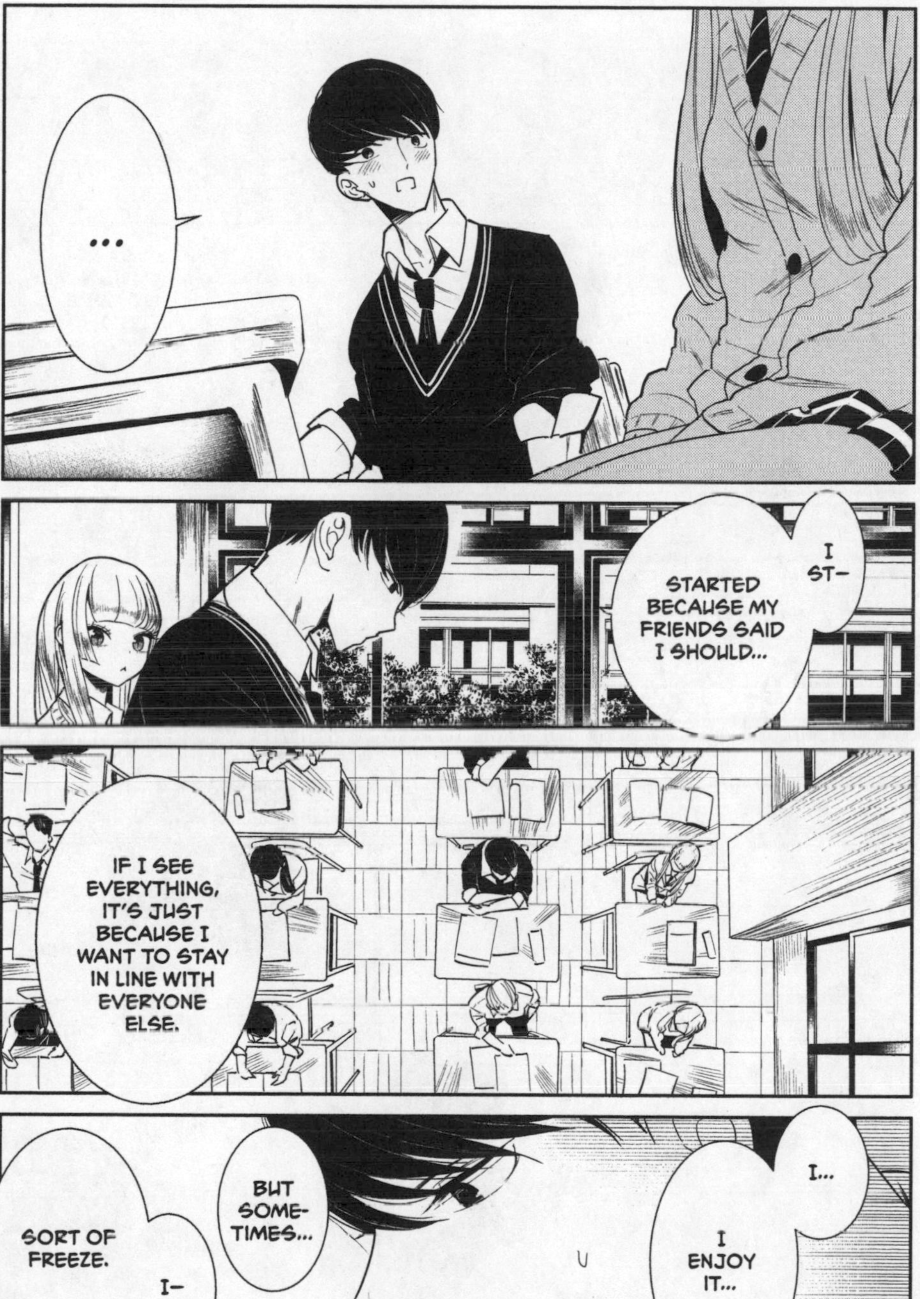
...
I ST—
STARTED BECAUSE MY FRIENDS SAID I SHOULD...
IF I SEE EVERYTHING, IT'S JUST BECAUSE I WANT TO STAY IN LINE WITH EVERYONE ELSE.
I...
I ENJOY IT...
BUT SOME-TIMES...
I—
SORT OF FREEZE.

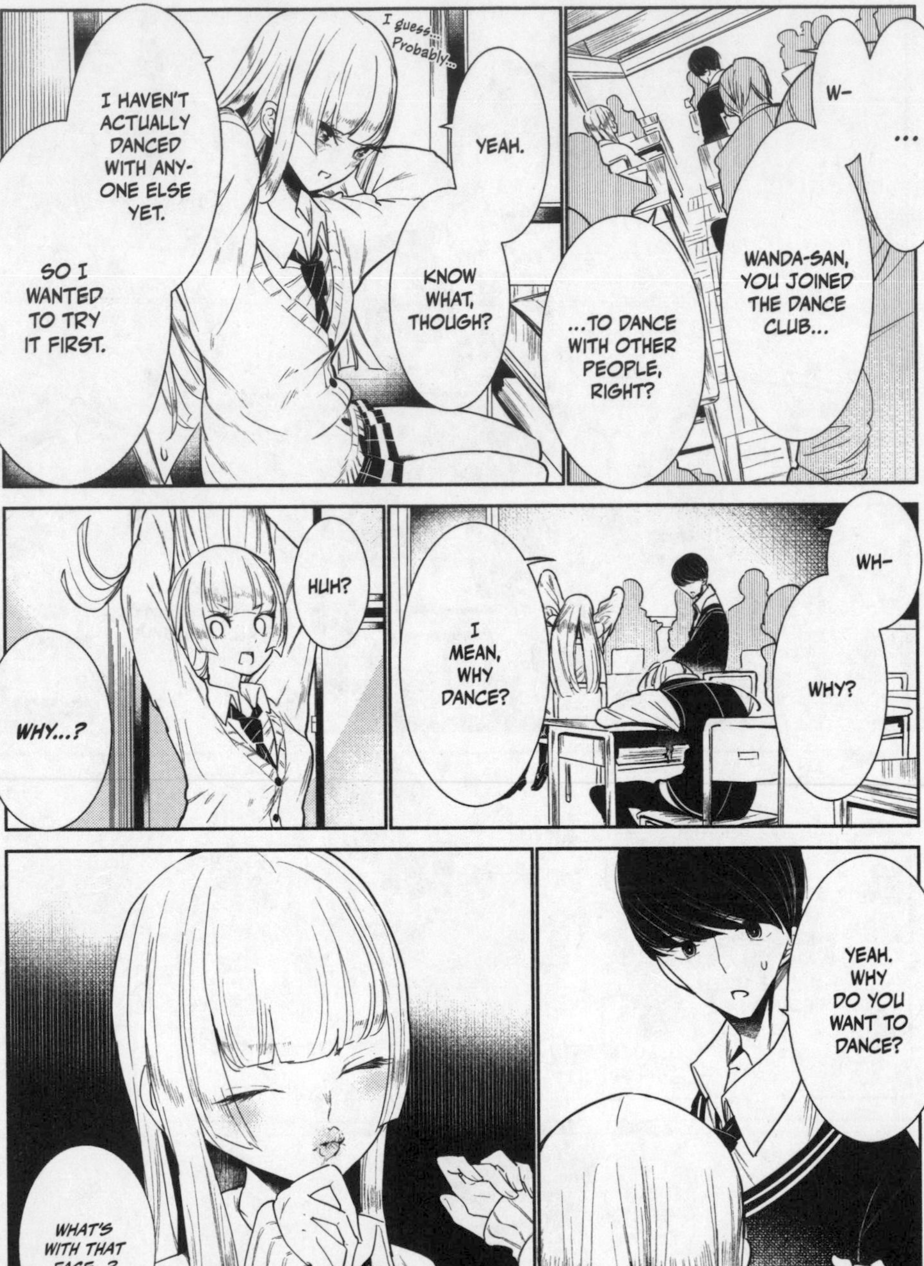
W-
...
WANDA-SAN, YOU JOINED THE DANCE CLUB...
...TO DANCE WITH OTHER PEOPLE, RIGHT?
YEAH.
I guess... Probably...
KNOW WHAT, THOUGH?
I HAVEN'T ACTUALLY DANCED WITH ANY-ONE ELSE YET.
SO I WANTED TO TRY IT FIRST.
WH-
WHY?
I MEAN, WHY DANCE?
HUH?
WHY...?
YEAH. WHY DO YOU WANT TO DANCE?
WHAT'S WITH THAT FACE...?

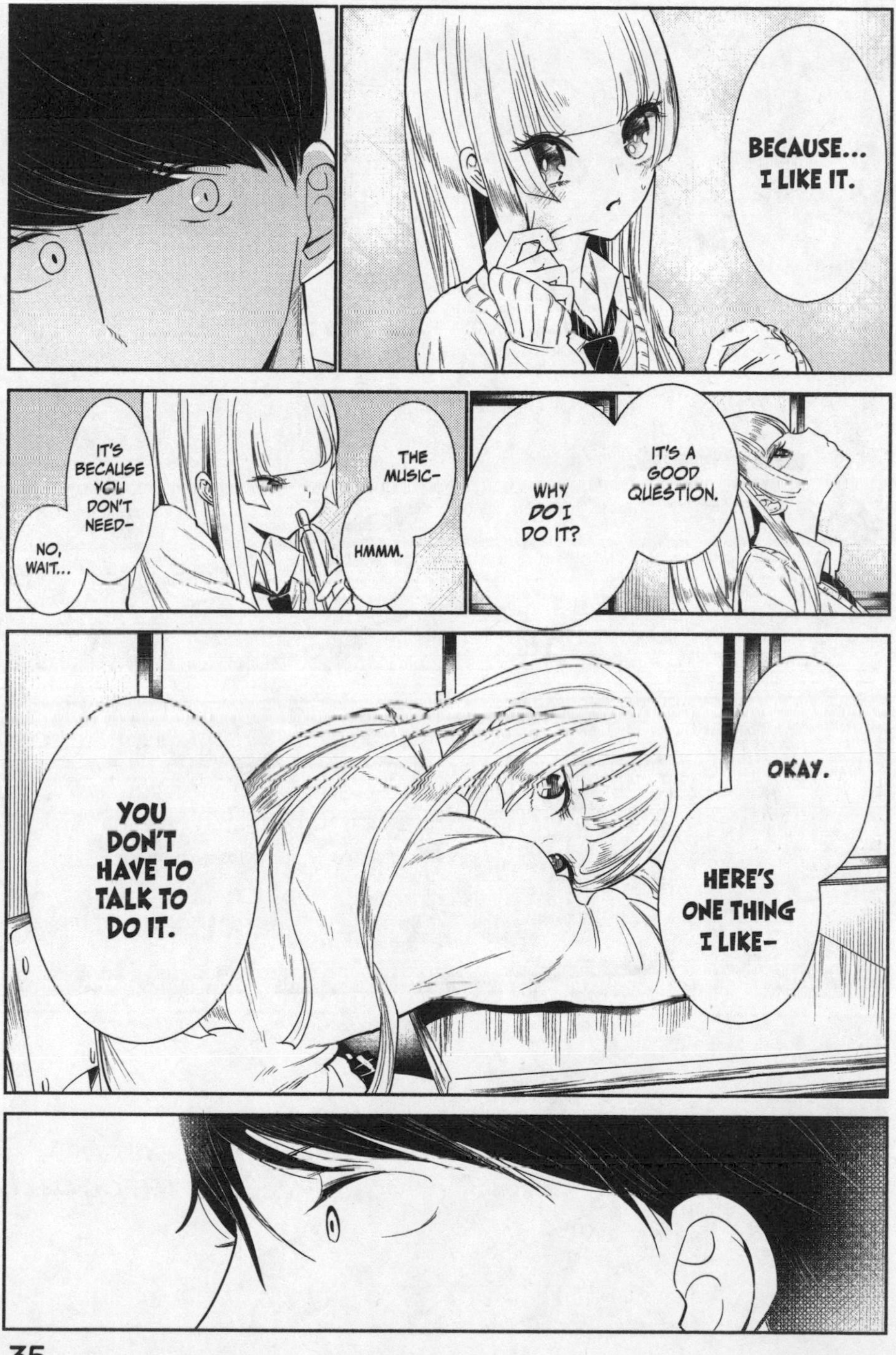
BECAUSE... I LIKE IT.
IT'S A GOOD QUESTION.
WHY *DO* I DO IT?
THE MUSIC-
HMMM.
IT'S BECAUSE YOU DON'T NEED-
NO, WAIT...
OKAY.
HERE'S ONE THING I LIKE-
YOU DON'T HAVE TO TALK TO DO IT.

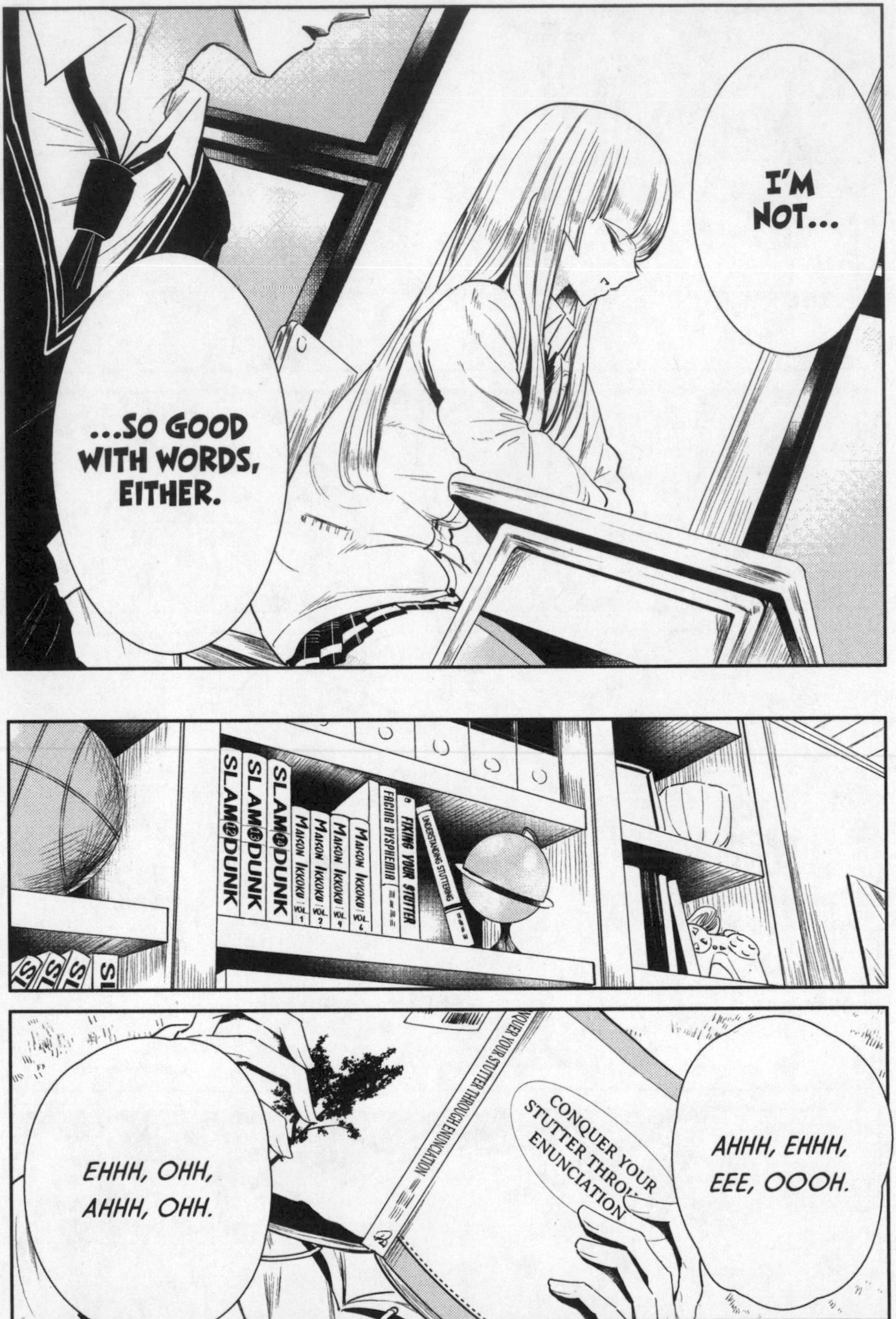
I'M NOT...
...SO GOOD WITH WORDS, EITHER.
UNDERSTANDING STUTTERING
FIXING YOUR STUTTER
FACING DYSPHEMIA
MAISON IKKOKU VOL. 6
MAISON IKKOKU VOL. 4
MAISON IKKOKU VOL. 2
MAISON IKKOKU VOL. 1
SLAM DUNK
SLAM DUNK
SLAM DUNK
AHHH, EHHH, EEE, OOOH.
CONQUER YOUR STUTTER THROUGH ENUNCIATION
EHHH, OHH, AHHH, OHH.

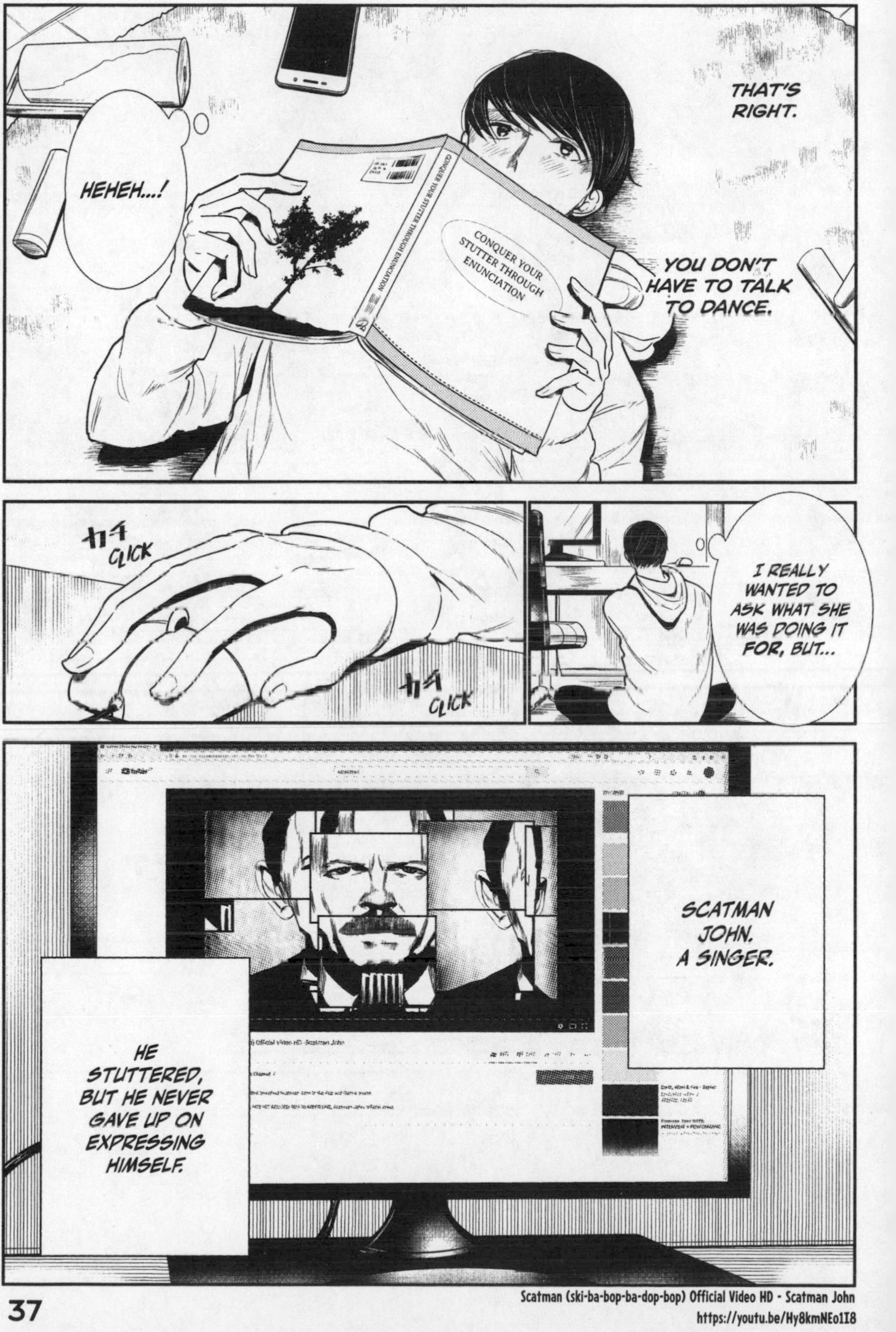
THAT'S RIGHT.
YOU DON'T HAVE TO TALK TO DANCE.
CONQUER YOUR STUTTER THROUGH ENUNCIATION
HEHEH...!
I REALLY WANTED TO ASK WHAT SHE WAS DOING IT FOR, BUT...
カチ CLICK
カチ CLICK
SCATMAN JOHN. A SINGER.
HE STUTTERED, BUT HE NEVER GAVE UP ON EXPRESSING HIMSELF.

Scatman (ski-ba-bop-ba-dop-bop) Official Video HD - Scatman John
https://youtu.be/Hy8kmNEo1I8

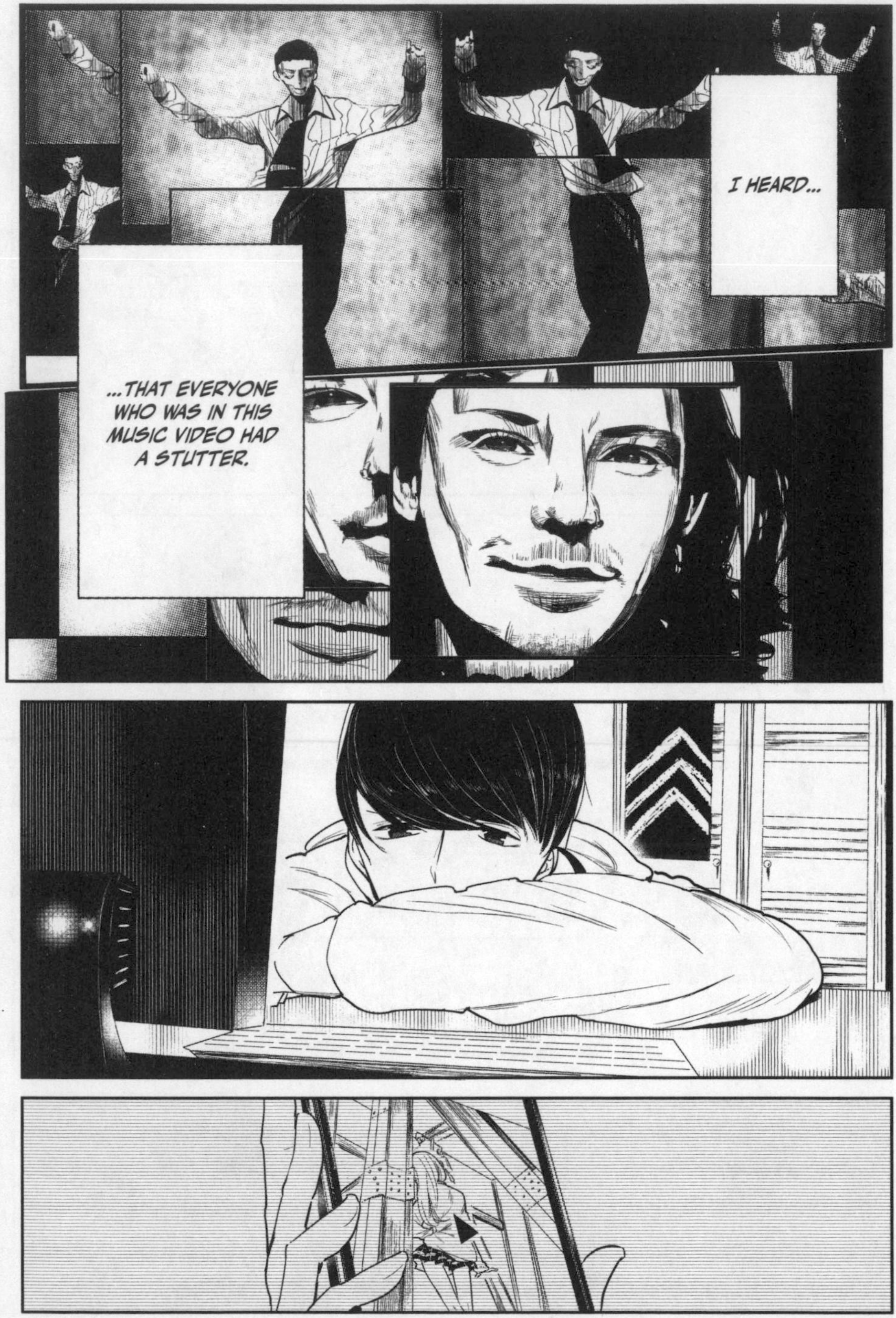
I HEARD...
...THAT EVERYONE WHO WAS IN THIS MUSIC VIDEO HAD A STUTTER.

I WANT TO SEE IT.

I WANT TO SEE WANDĀ-SAN DANCE.

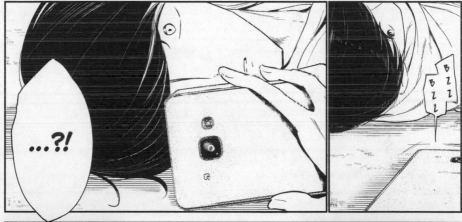

...?!

B Z Z Z

‹ Toyoball Class 14 (22)

Hoto

Witness the Ichirin winner!

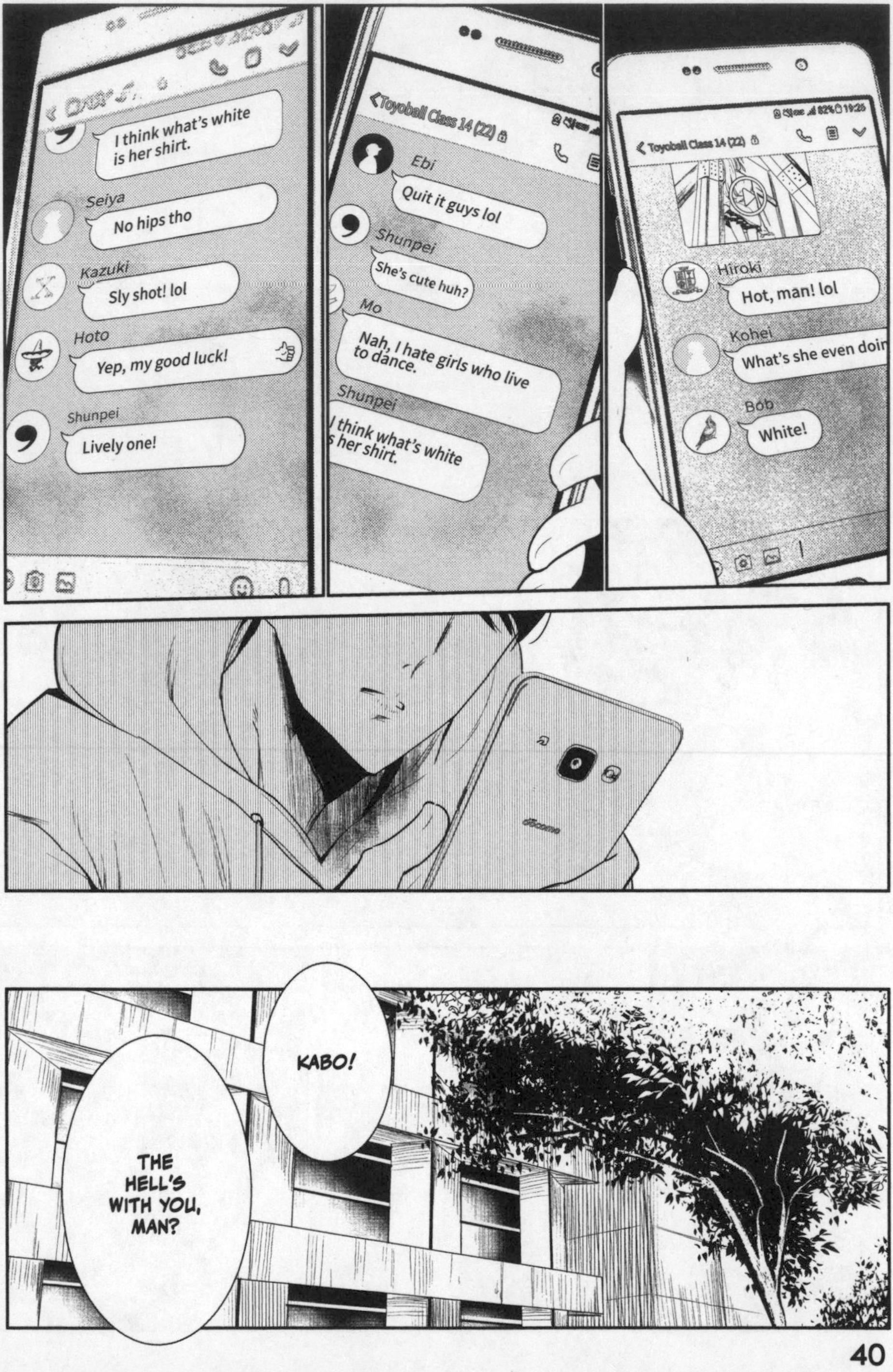
Toyoball Class 14 (22)
Hiroki
Hot, man! lol
Kohei
What's she even doin
Bob
White!
Toyoball Class 14 (22)
Ebi
Quit it guys lol
Shunpei
She's cute huh?
Mo
Nah, I hate girls who live to dance.
Shunpei
I think what's white s her shirt.
I think what's white is her shirt.
Seiya
No hips tho
Kazuki
Sly shot! lol
Hoto
Yep, my good luck!
Shunpei
Lively one!
KABO!
THE HELL'S WITH YOU, MAN?

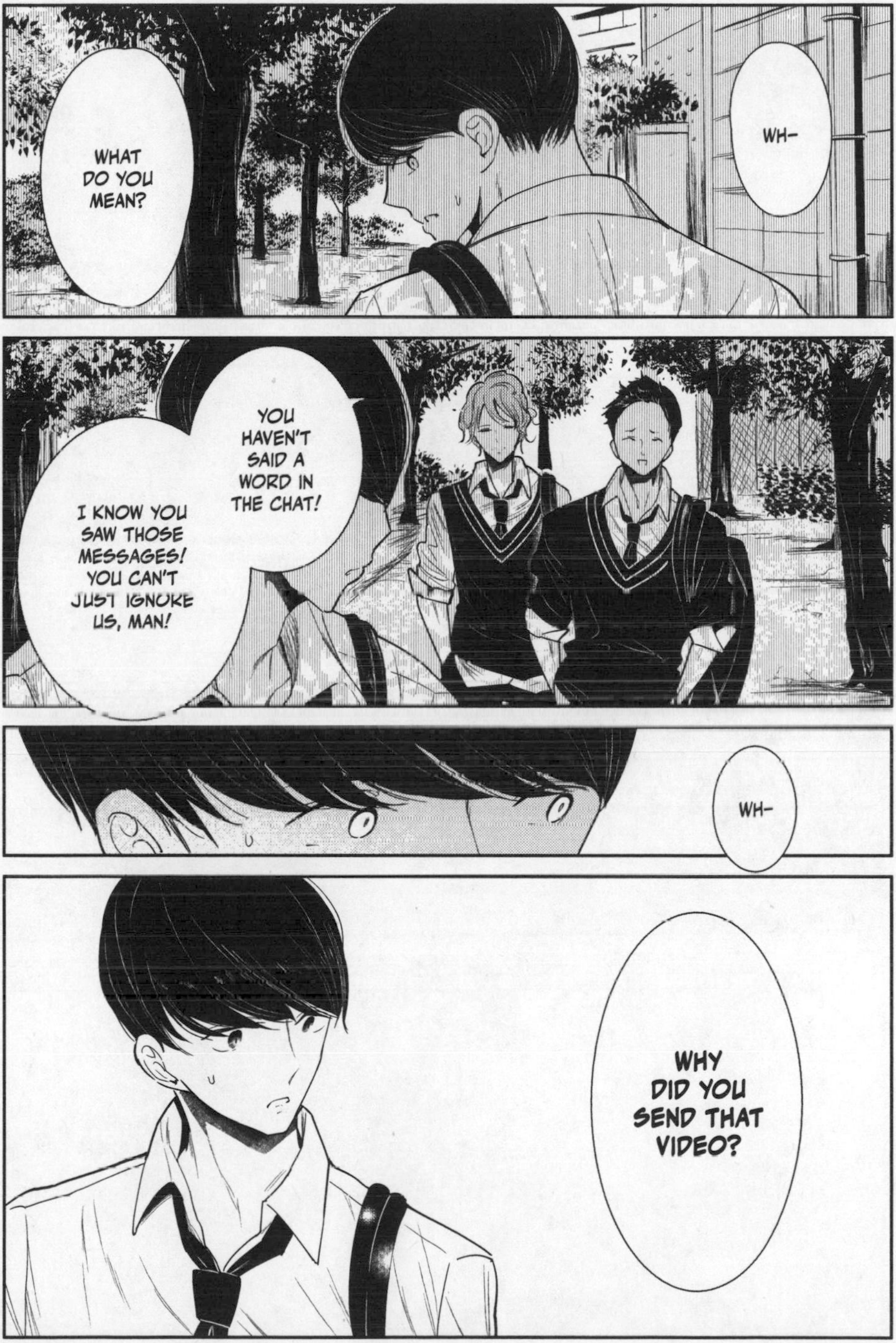
WH-
WHAT DO YOU MEAN?
YOU HAVEN'T SAID A WORD IN THE CHAT!
I KNOW YOU SAW THOSE MESSAGES! YOU CAN'T JUST IGNORE US, MAN!
WH-
WHY DID YOU SEND THAT VIDEO?

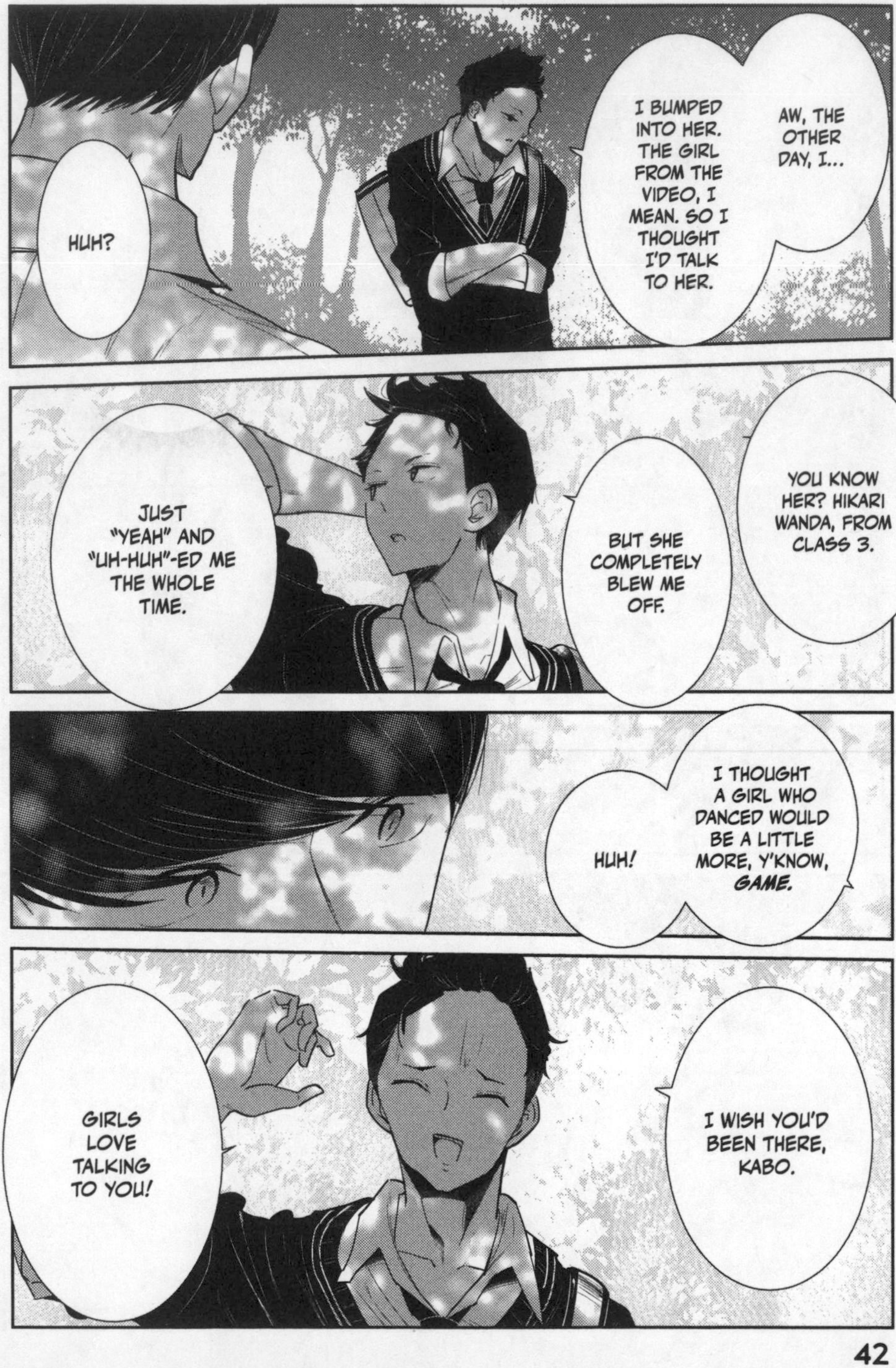
AW, THE OTHER DAY, I...
I BUMPED INTO HER. THE GIRL FROM THE VIDEO, I MEAN. SO I THOUGHT I'D TALK TO HER.
HUH?
YOU KNOW HER? HIKARI WANDA, FROM CLASS 3.
BUT SHE COMPLETELY BLEW ME OFF.
JUST "YEAH" AND "UH-HUH"-ED ME THE WHOLE TIME.
I THOUGHT A GIRL WHO DANCED WOULD BE A LITTLE MORE, Y'KNOW, *GAME.*
HUH!
I WISH YOU'D BEEN THERE, KABO.
GIRLS LOVE TALKING TO YOU!

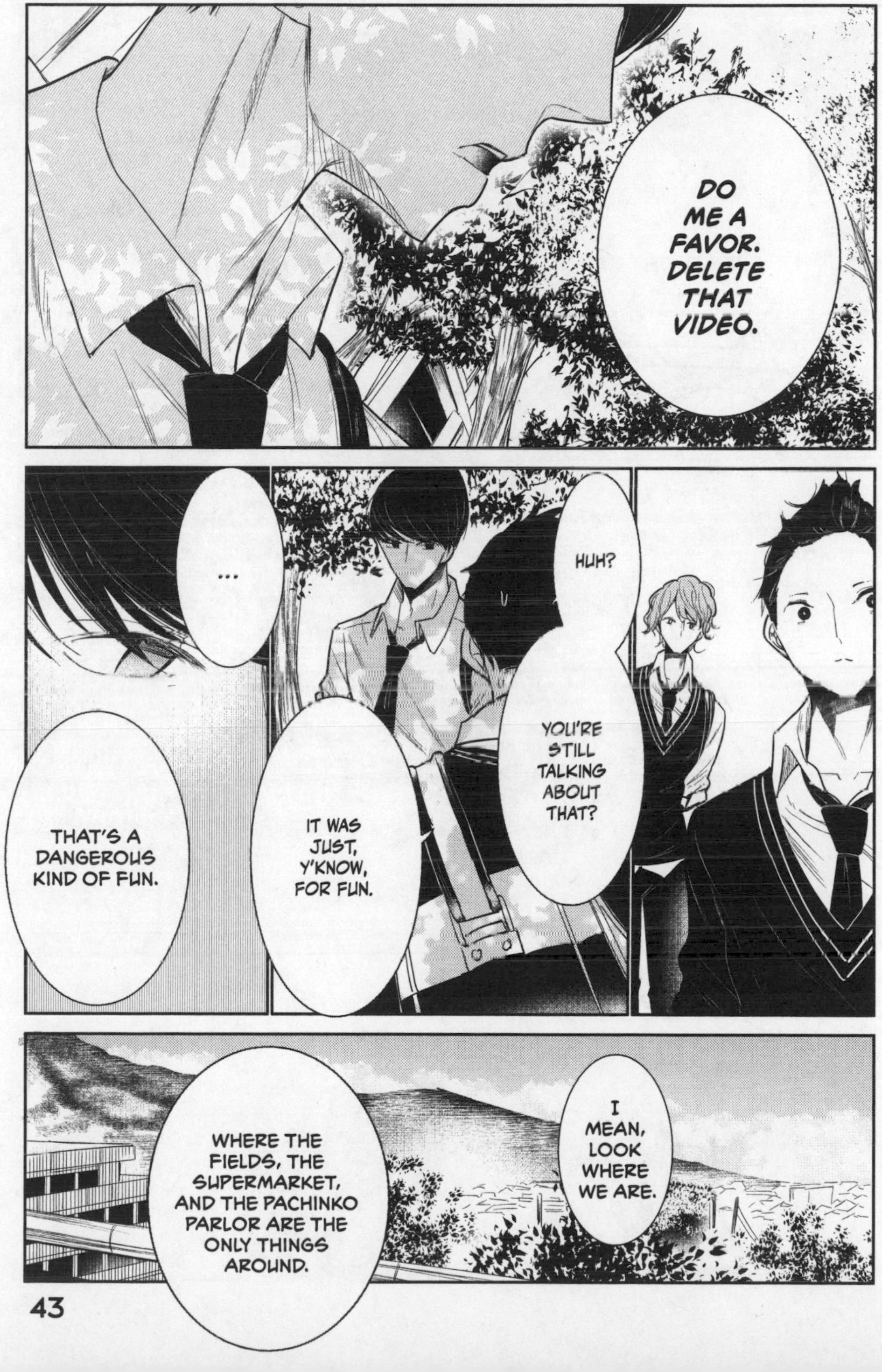
DO ME A FAVOR. DELETE THAT VIDEO.
HUH?
YOU'RE STILL TALKING ABOUT THAT?
IT WAS JUST, Y'KNOW, FOR FUN.
...
THAT'S A DANGEROUS KIND OF FUN.
I MEAN, LOOK WHERE WE ARE.
WHERE THE FIELDS, THE SUPERMARKET, AND THE PACHINKO PARLOR ARE THE ONLY THINGS AROUND.

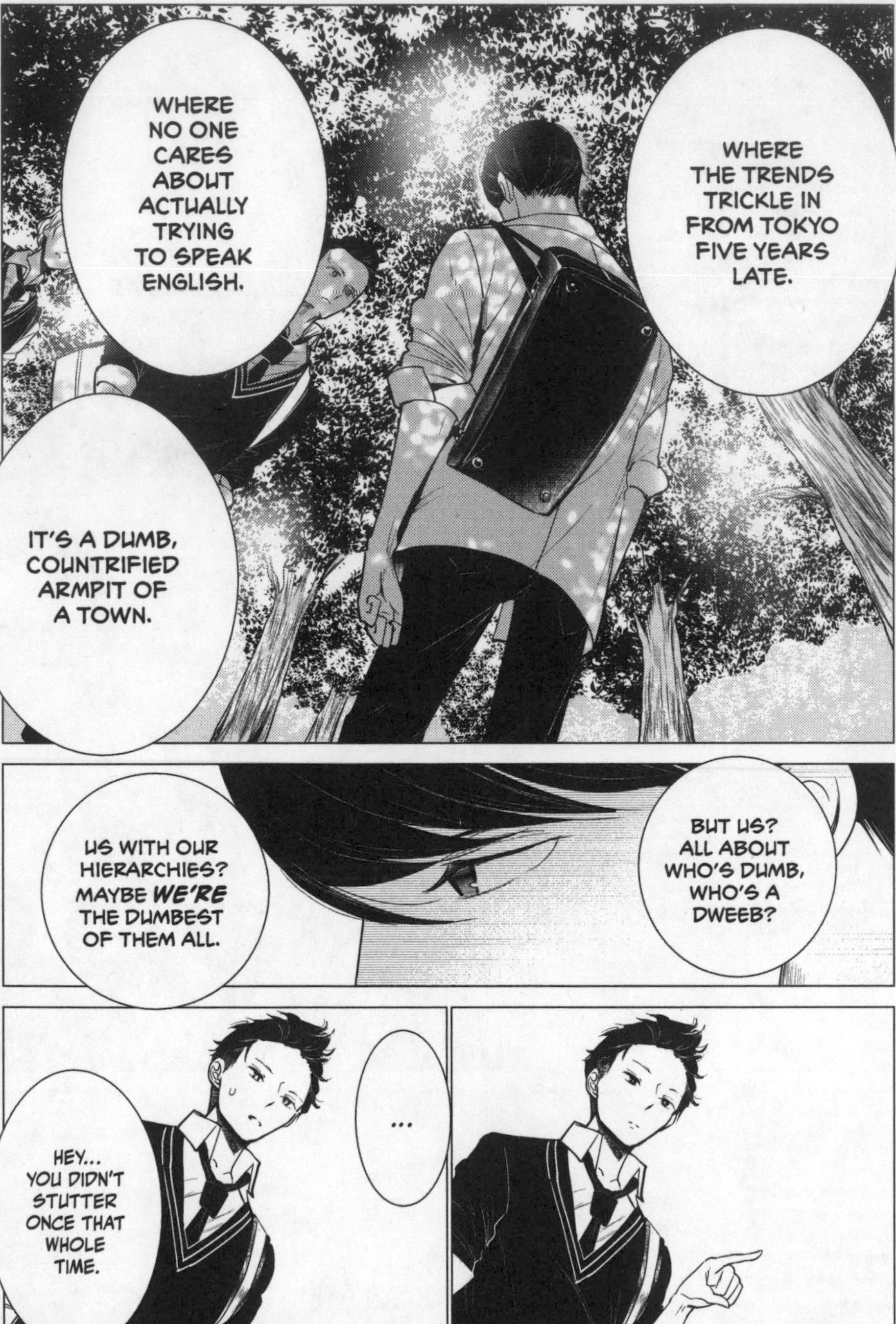
WHERE THE TRENDS TRICKLE IN FROM TOKYO FIVE YEARS LATE.
WHERE NO ONE CARES ABOUT ACTUALLY TRYING TO SPEAK ENGLISH.
IT'S A DUMB, COUNTRIFIED ARMPIT OF A TOWN.
BUT US? ALL ABOUT WHO'S DUMB, WHO'S A DWEEB?
US WITH OUR HIERARCHIES? MAYBE *WE'RE* THE DUMBEST OF THEM ALL.
...
HEY... YOU DIDN'T STUTTER ONCE THAT WHOLE TIME.

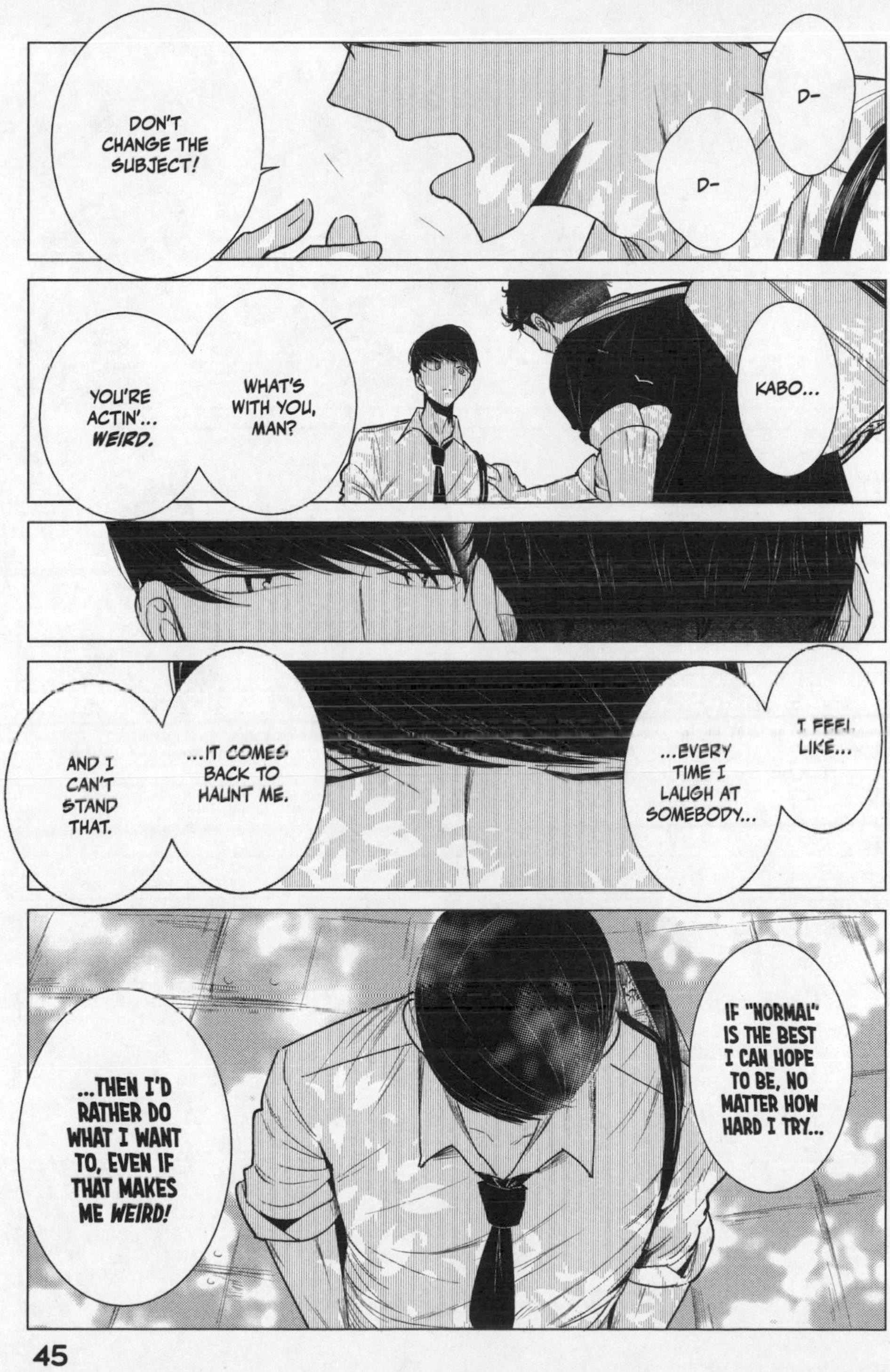
D-
D-
DON'T CHANGE THE SUBJECT!
KABO...
WHAT'S WITH YOU, MAN?
YOU'RE ACTIN'... *WEIRD.*
I FEEL LIKE...
...EVERY TIME I LAUGH AT SOMEBODY...
...IT COMES BACK TO HAUNT ME.
AND I CAN'T STAND THAT.
IF "NORMAL" IS THE BEST I CAN HOPE TO BE, NO MATTER HOW HARD I TRY...
...THEN I'D RATHER DO WHAT I WANT TO, EVEN IF THAT MAKES ME *WEIRD!*

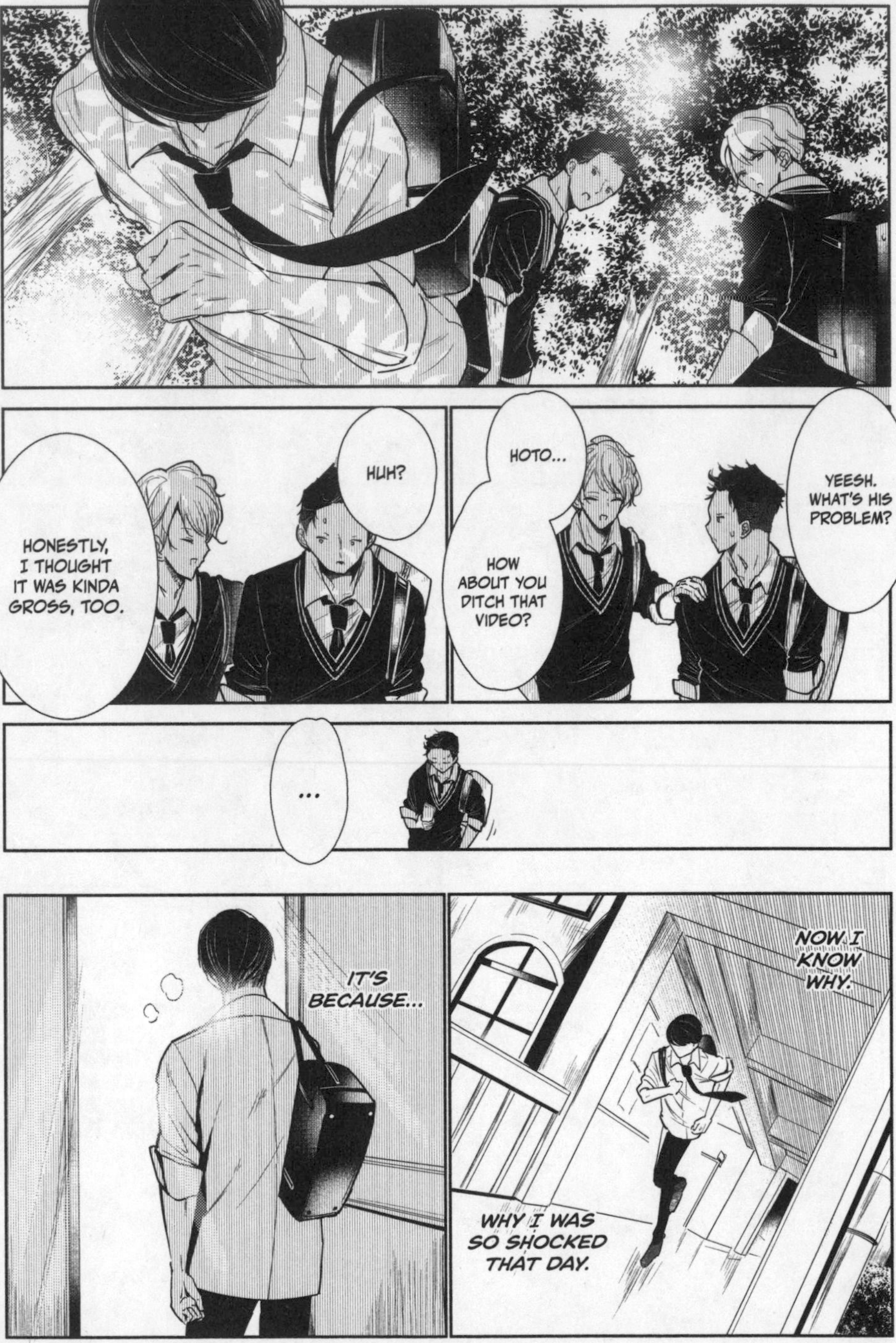
YEESH. WHAT'S HIS PROBLEM?
HOTO...
HOW ABOUT YOU DITCH THAT VIDEO?
HUH?
HONESTLY, I THOUGHT IT WAS KINDA GROSS, TOO.
...
NOW I KNOW WHY.
WHY I WAS SO SHOCKED THAT DAY.
IT'S BECAUSE...

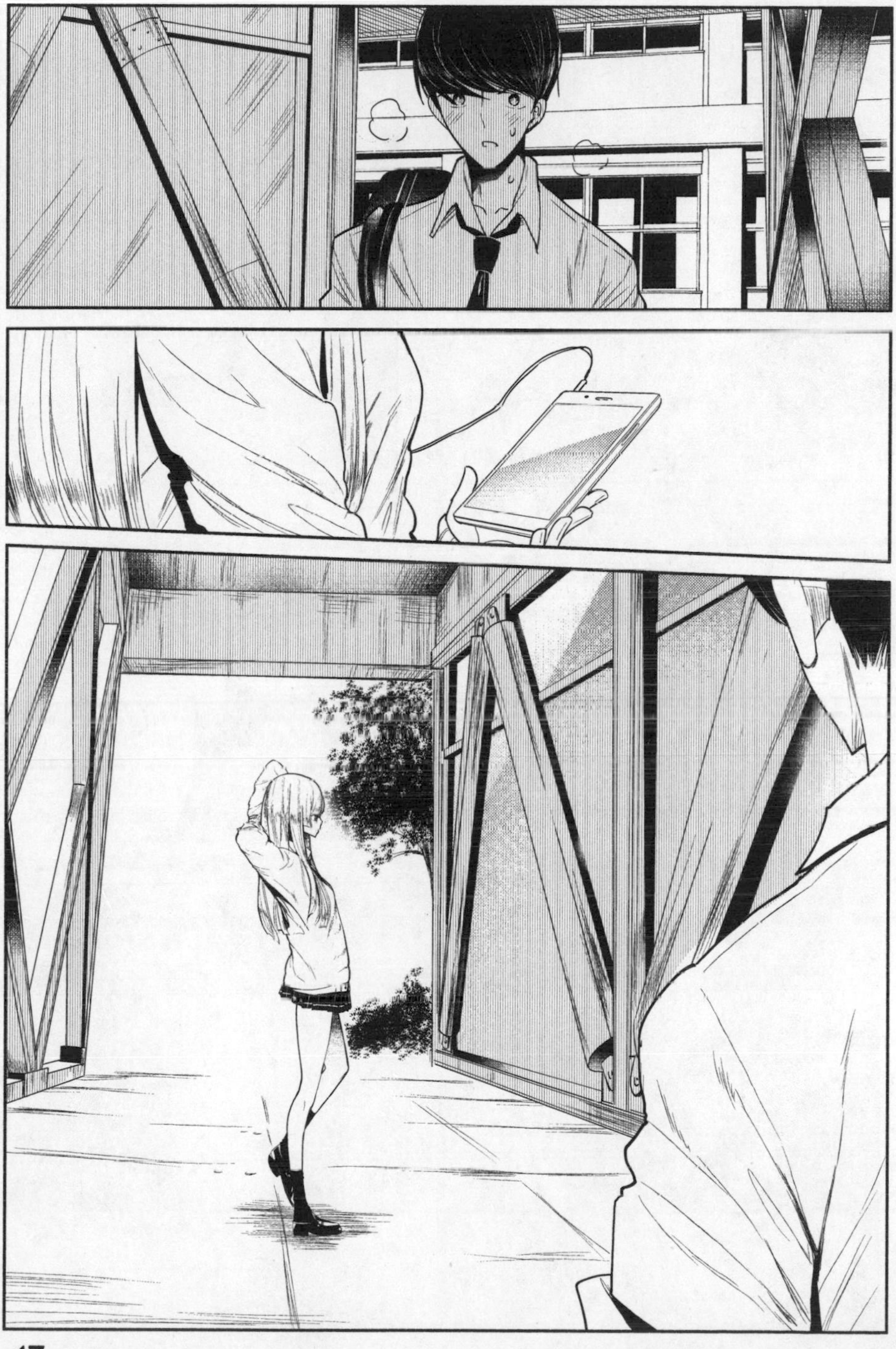

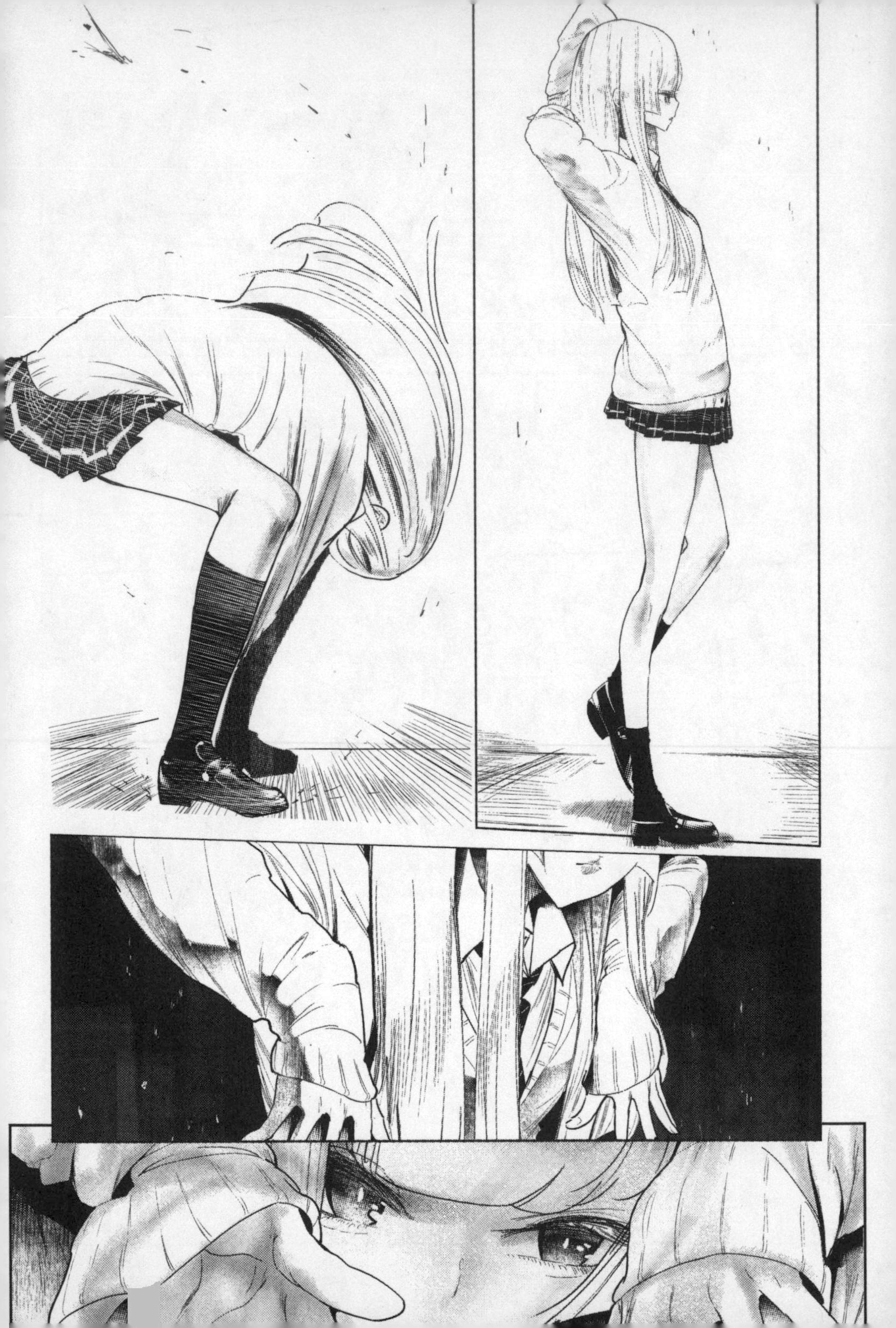

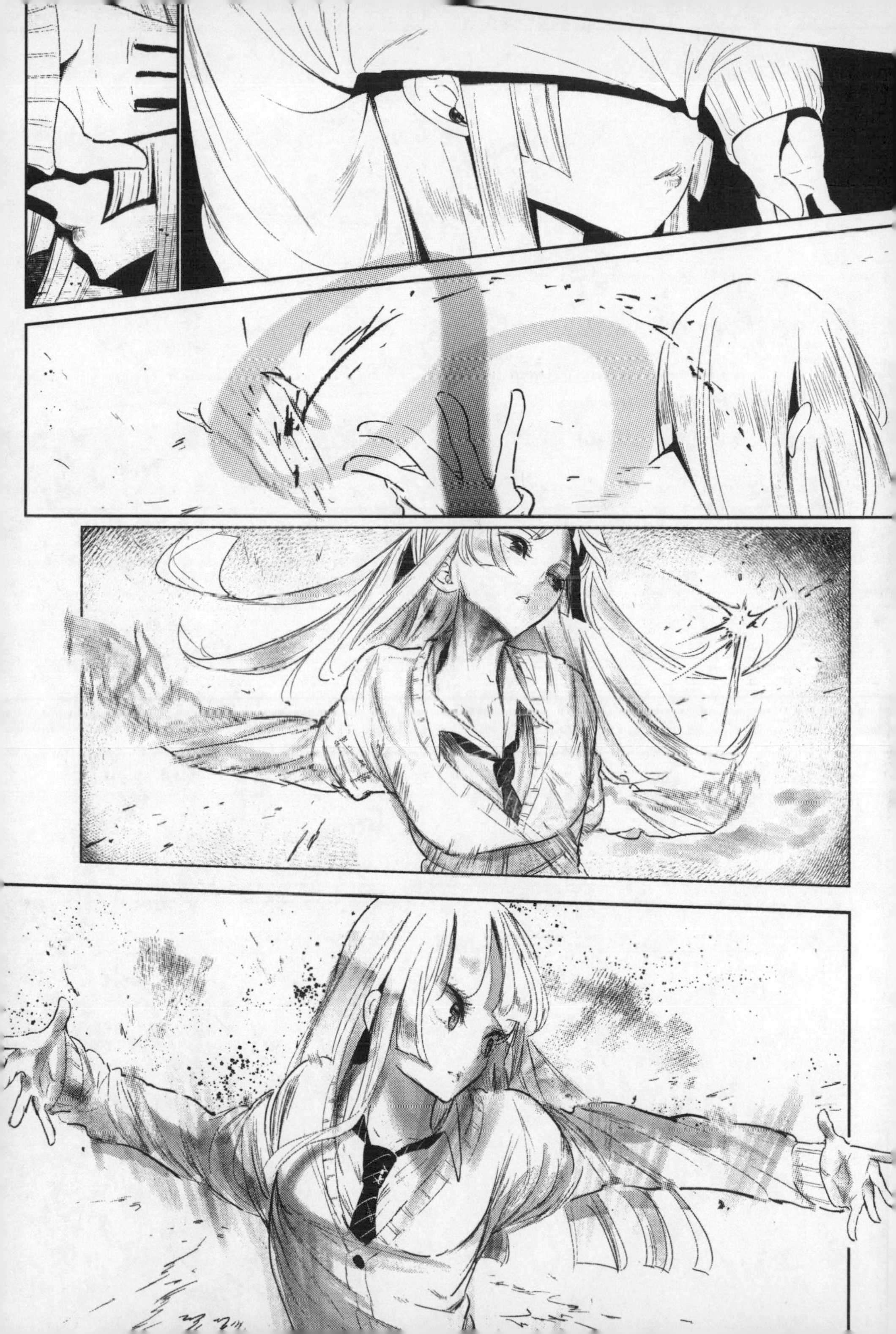

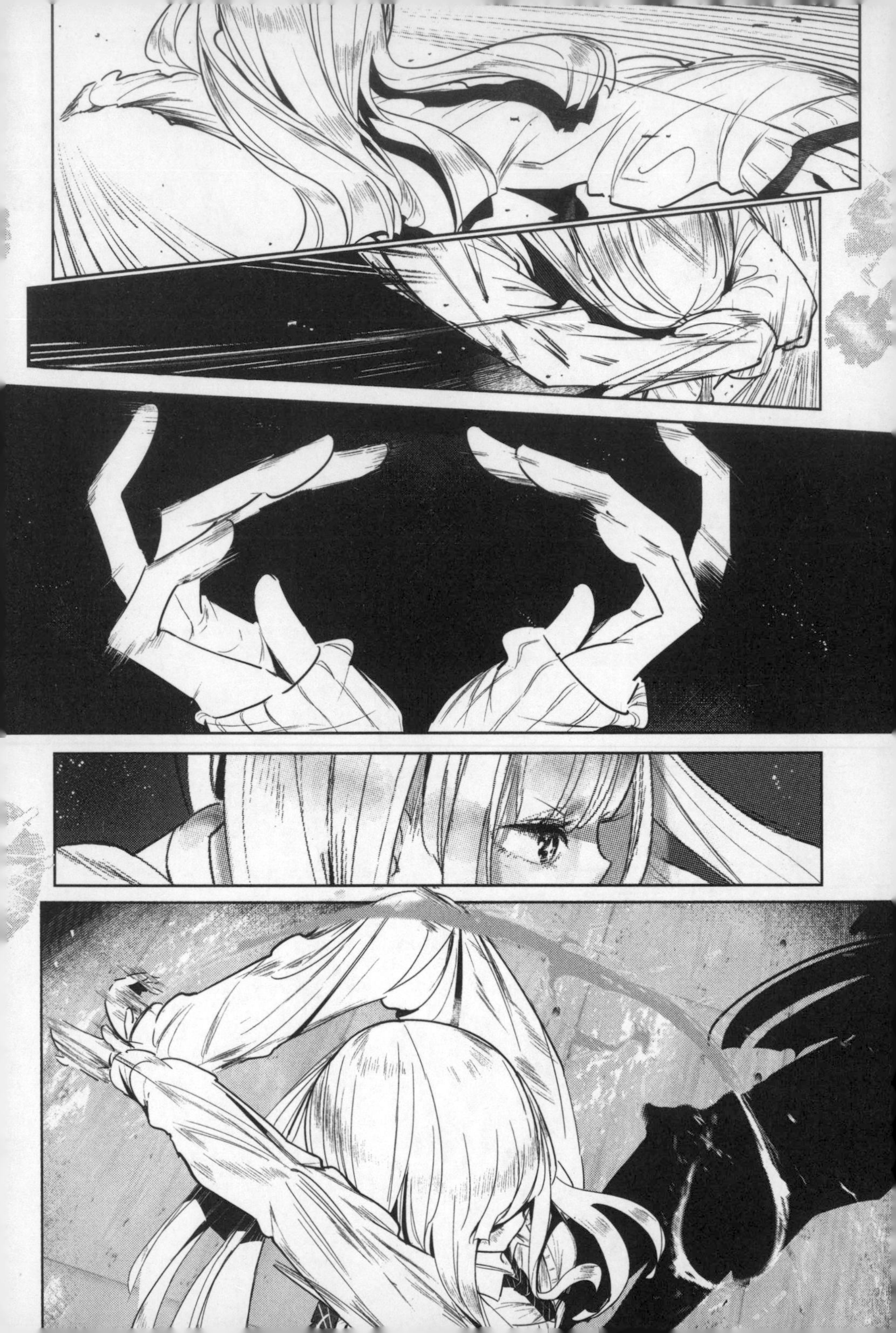

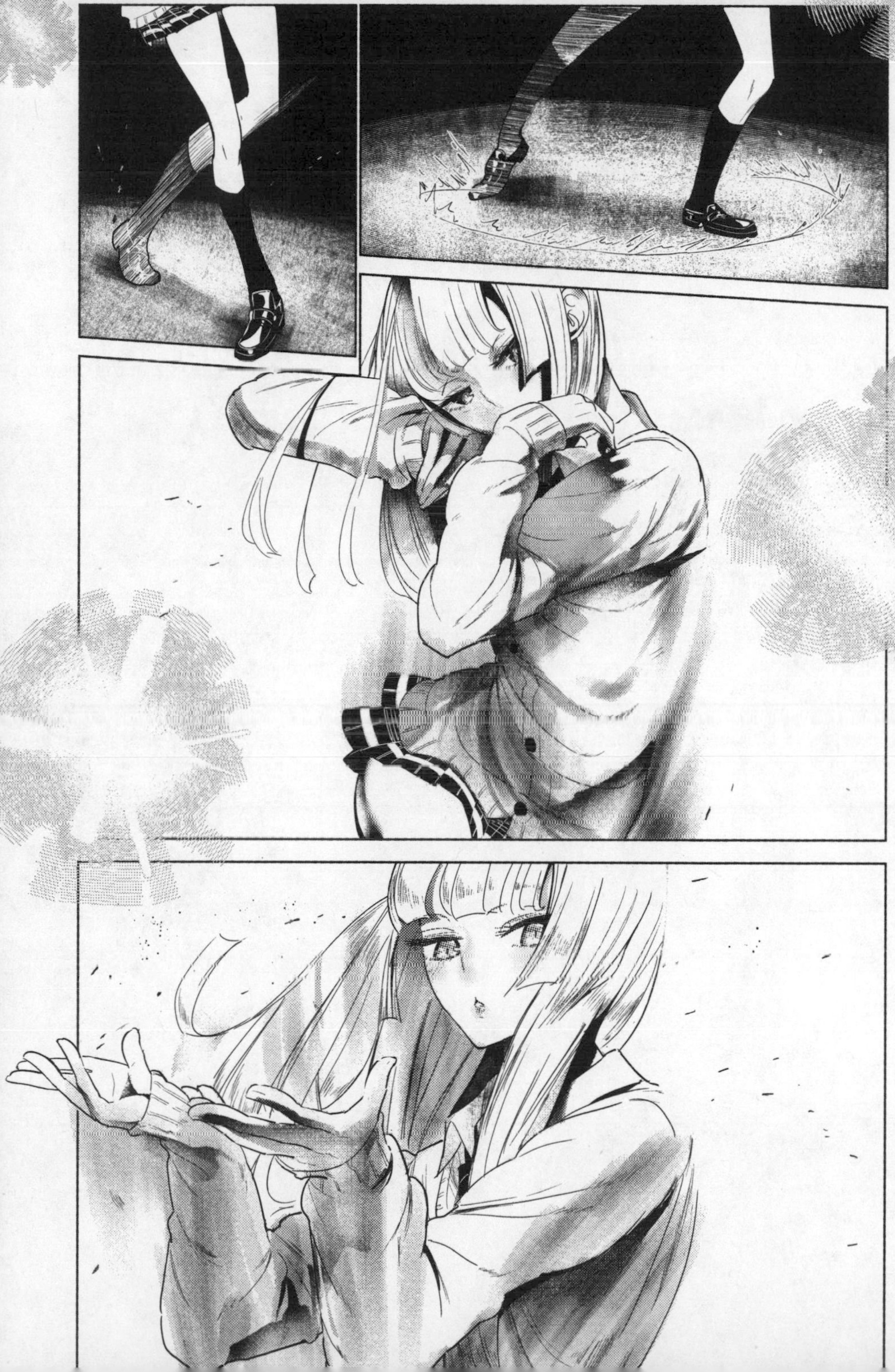

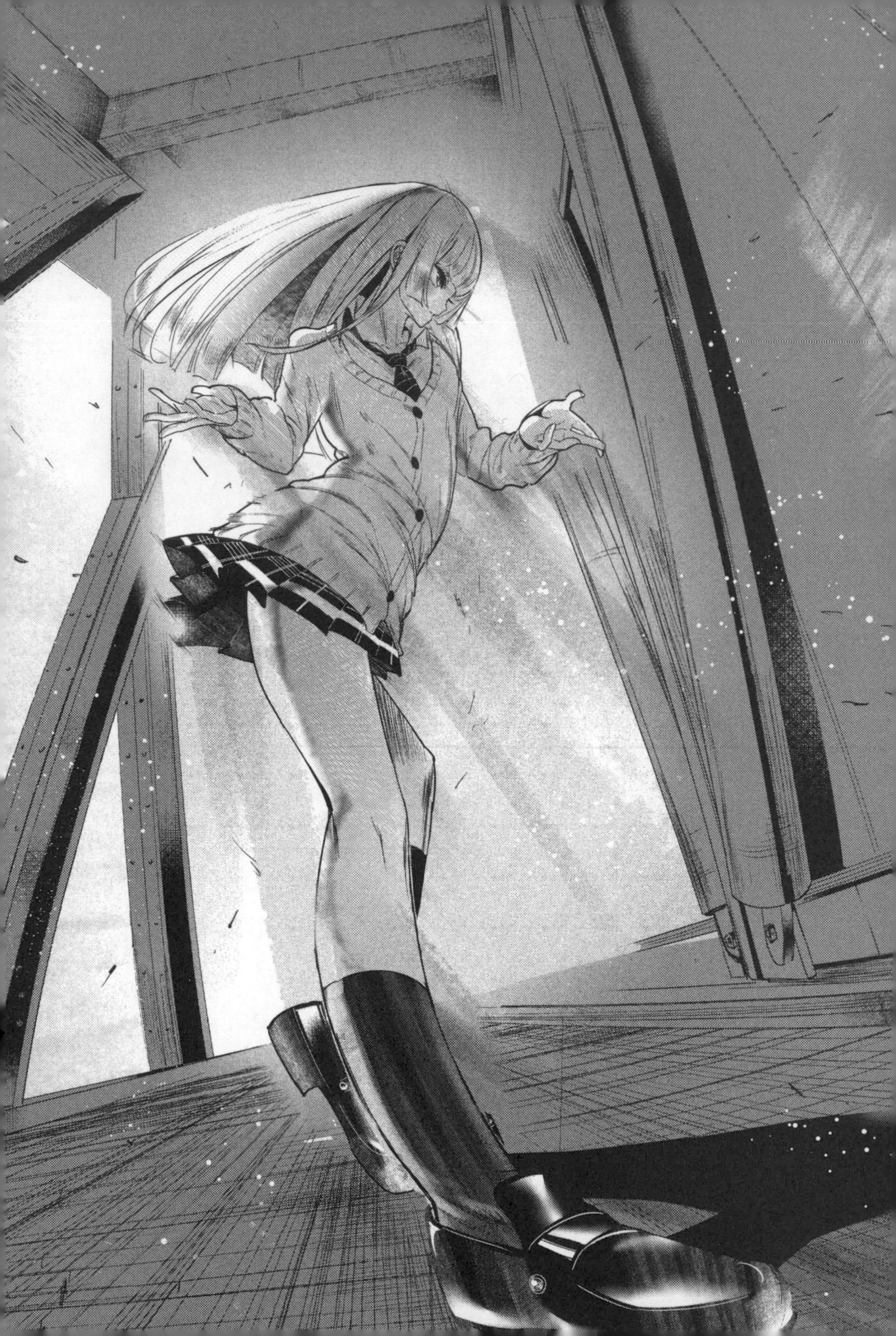

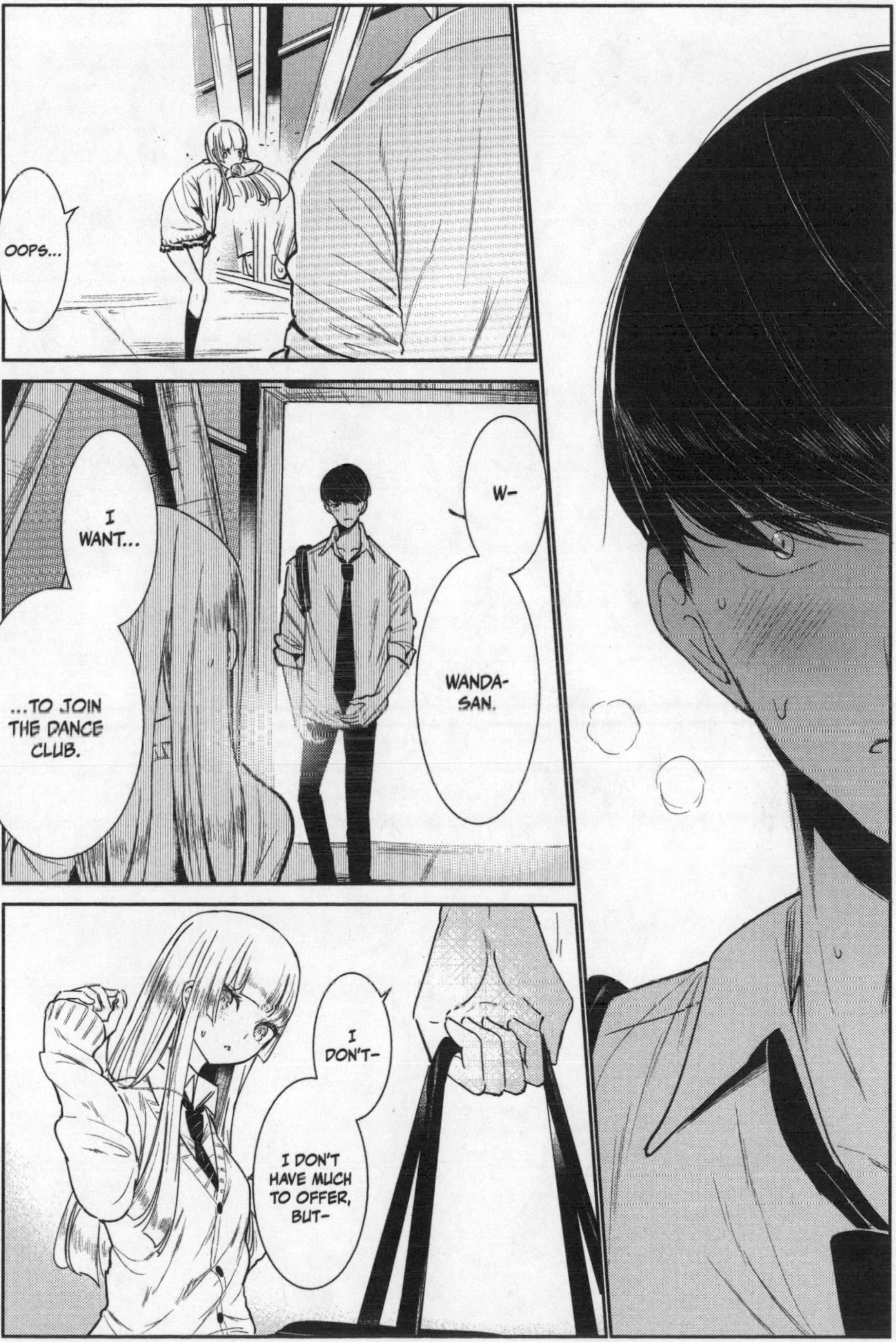
OOPS...
W-
WANDA-SAN.
I WANT...
...TO JOIN THE DANCE CLUB.
I DON'T-
I DON'T HAVE MUCH TO OFFER, BUT-

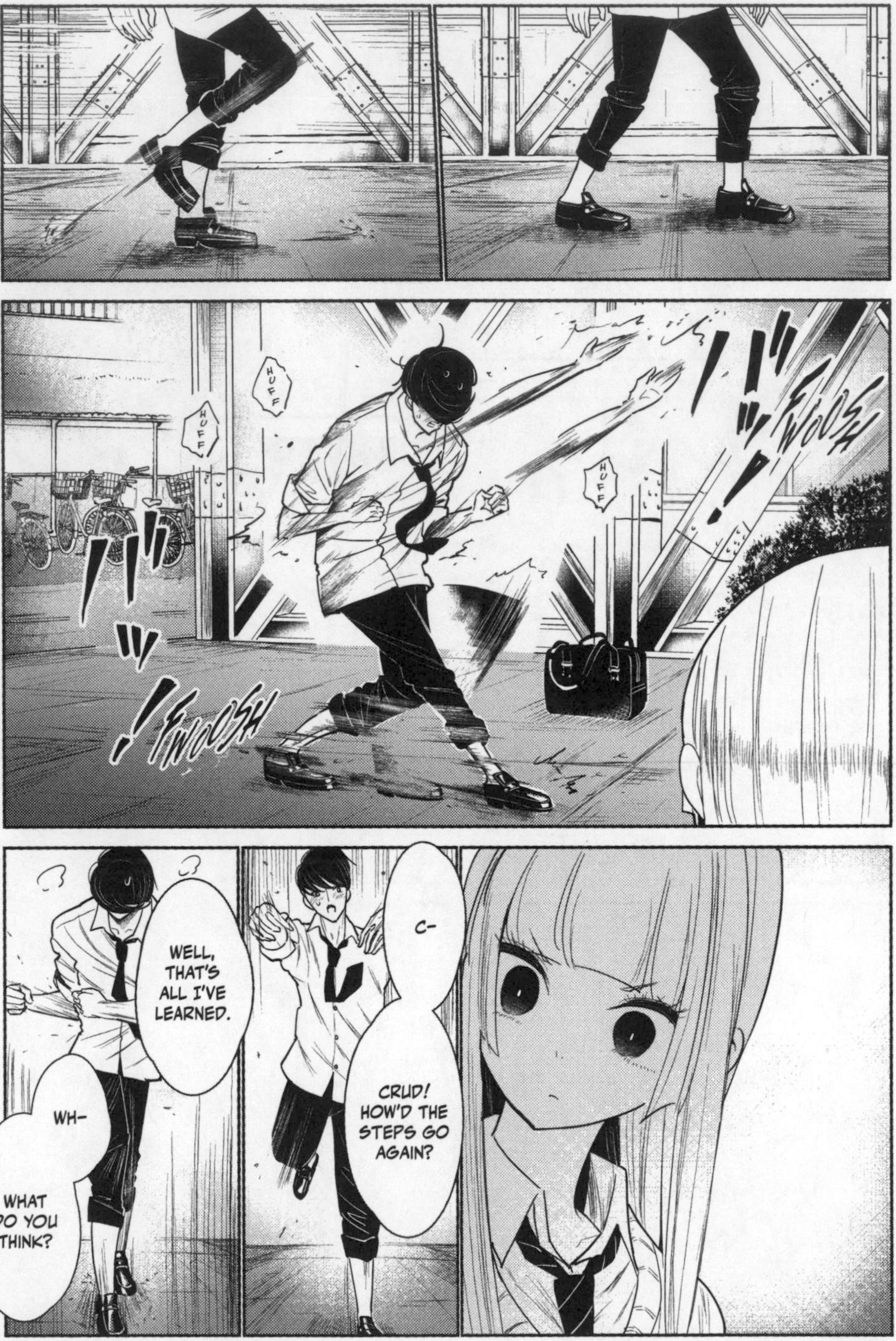
FWOOSH
HUFF
HUFF
HUFF
FWOOSH
C-
CRUD! HOW'D THE STEPS GO AGAIN?
WELL, THAT'S ALL I'VE LEARNED.
WH-
WHAT DO YOU THINK?

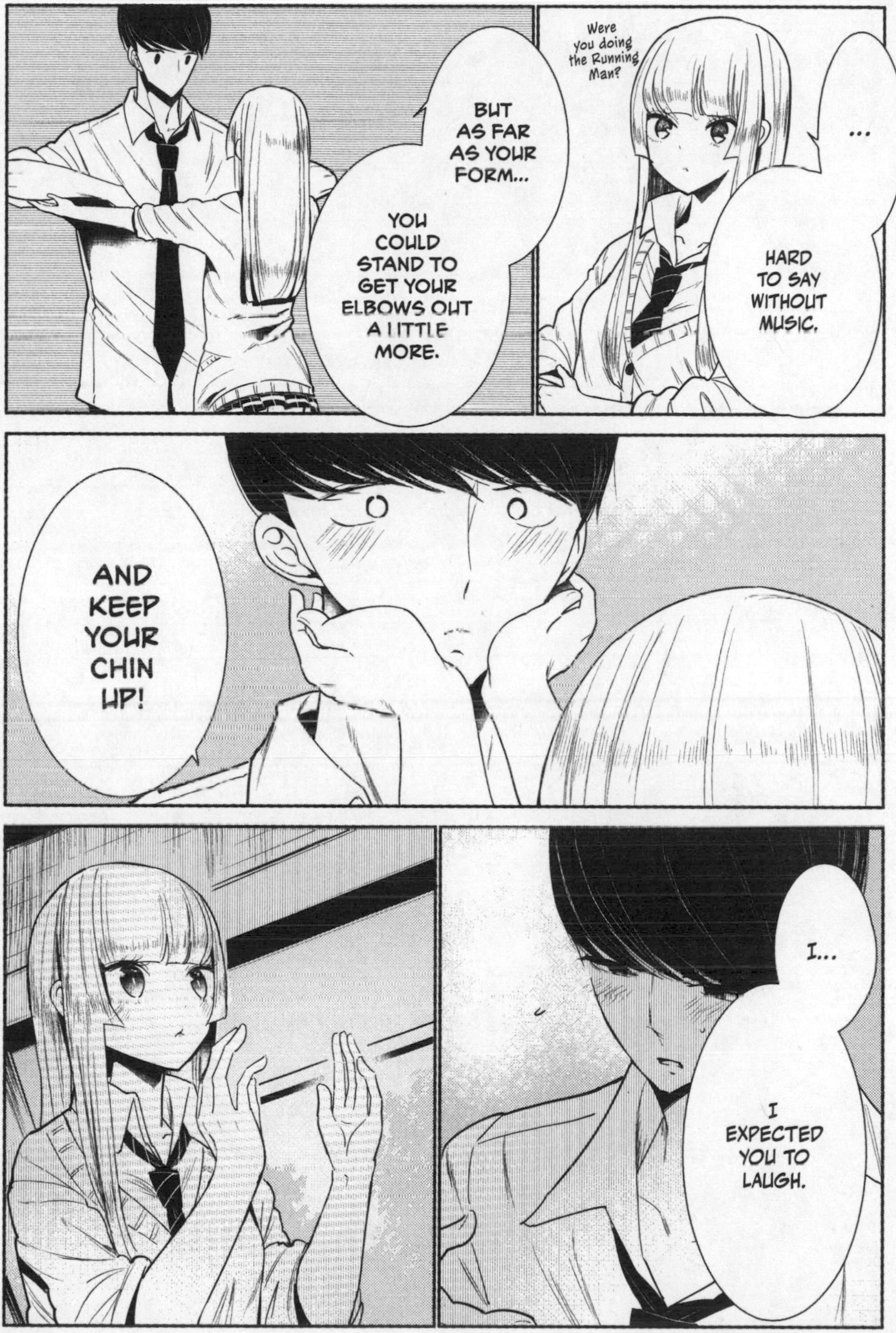
...
Were you doing the Running Man?
HARD TO SAY WITHOUT MUSIC.
BUT AS FAR AS YOUR FORM...
YOU COULD STAND TO GET YOUR ELBOWS OUT A LITTLE MORE.
AND KEEP YOUR CHIN UP!
I...
I EXPECTED YOU TO LAUGH.

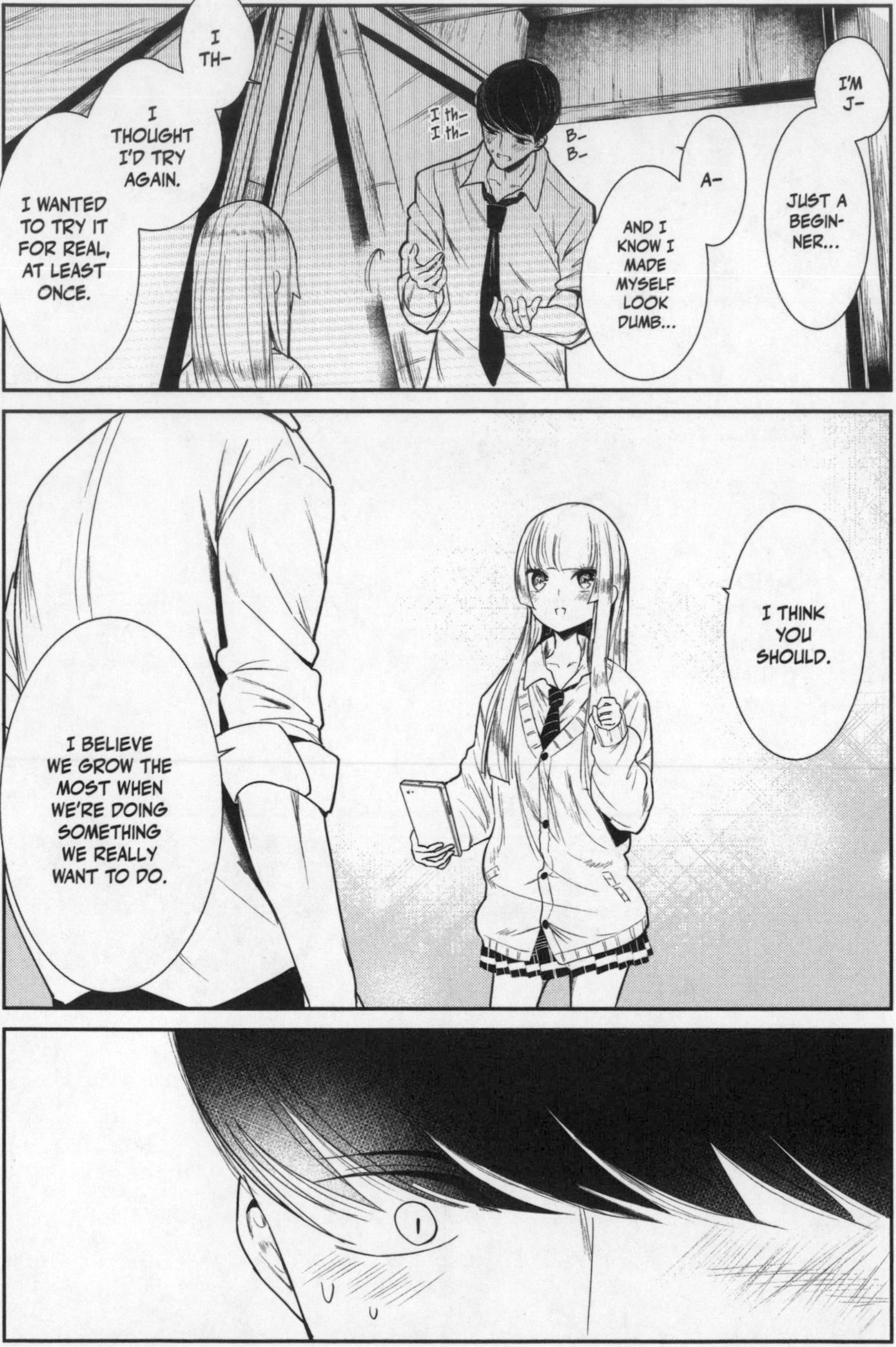
I'M J-
JUST A BEGINNER...
A-
AND I KNOW I MADE MYSELF LOOK DUMB...
B- B-
I th- I th-
I TH-
I THOUGHT I'D TRY AGAIN.
I WANTED TO TRY IT FOR REAL, AT LEAST ONCE.
I THINK YOU SHOULD.
I BELIEVE WE GROW THE MOST WHEN WE'RE DOING SOMETHING WE REALLY WANT TO DO.

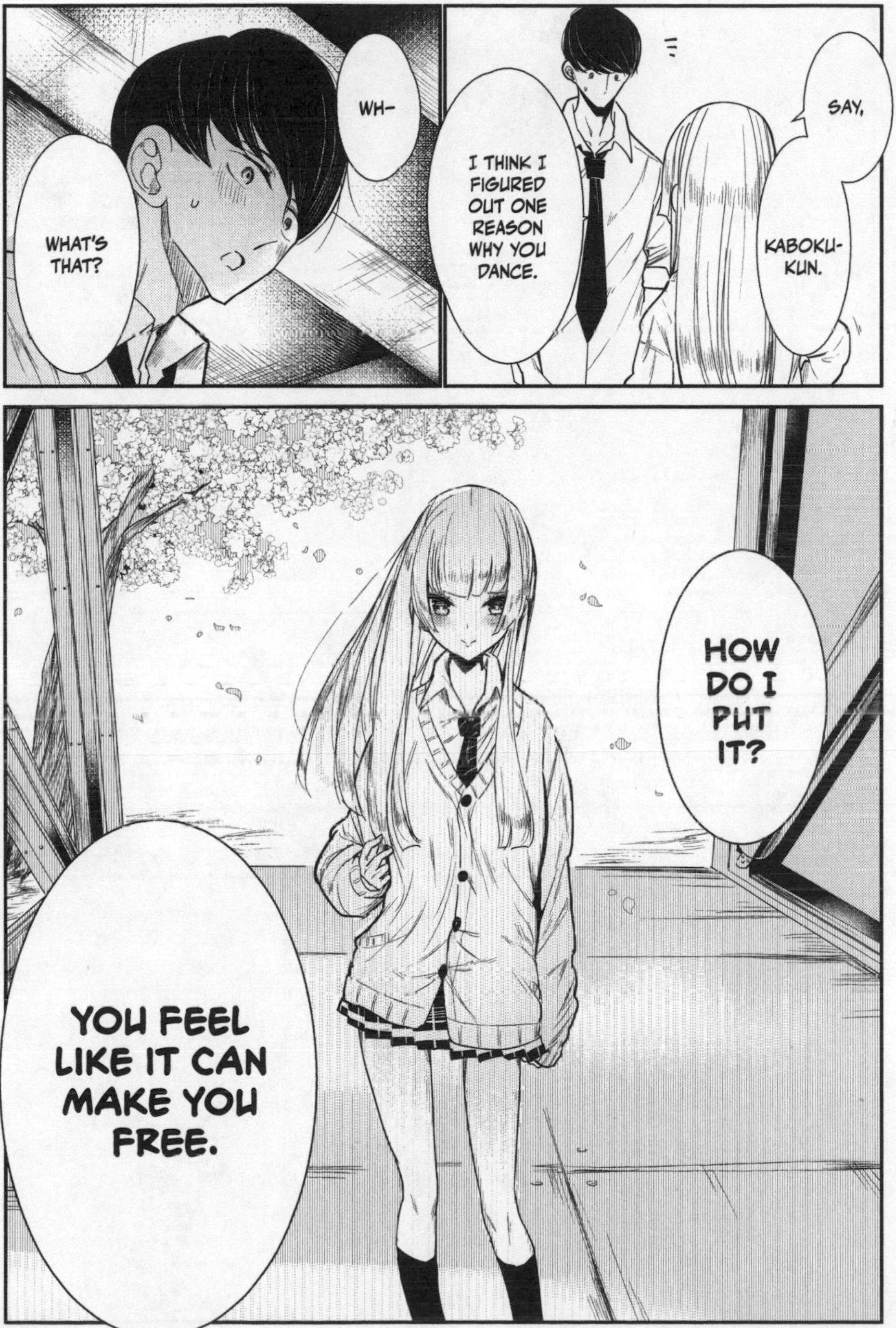

SAY,
KABOKU-KUN.
I THINK I FIGURED OUT ONE REASON WHY YOU DANCE.
WH-
WHAT'S THAT?
HOW DO I PUT IT?
YOU FEEL LIKE IT CAN MAKE YOU FREE.

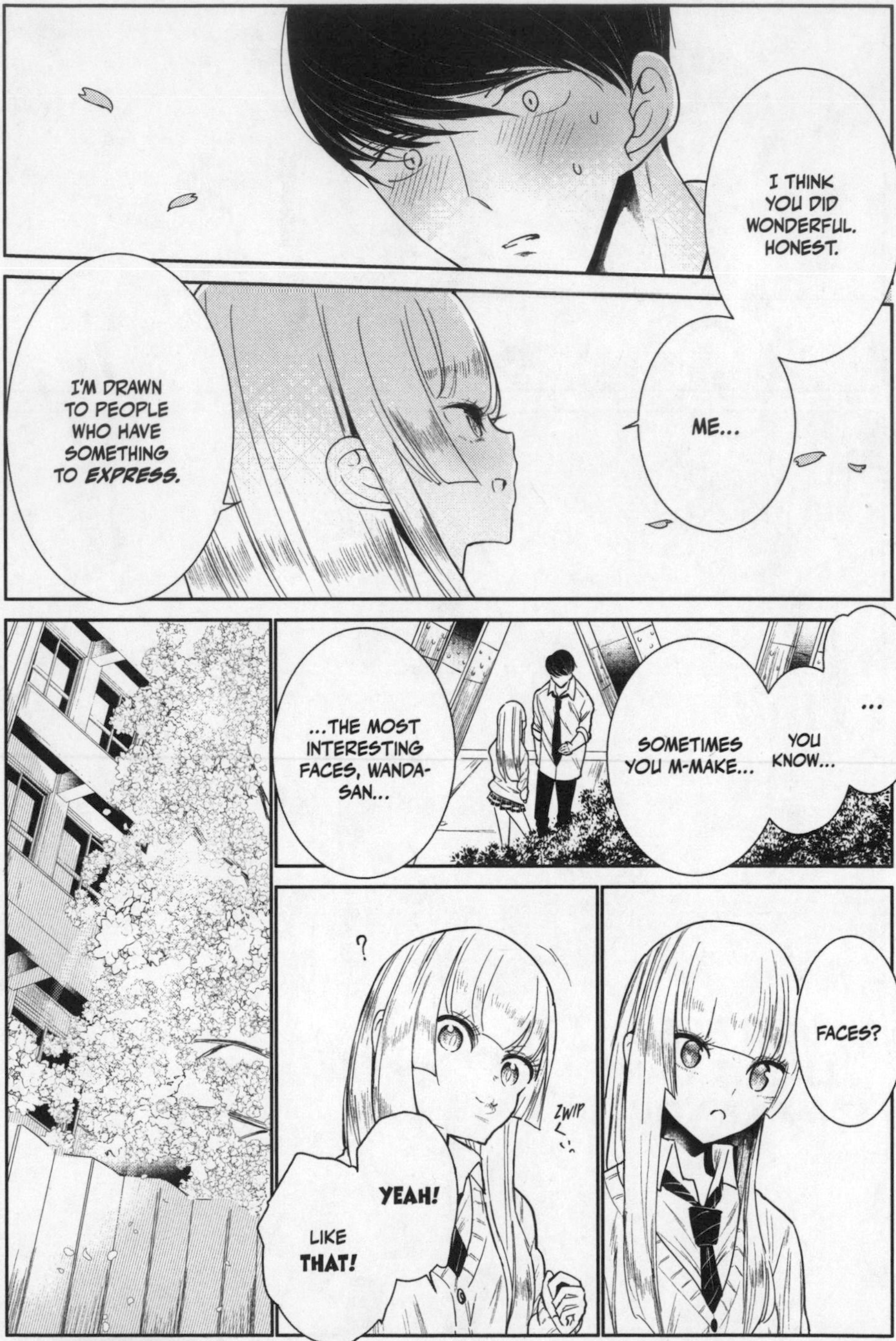
I THINK YOU DID WONDERFUL. HONEST.
ME...
I'M DRAWN TO PEOPLE WHO HAVE SOMETHING TO *EXPRESS.*
...
YOU KNOW...
SOMETIMES YOU M-MAKE...
...THE MOST INTERESTING FACES, WANDA-SAN...
FACES?
?
ZWIP
YEAH!
LIKE **THAT!**

Ch. 1: END

Ch. 2: The Dance Club's Boy/Girl Ratio

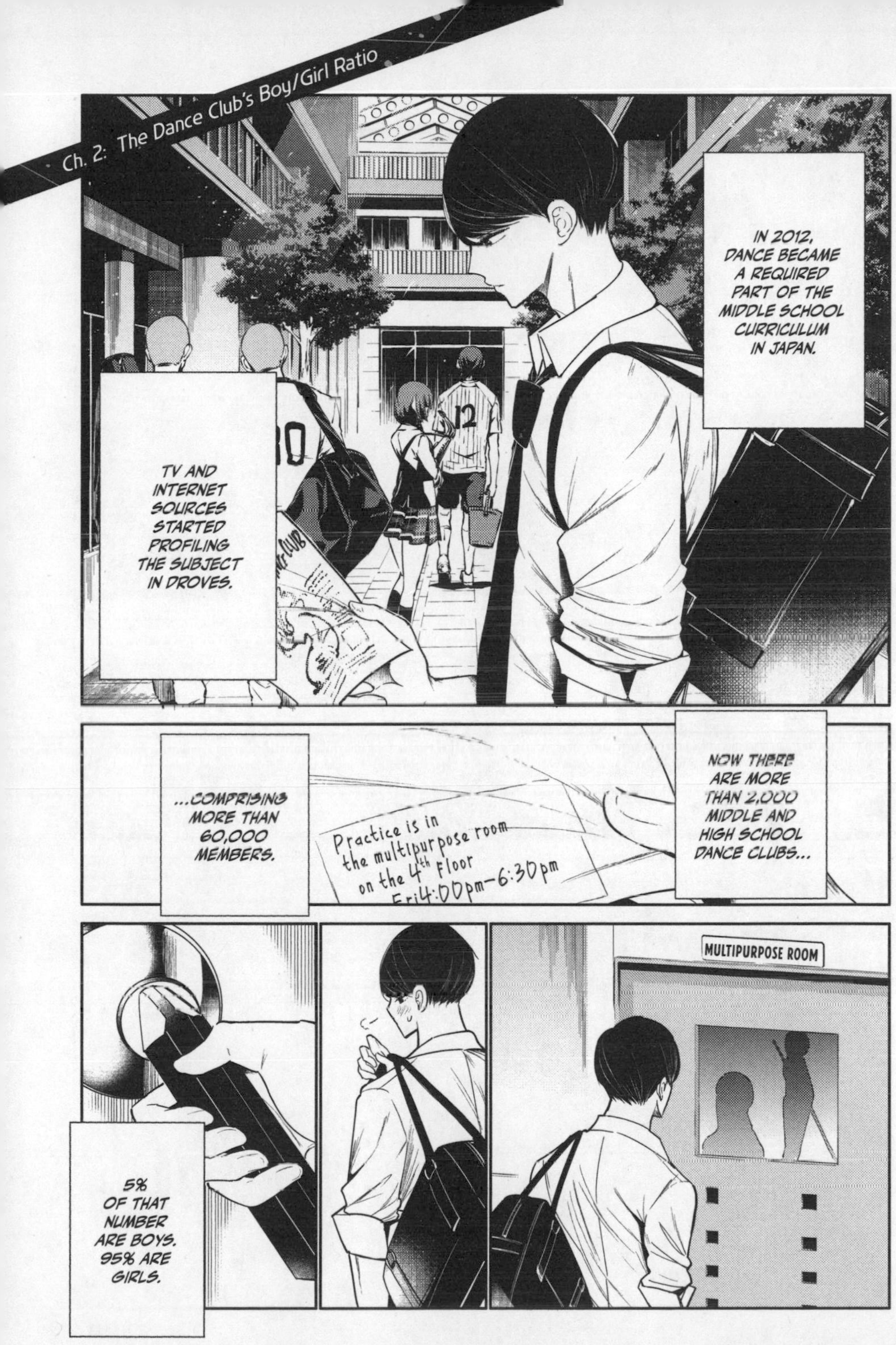
IN 2012, DANCE BECAME A REQUIRED PART OF THE MIDDLE SCHOOL CURRICULUM IN JAPAN.
TV AND INTERNET SOURCES STARTED PROFILING THE SUBJECT IN DROVES.
12
NOW THERE ARE MORE THAN 2,000 MIDDLE AND HIGH SCHOOL DANCE CLUBS...
Practice is in the multipurpose room on the 4th Floor Fri 4:00pm-6:30pm
...COMPRISING MORE THAN 60,000 MEMBERS.
MULTIPURPOSE ROOM
5% OF THAT NUMBER ARE BOYS. 95% ARE GIRLS.

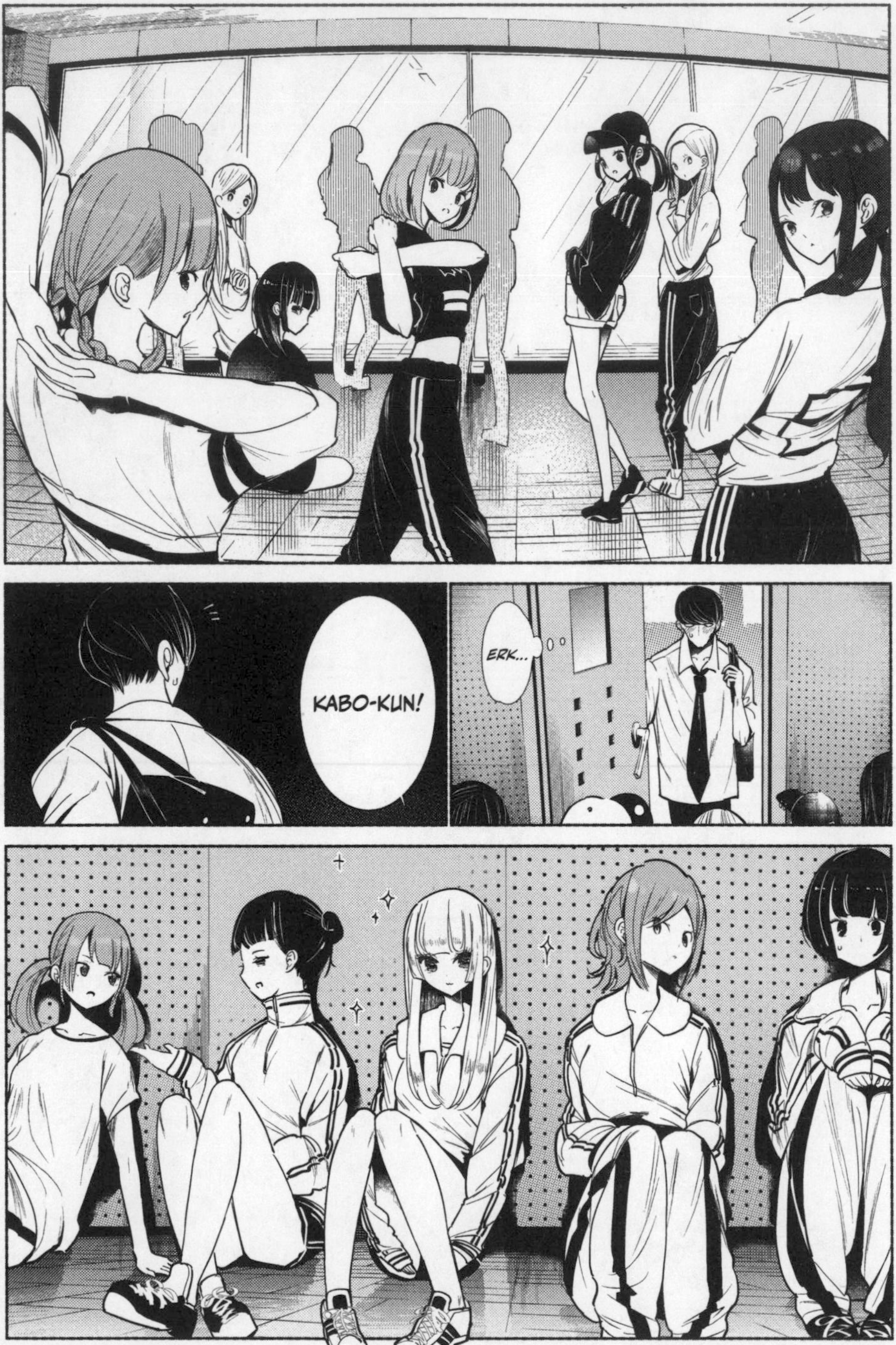
ERK...
KABO-KUN!

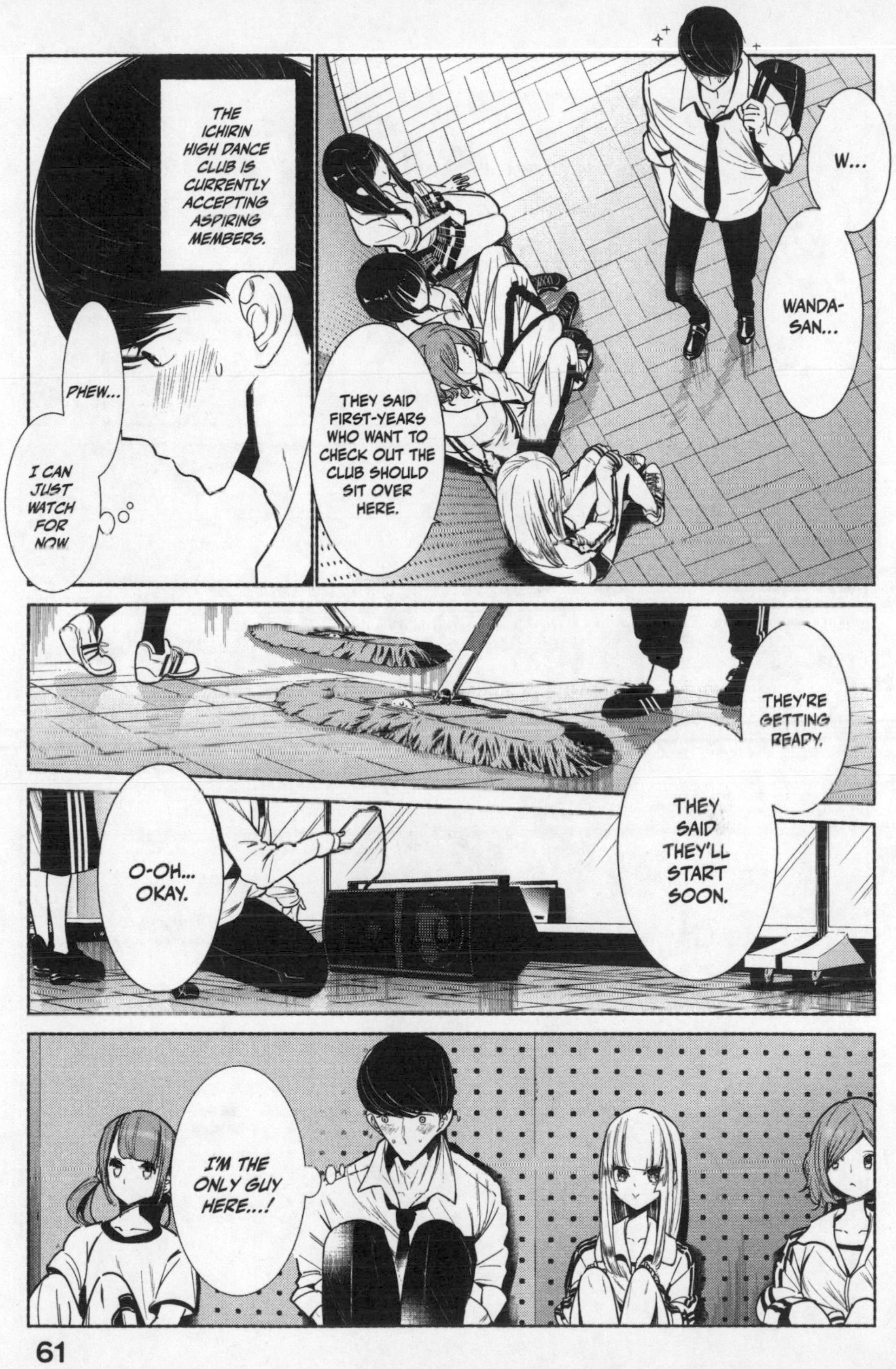
W...
WANDA-SAN...
THEY SAID FIRST-YEARS WHO WANT TO CHECK OUT THE CLUB SHOULD SIT OVER HERE.
THE ICHIRIN HIGH DANCE CLUB IS CURRENTLY ACCEPTING ASPIRING MEMBERS.
PHEW...
I CAN JUST WATCH FOR NOW.
THEY'RE GETTING READY.
THEY SAID THEY'LL START SOON.
O-OH... OKAY.
I'M THE ONLY GUY HERE...!

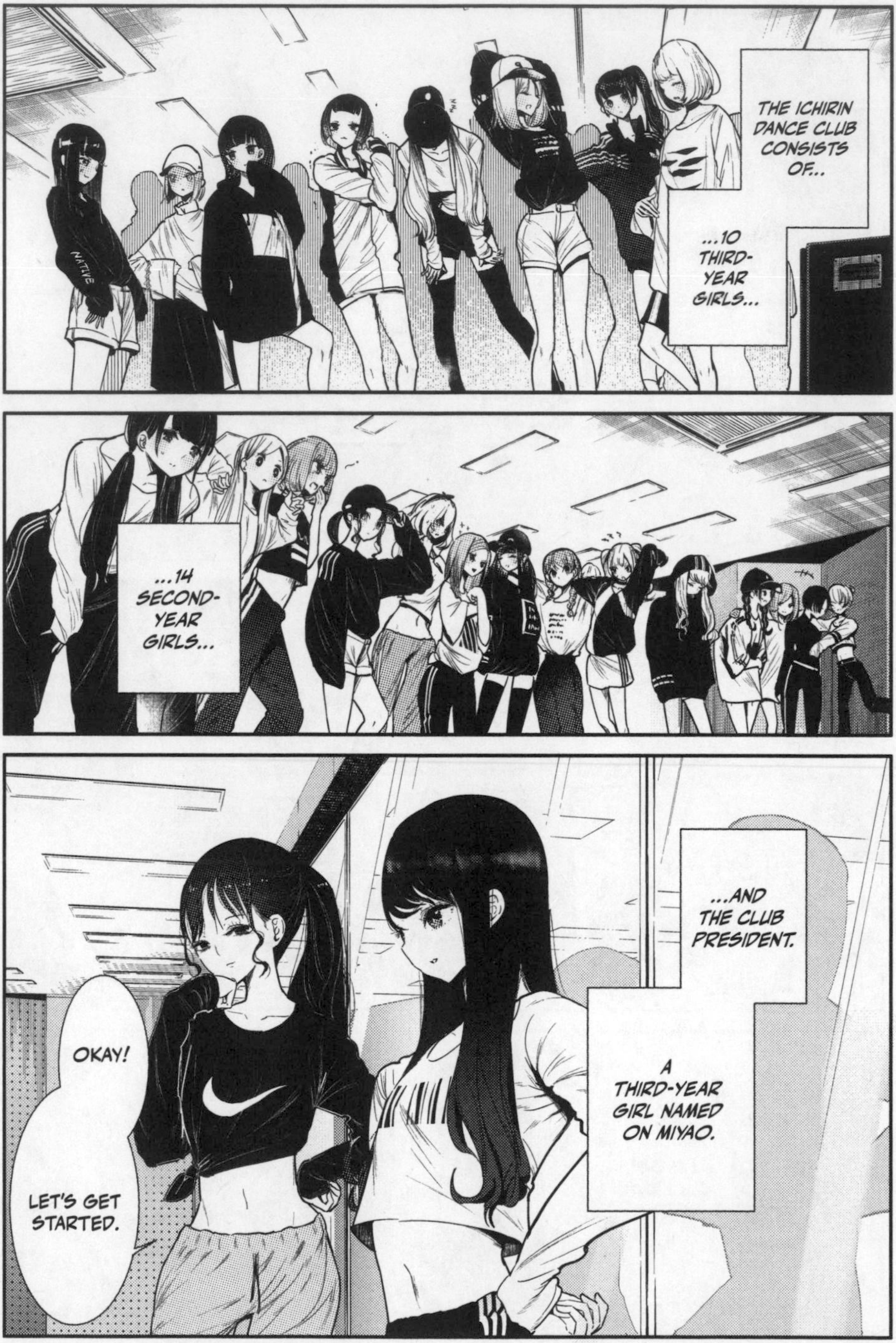
THE ICHIRIN DANCE CLUB CONSISTS OF...
...10 THIRD-YEAR GIRLS...
...14 SECOND-YEAR GIRLS...
...AND THE CLUB PRESIDENT.
A THIRD-YEAR GIRL NAMED ON MIYAO.
OKAY!
LET'S GET STARTED.

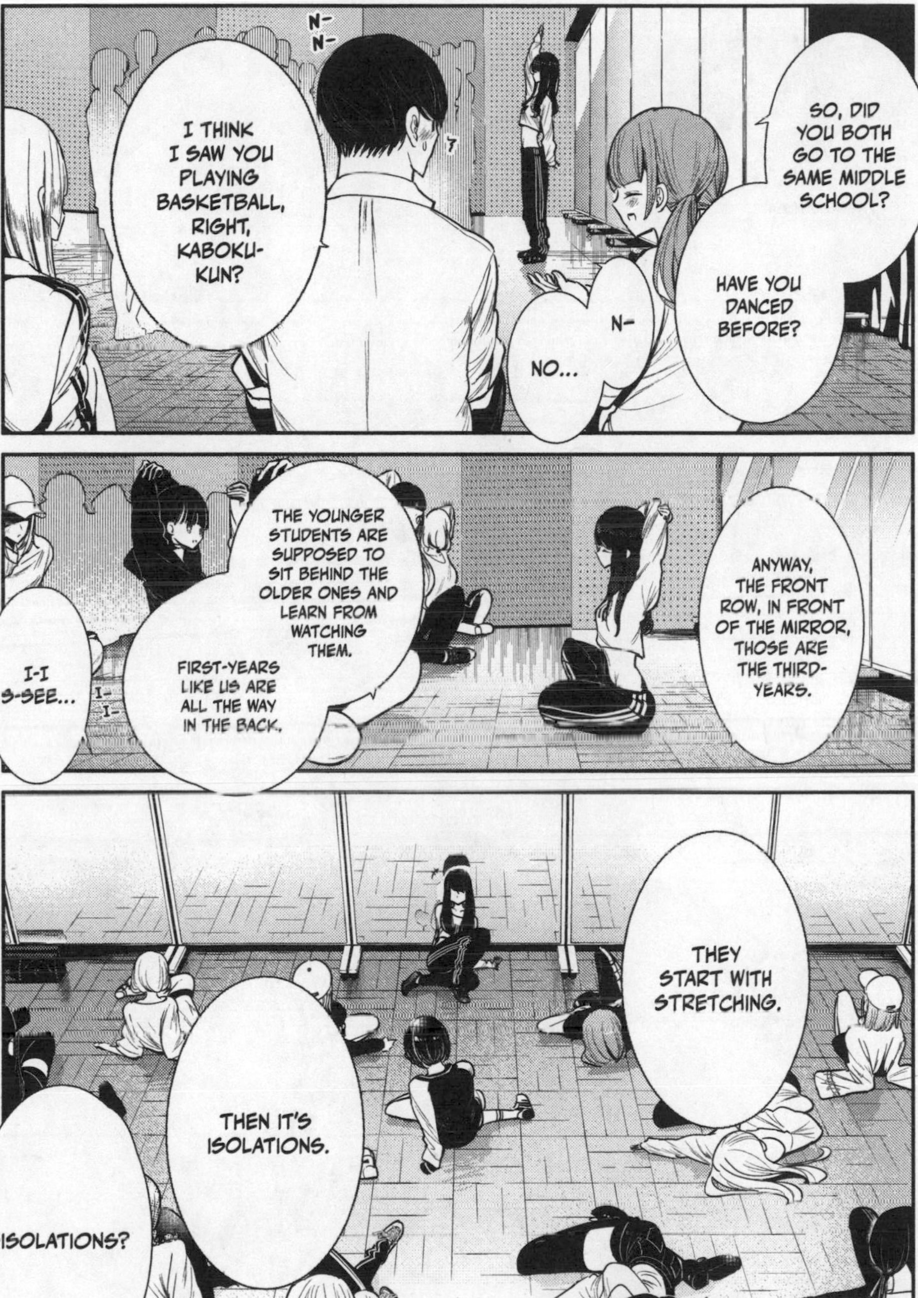
SO, DID YOU BOTH GO TO THE SAME MIDDLE SCHOOL?
HAVE YOU DANCED BEFORE?
N- NO...
N- N-
I THINK I SAW YOU PLAYING BASKETBALL, RIGHT, KABOKU-KUN?
ANYWAY, THE FRONT ROW, IN FRONT OF THE MIRROR, THOSE ARE THE THIRD-YEARS.
THE YOUNGER STUDENTS ARE SUPPOSED TO SIT BEHIND THE OLDER ONES AND LEARN FROM WATCHING THEM.
FIRST-YEARS LIKE US ARE ALL THE WAY IN THE BACK.
I- I-
I-I S-SEE...
THEY START WITH STRETCHING.
THEN IT'S ISOLATIONS.
I-ISOLATIONS?

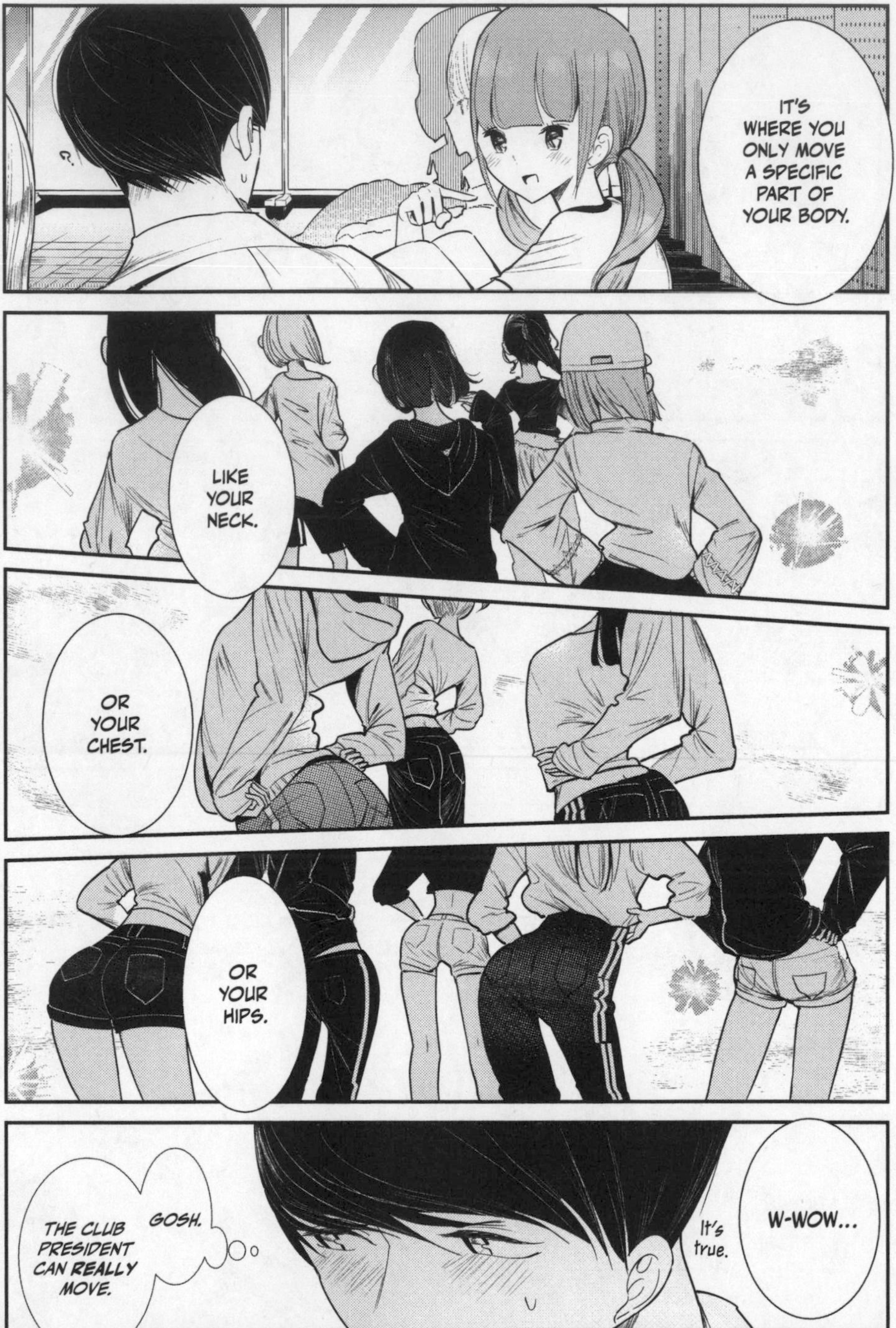
IT'S WHERE YOU ONLY MOVE A SPECIFIC PART OF YOUR BODY.
?
LIKE YOUR NECK.
OR YOUR CHEST.
OR YOUR HIPS.
W-WOW...
It's true.
GOSH.
THE CLUB PRESIDENT CAN REALLY MOVE.

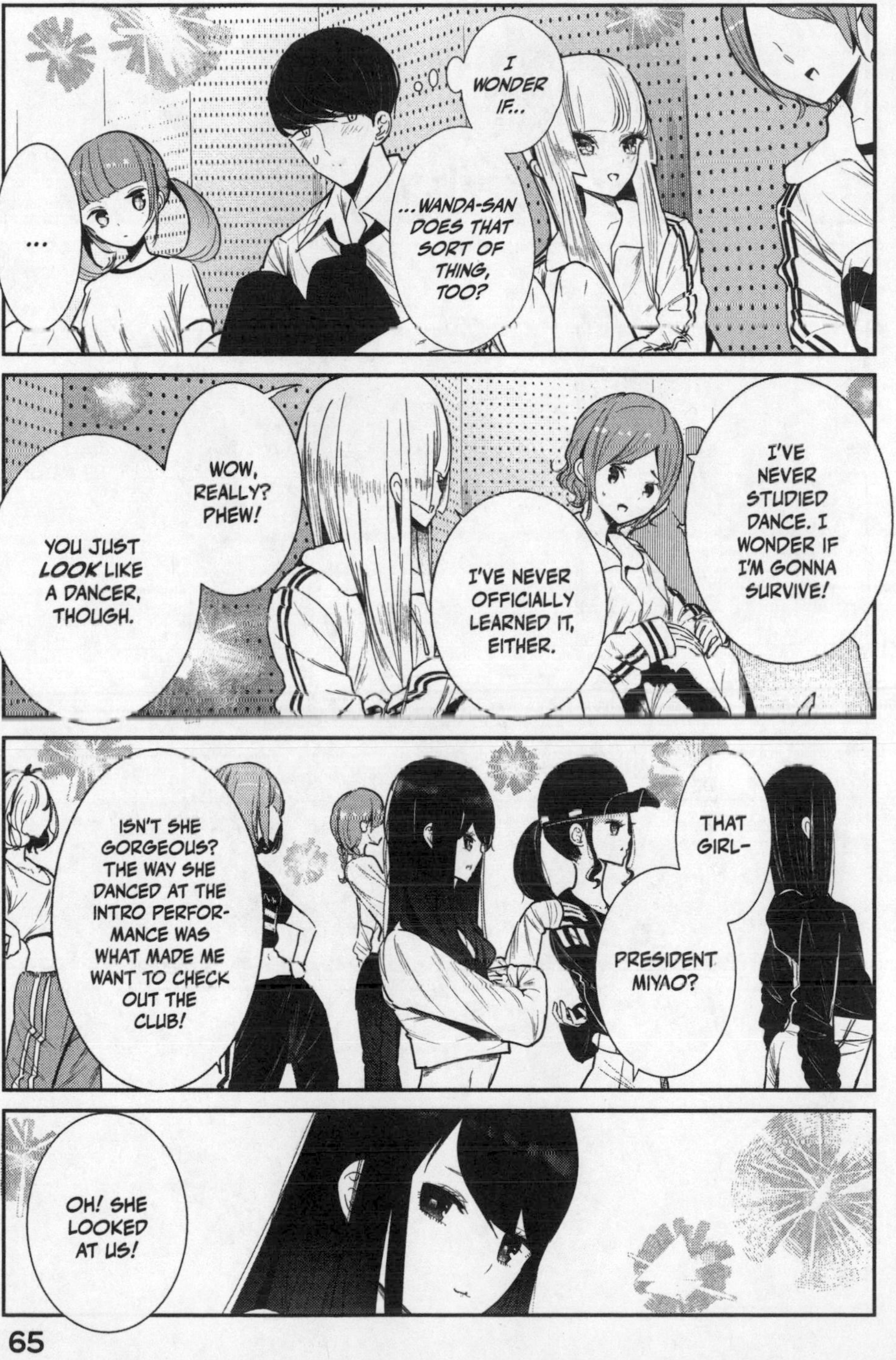
I WONDER IF...
...WANDA-SAN DOES THAT SORT OF THING, TOO?
...
I'VE NEVER STUDIED DANCE. I WONDER IF I'M GONNA SURVIVE!
I'VE NEVER OFFICIALLY LEARNED IT, EITHER.
WOW, REALLY? PHEW!
YOU JUST *LOOK* LIKE A DANCER, THOUGH.
THAT GIRL-
PRESIDENT MIYAO?
ISN'T SHE GORGEOUS? THE WAY SHE DANCED AT THE INTRO PERFORMANCE WAS WHAT MADE ME WANT TO CHECK OUT THE CLUB!
OH! SHE LOOKED AT US!

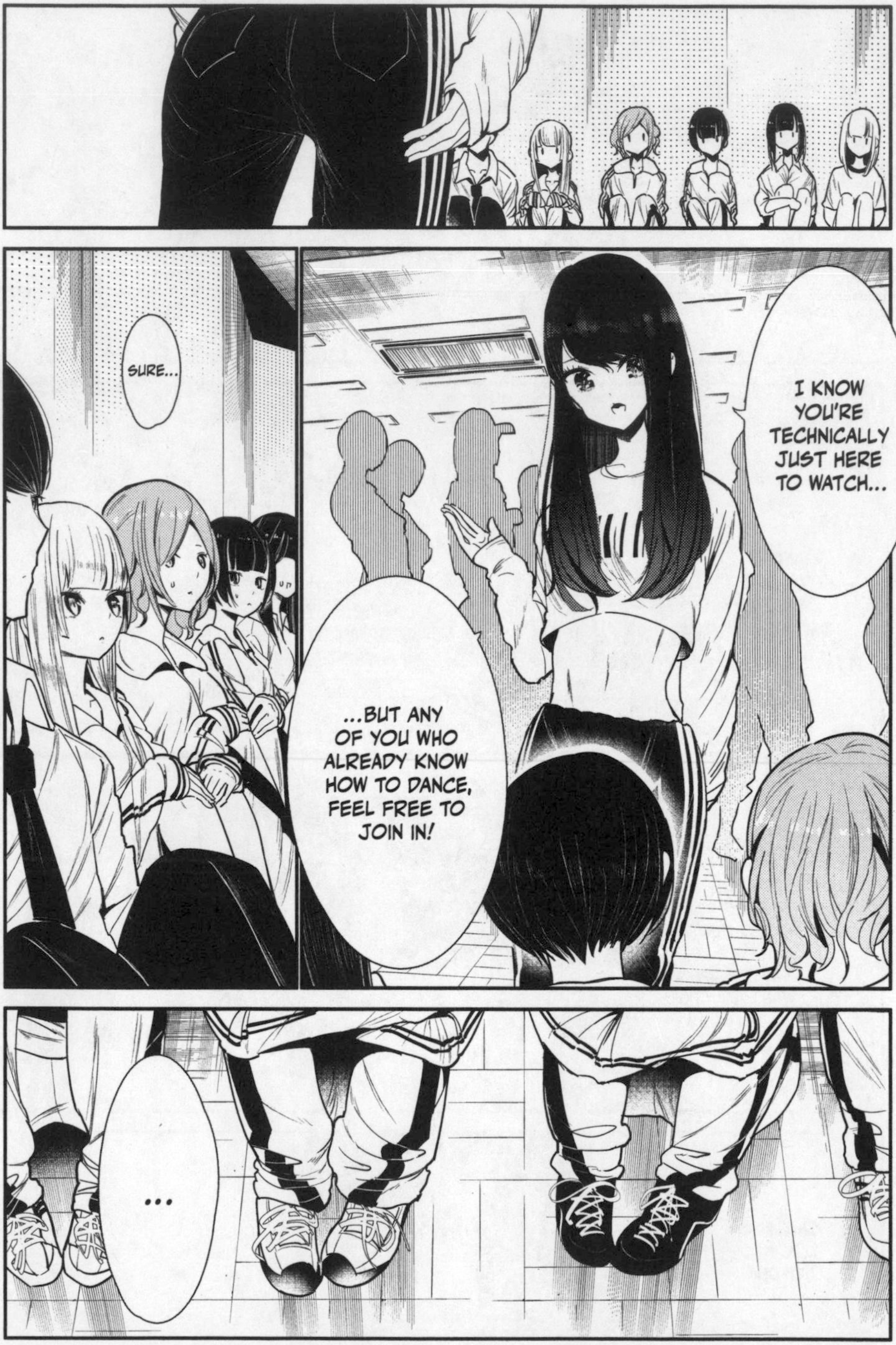
I KNOW YOU'RE TECHNICALLY JUST HERE TO WATCH...
...BUT ANY OF YOU WHO ALREADY KNOW HOW TO DANCE, FEEL FREE TO JOIN IN!
SURE...
...

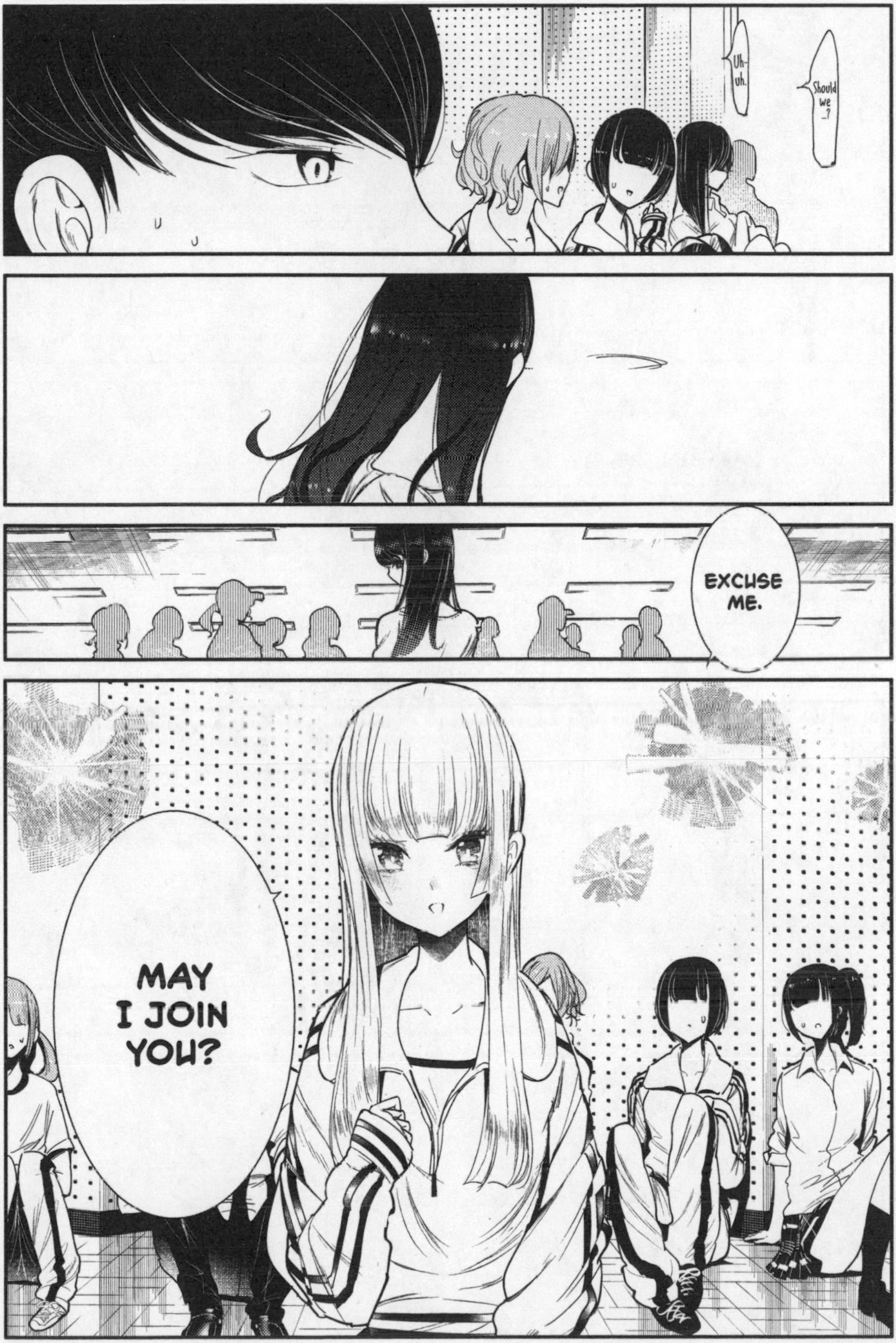
Should we _?
Uh-uh.
EXCUSE ME.
MAY I JOIN YOU?

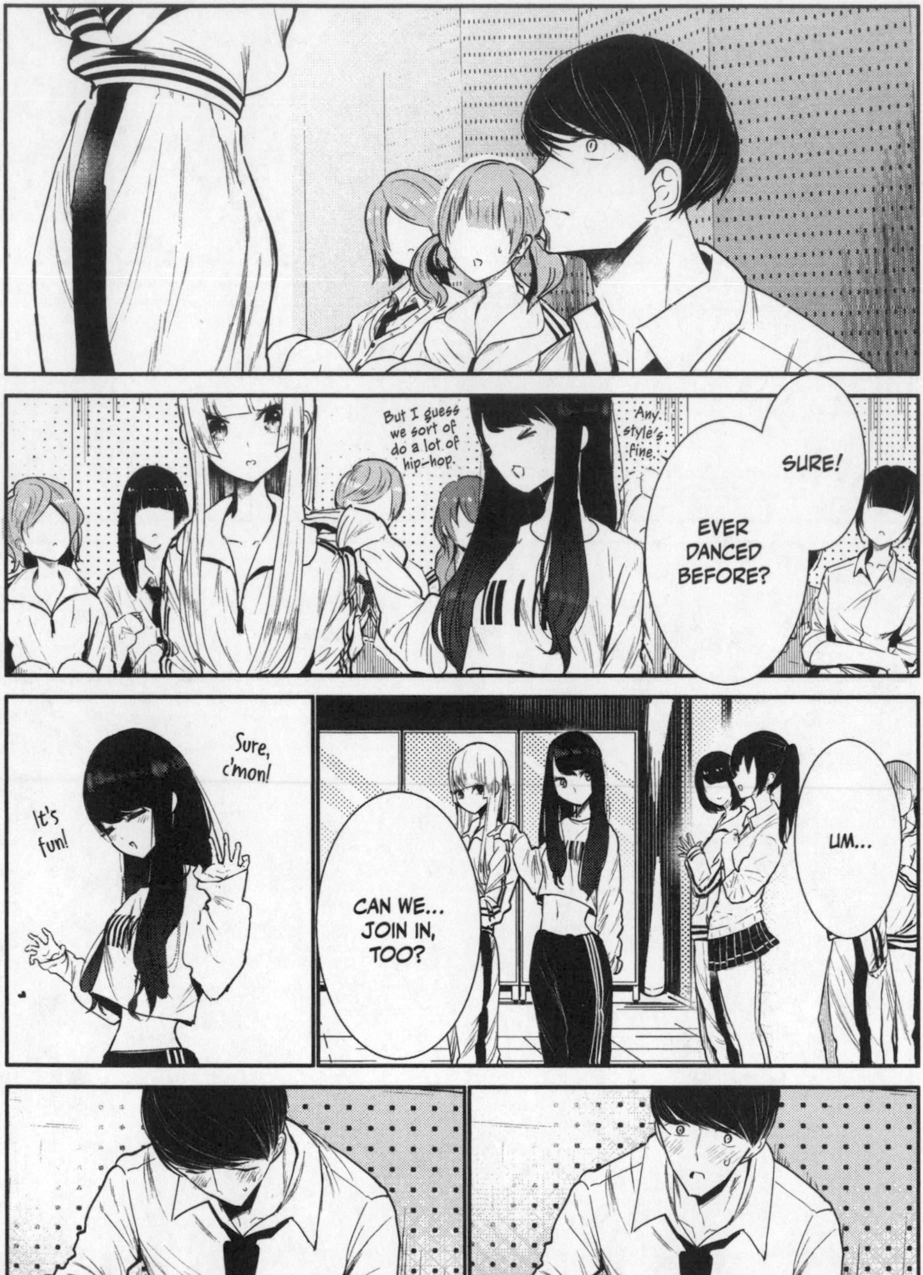
SURE! EVER DANCED BEFORE?
Any style's fine.
But I guess we sort of do a lot of hip-hop.
UM...
CAN WE... JOIN IN, TOO?
Sure, c'mon!
It's fun!

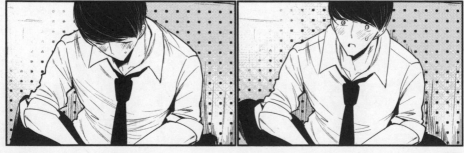

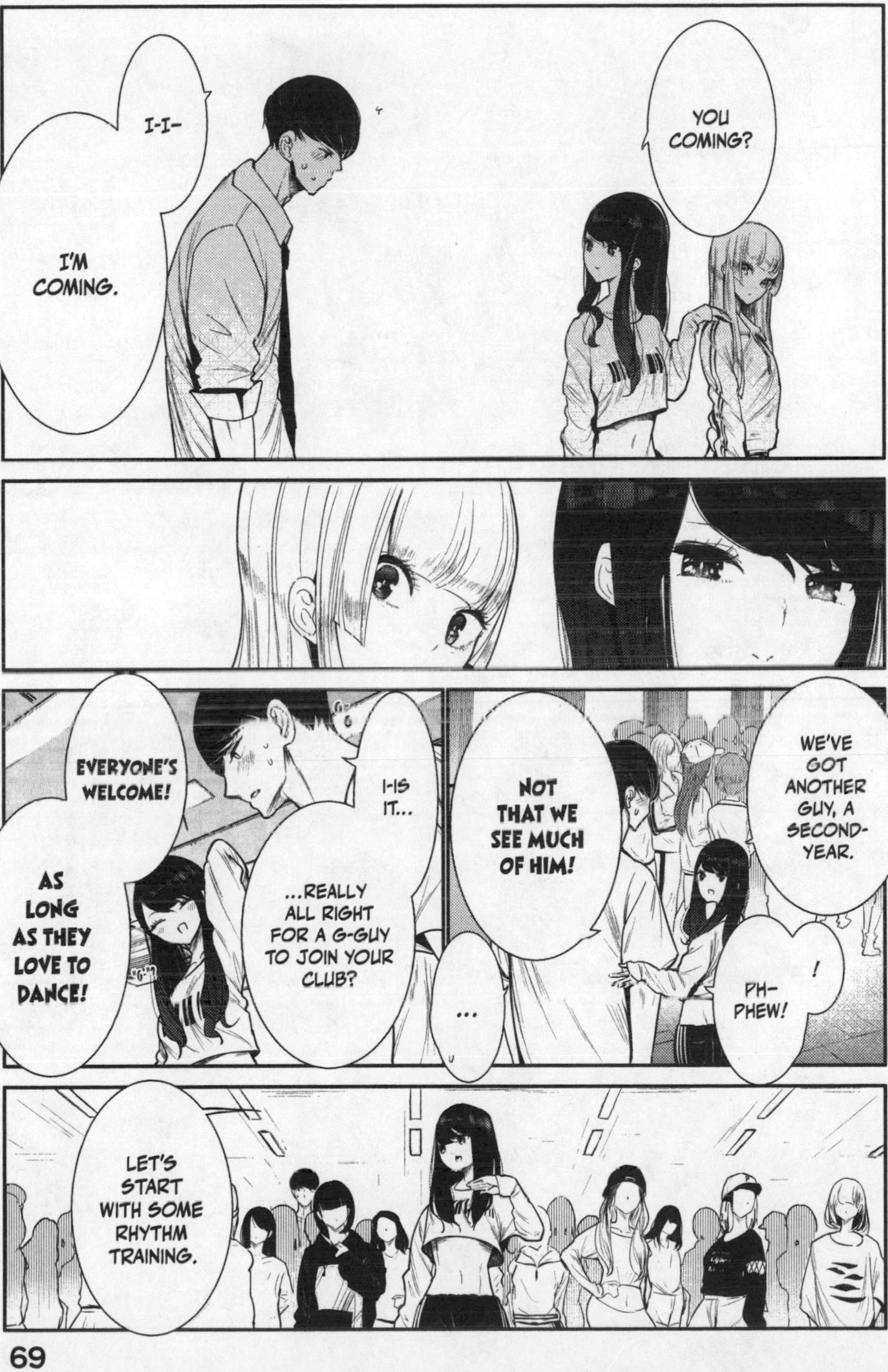
YOU COMING?
I-I-
I'M COMING.
WE'VE GOT ANOTHER GUY, A SECOND-YEAR.
NOT THAT WE SEE MUCH OF HIM!
!
PH-PHEW!
...
I-IS IT...
...REALLY ALL RIGHT FOR A G-GUY TO JOIN YOUR CLUB?
EVERYONE'S WELCOME!
AS LONG AS THEY LOVE TO DANCE!
LET'S START WITH SOME RHYTHM TRAINING.

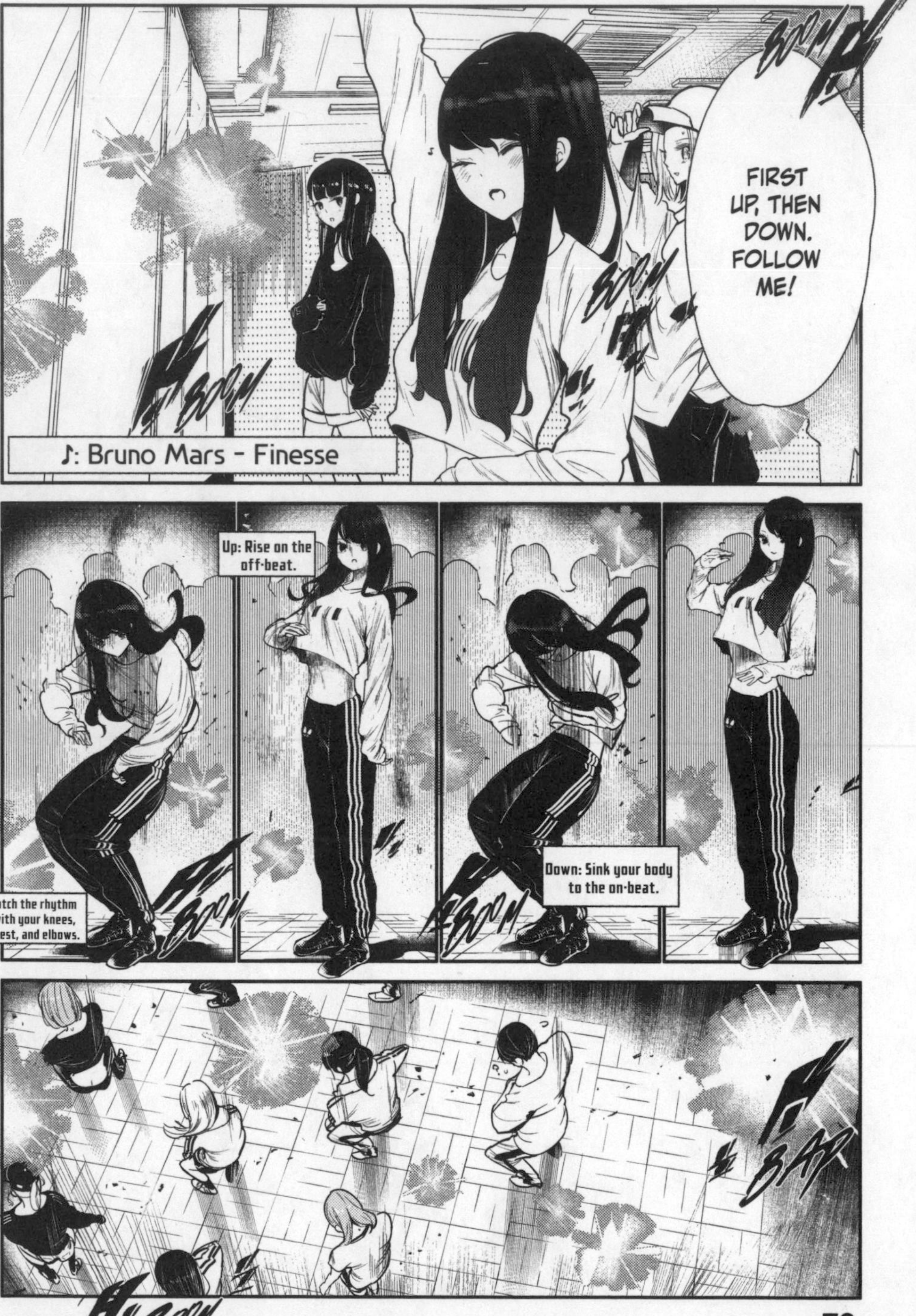
FIRST UP, THEN DOWN. FOLLOW ME!
♪: Bruno Mars - Finesse
Down: Sink your body to the on-beat.
Up: Rise on the off-beat.
Catch the rhythm with your knees, chest, and elbows.

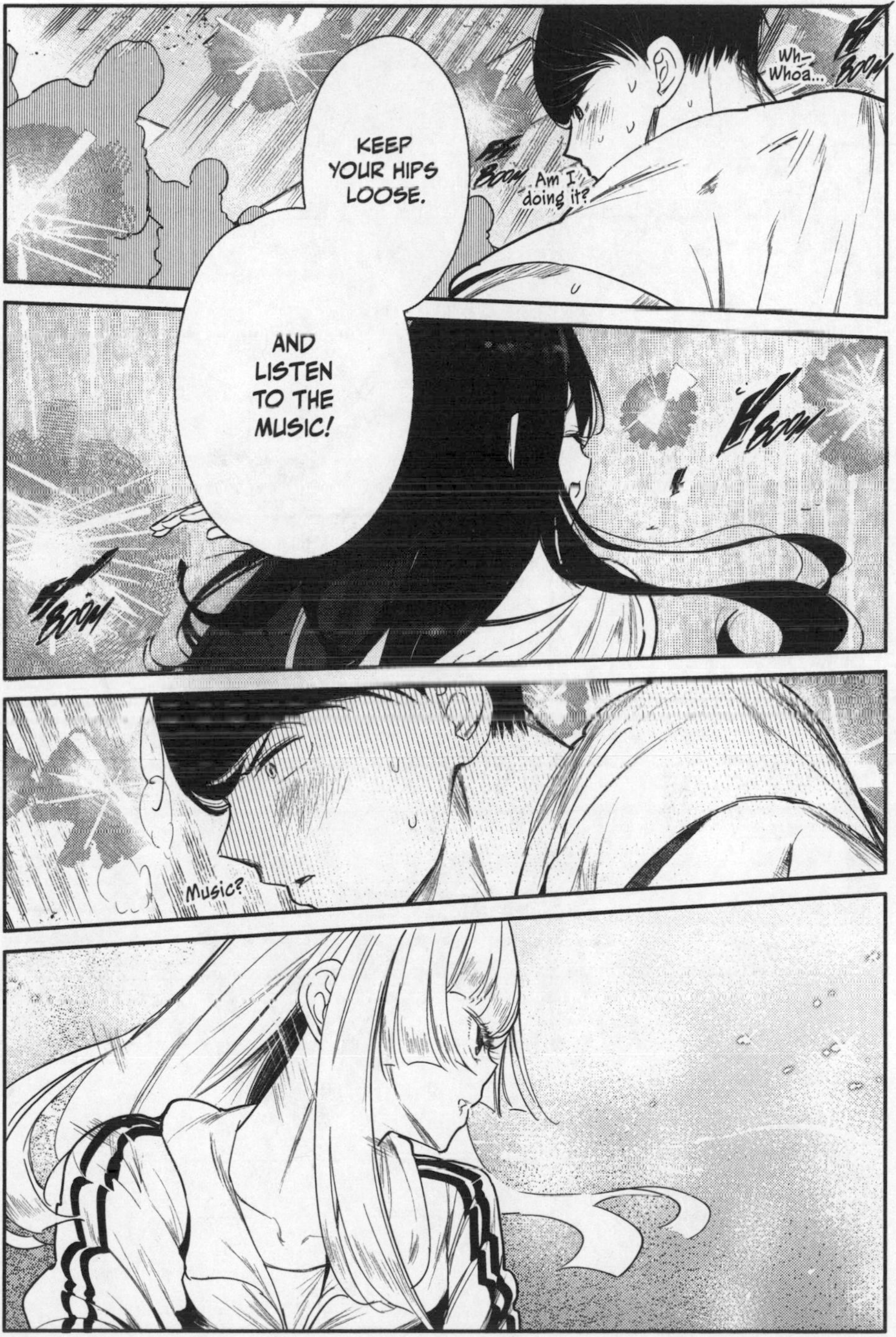
Wh— Whoa...
Am I doing it?
KEEP YOUR HIPS LOOSE.
AND LISTEN TO THE MUSIC!
Music?

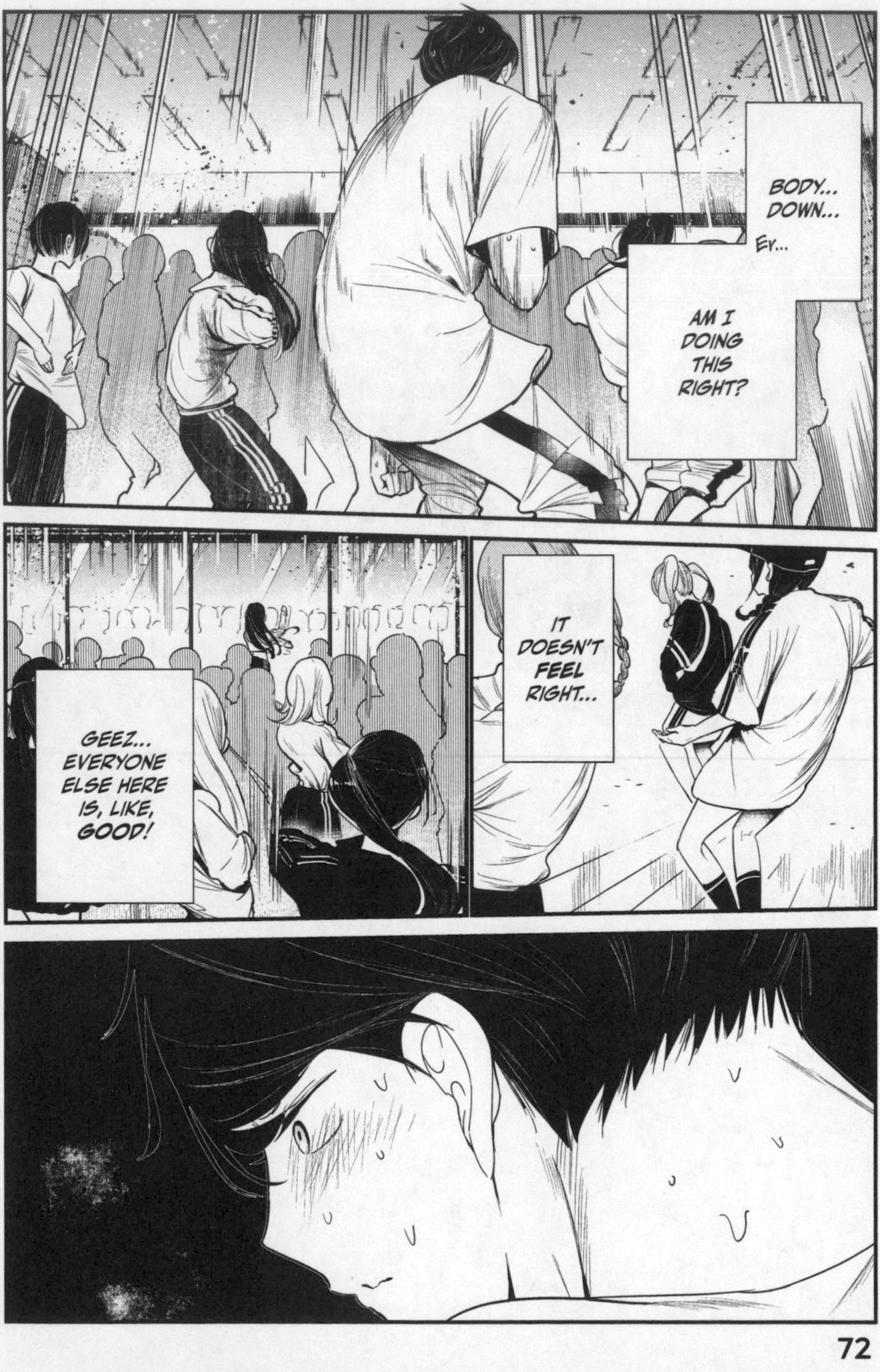
BODY... DOWN...
Er...
AM I DOING THIS RIGHT?
IT DOESN'T FEEL RIGHT...
GEEZ... EVERYONE ELSE HERE IS, LIKE, GOOD!

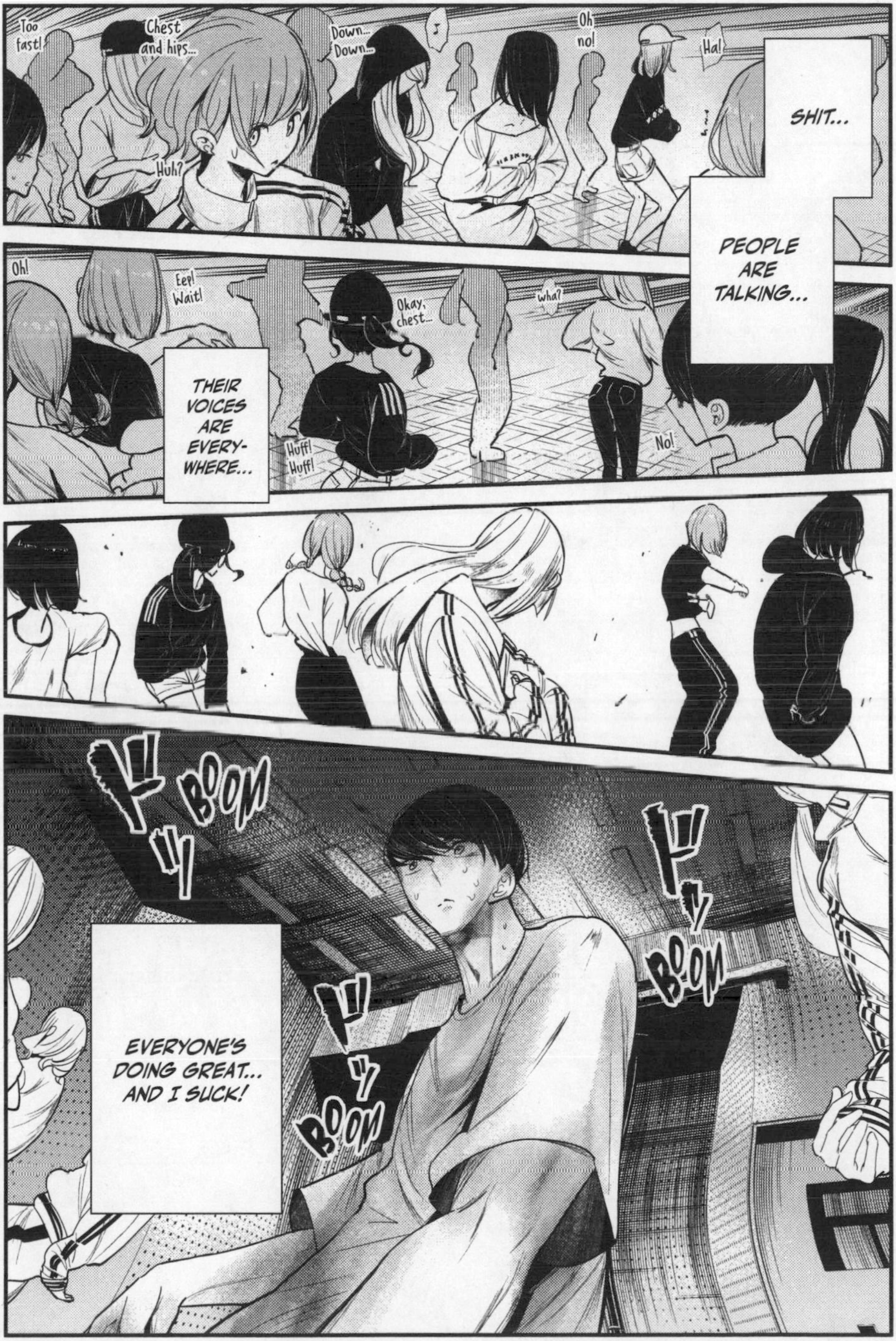
SHIT...
PEOPLE ARE TALKING...
Ha!
Oh no!
♪
Down... Down...
Huh?
Chest and hips...
Too fast!
Wha?
No!
Okay, chest...
Huff! Huff!
THEIR VOICES ARE EVERY-WHERE...
Eep! Wait!
Oh!
BOOM
BOOM
EVERYONE'S DOING GREAT... AND I SUCK!
BOOM

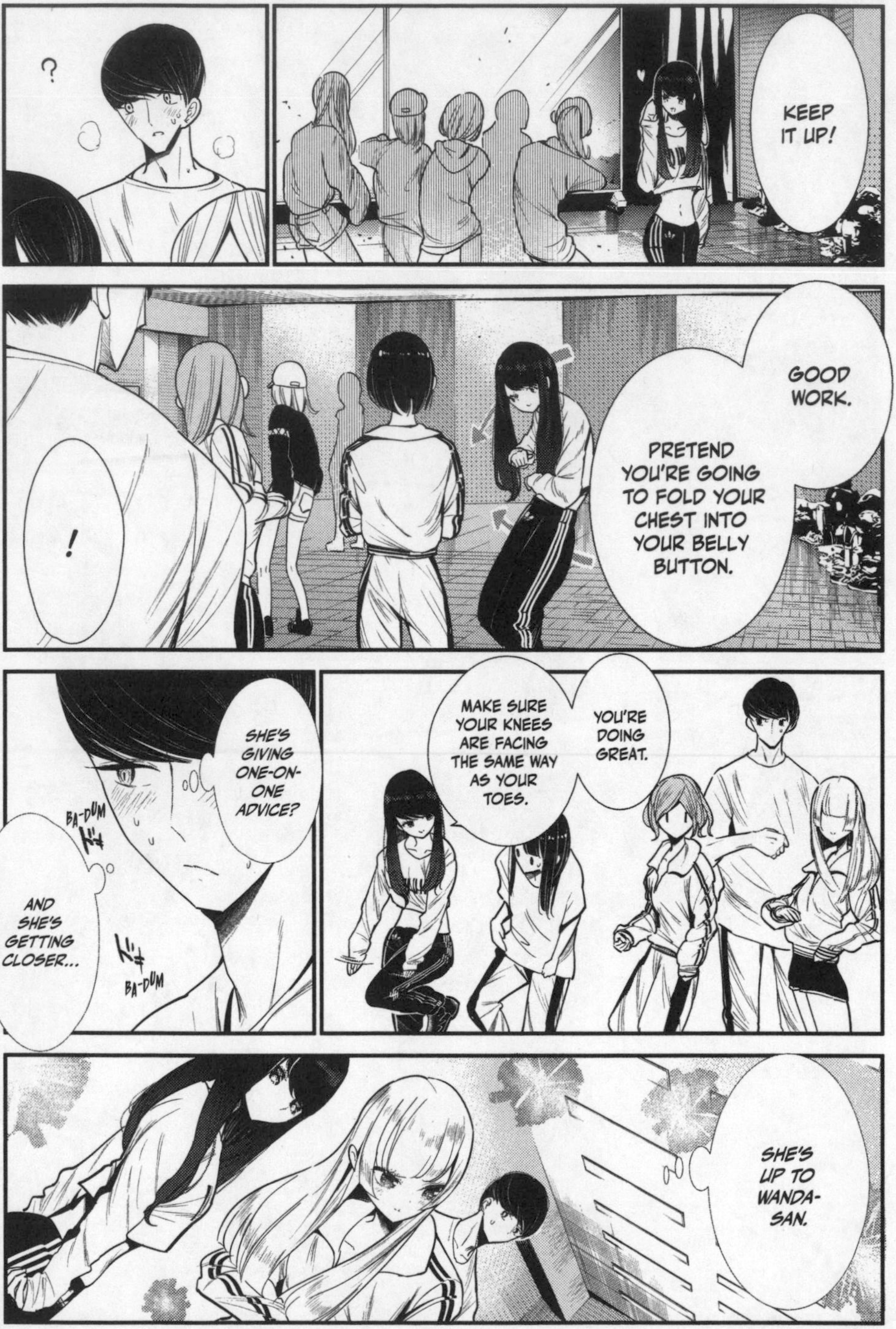
KEEP IT UP!
?
GOOD WORK.
PRETEND YOU'RE GOING TO FOLD YOUR CHEST INTO YOUR BELLY BUTTON.
!
YOU'RE DOING GREAT.
MAKE SURE YOUR KNEES ARE FACING THE SAME WAY AS YOUR TOES.
SHE'S GIVING ONE-ON-ONE ADVICE?
BA-DUM
ドキ
AND SHE'S GETTING CLOSER...
ドキ
BA-DUM
SHE'S UP TO WANDA-SAN.

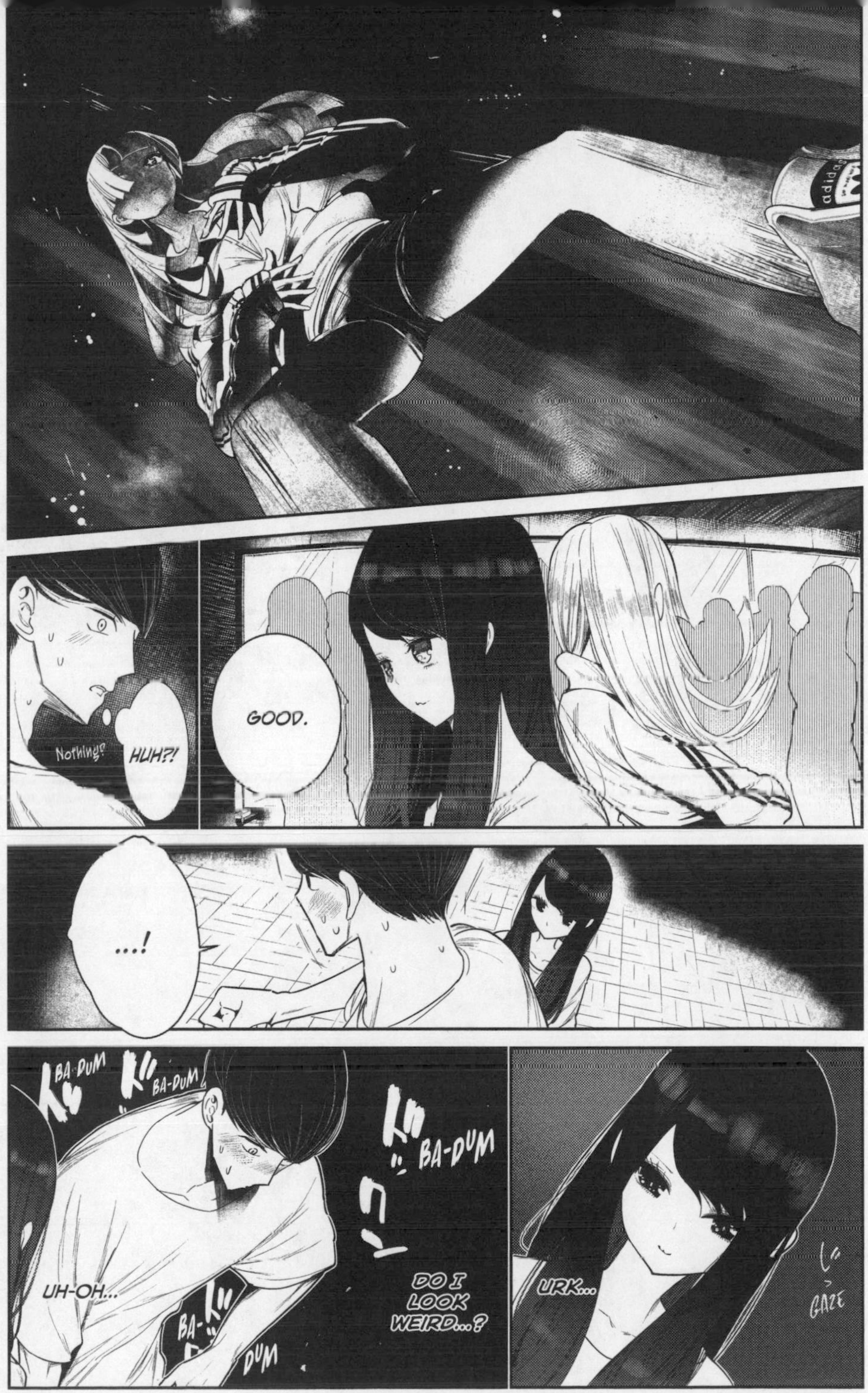
GOOD.
HUH?!
Nothing!?
...!
GAZE
URK...
BA-DUM
DO I LOOK WEIRD...?
BA-DUM
BA-DUM
UH-OH...
BA-DUM

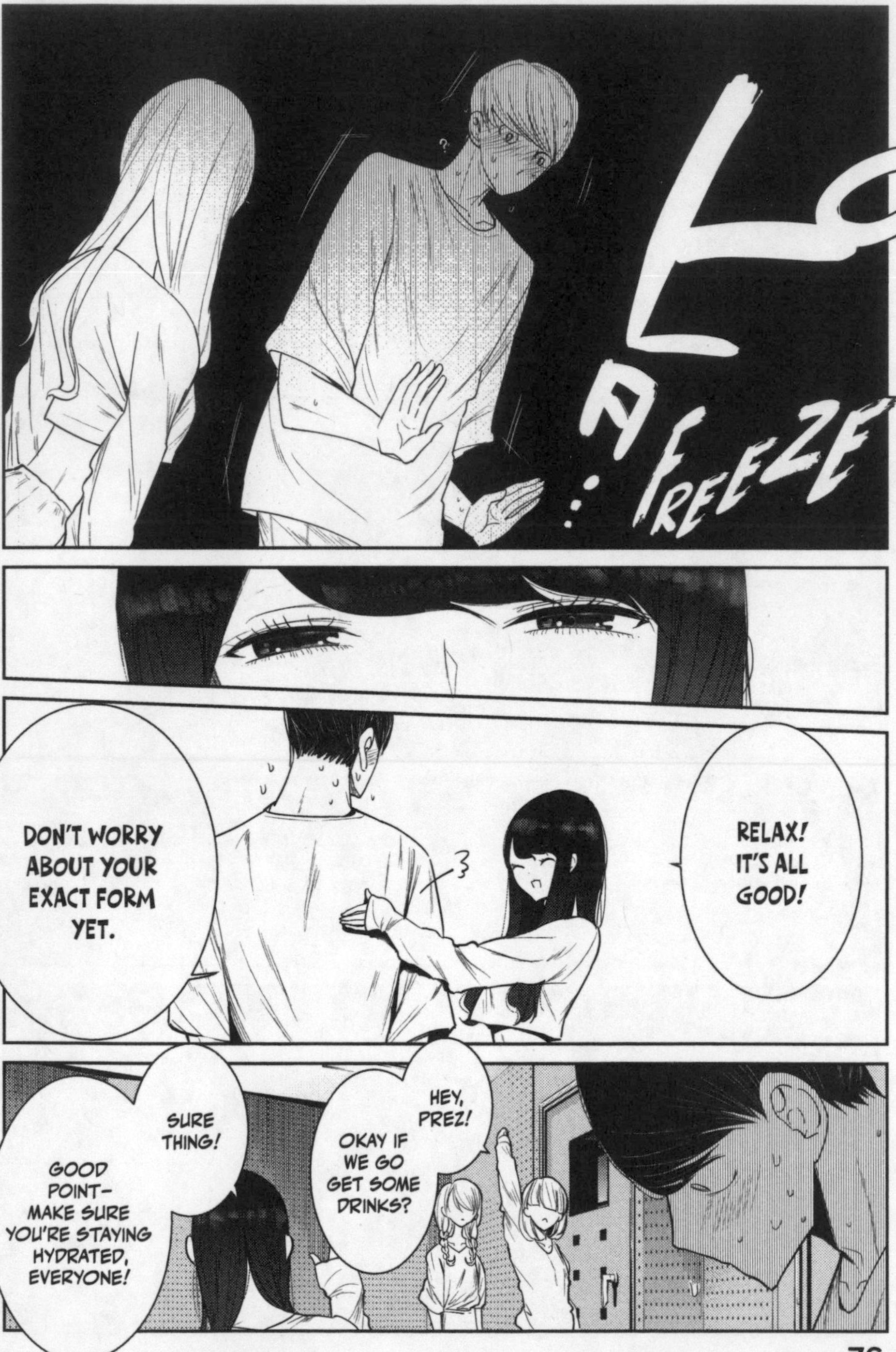
ピタ…
FREEZE
RELAX! IT'S ALL GOOD!
DON'T WORRY ABOUT YOUR EXACT FORM YET.
HEY, PREZ!
OKAY IF WE GO GET SOME DRINKS?
SURE THING!
GOOD POINT—MAKE SURE YOU'RE STAYING HYDRATED, EVERYONE!

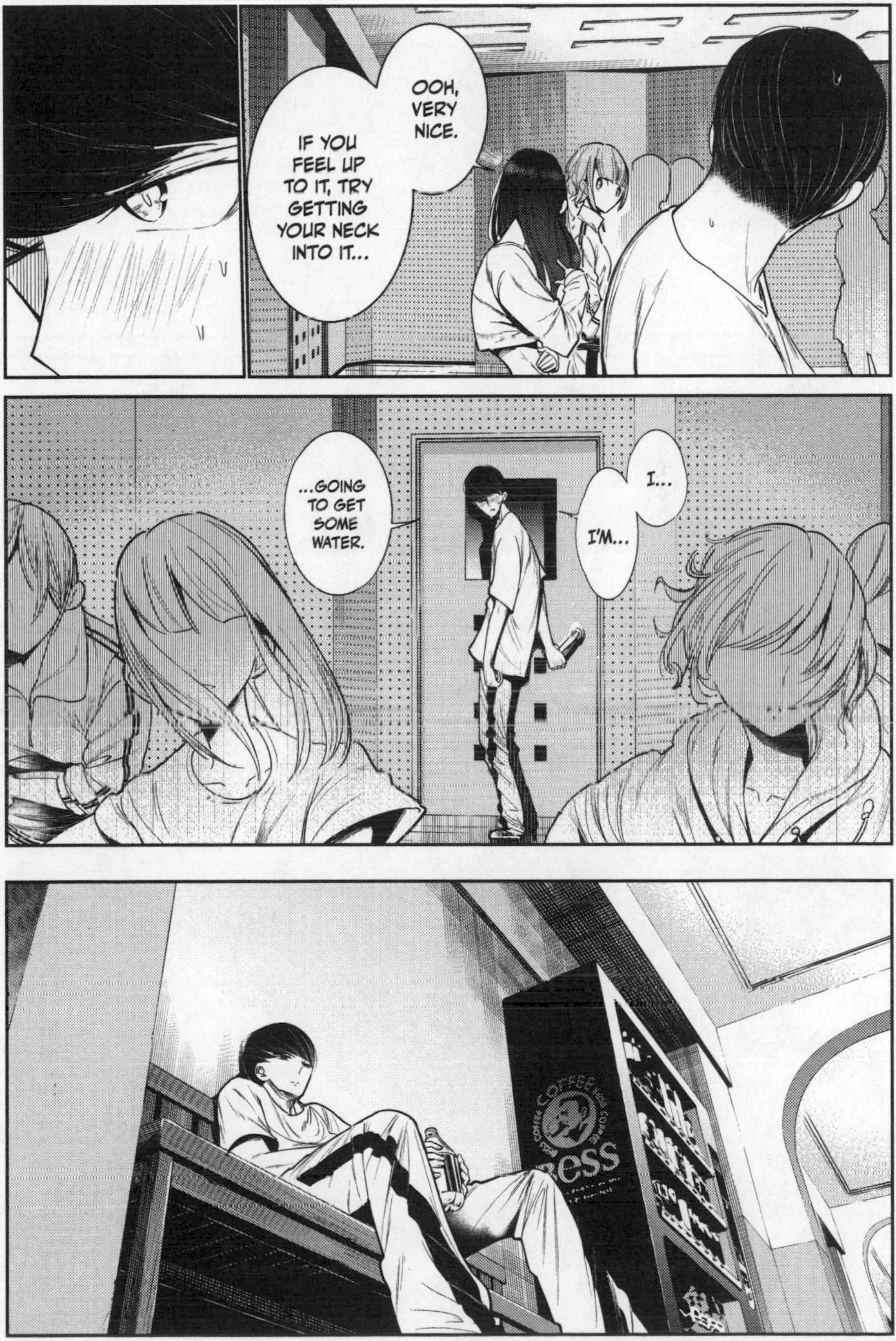
OOH, VERY NICE.
IF YOU FEEL UP TO IT, TRY GETTING YOUR NECK INTO IT...
I...
I'M...
...GOING TO GET SOME WATER.

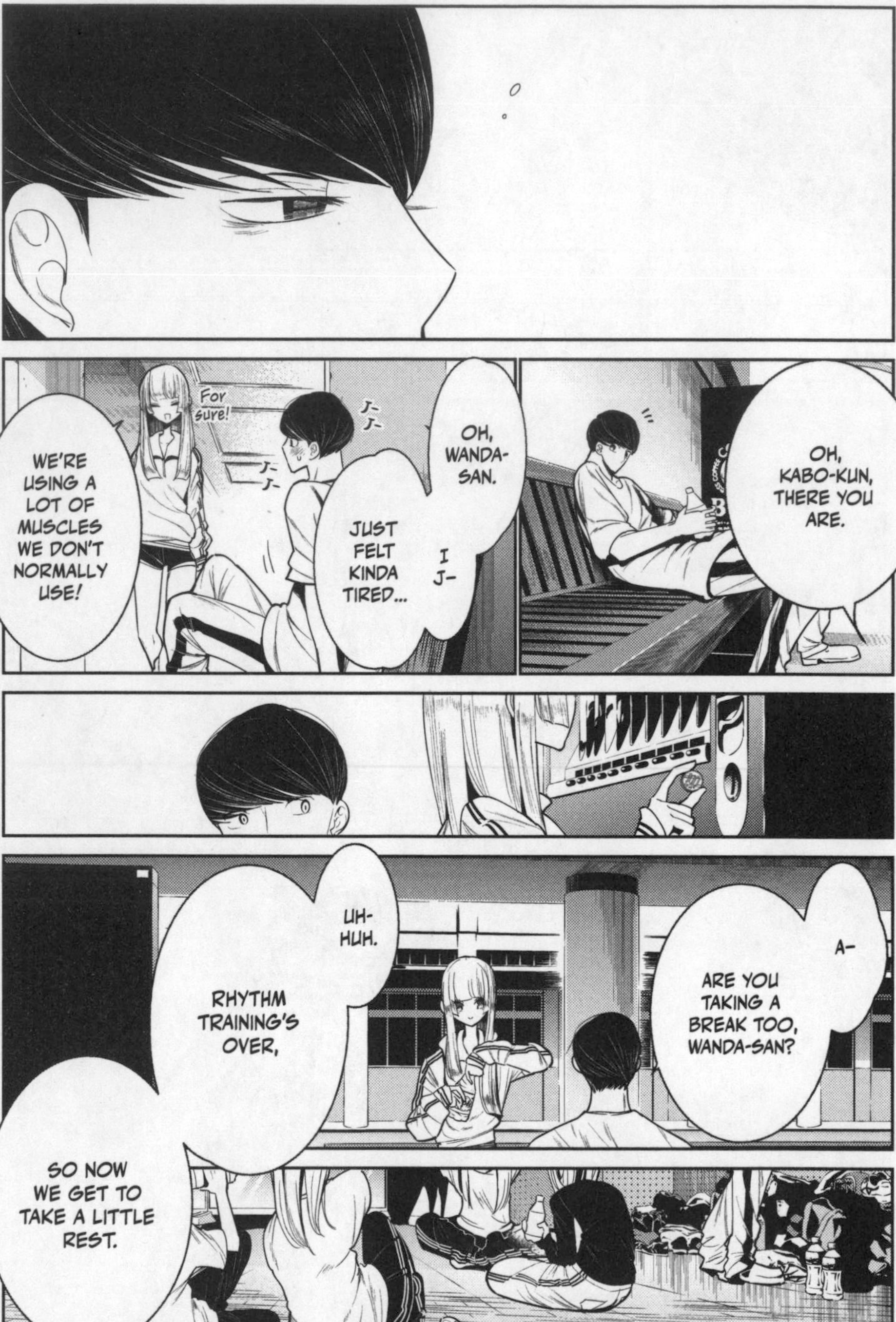
OH, KABO-KUN, THERE YOU ARE.
OH, WANDA-SAN.
J– J–
J– J–
I J–
JUST FELT KINDA TIRED...
For sure!
WE'RE USING A LOT OF MUSCLES WE DON'T NORMALLY USE!
A–
ARE YOU TAKING A BREAK TOO, WANDA-SAN?
UH-HUH.
RHYTHM TRAINING'S OVER,
SO NOW WE GET TO TAKE A LITTLE REST.

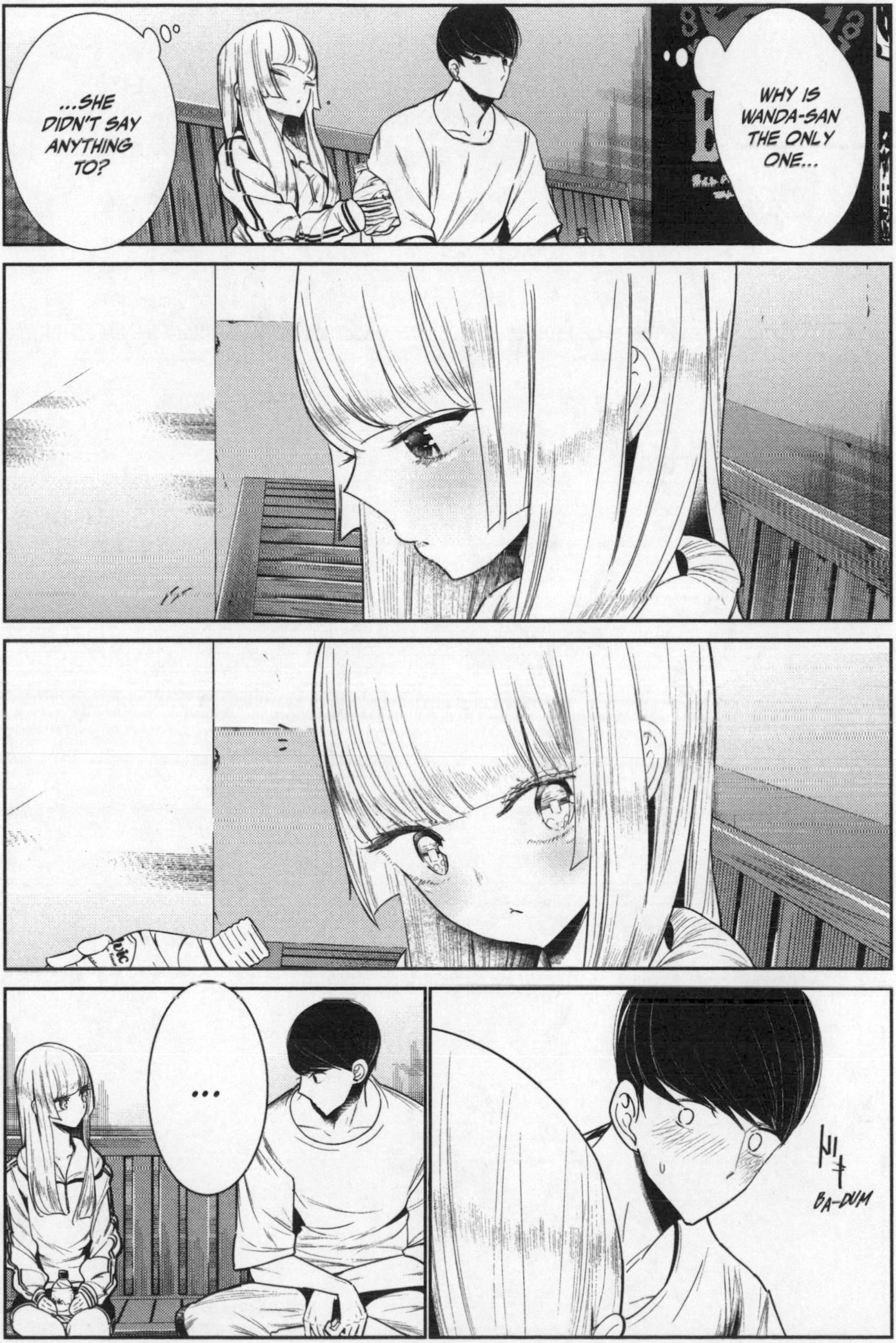
WHY IS WANDA-SAN THE ONLY ONE...
...SHE DIDN'T SAY ANYTHING TO?
BA-DUM
...

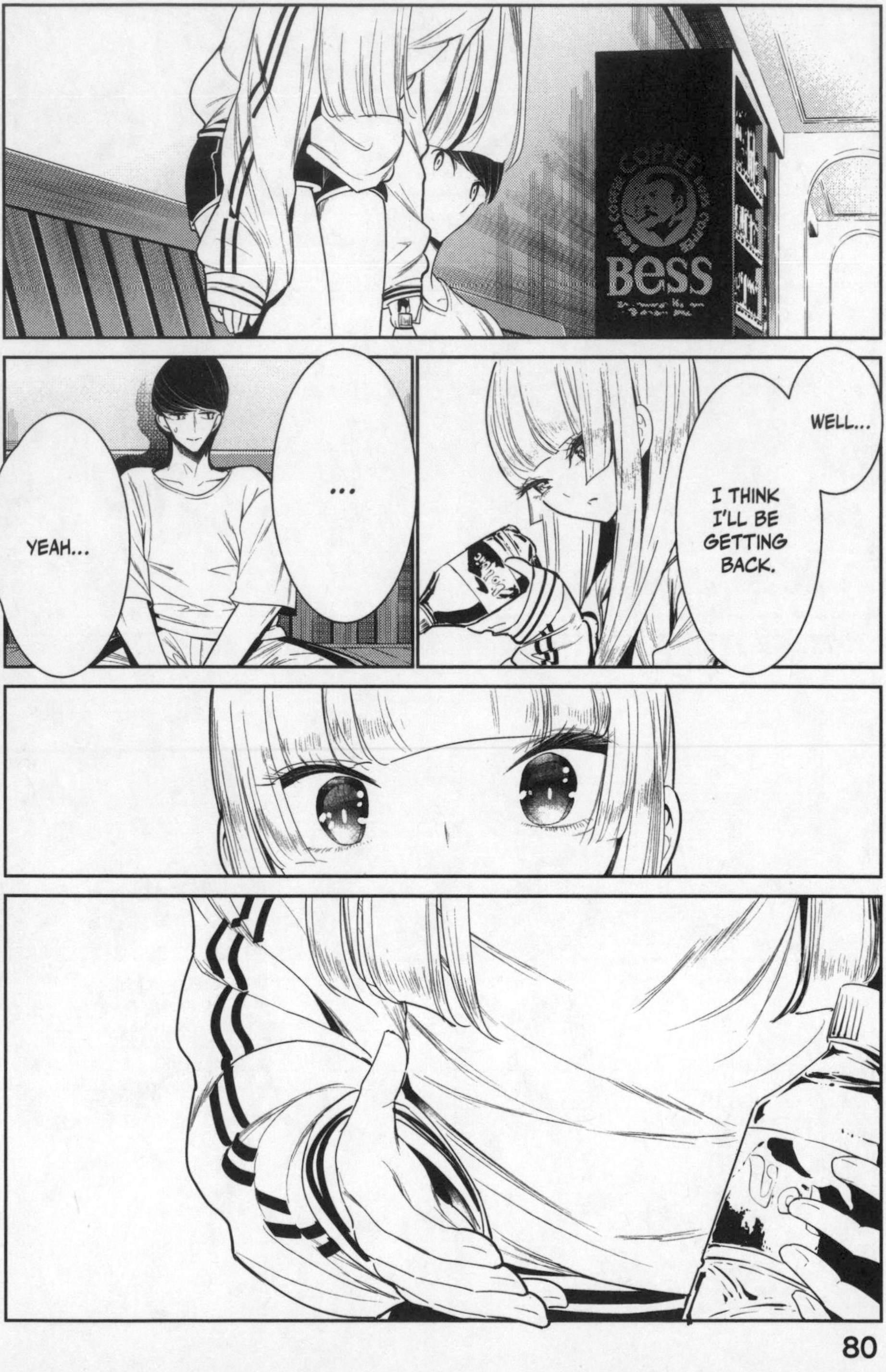
COFFEE
BeSS
WELL...
I THINK I'LL BE GETTING BACK.
...
YEAH...

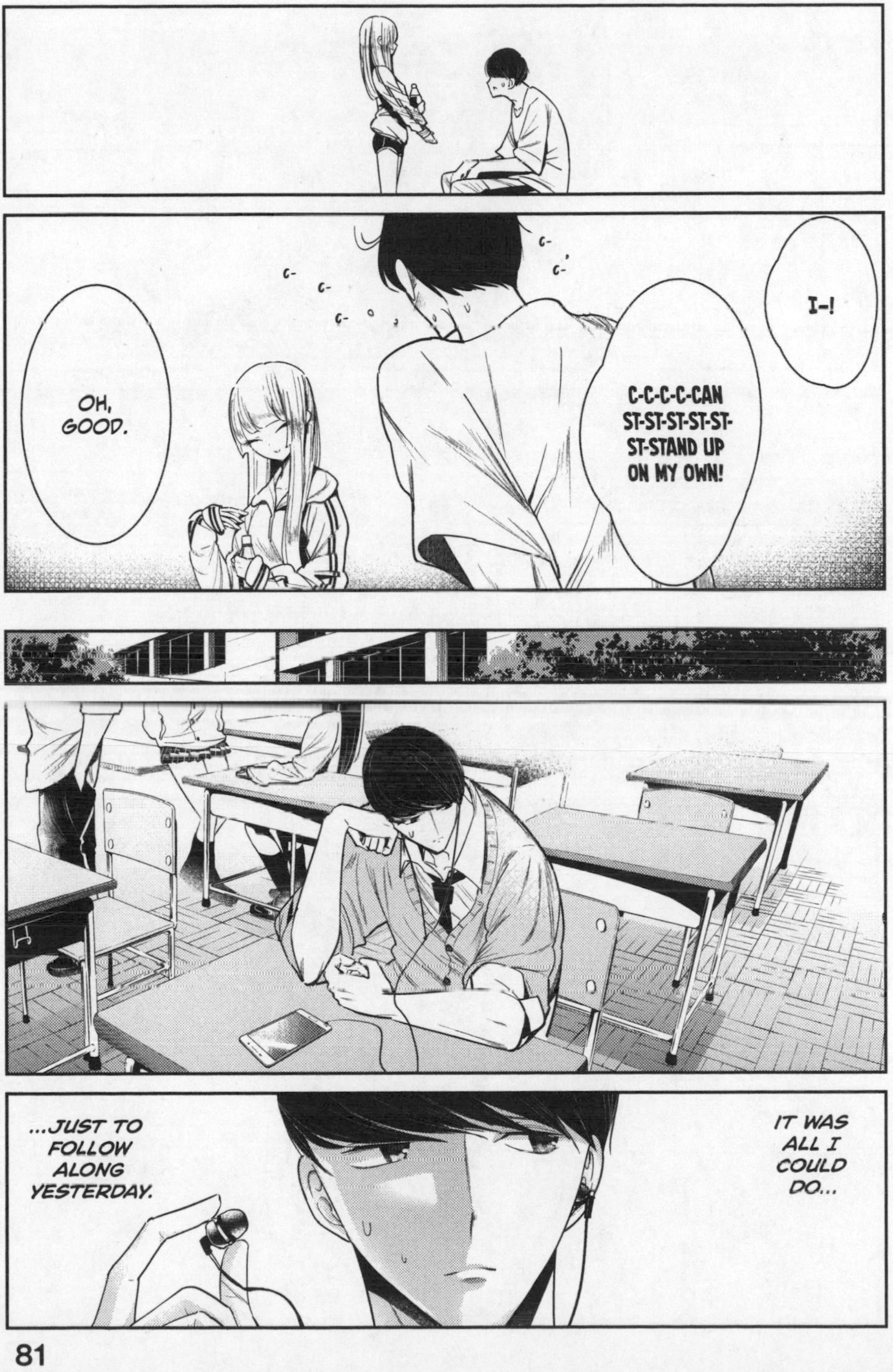

I–!
C-C-C-C-CAN ST-ST-ST-ST-ST-ST-STAND UP ON MY OWN!
OH, GOOD.
IT WAS ALL I COULD DO...
...JUST TO FOLLOW ALONG YESTERDAY.

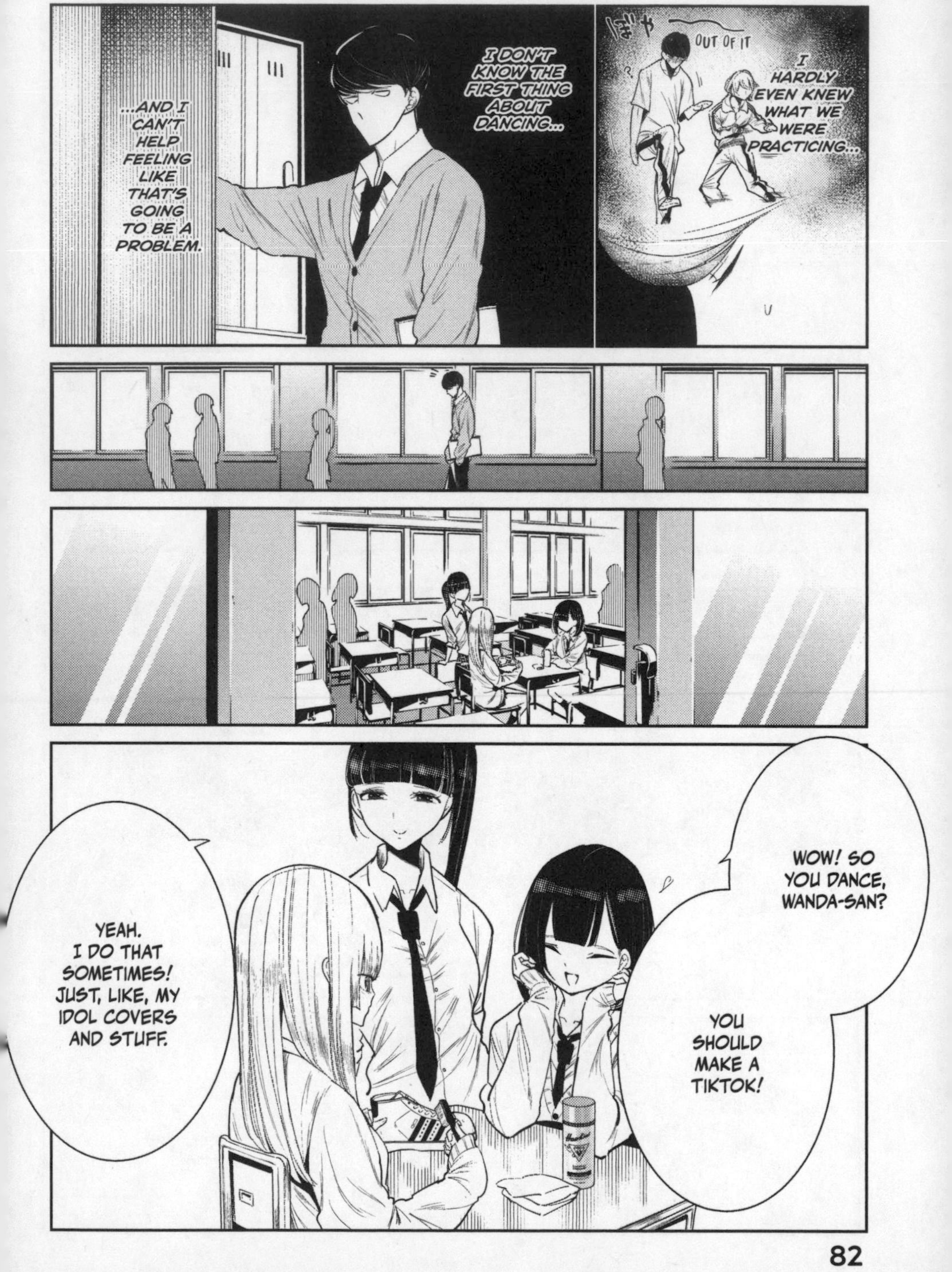
OUT OF IT
I HARDLY EVEN KNEW WHAT WE WERE PRACTICING...
I DON'T KNOW THE FIRST THING ABOUT DANCING...
...AND I CAN'T HELP FEELING LIKE THAT'S GOING TO BE A PROBLEM.
WOW! SO YOU DANCE, WANDA-SAN?
YOU SHOULD MAKE A TIKTOK!
YEAH. I DO THAT SOMETIMES! JUST, LIKE, MY IDOL COVERS AND STUFF.

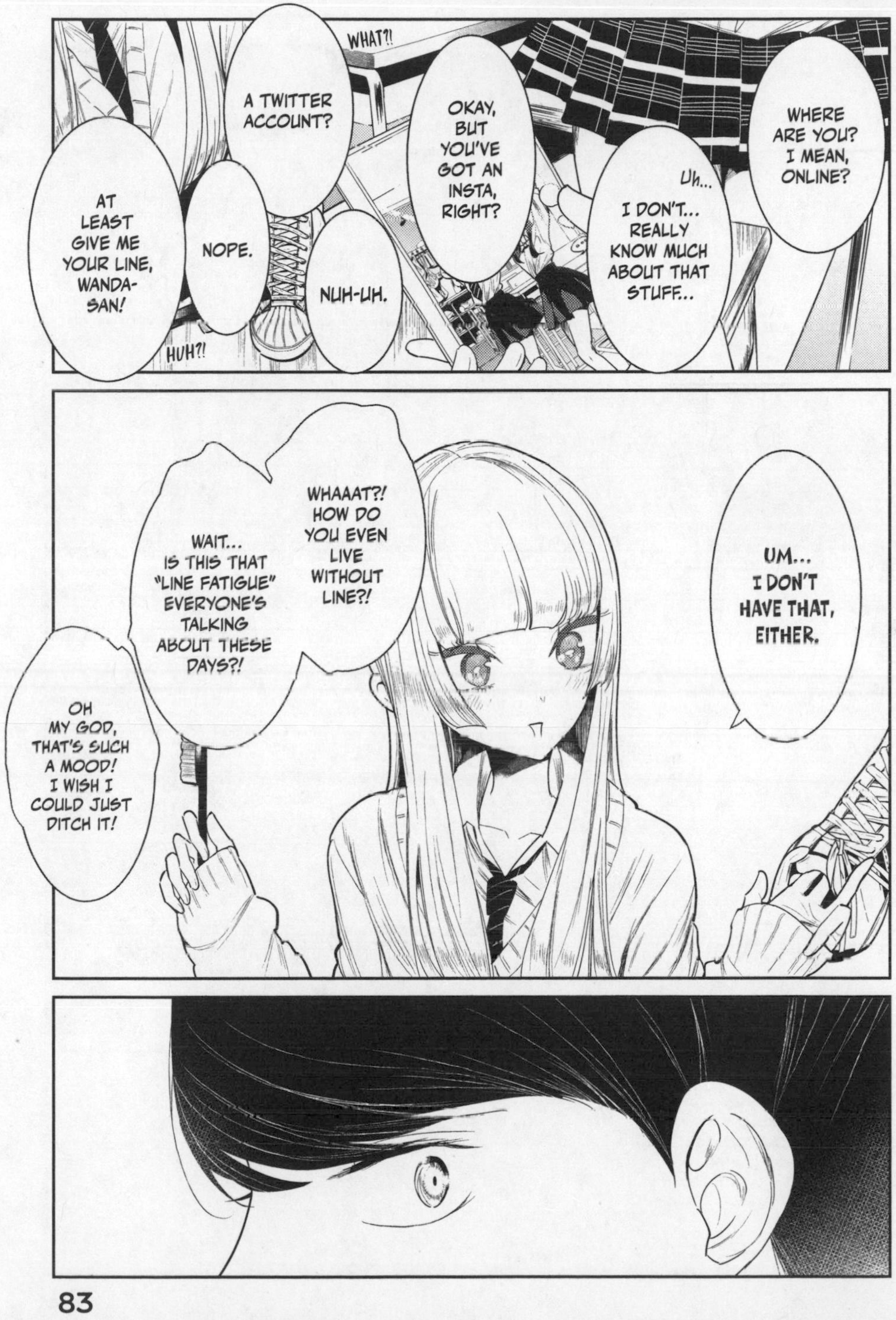
WHERE ARE YOU? I MEAN, ONLINE?
Uh...
I DON'T... REALLY KNOW MUCH ABOUT THAT STUFF...
OKAY, BUT YOU'VE GOT AN INSTA, RIGHT?
NUH-UH.
WHAT?!
A TWITTER ACCOUNT?
NOPE.
AT LEAST GIVE ME YOUR LINE, WANDA-SAN!
HUH?!
UM... I DON'T HAVE THAT, EITHER.
WHAAAT?! HOW DO YOU EVEN LIVE WITHOUT LINE?!
WAIT... IS THIS THAT "LINE FATIGUE" EVERYONE'S TALKING ABOUT THESE DAYS?!
OH MY GOD, THAT'S SUCH A MOOD! I WISH I COULD JUST DITCH IT!

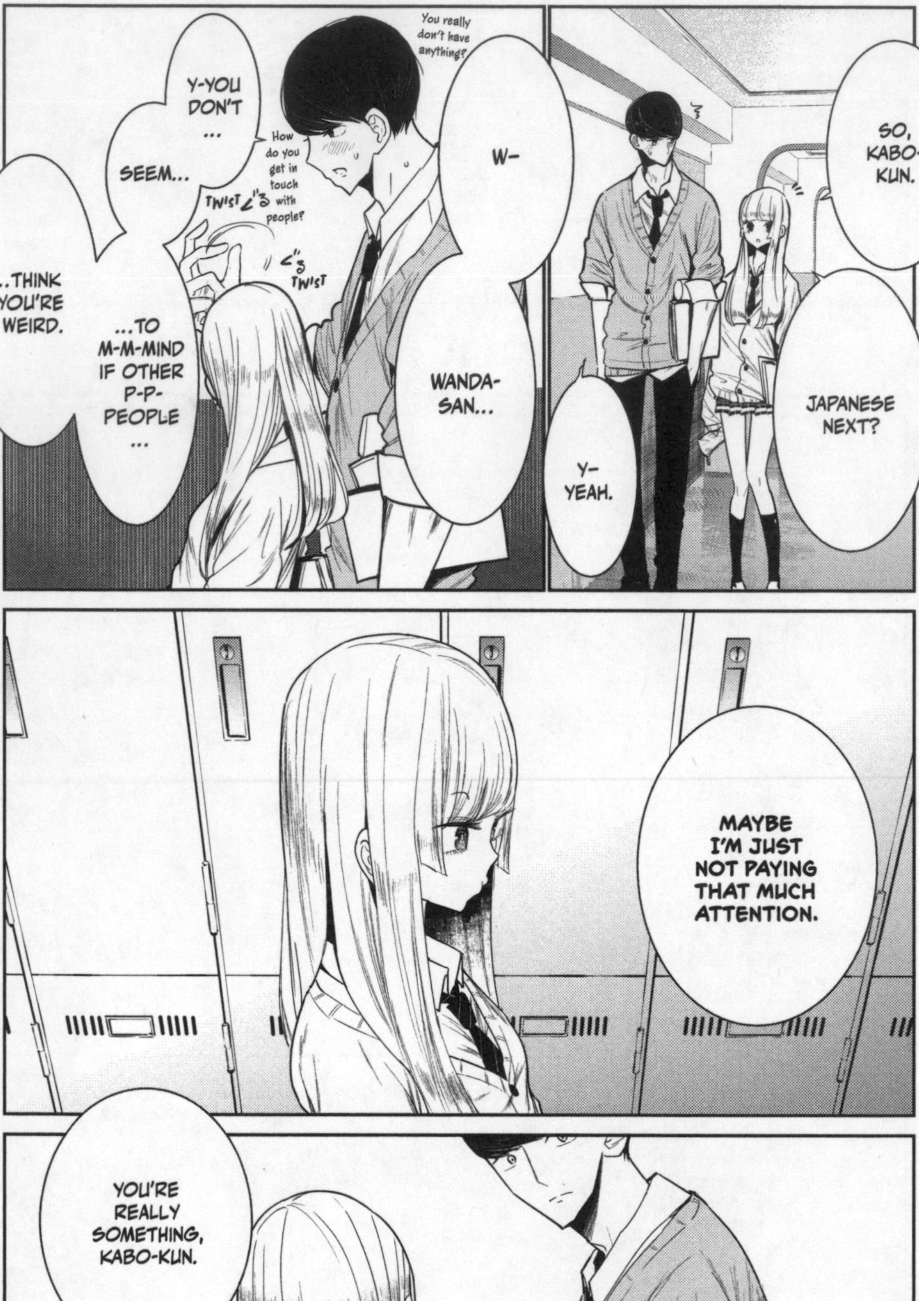
SO, KABO-KUN.
JAPANESE NEXT?
Y-YEAH.
You really don't have anything?
W-
WANDA-SAN...
How do you get in touch with people?
Y-YOU DON'T ... SEEM...
TWIST
TWIST
...TO M-M-MIND IF OTHER P-P-PEOPLE ...
...THINK YOU'RE WEIRD.
MAYBE I'M JUST NOT PAYING THAT MUCH ATTENTION.
YOU'RE REALLY SOMETHING, KABO-KUN.

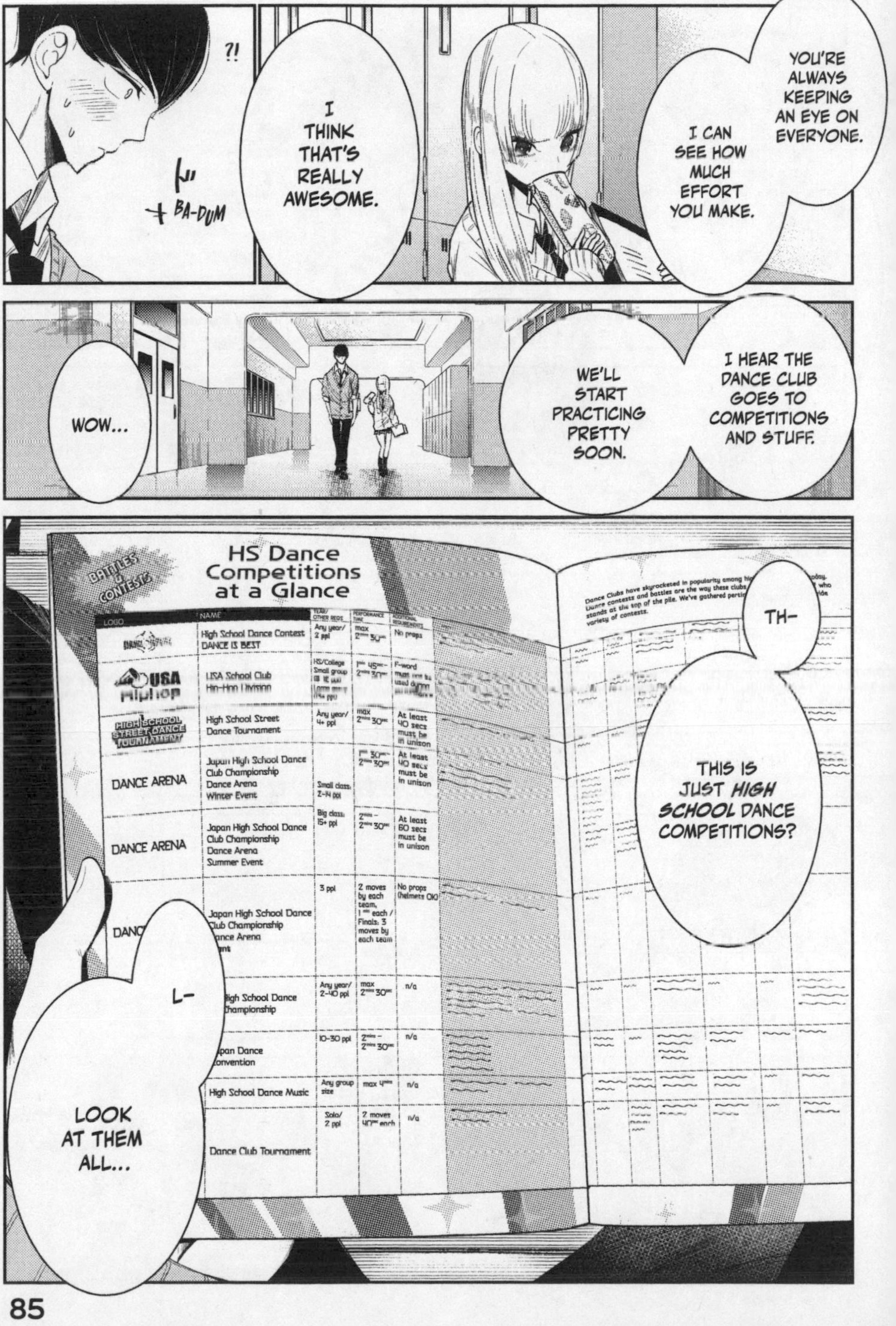
YOU'RE ALWAYS KEEPING AN EYE ON EVERYONE.
I CAN SEE HOW MUCH EFFORT YOU MAKE.
I THINK THAT'S REALLY AWESOME.
?!
BA-DUM
I HEAR THE DANCE CLUB GOES TO COMPETITIONS AND STUFF.
WE'LL START PRACTICING PRETTY SOON.
WOW...
HS Dance Competitions at a Glance
BATTLES & CONTESTS
LOGO
NAME
High School Dance Contest DANCE IS BEST
High School Street Dance Tournament
DANCE ARENA
Japan High School Dance Club Championship Dance Arena Winter Event
DANCE ARENA
Japan High School Dance Club Championship Dance Arena Summer Event
High School Dance Music
Dance Club Tournament
TH-
THIS IS JUST *HIGH SCHOOL* DANCE COMPETITIONS?
L-
LOOK AT THEM ALL...

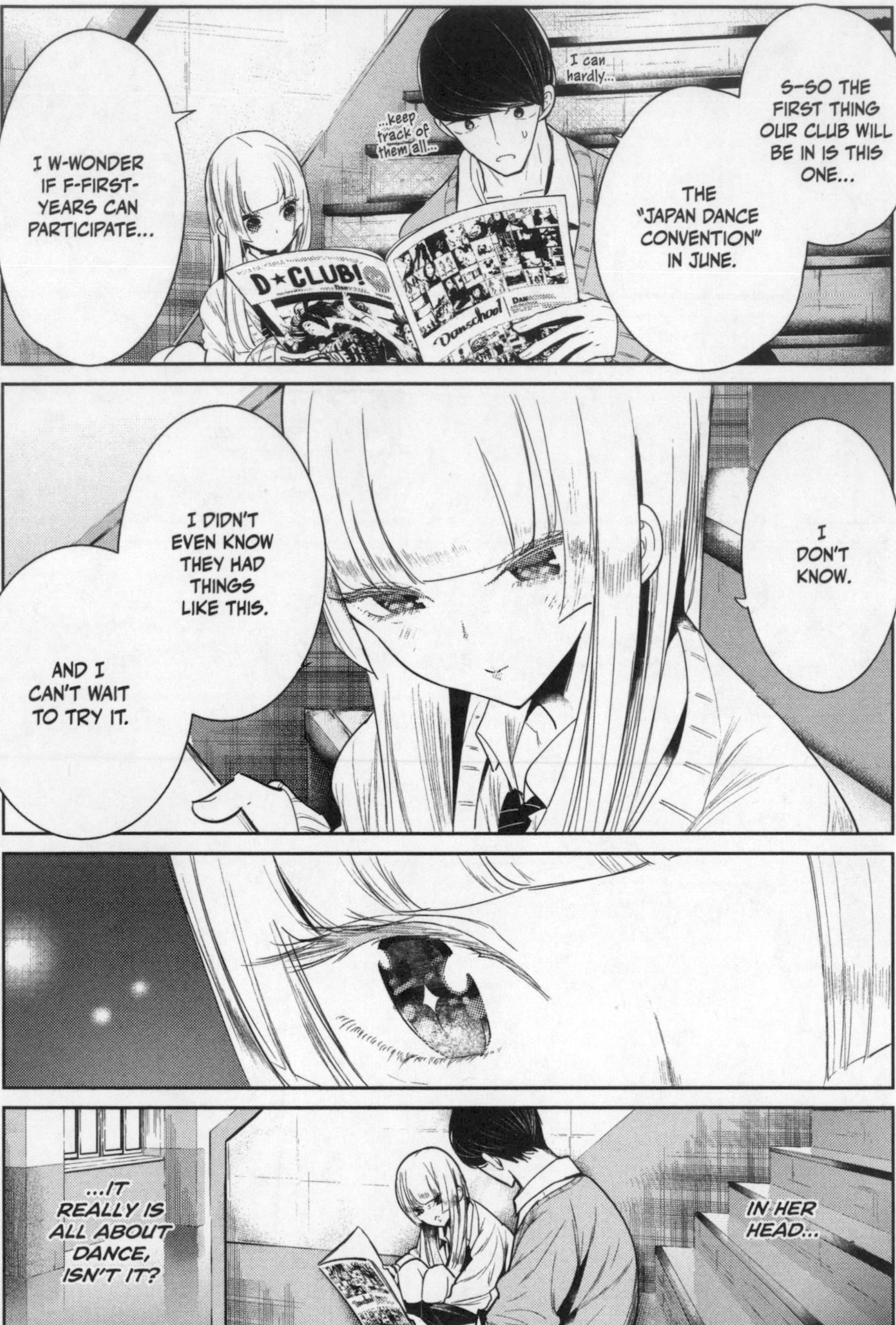
S-SO THE FIRST THING OUR CLUB WILL BE IN IS THIS ONE...
THE "JAPAN DANCE CONVENTION" IN JUNE.
I can hardly...
...keep track of them all...
D★CLUB!
Danschool
I W-WONDER IF F-FIRST-YEARS CAN PARTICIPATE...
I DON'T KNOW.
I DIDN'T EVEN KNOW THEY HAD THINGS LIKE THIS.
AND I CAN'T WAIT TO TRY IT.
IN HER HEAD...
...IT REALLY IS ALL ABOUT DANCE, ISN'T IT?

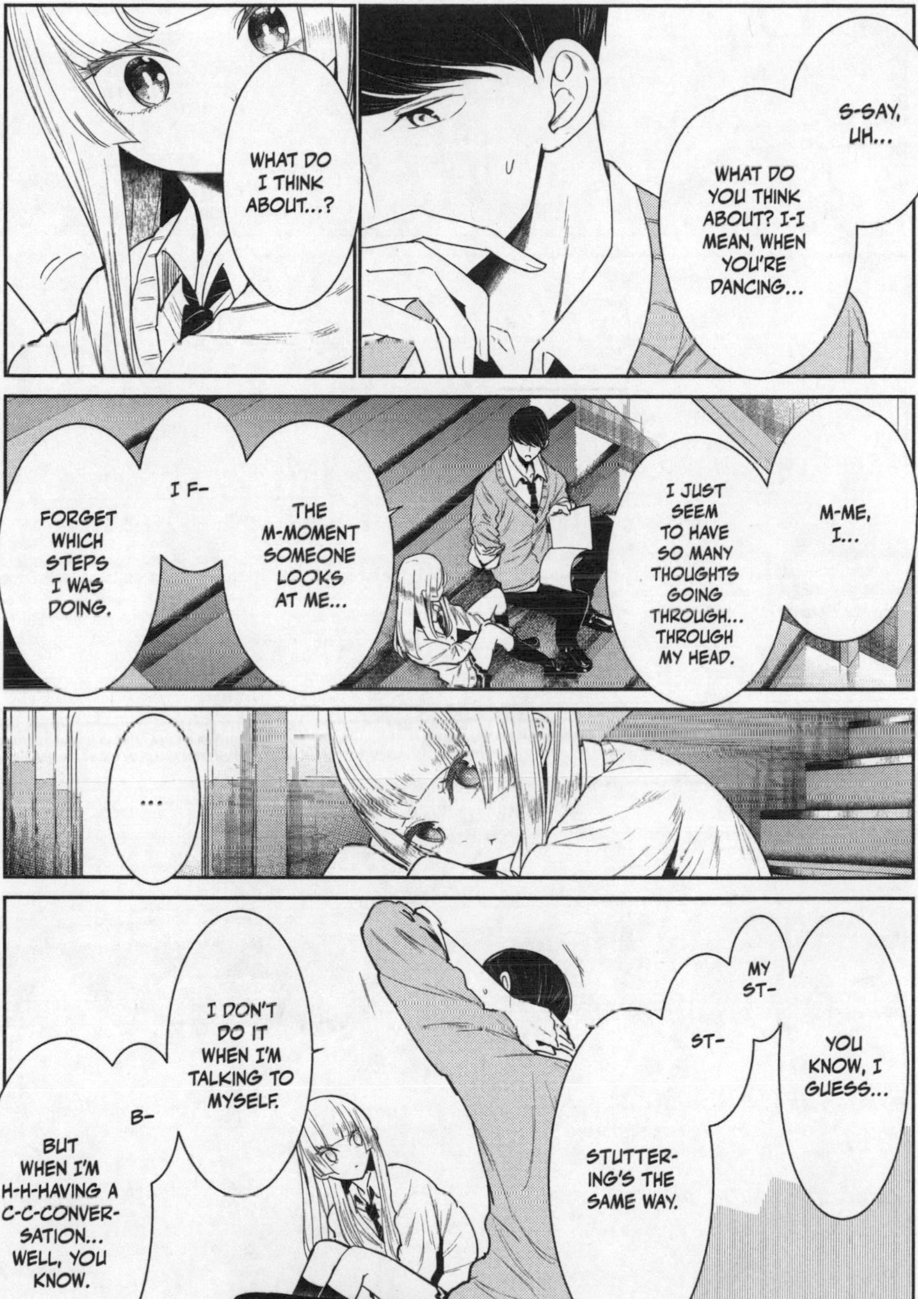
S-SAY, UH...
WHAT DO YOU THINK ABOUT? I-I MEAN, WHEN YOU'RE DANCING...
WHAT DO I THINK ABOUT...?
M-ME, I...
I JUST SEEM TO HAVE SO MANY THOUGHTS GOING THROUGH... THROUGH MY HEAD.
THE M-MOMENT SOMEONE LOOKS AT ME...
I F-
FORGET WHICH STEPS I WAS DOING.
...
YOU KNOW, I GUESS...
MY ST-
ST-
STUTTER-ING'S THE SAME WAY.
I DON'T DO IT WHEN I'M TALKING TO MYSELF.
B-
BUT WHEN I'M H-H-HAVING A C-C-CONVER-SATION... WELL, YOU KNOW.

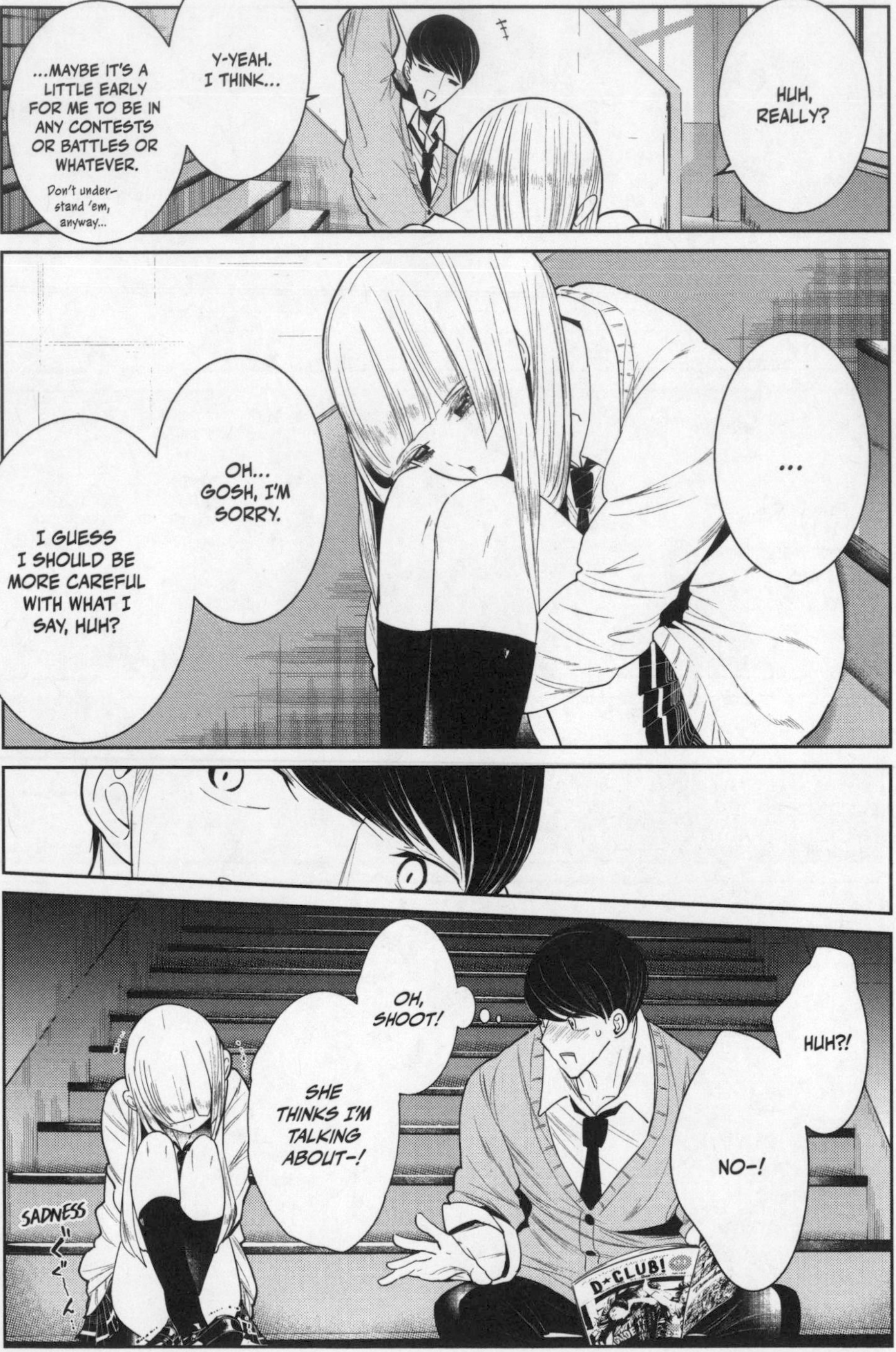
HUH, REALLY?
Y-YEAH. I THINK...
...MAYBE IT'S A LITTLE EARLY FOR ME TO BE IN ANY CONTESTS OR BATTLES OR WHATEVER.
Don't under-stand 'em, anyway...
...
OH... GOSH, I'M SORRY.
I GUESS I SHOULD BE MORE CAREFUL WITH WHAT I SAY, HUH?
HUH?!
NO-!
OH, SHOOT!
SHE THINKS I'M TALKING ABOUT-!
SADNESS
D☆CLUB!

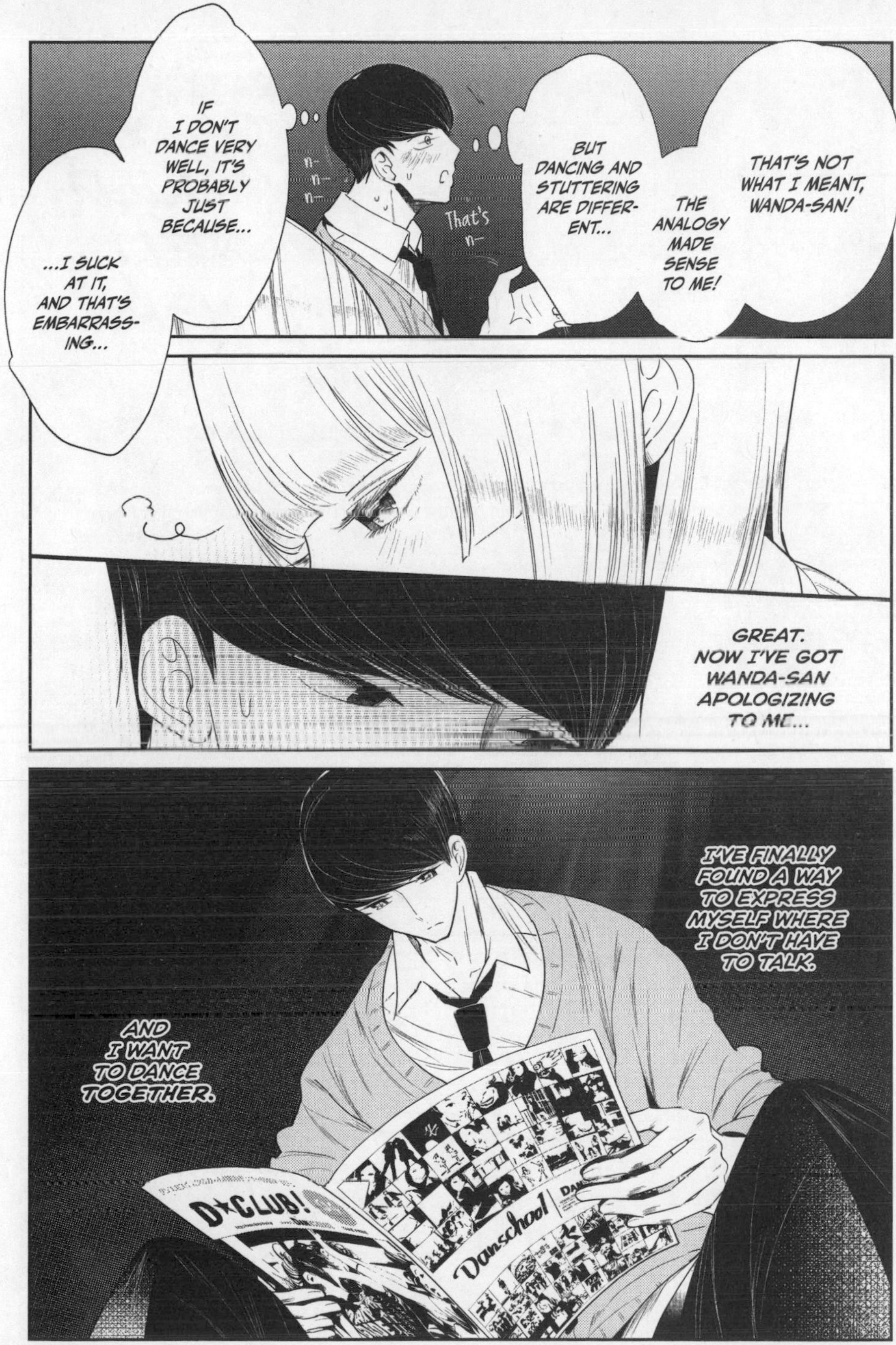
THAT'S NOT WHAT I MEANT, WANDA-SAN!
THE ANALOGY MADE SENSE TO ME!
BUT DANCING AND STUTTERING ARE DIFFER-ENT...
That's n–
n– n– n–
IF I DON'T DANCE VERY WELL, IT'S PROBABLY JUST BECAUSE...
...I SUCK AT IT, AND THAT'S EMBARRASS-ING...
GREAT. NOW I'VE GOT WANDA-SAN APOLOGIZING TO ME...
I'VE FINALLY FOUND A WAY TO EXPRESS MYSELF WHERE I DON'T HAVE TO TALK.
AND I WANT TO DANCE TOGETHER.
D☆CLUB!
Danschool
Danschool

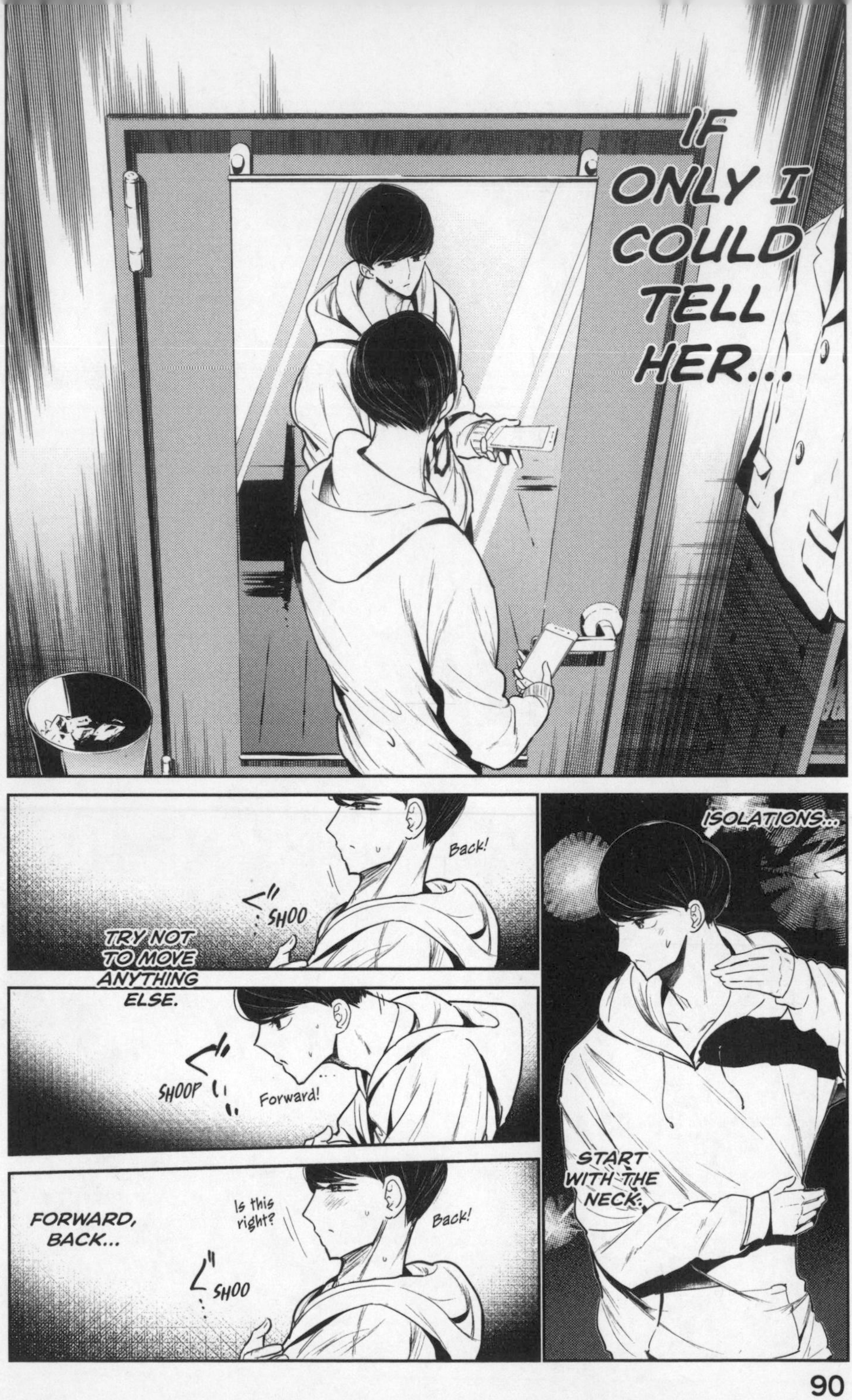
IF ONLY I COULD TELL HER...
ISOLATIONS...
START WITH THE NECK.
Back!
SHOO
TRY NOT TO MOVE ANYTHING ELSE.
Forward!
SHOOP
Is this right?
Back!
FORWARD, BACK...
SHOO

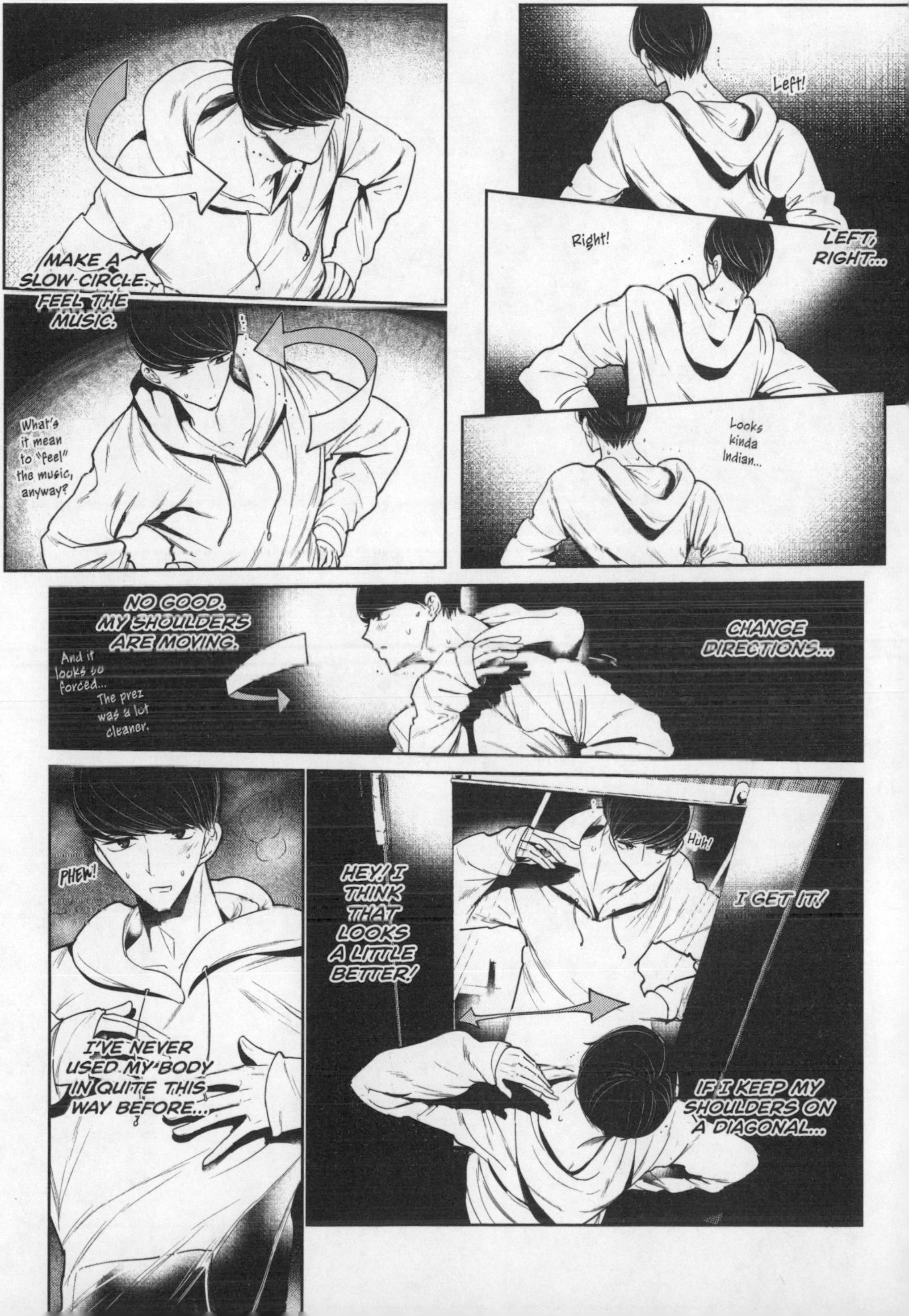
Left!
LEFT, RIGHT...
Right!
Looks kinda Indian...
MAKE A SLOW CIRCLE. FEEL THE MUSIC.
What's it mean to "feel" the music, anyway?
CHANGE DIRECTIONS...
NO GOOD. MY SHOULDERS ARE MOVING.
And it looks so forced...
The prez was a lot cleaner.
Huh!
I GET IT!
HEY! I THINK THAT LOOKS A LITTLE BETTER!
IF I KEEP MY SHOULDERS ON A DIAGONAL...
PHEW!
I'VE NEVER USED MY BODY IN QUITE THIS WAY BEFORE...

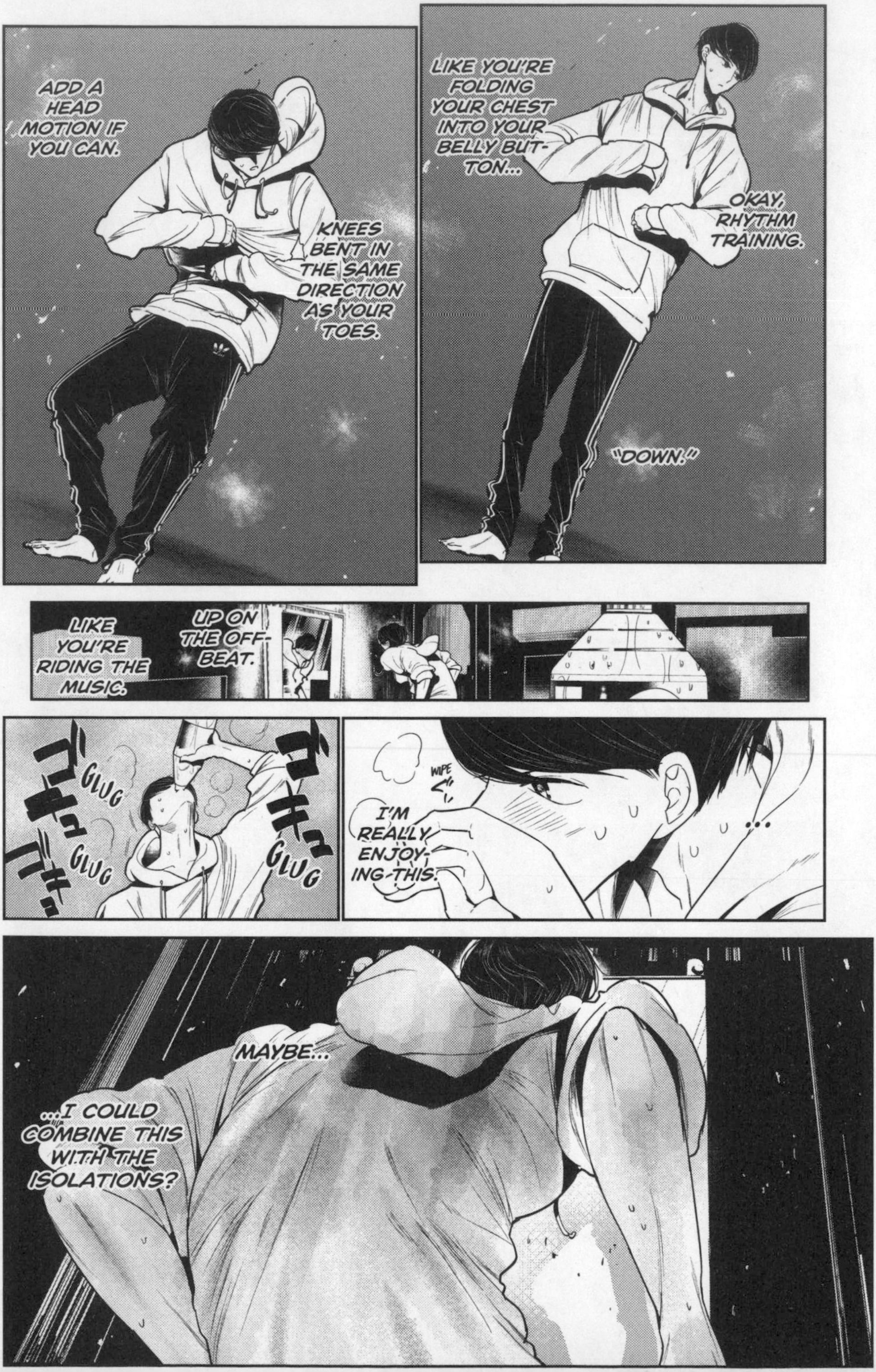
OKAY, RHYTHM TRAINING.
"DOWN."
LIKE YOU'RE FOLDING YOUR CHEST INTO YOUR BELLY BUTTON...
KNEES BENT IN THE SAME DIRECTION AS YOUR TOES.
ADD A HEAD MOTION IF YOU CAN.
UP ON THE OFF-BEAT.
LIKE YOU'RE RIDING THE MUSIC.
...
ぐい WIPE
I'M REALLY ENJOYING THIS.
ゴキュ GLUG
ゴキュ GLUG
ゴキュ GLUG
MAYBE...
...I COULD COMBINE THIS WITH THE ISOLATIONS?

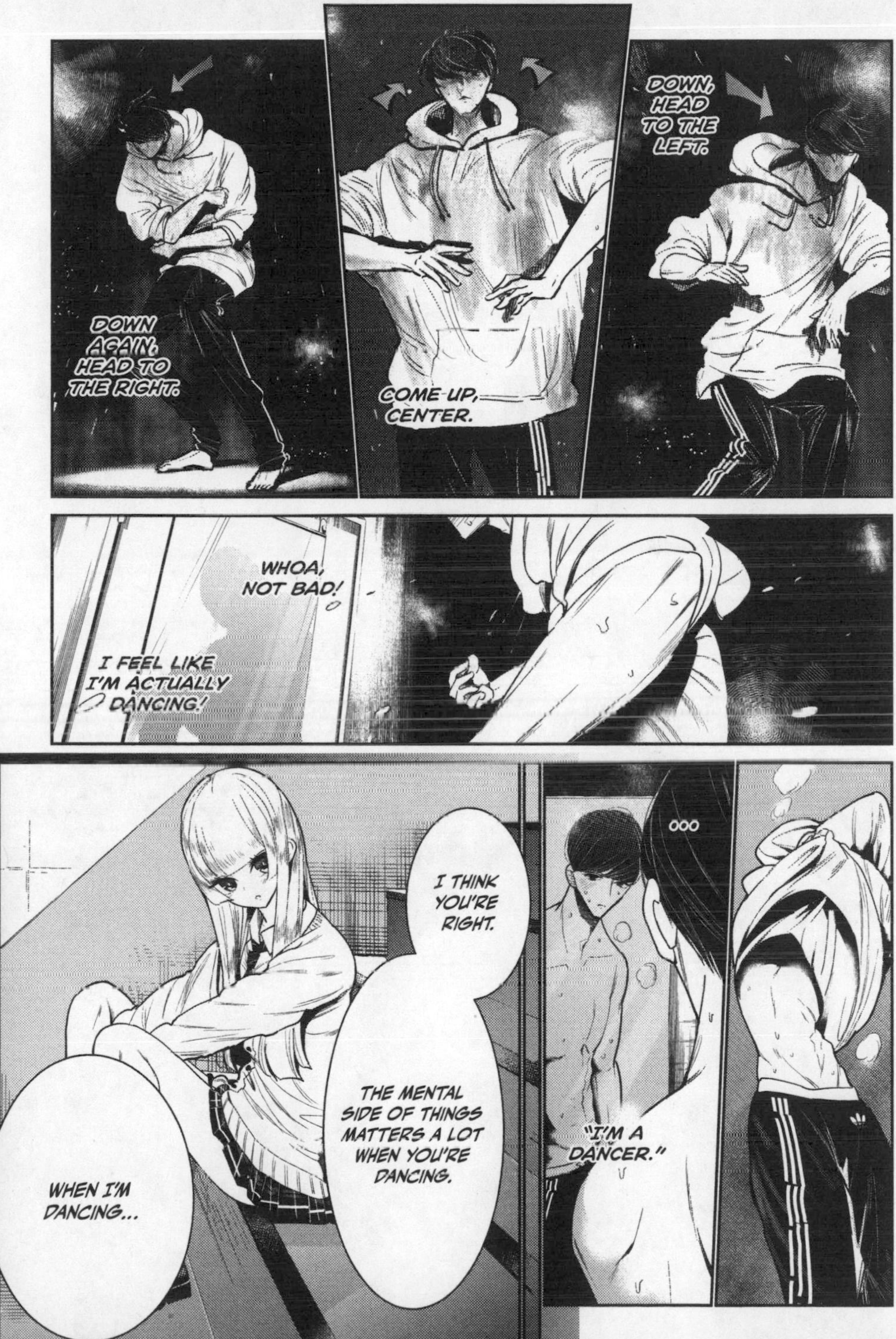
DOWN, HEAD TO THE LEFT.
COME UP, CENTER.
DOWN AGAIN, HEAD TO THE RIGHT.
WHOA, NOT BAD!
I FEEL LIKE I'M ACTUALLY DANCING!
...
"I'M A DANCER."
I THINK YOU'RE RIGHT.
THE MENTAL SIDE OF THINGS MATTERS A LOT WHEN YOU'RE DANCING.
WHEN I'M DANCING...

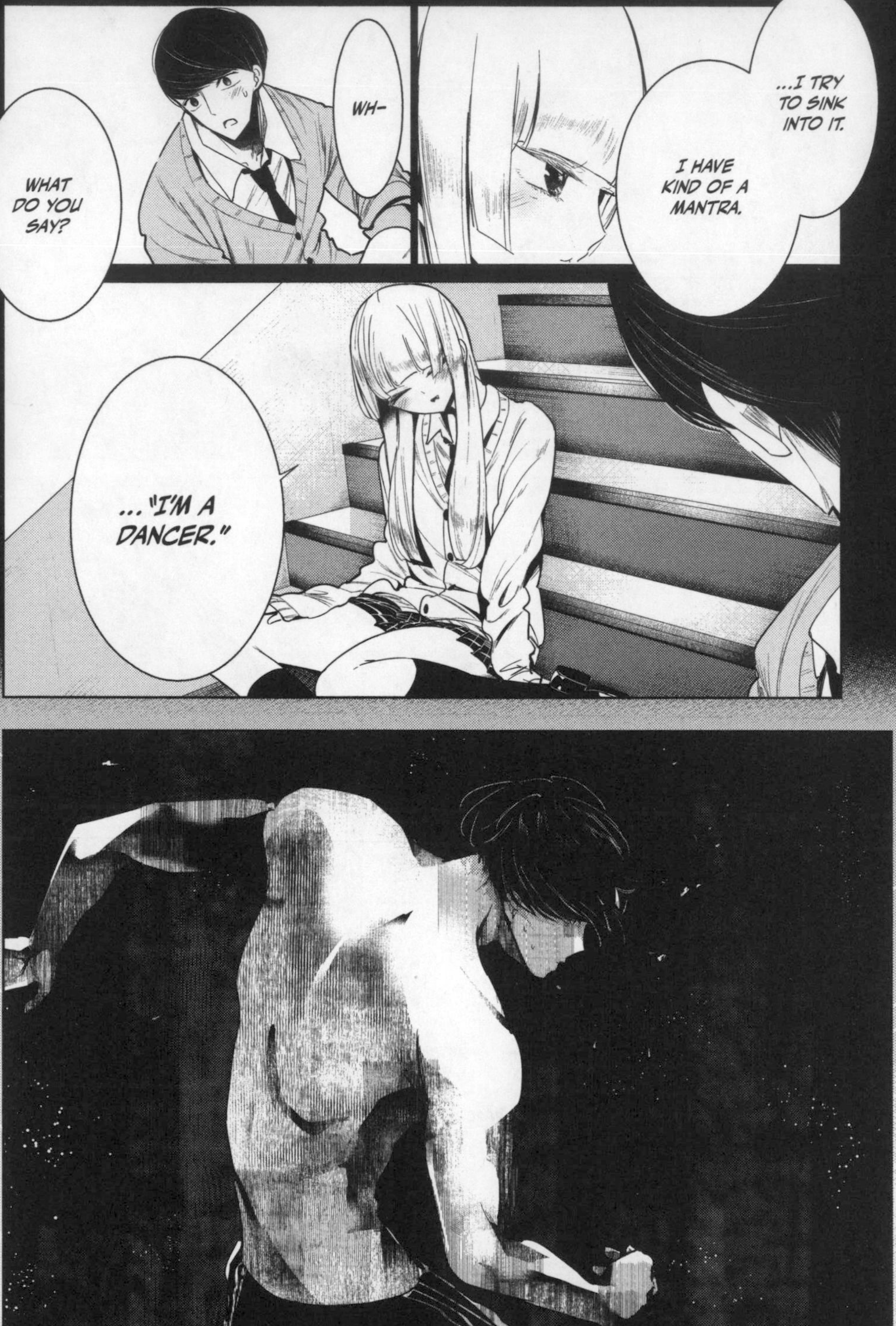

...I TRY TO SINK INTO IT.
I HAVE KIND OF A MANTRA.
WH-
WHAT DO YOU SAY?
..."I'M A DANCER."

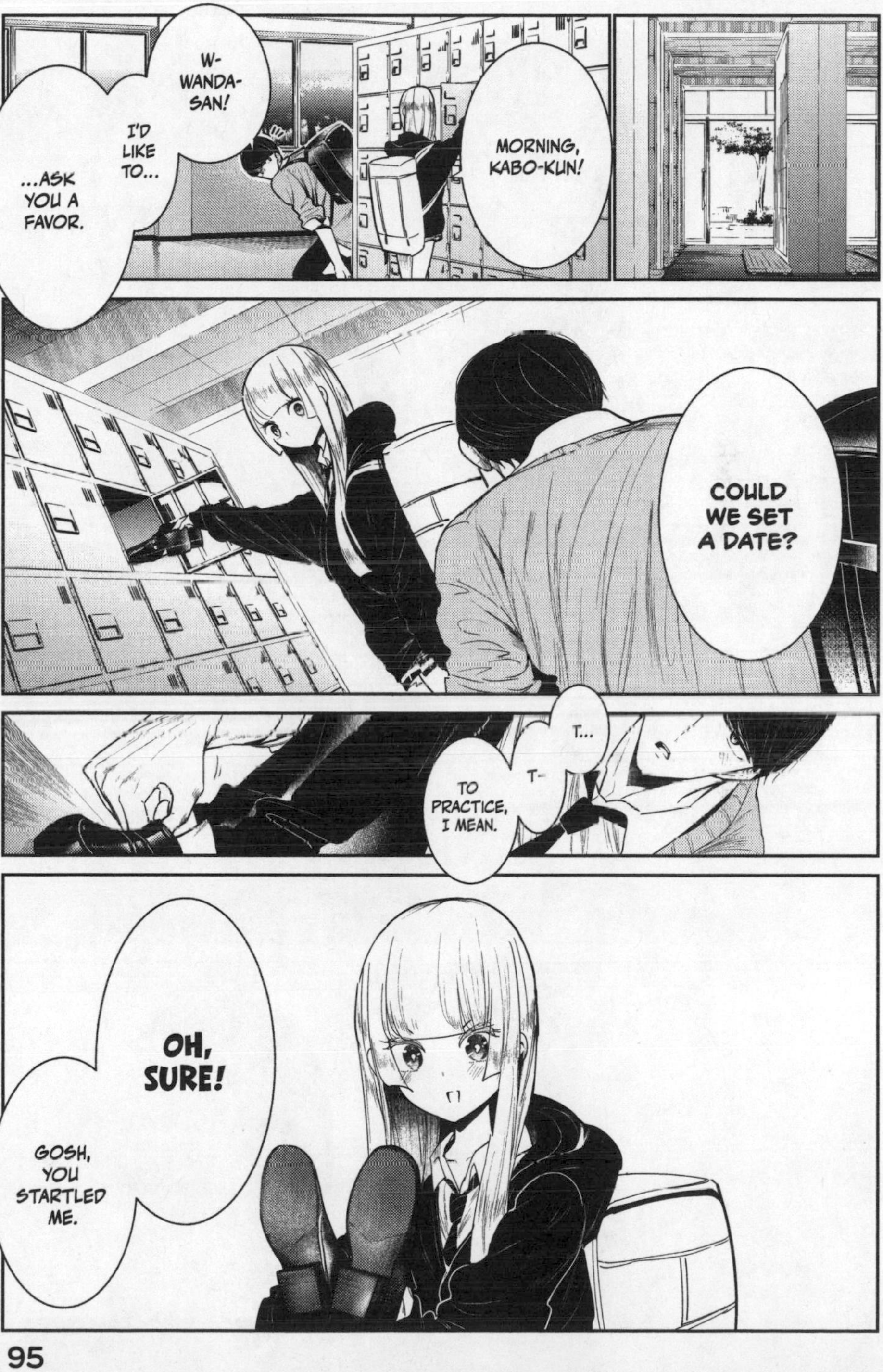
MORNING, KABO-KUN!
W-WANDA-SAN!
I'D LIKE TO...
...ASK YOU A FAVOR.
COULD WE SET A DATE?
T...
T-
TO PRACTICE, I MEAN.
OH, SURE!
GOSH, YOU STARTLED ME.

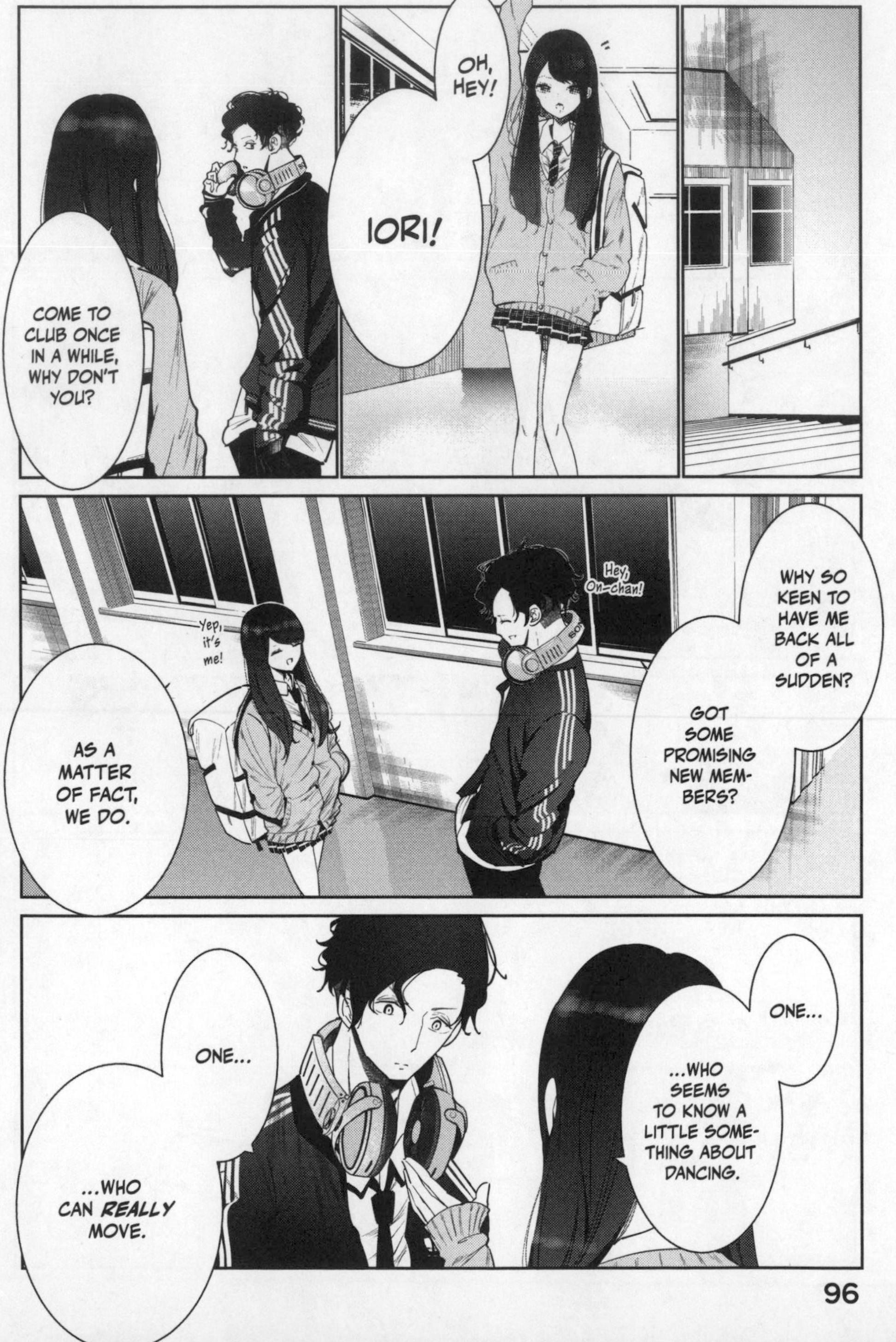
OH, HEY!
IORI!
COME TO CLUB ONCE IN A WHILE, WHY DON'T YOU?
WHY SO KEEN TO HAVE ME BACK ALL OF A SUDDEN?
GOT SOME PROMISING NEW MEM-BERS?
Hey, On-chan!
Yep, it's me!
AS A MATTER OF FACT, WE DO.
ONE...
...WHO SEEMS TO KNOW A LITTLE SOME-THING ABOUT DANCING.
ONE...
...WHO CAN *REALLY* MOVE.

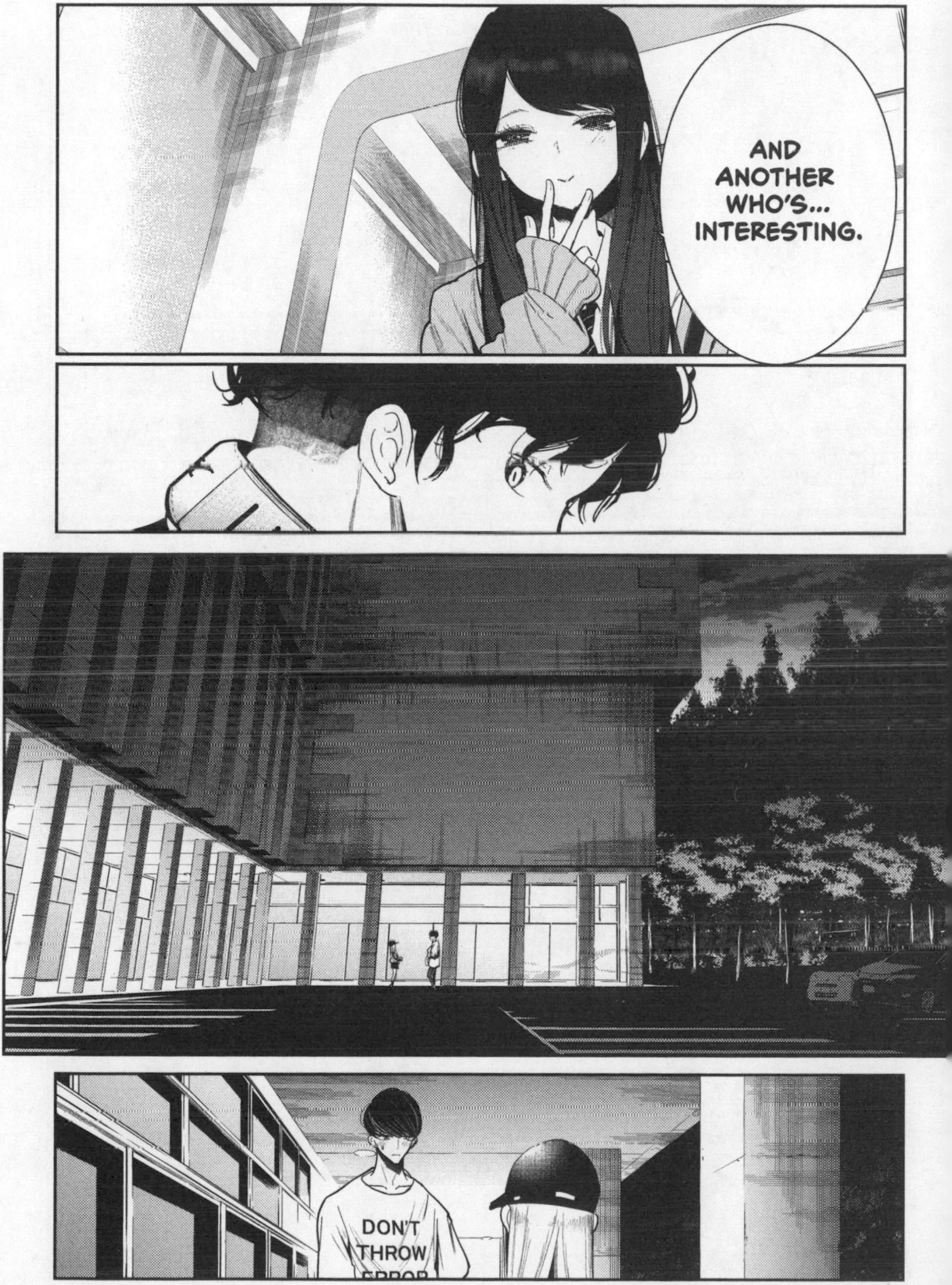
AND ANOTHER WHO'S... INTERESTING.
DON'T
THROW

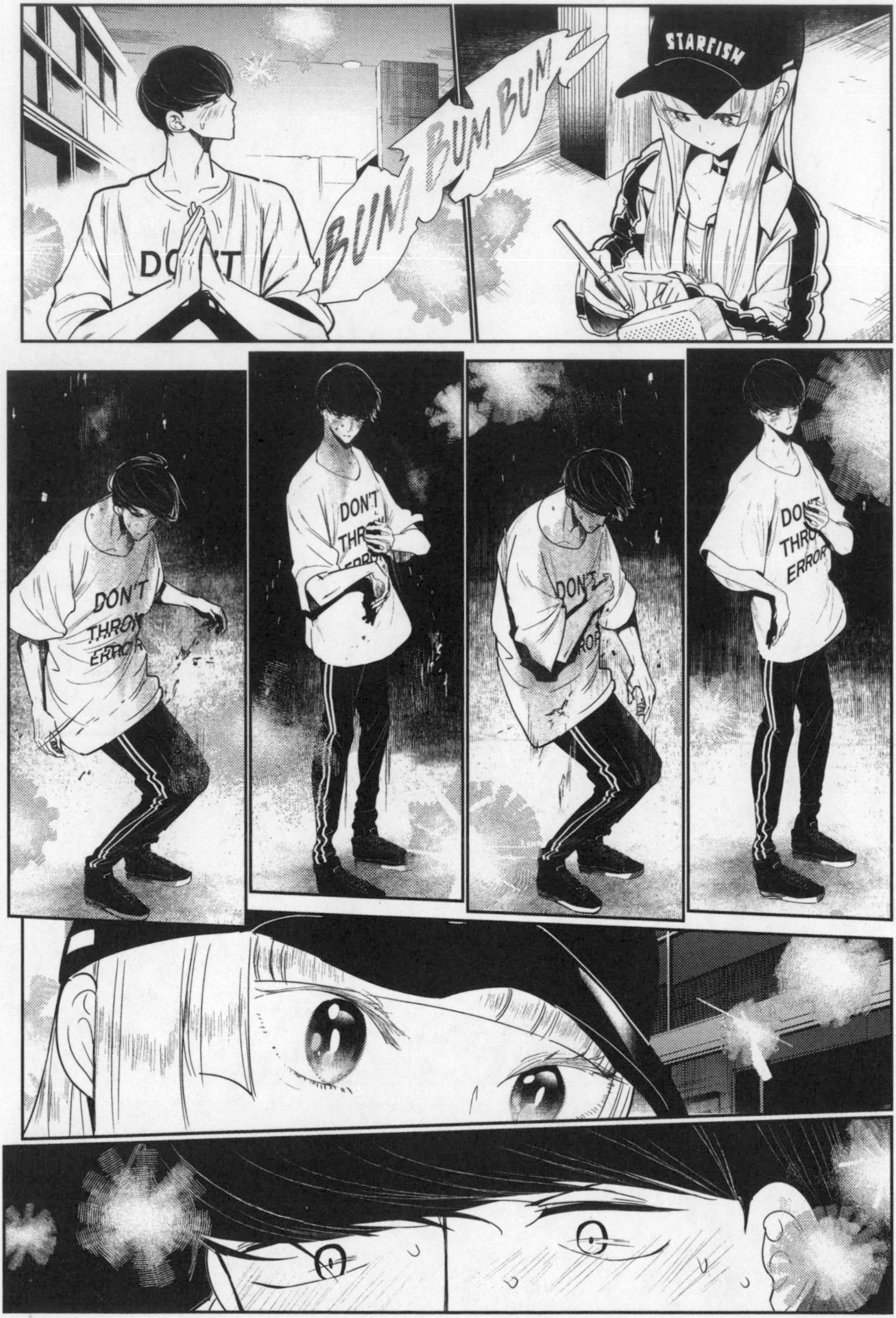
STARFISH
BUM BUM BUM

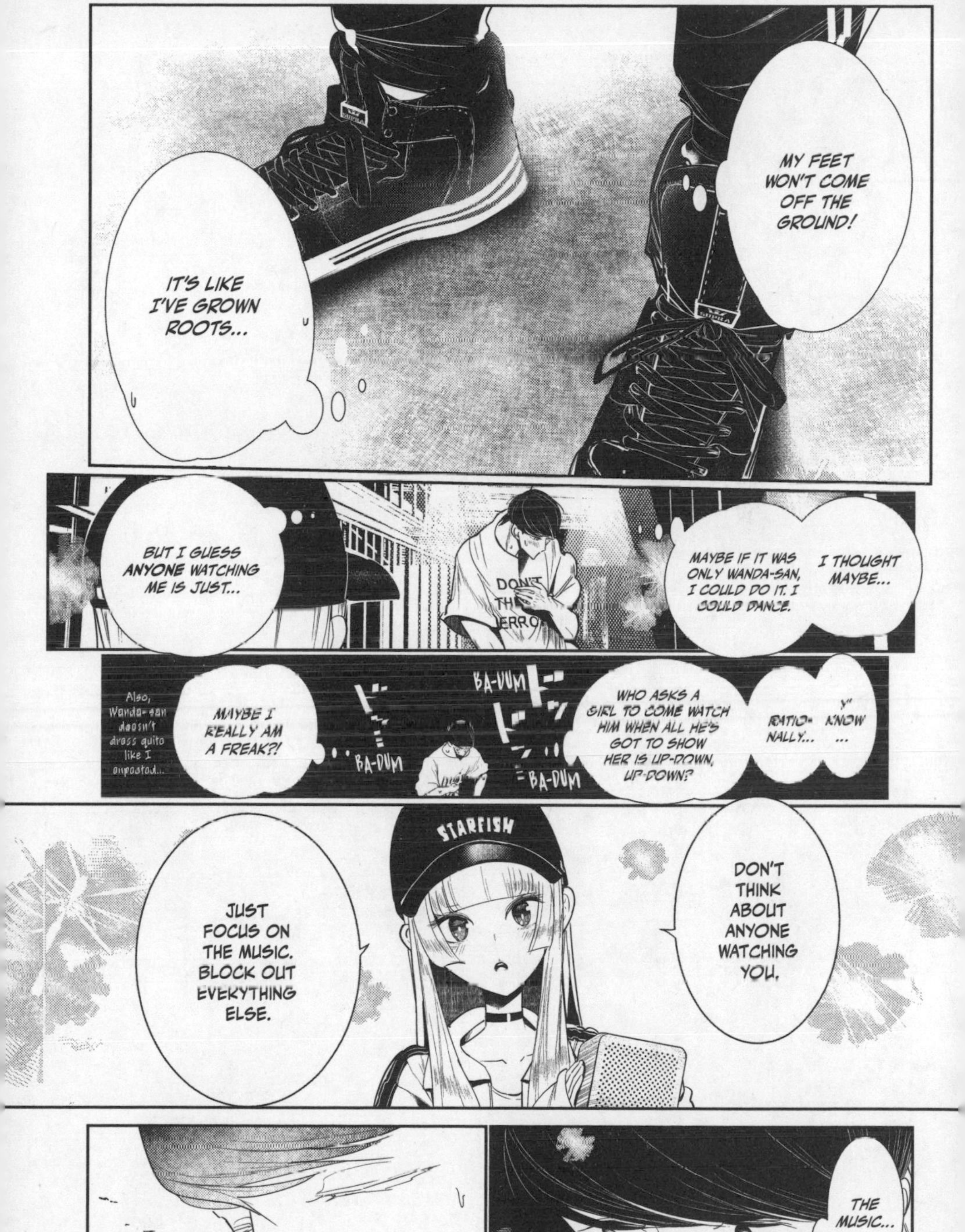
MY FEET WON'T COME OFF THE GROUND!
IT'S LIKE I'VE GROWN ROOTS...
I THOUGHT MAYBE...
MAYBE IF IT WAS ONLY WANDA-SAN, I COULD DO IT. I COULD DANCE.
BUT I GUESS ANYONE WATCHING ME IS JUST...
Y' KNOW ...
RATIO-NALLY...
WHO ASKS A GIRL TO COME WATCH HIM WHEN ALL HE'S GOT TO SHOW HER IS UP-DOWN, UP-DOWN?
BA-DUM
BA-DUM
BA-DUM
MAYBE I REALLY AM A FREAK?!
Also, Wanda-san doesn't dress quite like I expected...
STARFISH
DON'T THINK ABOUT ANYONE WATCHING YOU.
JUST FOCUS ON THE MUSIC. BLOCK OUT EVERYTHING ELSE.
THE MUSIC...

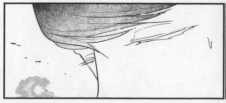

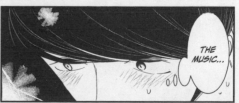

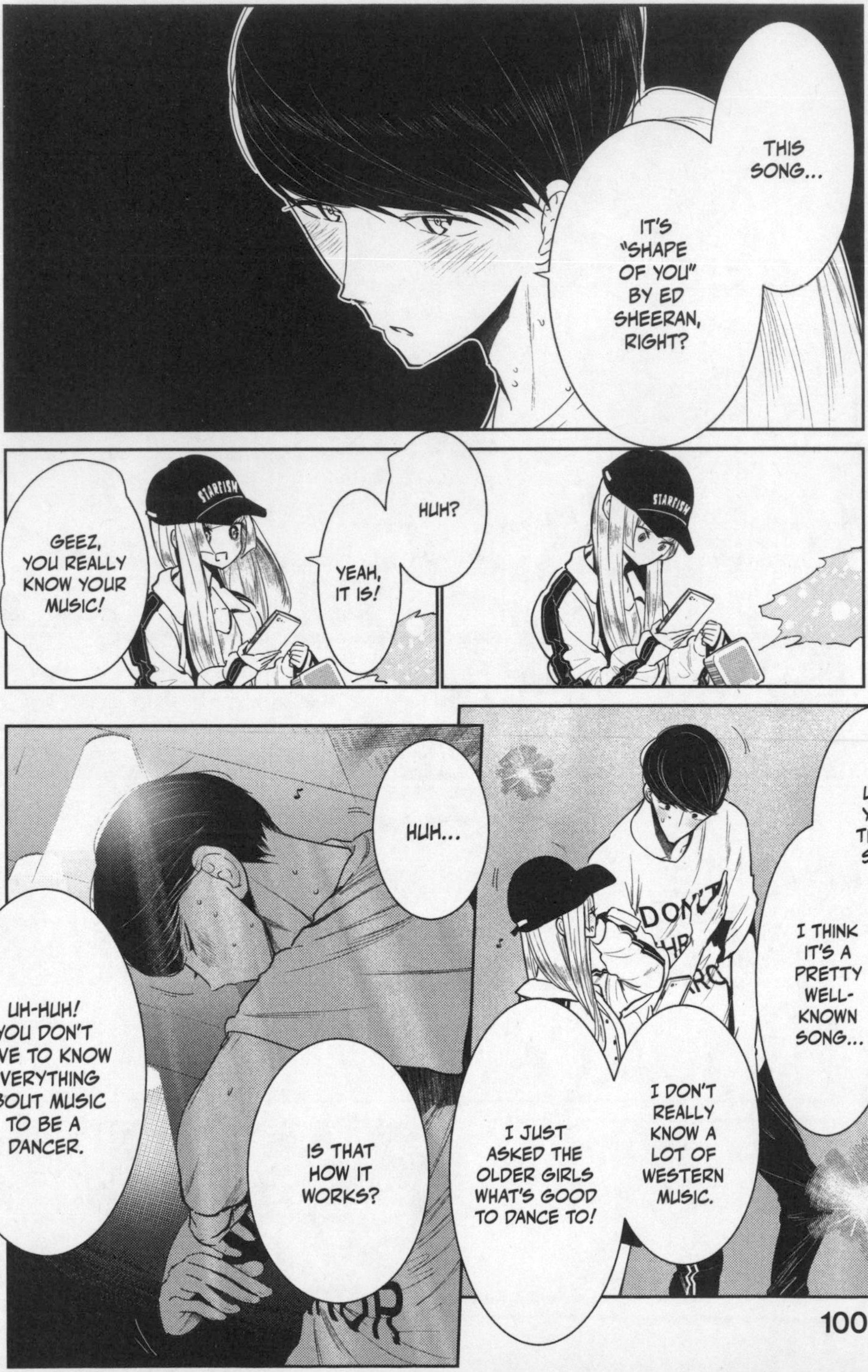
THIS SONG...
IT'S "SHAPE OF YOU" BY ED SHEERAN, RIGHT?
STARFISH
HUH?
YEAH, IT IS!
GEEZ, YOU REALLY KNOW YOUR MUSIC!
UH... YOU THINK SO?
I THINK IT'S A PRETTY WELL-KNOWN SONG...
I DON'T REALLY KNOW A LOT OF WESTERN MUSIC.
I JUST ASKED THE OLDER GIRLS WHAT'S GOOD TO DANCE TO!
HUH...
IS THAT HOW IT WORKS?
UH-HUH! YOU DON'T HAVE TO KNOW EVERYTHING ABOUT MUSIC TO BE A DANCER.

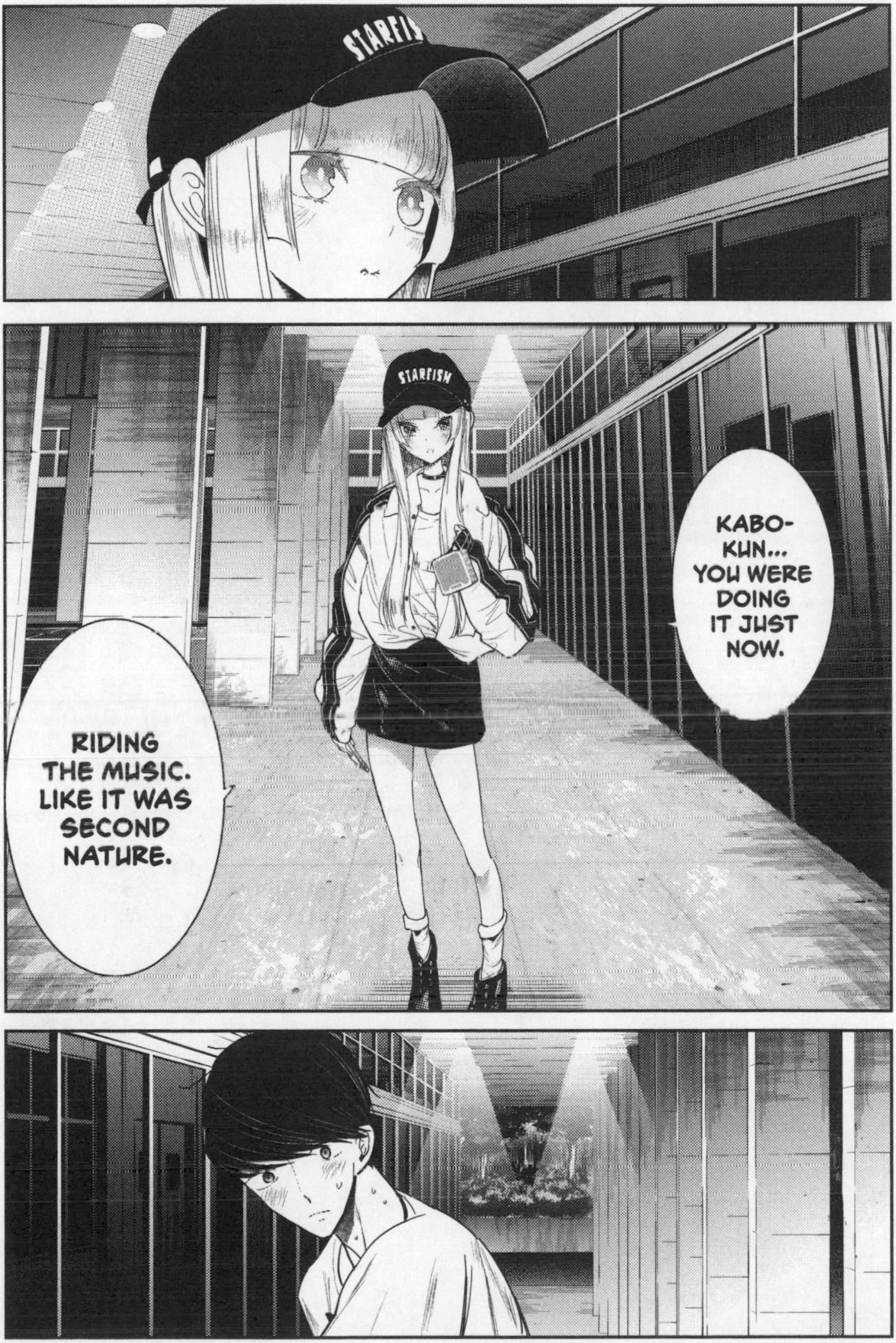
STARFISH
KABO-KUN... YOU WERE DOING IT JUST NOW.
RIDING THE MUSIC. LIKE IT WAS SECOND NATURE.

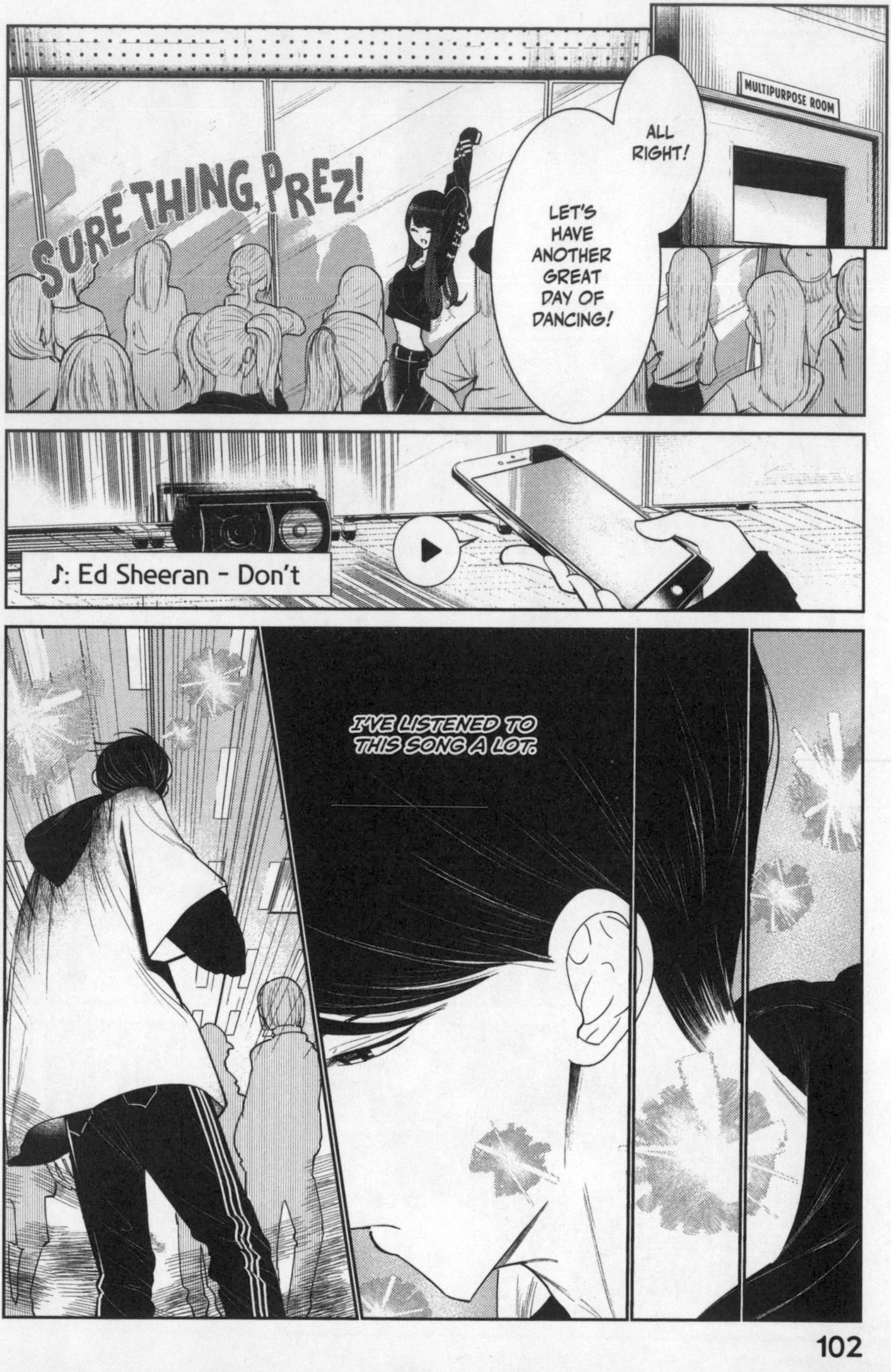
MULTIPURPOSE ROOM
ALL RIGHT!
LET'S HAVE ANOTHER GREAT DAY OF DANCING!
SURE THING, PREZ!
♪: Ed Sheeran - Don't
I'VE LISTENED TO THIS SONG A LOT.

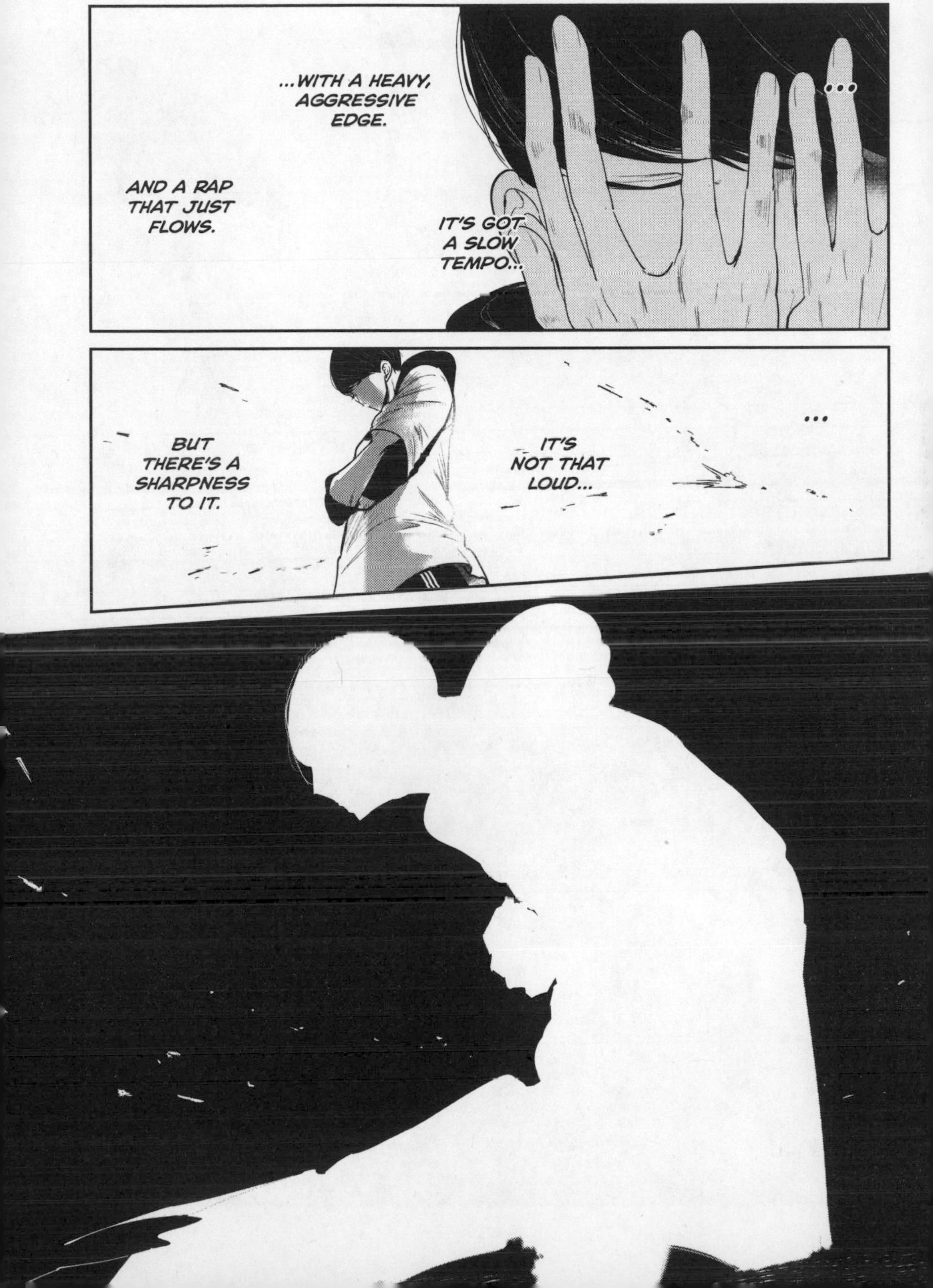
...
IT'S GOT A SLOW TEMPO...
...WITH A HEAVY, AGGRESSIVE EDGE.
AND A RAP THAT JUST FLOWS.
...
IT'S NOT THAT LOUD...
BUT THERE'S A SHARPNESS TO IT.

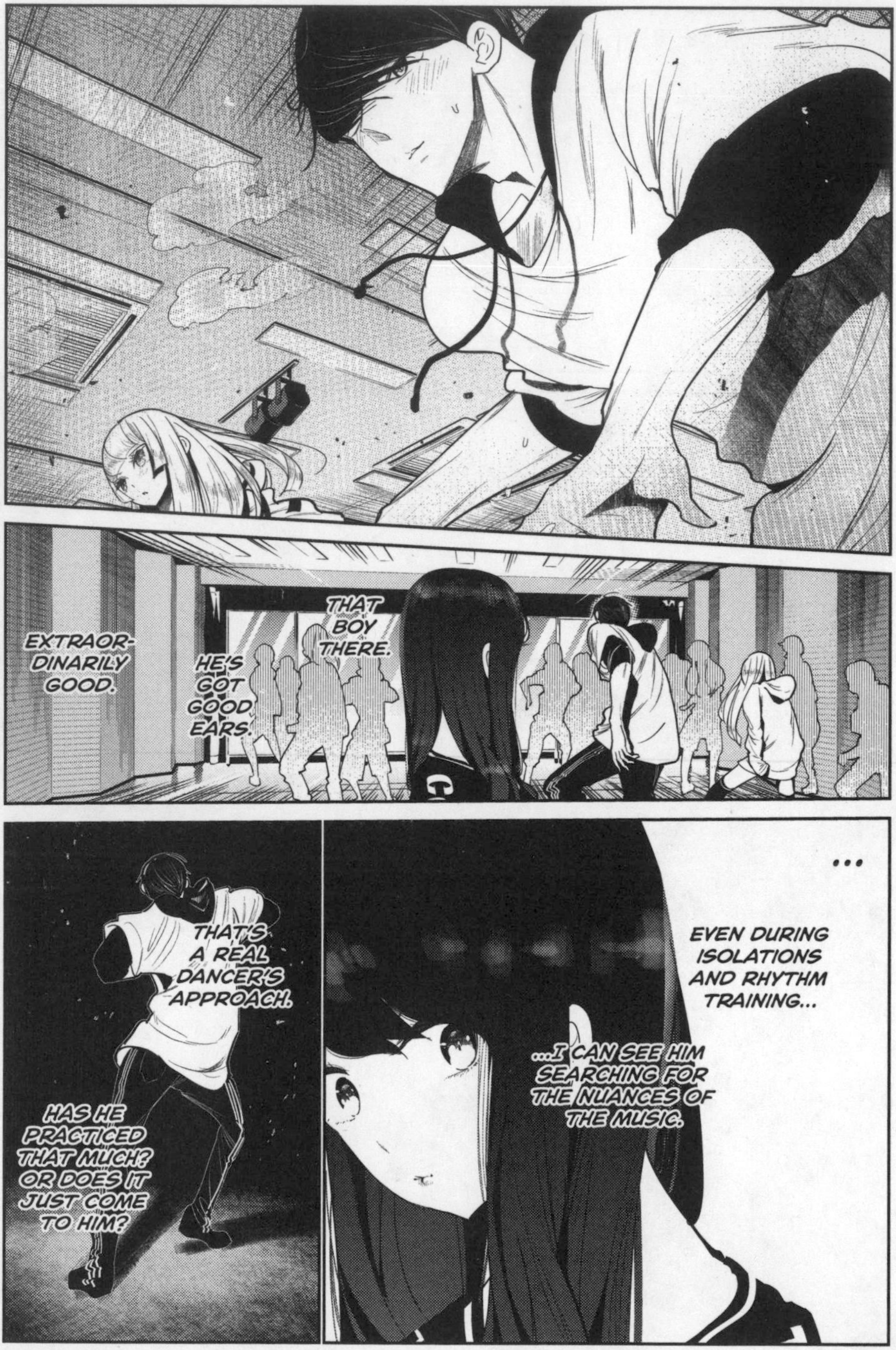
THAT BOY THERE.
HE'S GOT GOOD EARS.
EXTRAOR-DINARILY GOOD.
...
EVEN DURING ISOLATIONS AND RHYTHM TRAINING...
...I CAN SEE HIM SEARCHING FOR THE NUANCES OF THE MUSIC.
THAT'S A REAL DANCER'S APPROACH.
HAS HE PRACTICED THAT MUCH? OR DOES IT JUST COME TO HIM?

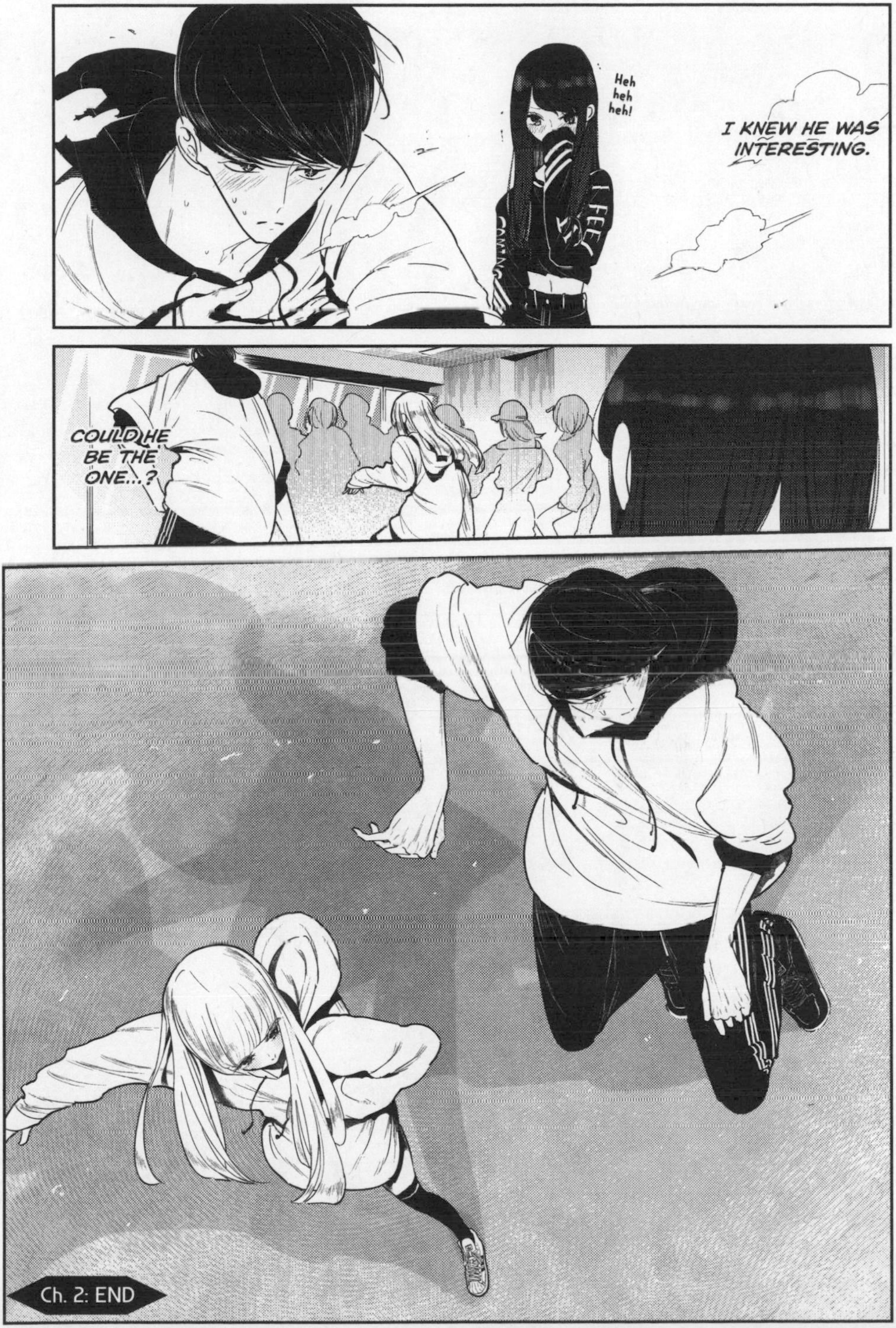
I KNEW HE WAS INTERESTING.
Heh heh heh!
COULD HE BE THE ONE...?
Ch. 2: END

WANDANCE

Ch. 3: The Audition

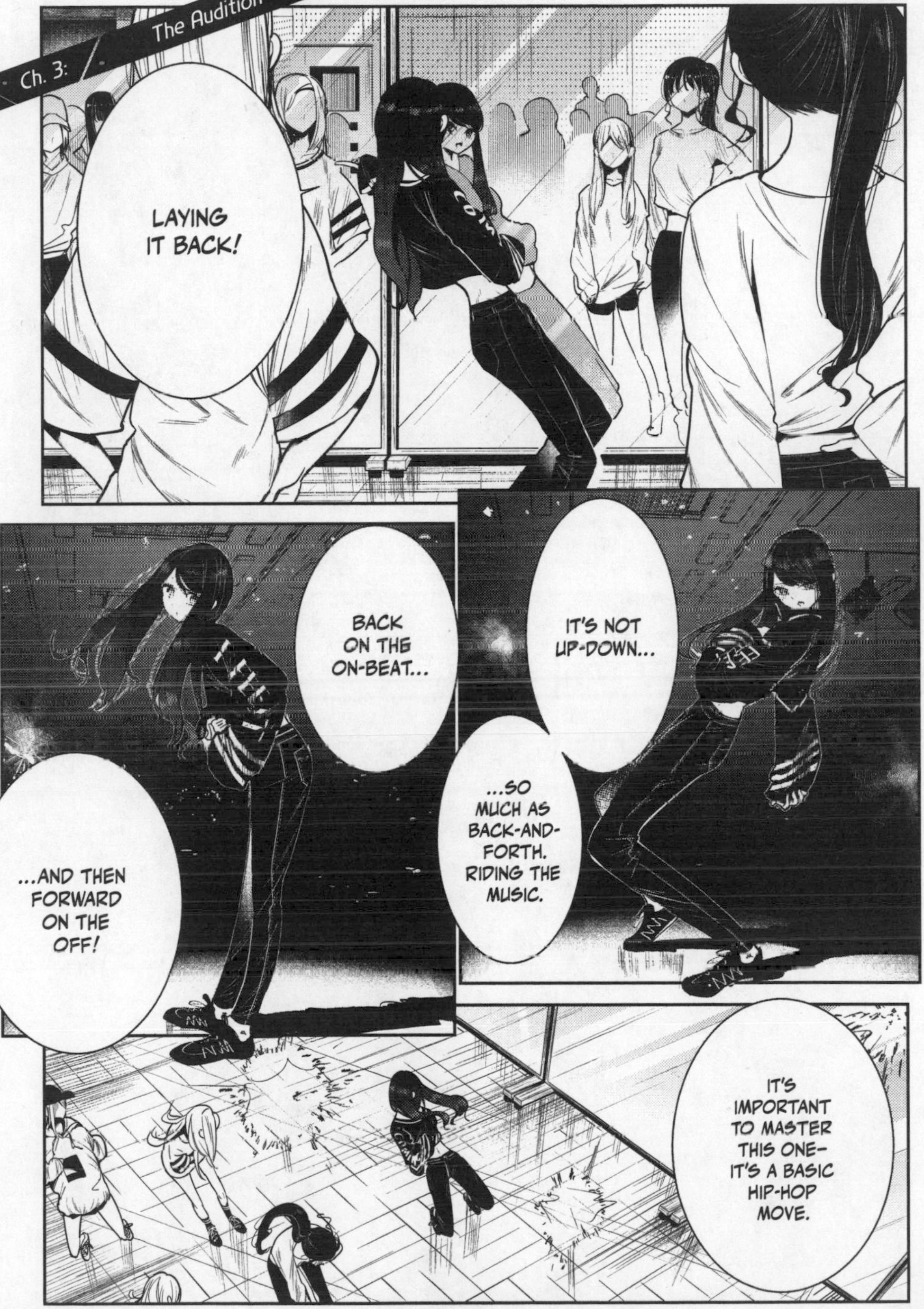

LAYING IT BACK!
IT'S NOT UP-DOWN...
...SO MUCH AS BACK-AND-FORTH. RIDING THE MUSIC.
BACK ON THE ON-BEAT...
...AND THEN FORWARD ON THE OFF!
IT'S IMPORTANT TO MASTER THIS ONE—IT'S A BASIC HIP-HOP MOVE.

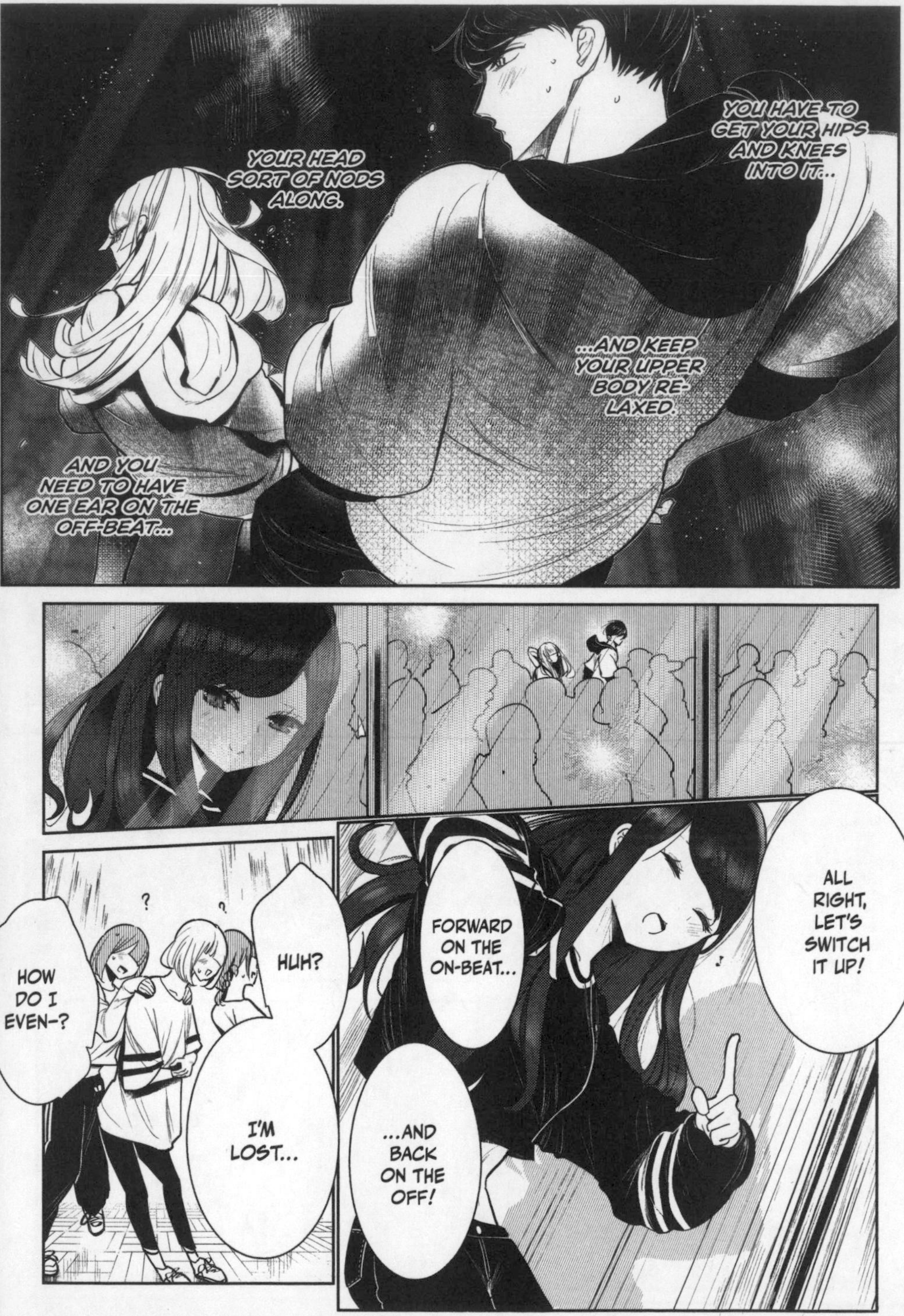
YOU HAVE TO GET YOUR HIPS AND KNEES INTO IT...
YOUR HEAD SORT OF NODS ALONG.
...AND KEEP YOUR UPPER BODY RE-LAXED.
AND YOU NEED TO HAVE ONE EAR ON THE OFF-BEAT...
ALL RIGHT, LET'S SWITCH IT UP!
FORWARD ON THE ON-BEAT...
...AND BACK ON THE OFF!
HUH?
I'M LOST...
HOW DO I EVEN-?

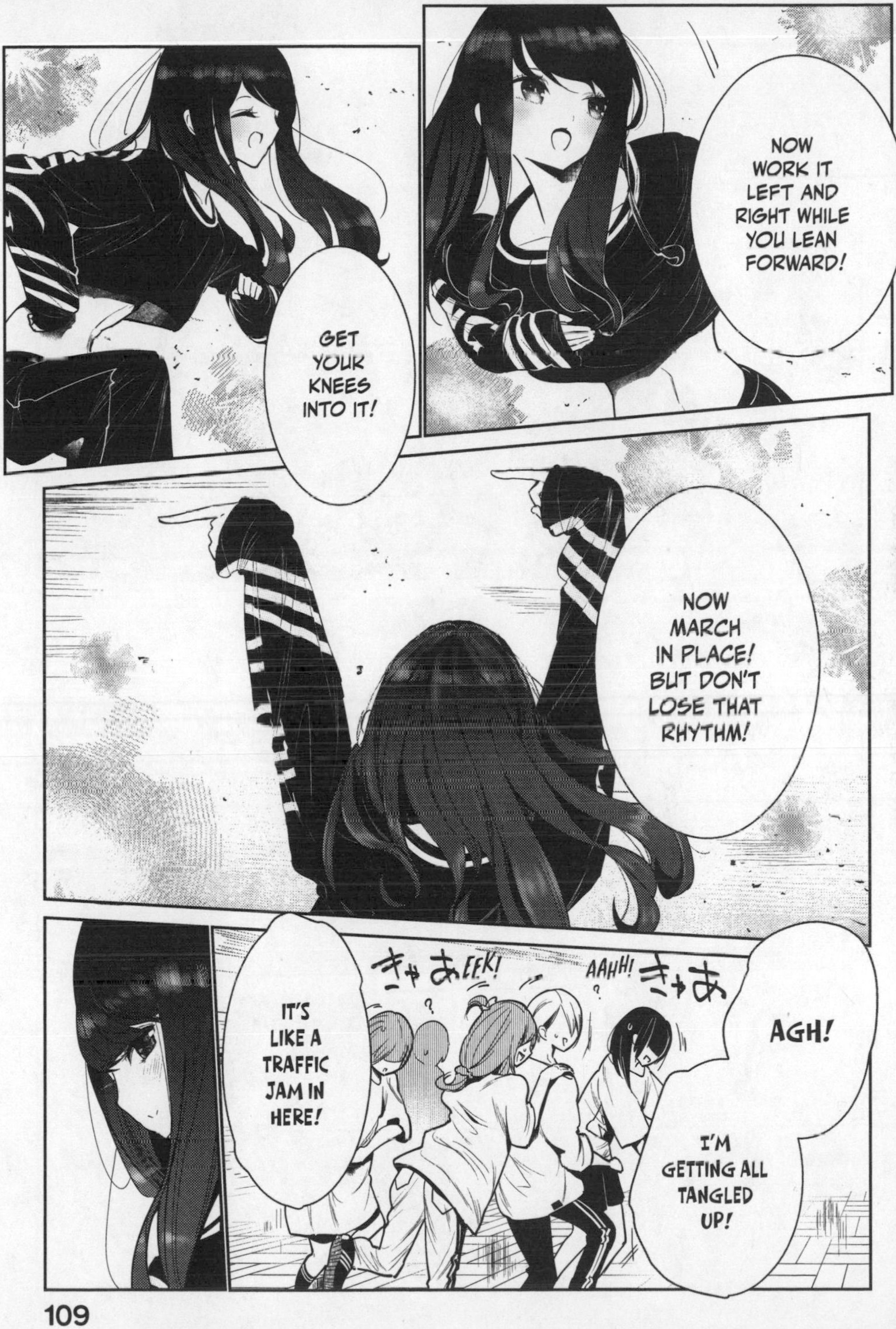
NOW WORK IT LEFT AND RIGHT WHILE YOU LEAN FORWARD!
GET YOUR KNEES INTO IT!
NOW MARCH IN PLACE! BUT DON'T LOSE THAT RHYTHM!
AGH!
I'M GETTING ALL TANGLED UP!
きゃあ
AAHH!
きゃあ EEK!
IT'S LIKE A TRAFFIC JAM IN HERE!

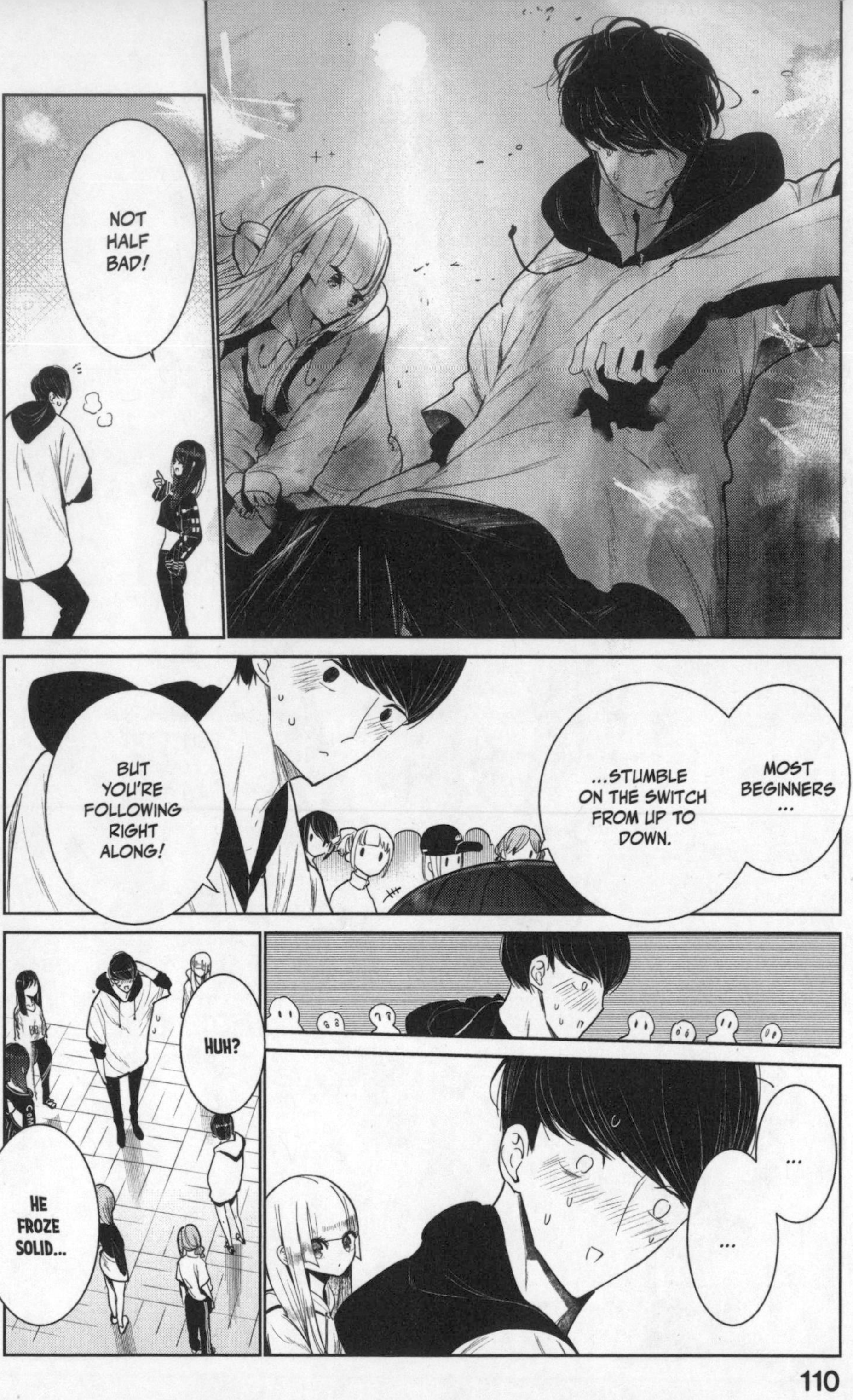
NOT HALF BAD!
MOST BEGINNERS ...
...STUMBLE ON THE SWITCH FROM UP TO DOWN.
BUT YOU'RE FOLLOWING RIGHT ALONG!
...
...
HUH?
HE FROZE SOLID...

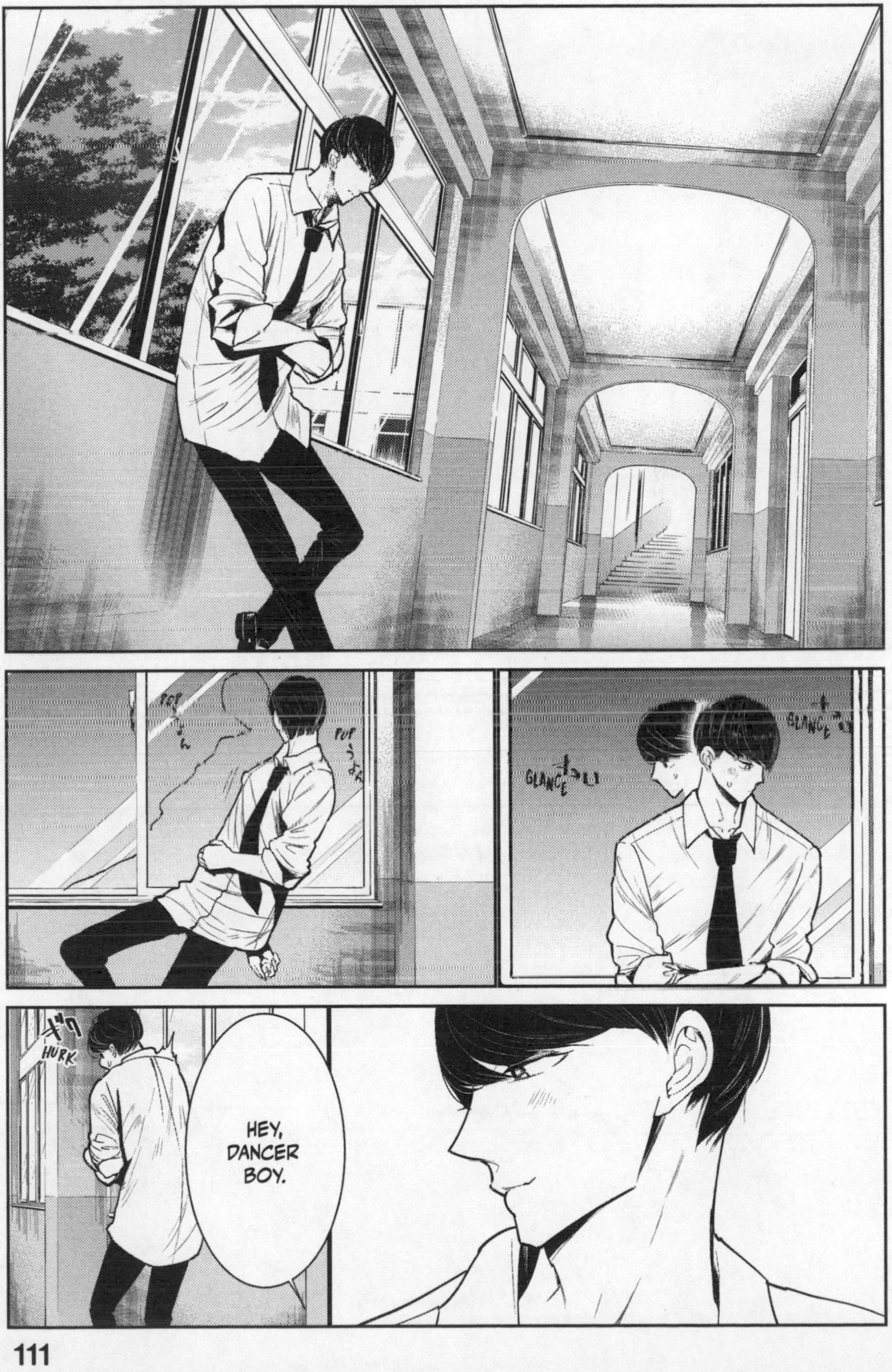
GLANCE
GLANCE
POP
POP
HEY, DANCER BOY.
HURK

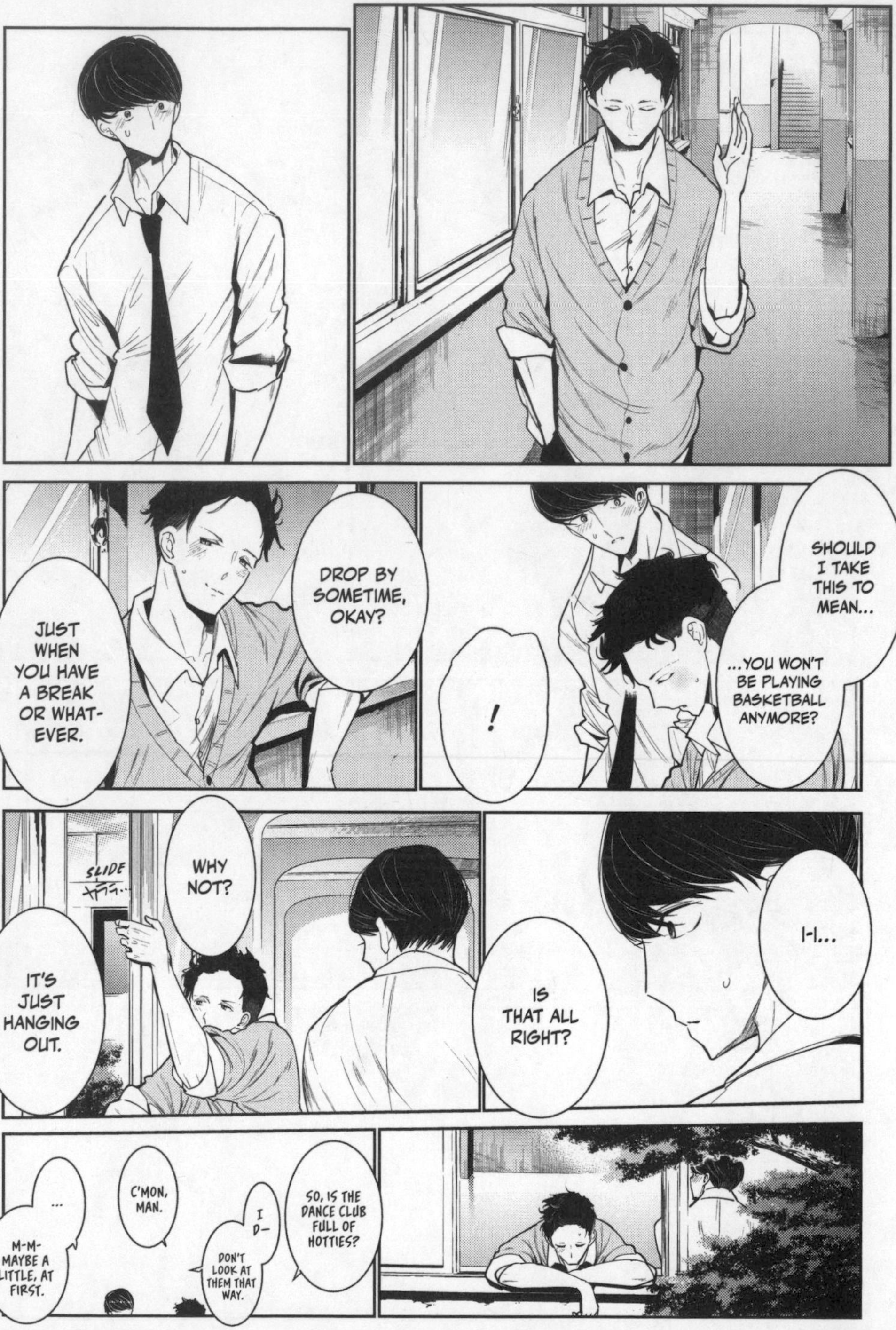
SHOULD I TAKE THIS TO MEAN...
...YOU WON'T BE PLAYING BASKETBALL ANYMORE?
!
DROP BY SOMETIME, OKAY?
JUST WHEN YOU HAVE A BREAK OR WHAT-EVER.
I-I...
IS THAT ALL RIGHT?
WHY NOT?
SLIDE
IT'S JUST HANGING OUT.
SO, IS THE DANCE CLUB FULL OF HOTTIES?
I D—
DON'T LOOK AT THEM THAT WAY.
C'MON, MAN.
...
M-M-MAYBE A LITTLE, AT FIRST.

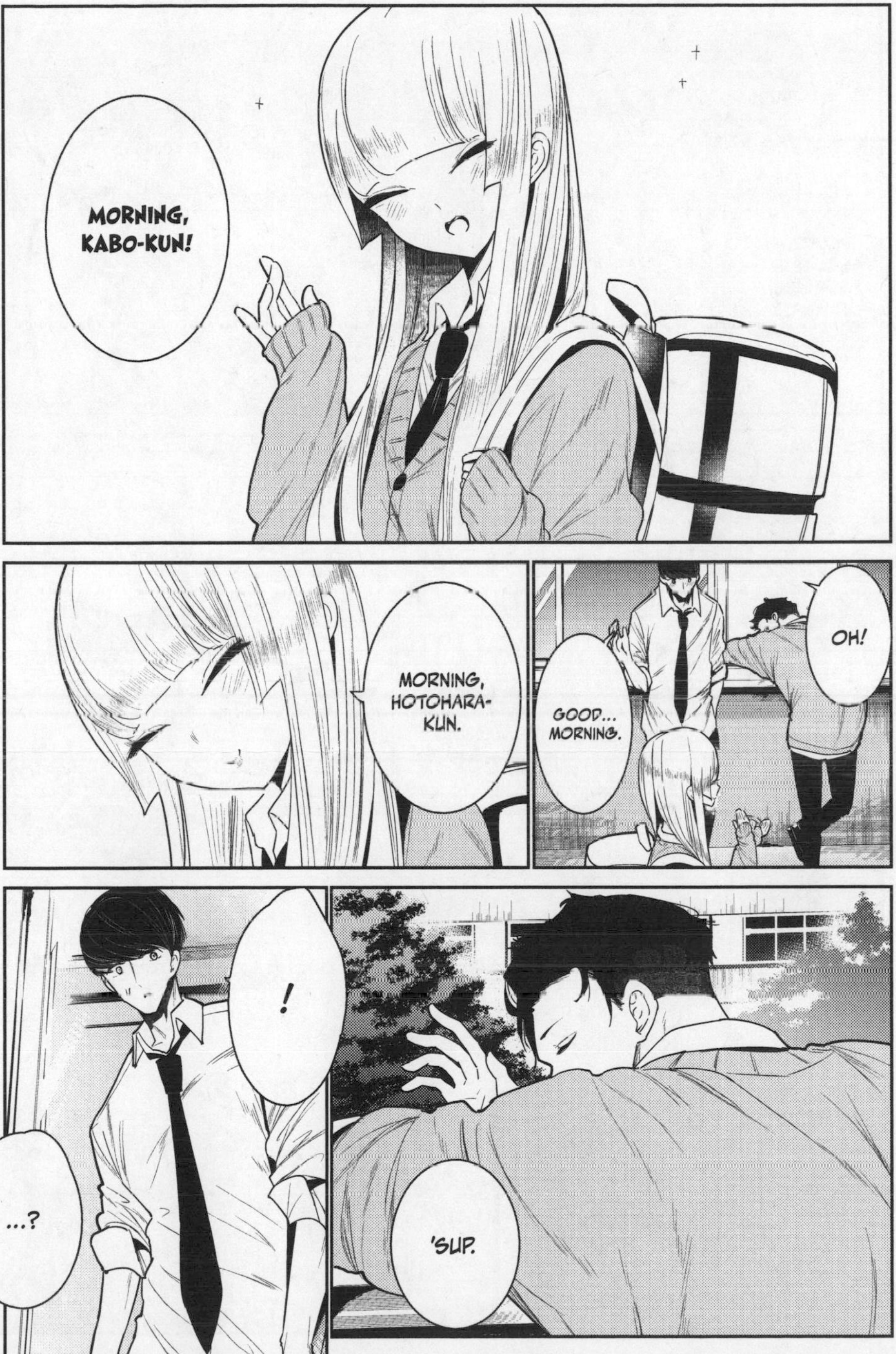
MORNING, KABO-KUN!
OH!
GOOD... MORNING.
MORNING, HOTOHARA-KUN.
'SUP.
!
...?

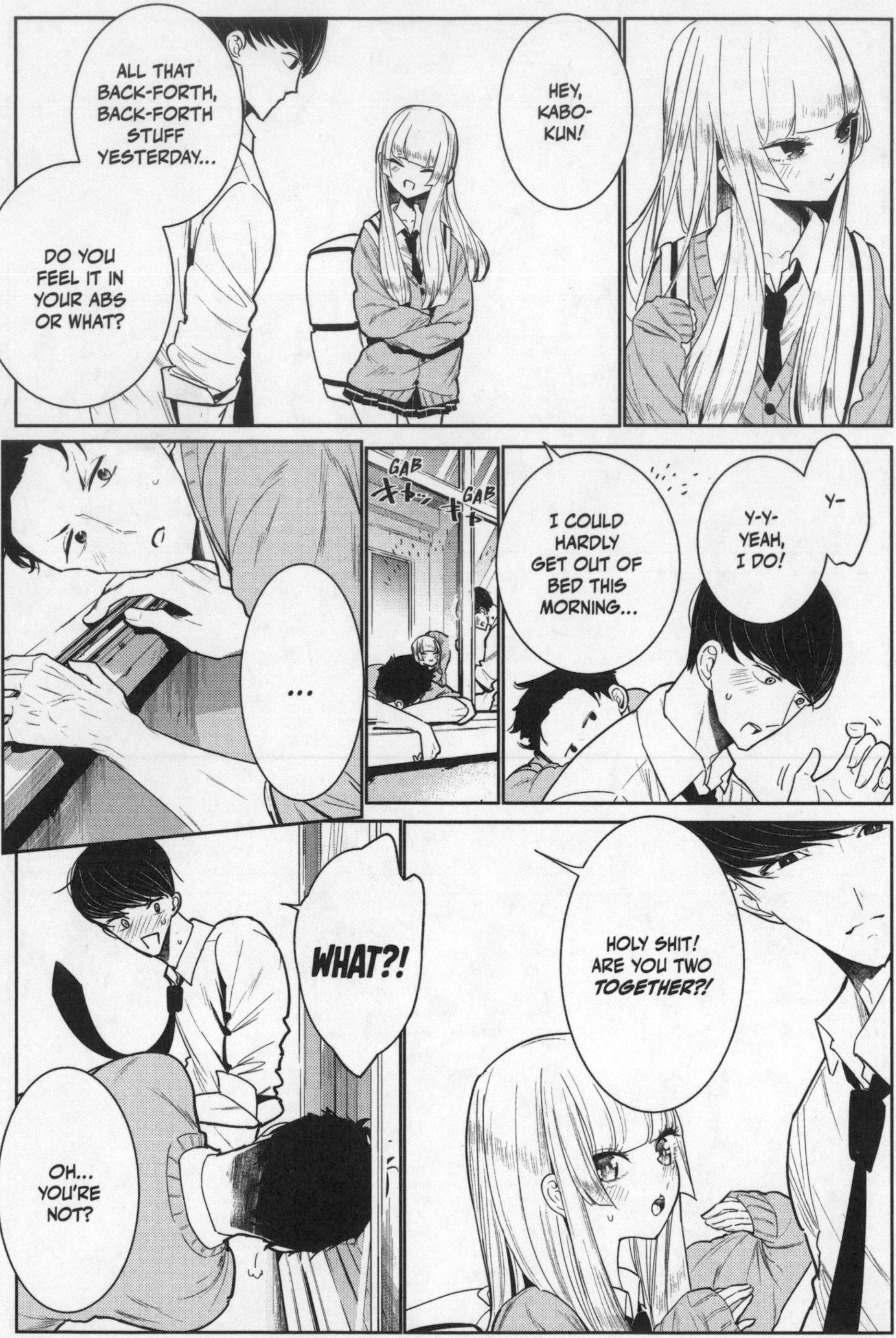
HEY, KABO-KUN!
ALL THAT BACK-FORTH, BACK-FORTH STUFF YESTERDAY...
DO YOU FEEL IT IN YOUR ABS OR WHAT?
Y- Y-Y- YEAH, I DO!
I COULD HARDLY GET OUT OF BED THIS MORNING...
GAB
GAB
...
HOLY SHIT! ARE YOU TWO TOGETHER?!
WHAT?!
OH... YOU'RE NOT?

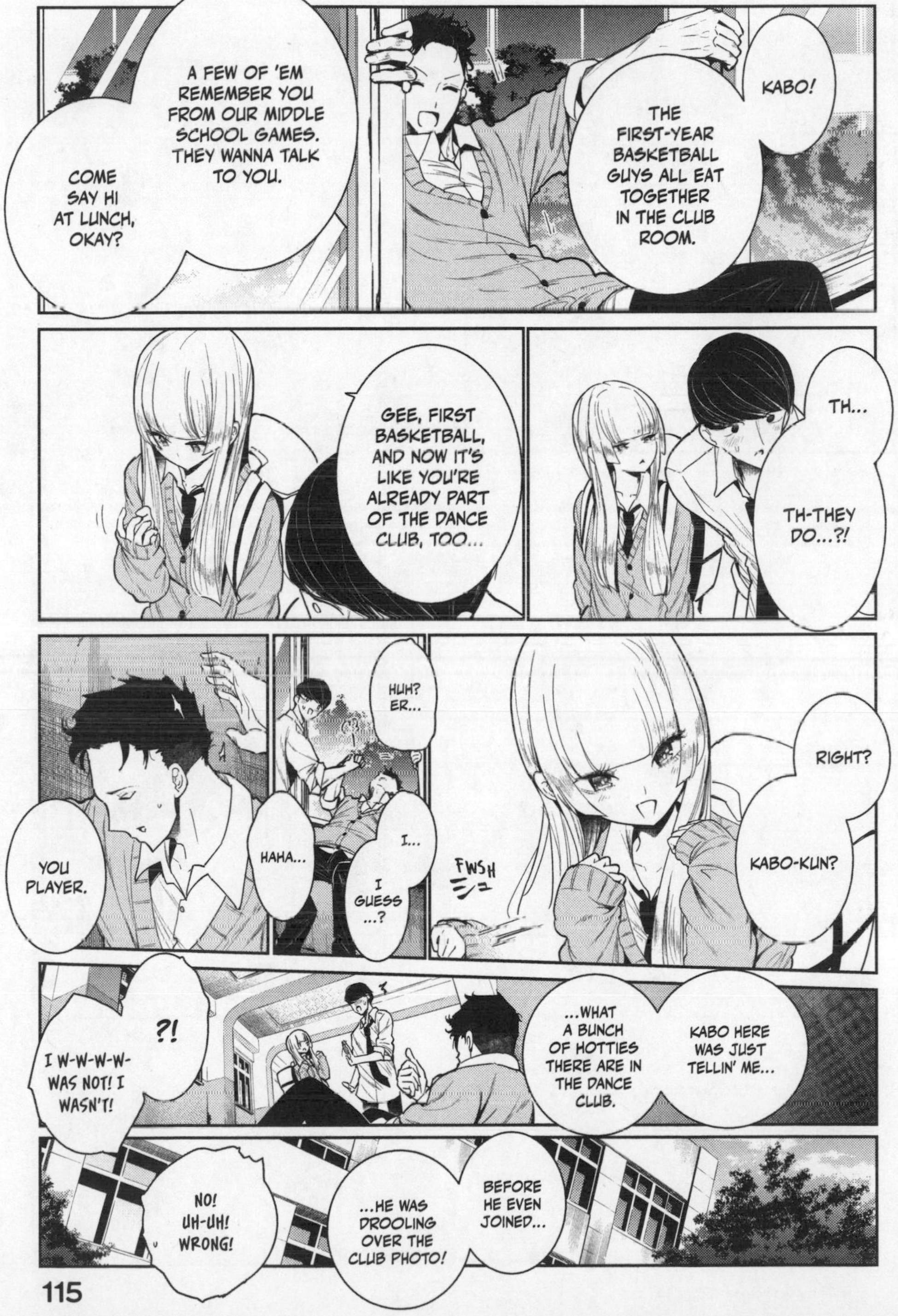
KABO!
THE FIRST-YEAR BASKETBALL GUYS ALL EAT TOGETHER IN THE CLUB ROOM.
A FEW OF 'EM REMEMBER YOU FROM OUR MIDDLE SCHOOL GAMES. THEY WANNA TALK TO YOU.
COME SAY HI AT LUNCH, OKAY?
TH...
TH-THEY DO...?!
GEE, FIRST BASKETBALL, AND NOW IT'S LIKE YOU'RE ALREADY PART OF THE DANCE CLUB, TOO...
RIGHT?
KABO-KUN?
FWSH
HUH? ER...
I... I GUESS ...?
HAHA...
YOU PLAYER.
KABO HERE WAS JUST TELLIN' ME...
...WHAT A BUNCH OF HOTTIES THERE ARE IN THE DANCE CLUB.
?!
I W-W-W-W-WAS NOT! I WASN'T!
BEFORE HE EVEN JOINED...
...HE WAS DROOLING OVER THE CLUB PHOTO!
NO! UH-UH! WRONG!

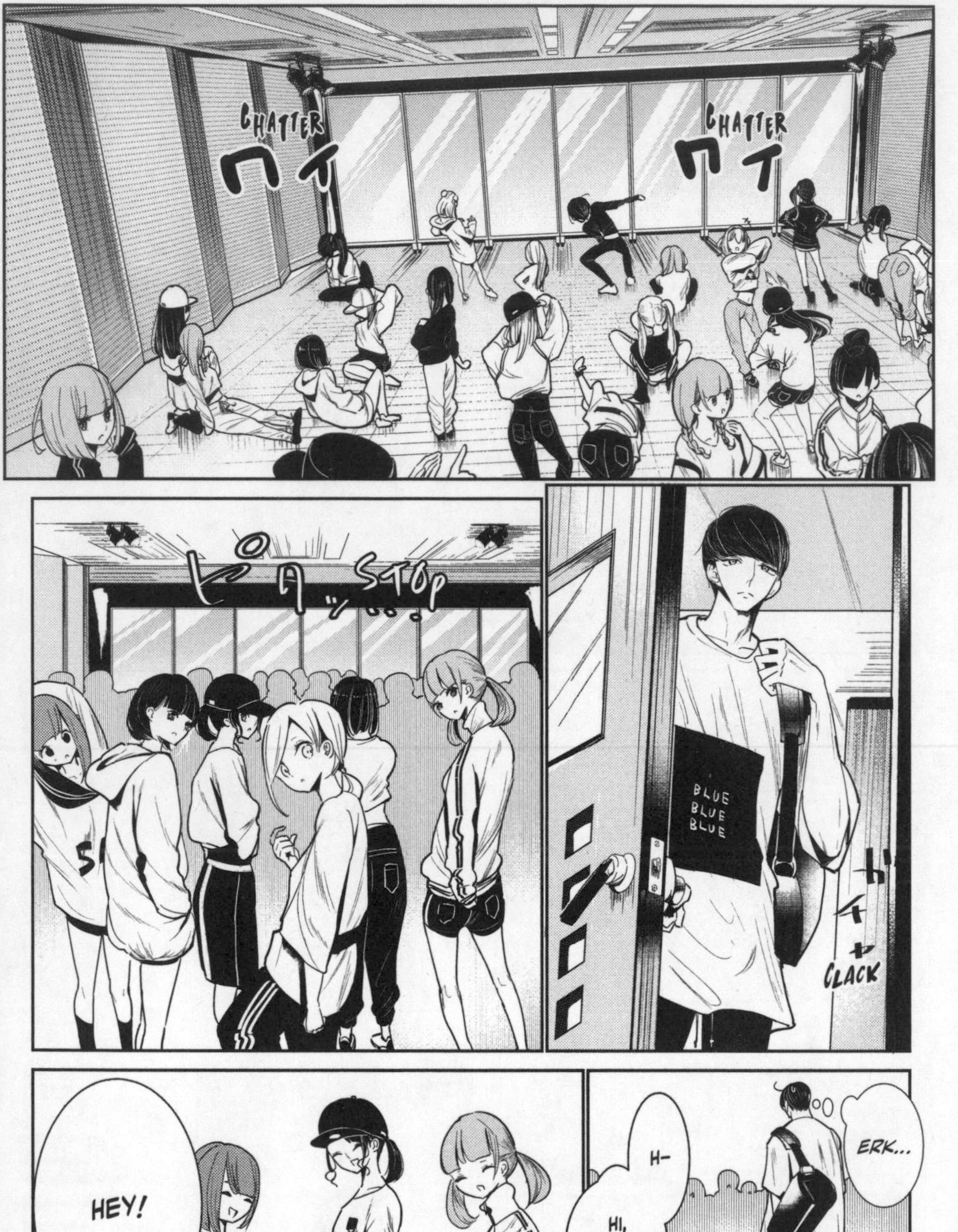
CHATTER
ワイ
CHATTER
ワイ
ガチャ
CLACK
ピタッ
STOP
ERK...
H-
HI, EVERY-ONE.
HEY!

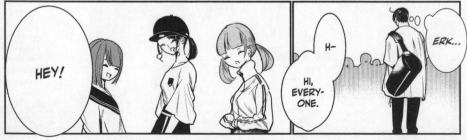

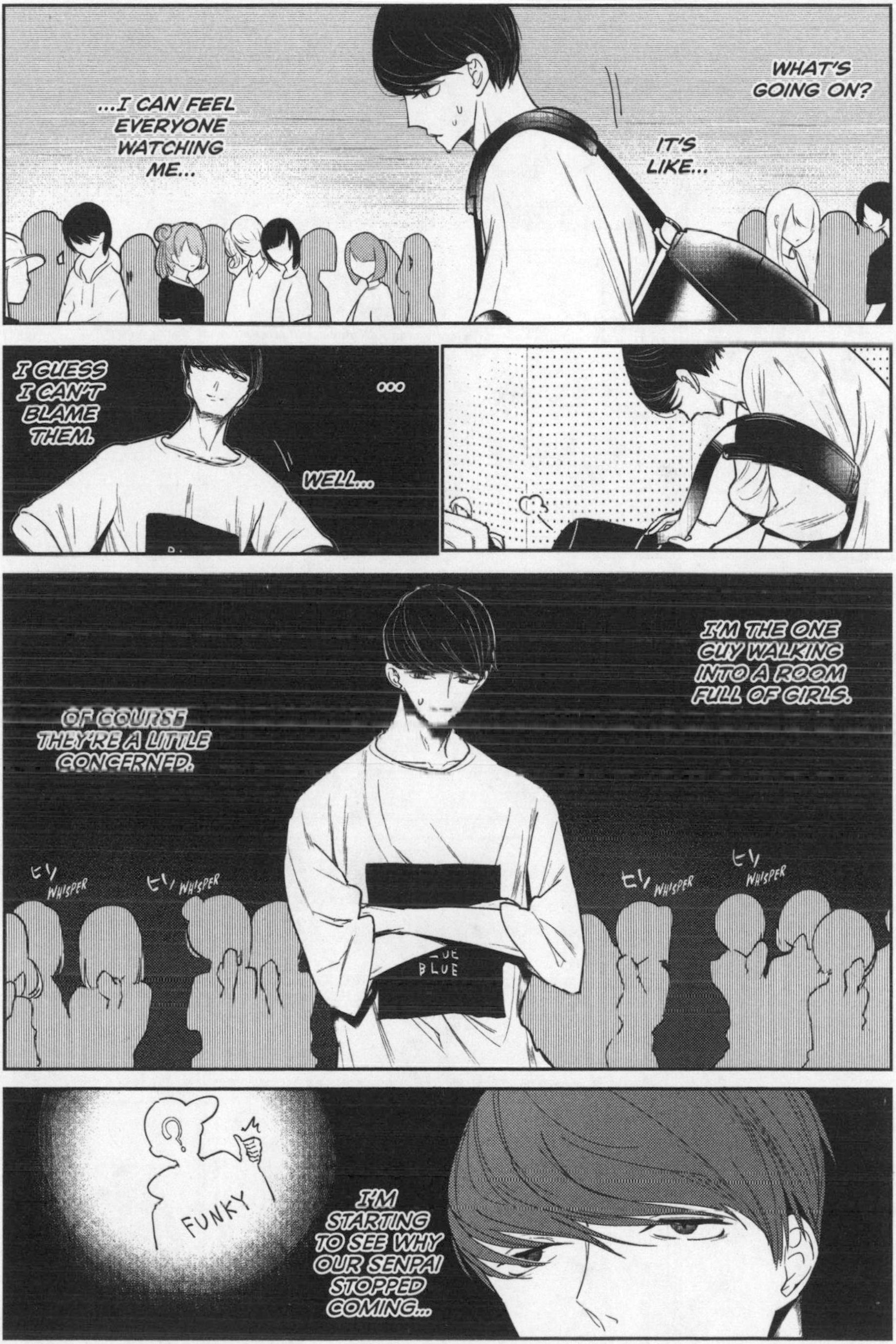
WHAT'S GOING ON?
IT'S LIKE...
...I CAN FEEL EVERYONE WATCHING ME...
...
WELL...
I GUESS I CAN'T BLAME THEM.
I'M THE ONE GUY WALKING INTO A ROOM FULL OF GIRLS.
OF COURSE THEY'RE A LITTLE CONCERNED.
ヒソ WHISPER
ヒソ WHISPER
ヒソ WHISPER
ヒソ WHISPER
BLUE
I'M STARTING TO SEE WHY OUR SENPAI STOPPED COMING...
FUNKY

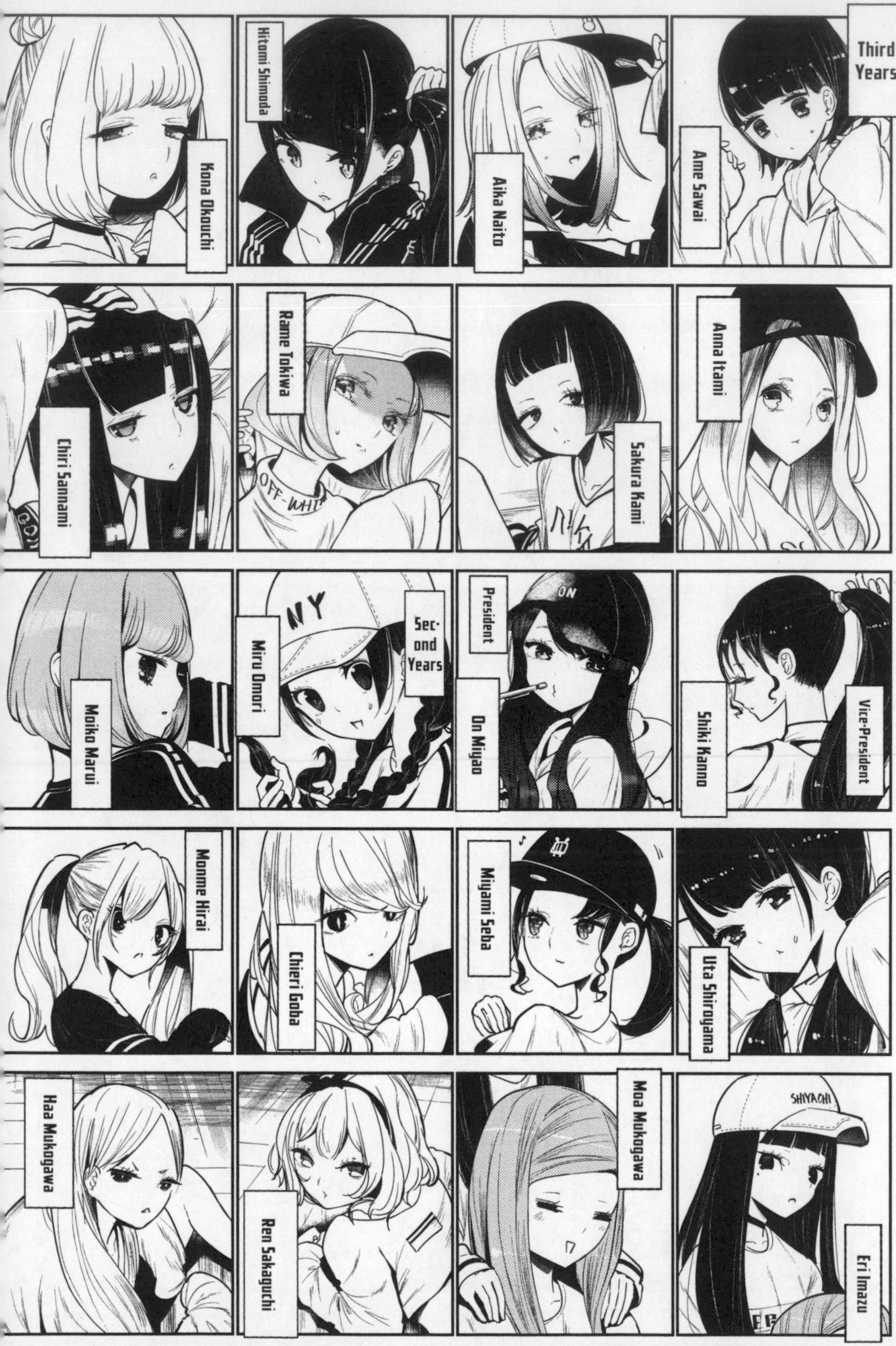
Third Years
Ame Sawai
Aika Naito
Hitomi Shimoda
Kona Okouchi
Anna Itami
Sakura Kami
Rame Tokiwa
Chiri Sannami
Vice-President
Shiki Kanno
ON
President
On Miyao
Sec-ond Years
NY
Miru Omori
Moiko Marui
Uta Shiroyama
Miyami Seba
Chieri Goba
Monme Hirai
SHIYACHI
Eri Imazu
Moa Mukogawa
Ren Sakaguchi
Haa Mukogawa

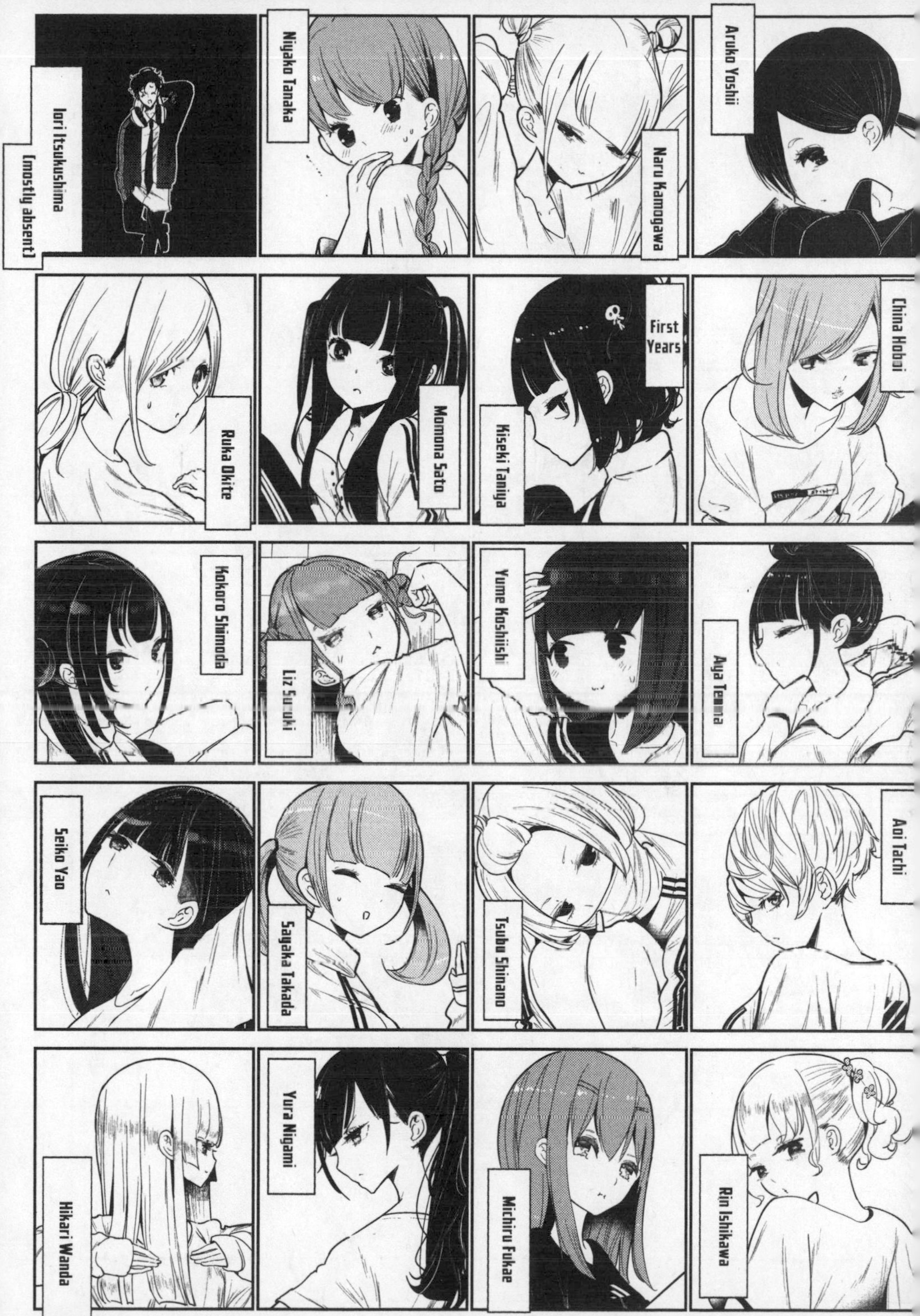

Aruko Yoshii
Naru Kamogawa
Niyako Tanaka
Iori Itsukushima
[mostly absent]
China Hobai
First Years
Kiseki Taniya
Momona Sato
Ruka Okite
Aya Tenma
Yume Koshiishi
Liz Suzuki
Kokoro Shimoda
Aoi Tachi
Tsubo Shinano
Sayaka Takada
Seiko Yao
Rin Ishikawa
Michiru Fukae
Yura Nigami
Hikari Wanda

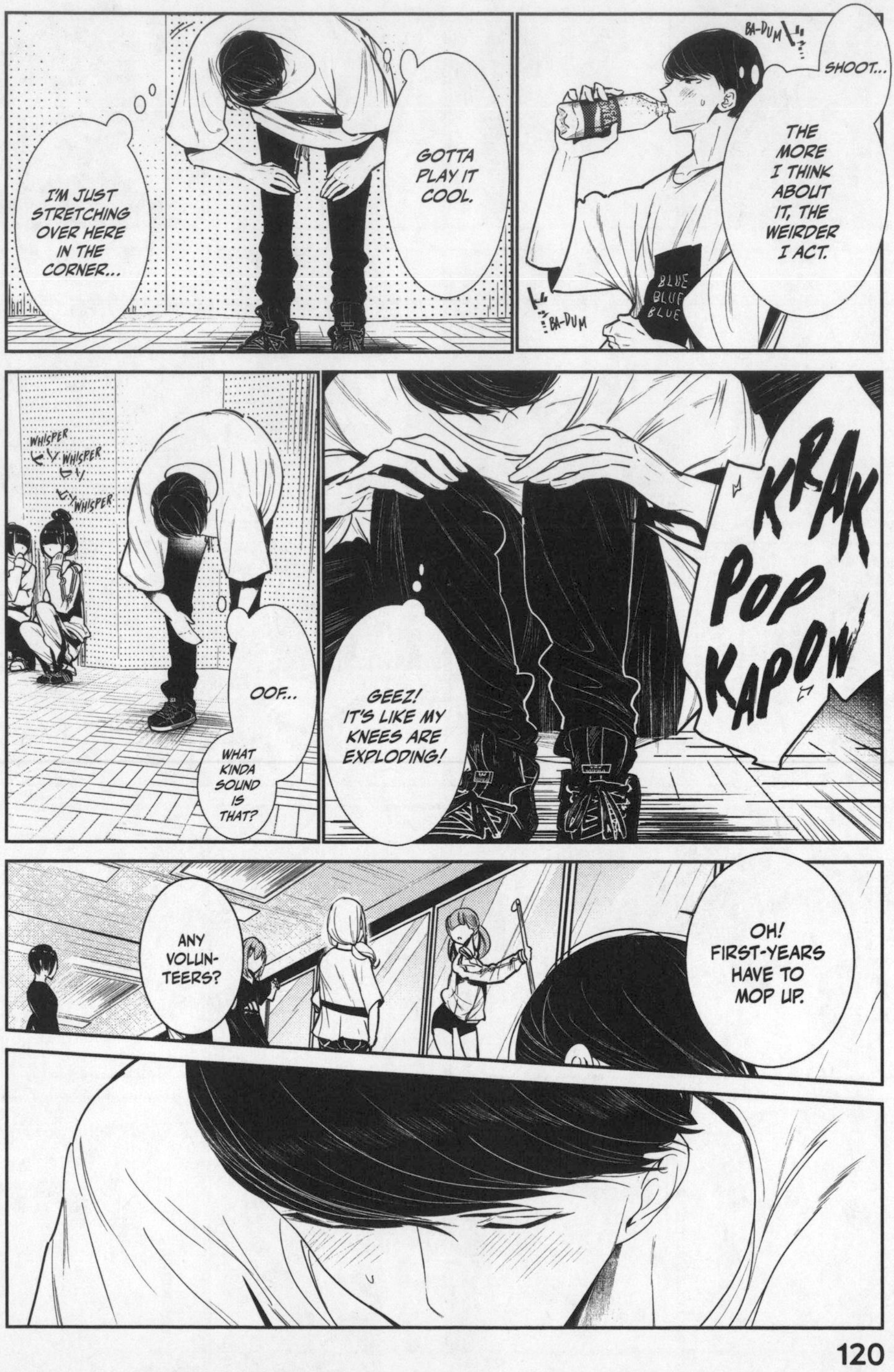
BA-DUM
SHOOT...
THE MORE I THINK ABOUT IT, THE WEIRDER I ACT.
BA-DUM
GOTTA PLAY IT COOL.
I'M JUST STRETCHING OVER HERE IN THE CORNER...
KRAK POP KAPOW
GEEZ! IT'S LIKE MY KNEES ARE EXPLODING!
OOF...
WHISPER WHISPER WHISPER
WHAT KINDA SOUND IS THAT?
OH! FIRST-YEARS HAVE TO MOP UP.
ANY VOLUN-TEERS?

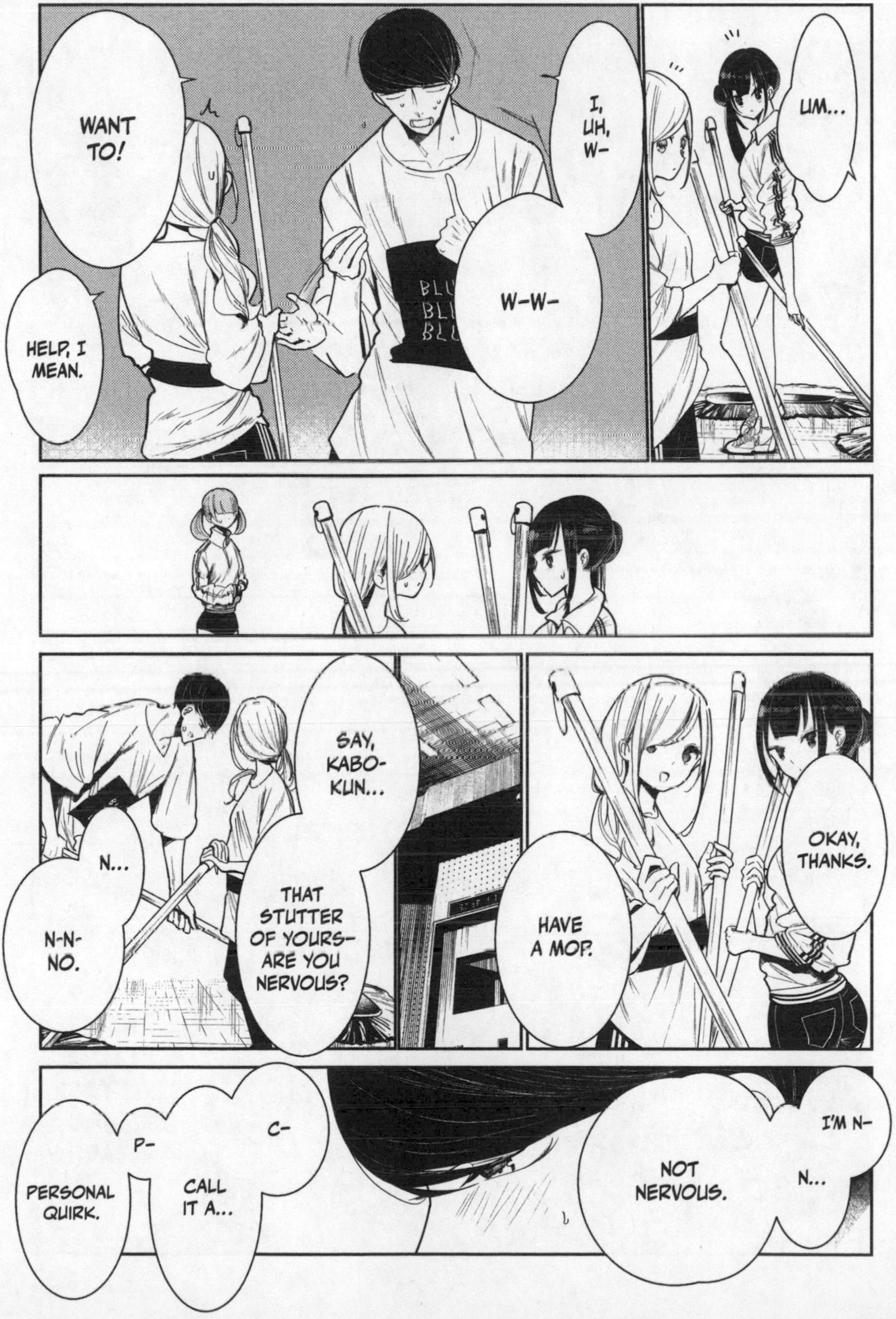
UM...
I, UH, W-
W-W-
WANT TO!
HELP, I MEAN.
OKAY, THANKS.
HAVE A MOP.
SAY, KABO-KUN...
THAT STUTTER OF YOURS- ARE YOU NERVOUS?
N...
N-N-NO.
I'M N-
N...
NOT NERVOUS.
C-
CALL IT A...
P-
PERSONAL QUIRK.

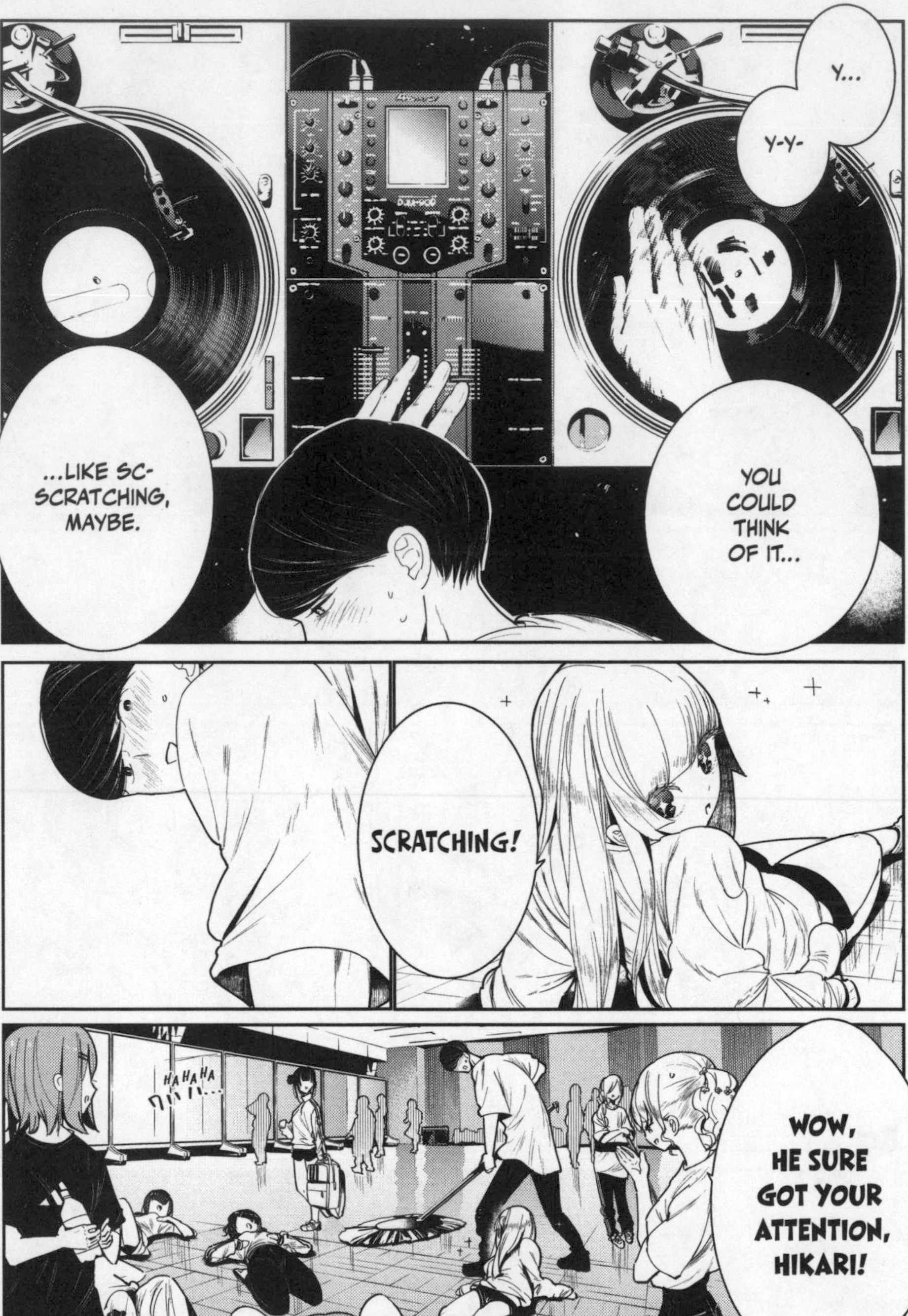
Y...
Y-Y-
YOU COULD THINK OF IT...
...LIKE SC-SCRATCHING, MAYBE.
SCRATCHING!
WOW, HE SURE GOT YOUR ATTENTION, HIKARI!
HAHAHA

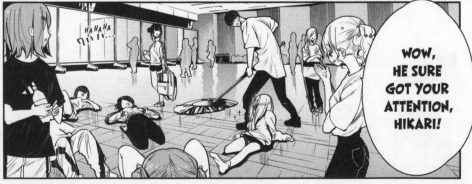

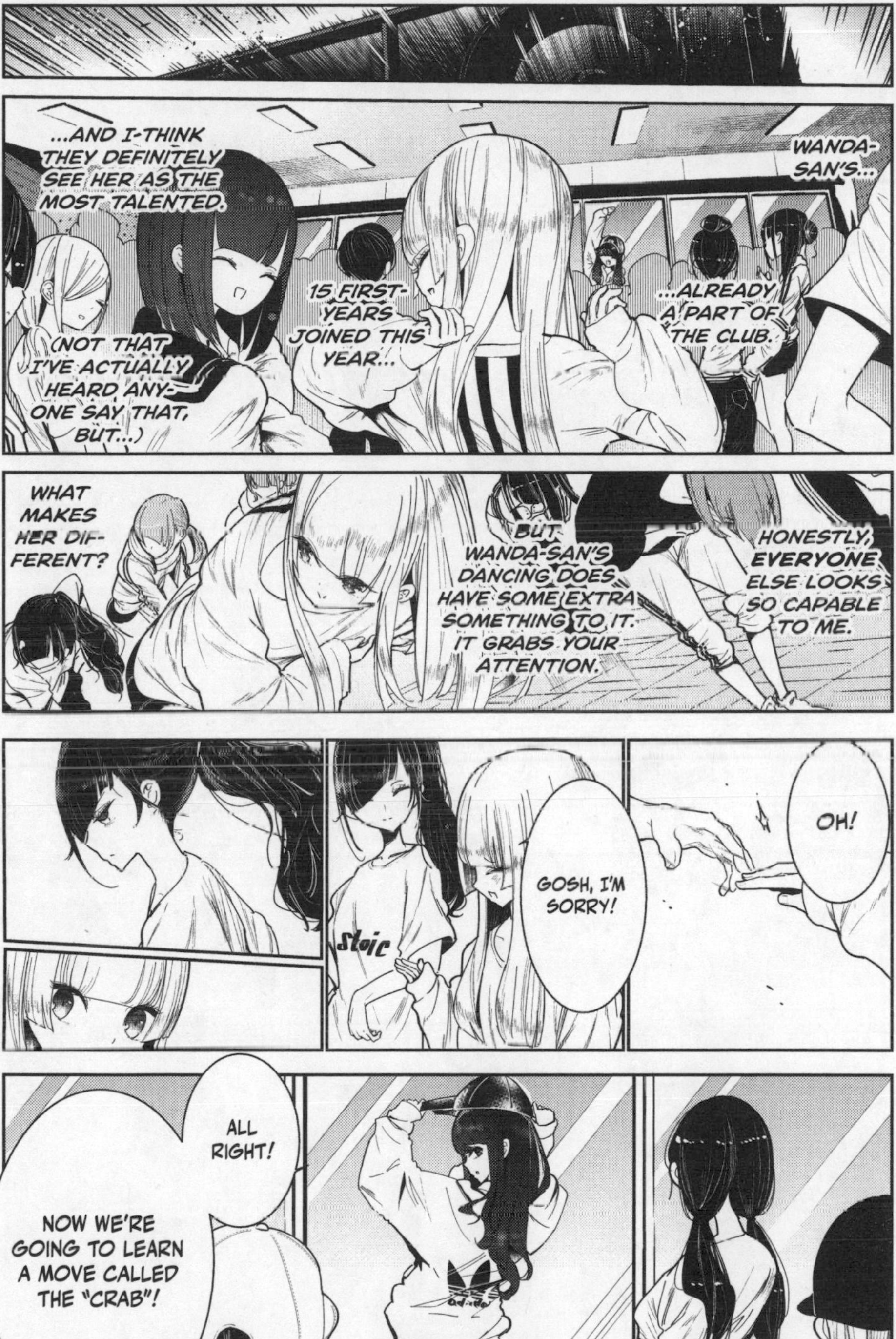
WANDA-SAN'S...
...ALREADY A PART OF THE CLUB.
15 FIRST-YEARS JOINED THIS YEAR...
...AND I-THINK THEY DEFINITELY SEE HER AS THE MOST TALENTED.
(NOT THAT I'VE ACTUALLY HEARD ANY-ONE SAY THAT, BUT...)
HONESTLY, EVERYONE ELSE LOOKS SO CAPABLE TO ME.
BUT WANDA-SAN'S DANCING DOES HAVE SOME EXTRA SOMETHING TO IT. IT GRABS YOUR ATTENTION.
WHAT MAKES HER DIF-FERENT?
OH!
GOSH, I'M SORRY!
stoic
ALL RIGHT!
NOW WE'RE GOING TO LEARN A MOVE CALLED THE "CRAB"!

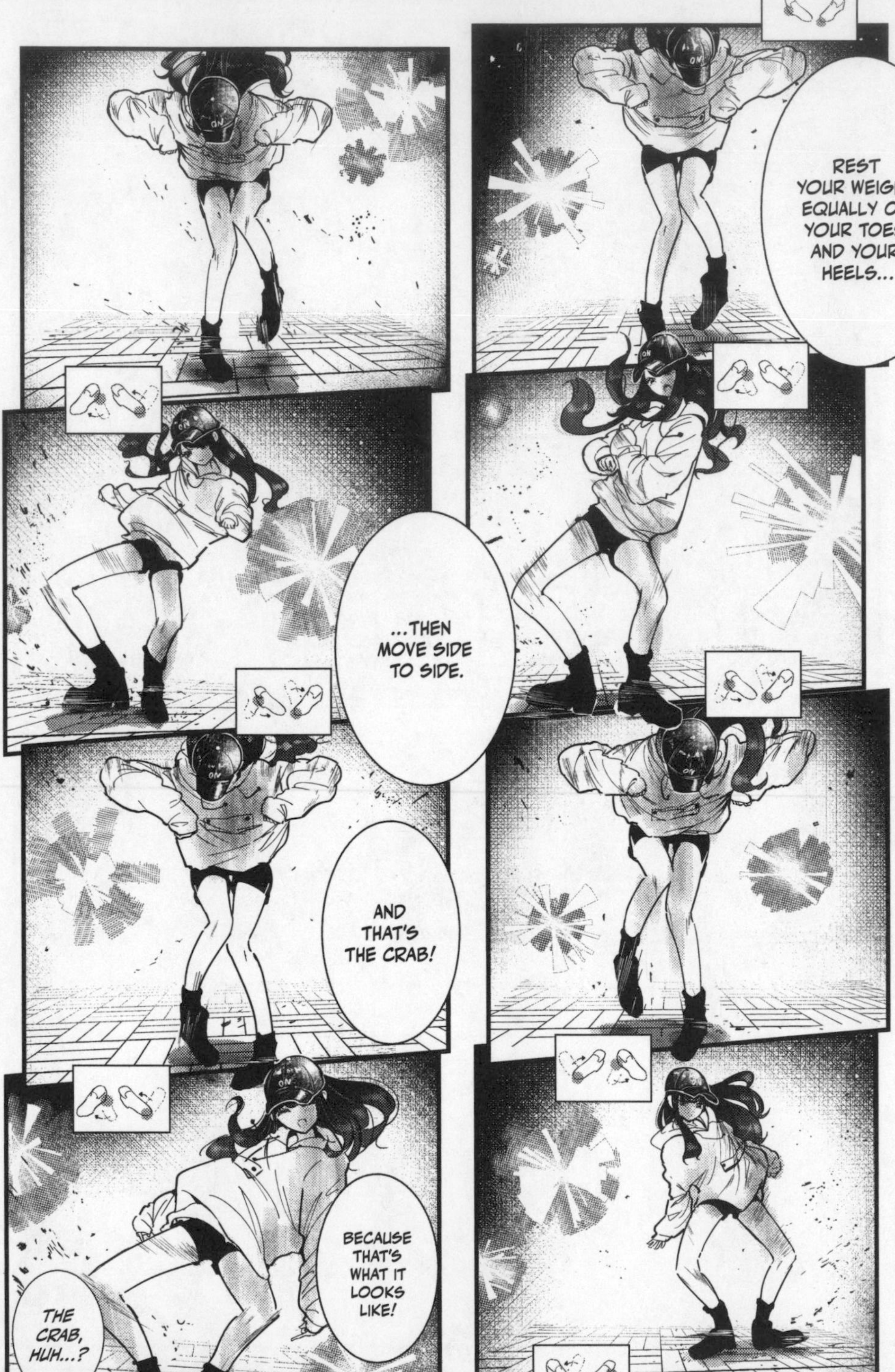
REST YOUR WEIGHT EQUALLY ON YOUR TOES AND YOUR HEELS...
...THEN MOVE SIDE TO SIDE.
AND THAT'S THE CRAB!
BECAUSE THAT'S WHAT IT LOOKS LIKE!
THE CRAB, HUH...?

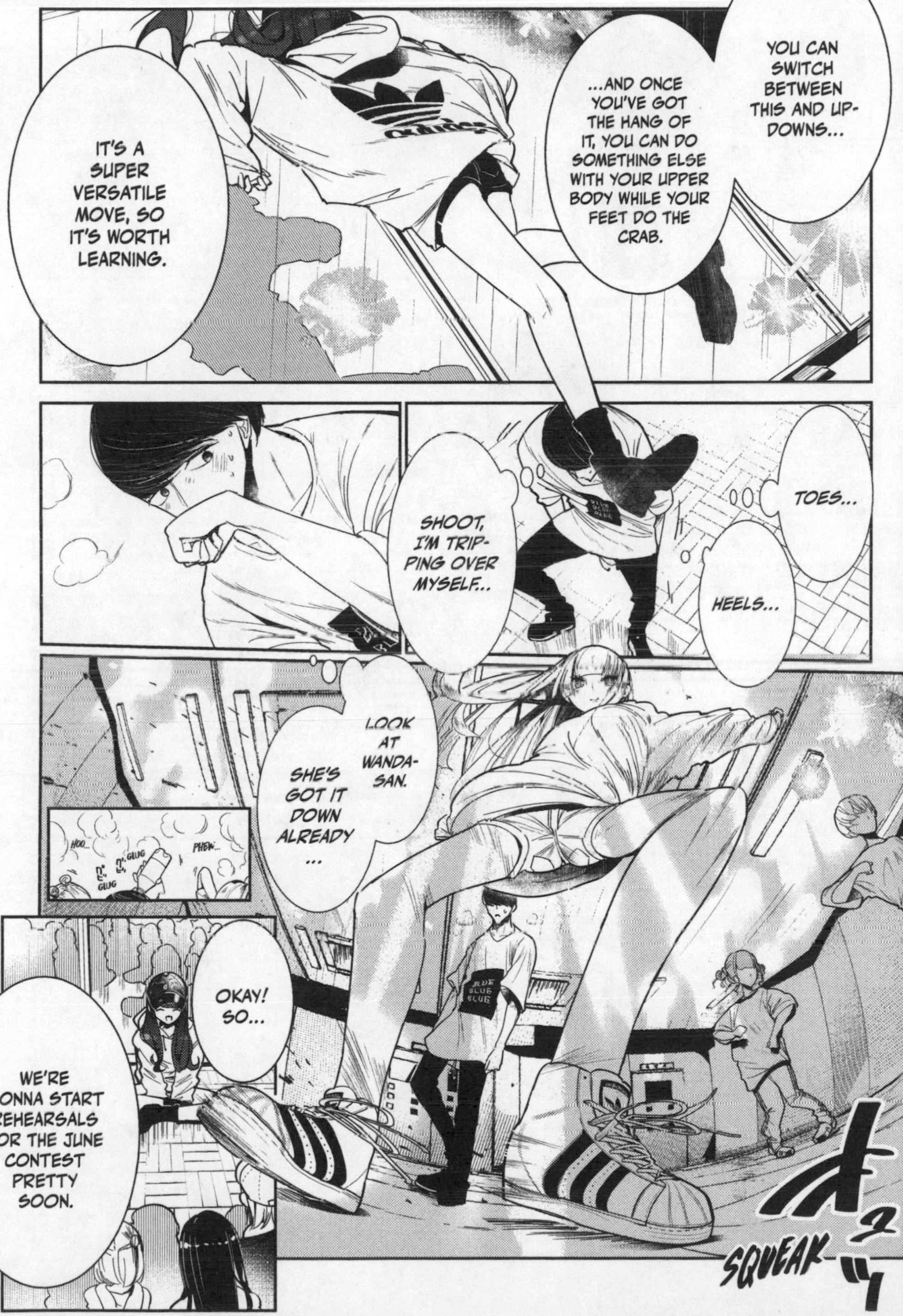

YOU CAN SWITCH BETWEEN THIS AND UP-DOWNS...
...AND ONCE YOU'VE GOT THE HANG OF IT, YOU CAN DO SOMETHING ELSE WITH YOUR UPPER BODY WHILE YOUR FEET DO THE CRAB.
IT'S A SUPER VERSATILE MOVE, SO IT'S WORTH LEARNING.
TOES...
HEELS...
SHOOT, I'M TRIP-PING OVER MYSELF...
LOOK AT WANDA-SAN.
SHE'S GOT IT DOWN ALREADY...
PHEW...
GLUG
GLUG
HOO...
OKAY! SO...
WE'RE GONNA START REHEARSALS FOR THE JUNE CONTEST PRETTY SOON.
SQUEAK

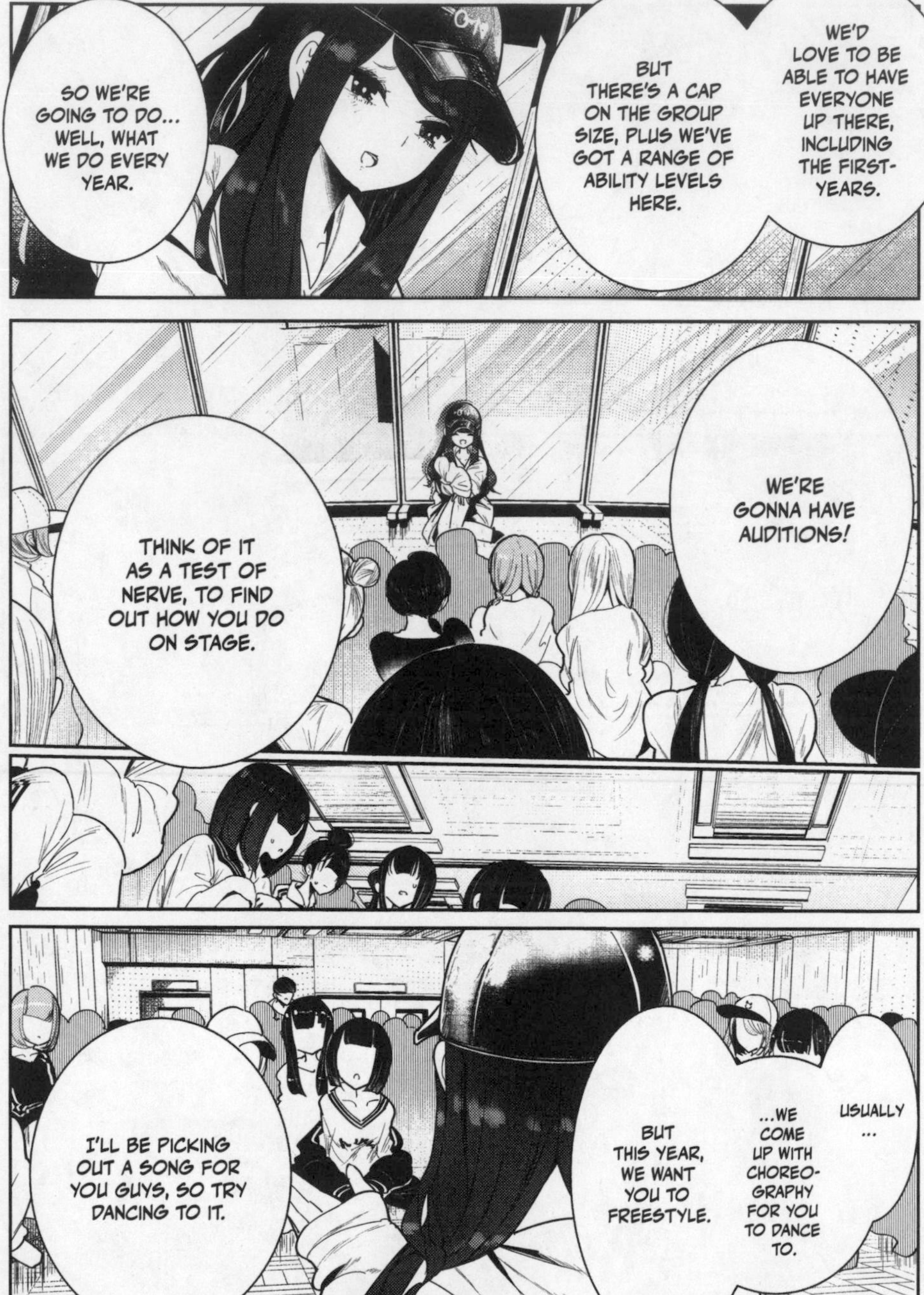

WE'D LOVE TO BE ABLE TO HAVE EVERYONE UP THERE, INCLUDING THE FIRST-YEARS.
BUT THERE'S A CAP ON THE GROUP SIZE, PLUS WE'VE GOT A RANGE OF ABILITY LEVELS HERE.
SO WE'RE GOING TO DO... WELL, WHAT WE DO EVERY YEAR.
WE'RE GONNA HAVE AUDITIONS!
THINK OF IT AS A TEST OF NERVE, TO FIND OUT HOW YOU DO ON STAGE.
USUALLY...
...WE COME UP WITH CHOREOGRAPHY FOR YOU TO DANCE TO.
BUT THIS YEAR, WE WANT YOU TO FREESTYLE.
I'LL BE PICKING OUT A SONG FOR YOU GUYS, SO TRY DANCING TO IT.

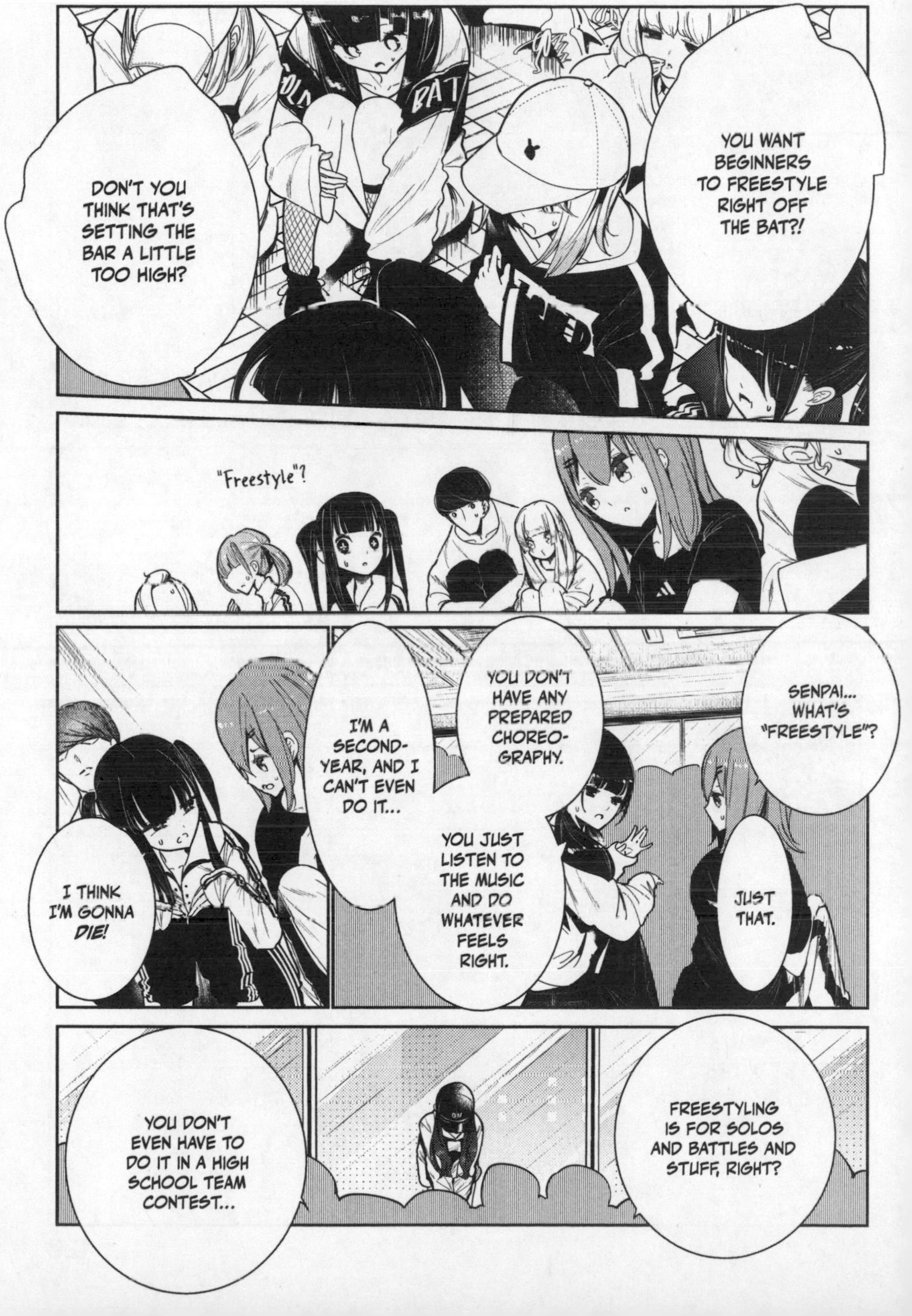
YOU WANT BEGINNERS TO FREESTYLE RIGHT OFF THE BAT?!
DON'T YOU THINK THAT'S SETTING THE BAR A LITTLE TOO HIGH?
"Freestyle"?
SENPAI... WHAT'S "FREESTYLE"?
YOU DON'T HAVE ANY PREPARED CHOREOGRAPHY.
YOU JUST LISTEN TO THE MUSIC AND DO WHATEVER FEELS RIGHT.
JUST THAT.
I'M A SECOND-YEAR, AND I CAN'T EVEN DO IT...
I THINK I'M GONNA *DIE!*
FREESTYLING IS FOR SOLOS AND BATTLES AND STUFF, RIGHT?
YOU DON'T EVEN HAVE TO DO IT IN A HIGH SCHOOL TEAM CONTEST...

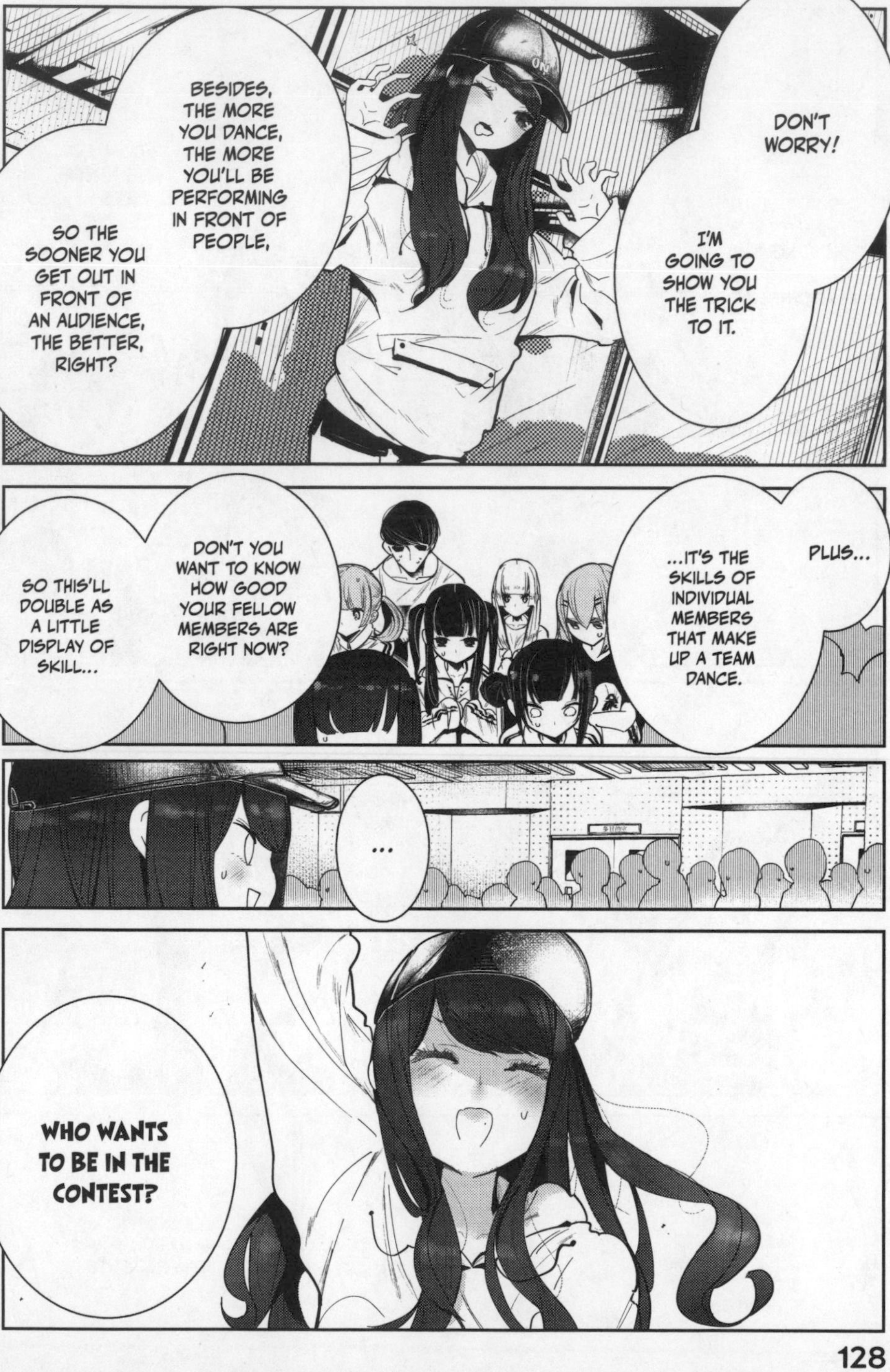
DON'T WORRY!
I'M GOING TO SHOW YOU THE TRICK TO IT.
BESIDES, THE MORE YOU DANCE, THE MORE YOU'LL BE PERFORMING IN FRONT OF PEOPLE,
SO THE SOONER YOU GET OUT IN FRONT OF AN AUDIENCE, THE BETTER, RIGHT?
PLUS...
...IT'S THE SKILLS OF INDIVIDUAL MEMBERS THAT MAKE UP A TEAM DANCE.
DON'T YOU WANT TO KNOW HOW GOOD YOUR FELLOW MEMBERS ARE RIGHT NOW?
SO THIS'LL DOUBLE AS A LITTLE DISPLAY OF SKILL...
...
WHO WANTS TO BE IN THE CONTEST?

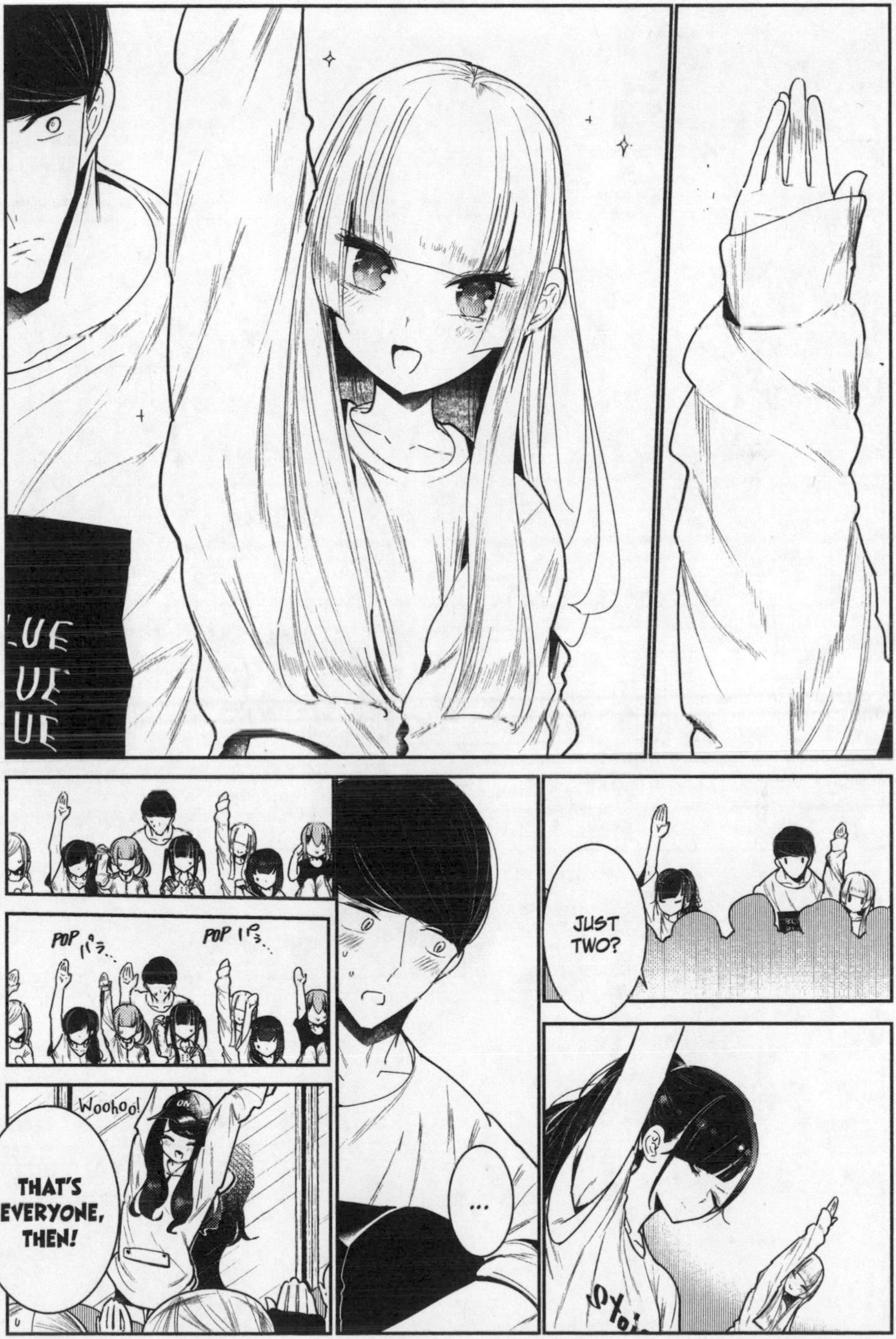
JUST TWO?
...
POP パラ…
POP パラ…
Woohoo!
THAT'S EVERYONE, THEN!

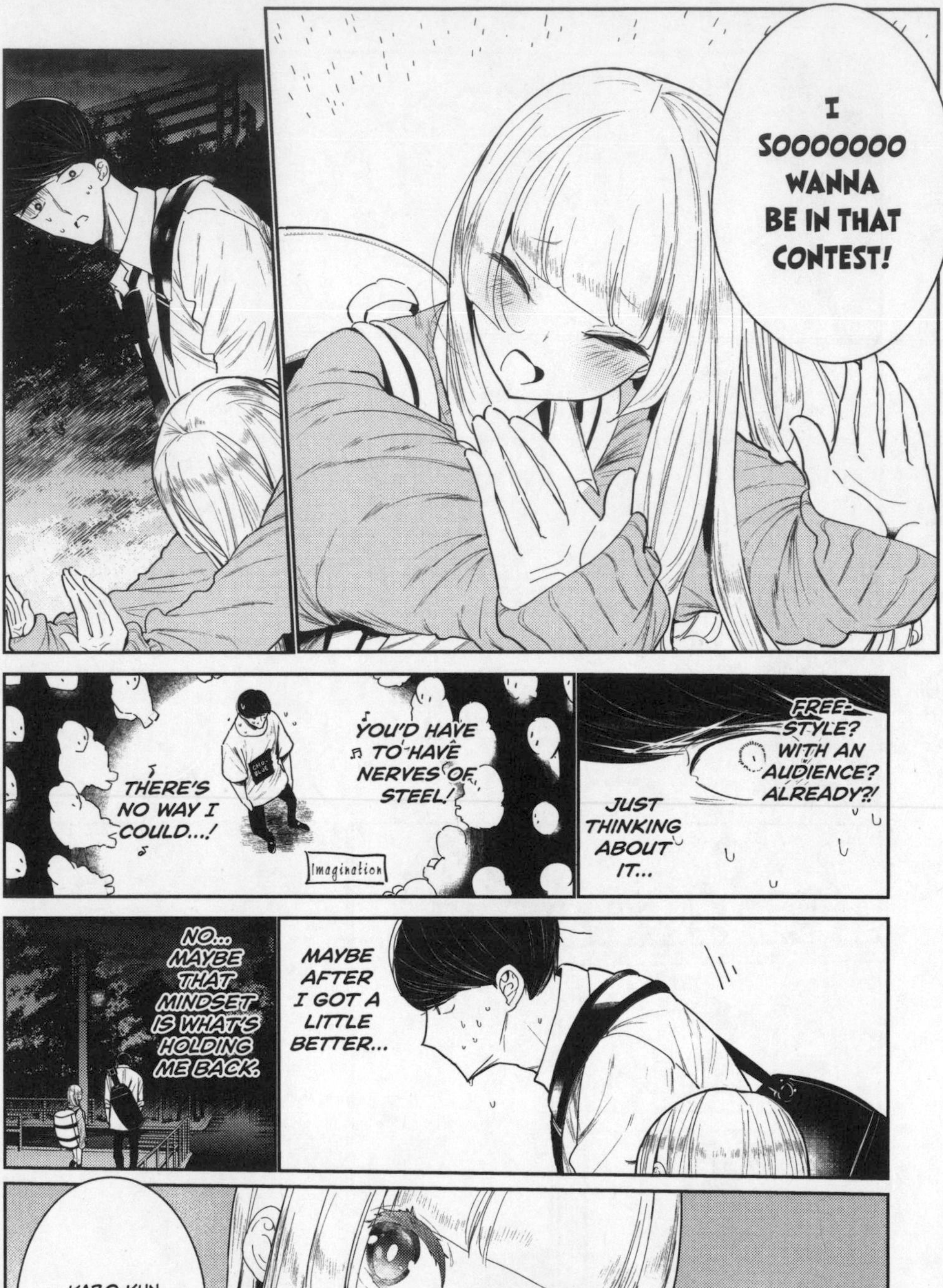
I SOOOOOOO WANNA BE IN THAT CONTEST!
FREE-STYLE? WITH AN AUDIENCE? ALREADY?!
JUST THINKING ABOUT IT...
YOU'D HAVE TO HAVE NERVES OF STEEL!
THERE'S NO WAY I COULD...!
Imagination
MAYBE AFTER I GOT A LITTLE BETTER...
NO... MAYBE THAT MINDSET IS WHAT'S HOLDING ME BACK.
KABO-KUN, ARE YOU NERVOUS?

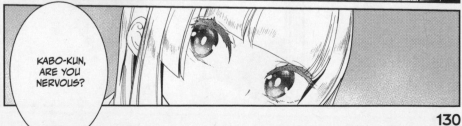

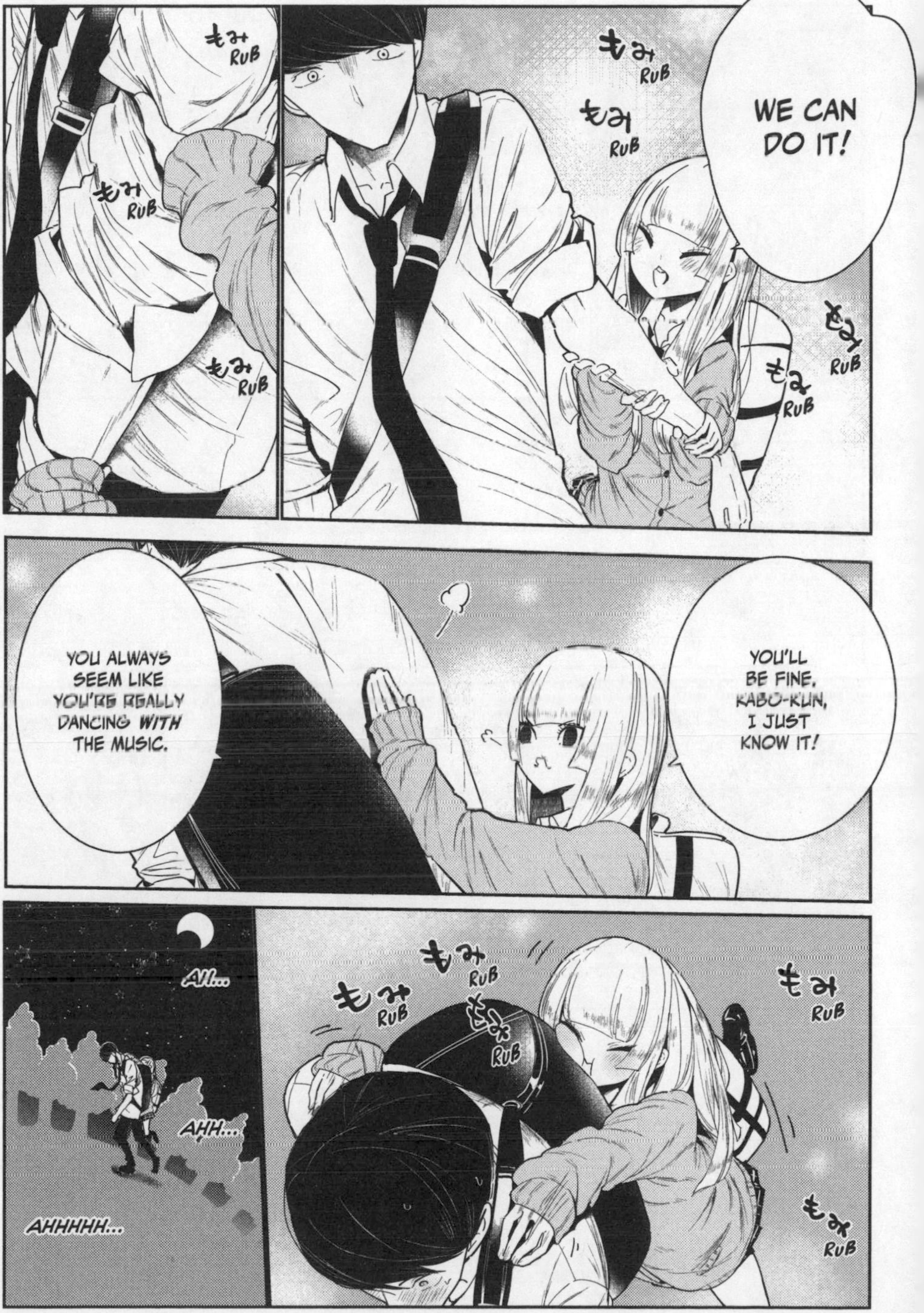
WE CAN DO IT!
もみ RUB
もみ RUB
もみ RUB
もみ RUB
もみ RUB
もみ RUB
もみ RUB
もみ RUB
YOU'LL BE FINE, KABO-KUN, I JUST KNOW IT!
YOU ALWAYS SEEM LIKE YOU'RE REALLY DANCING WITH THE MUSIC.
もみ RUB
もみ RUB
もみ RUB
もみ RUB
もみ RUB
AH...
AHH...
AHHHHH...

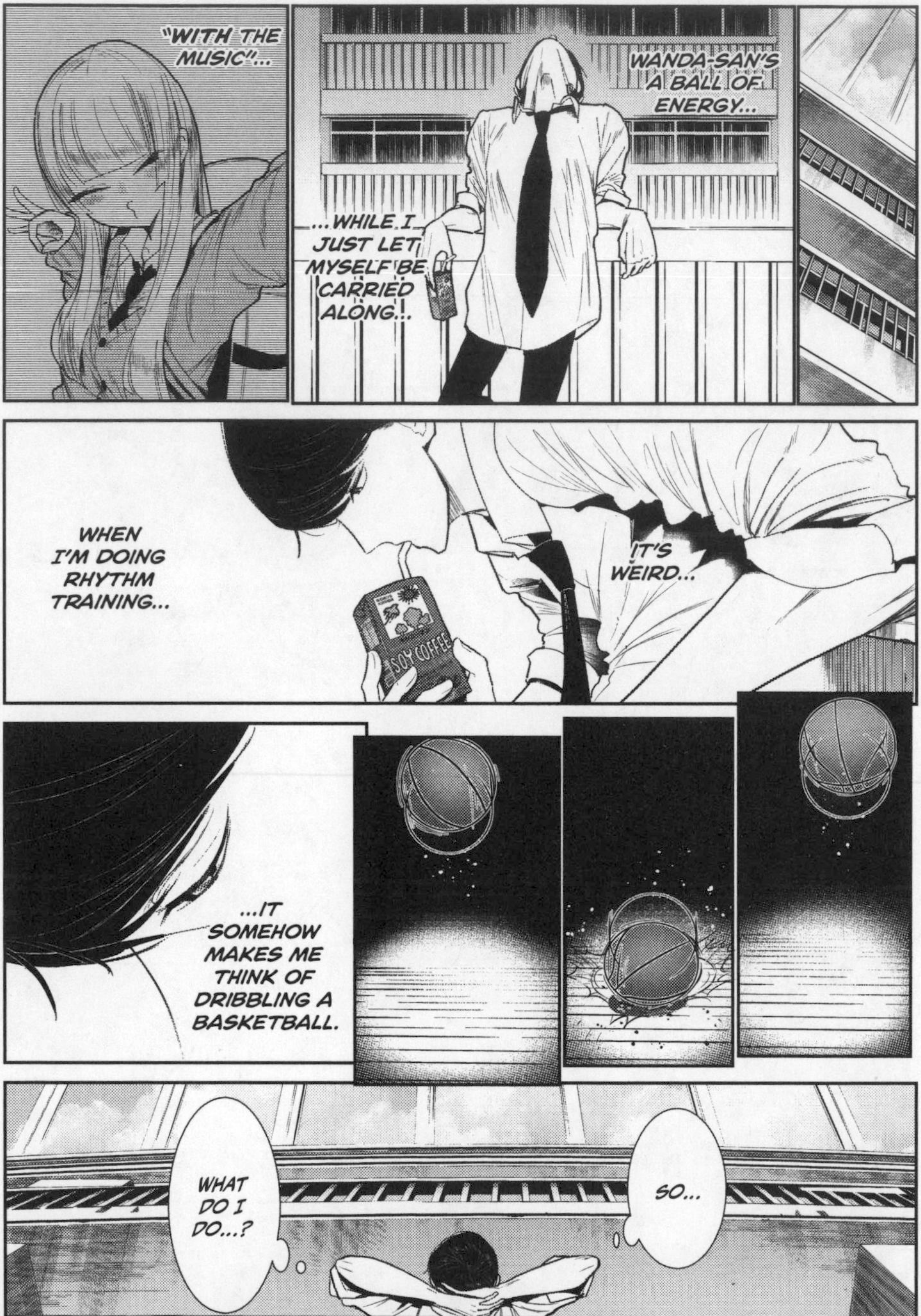
WANDA-SAN'S A BALL OF ENERGY...
...WHILE I JUST LET MYSELF BE CARRIED ALONG...
"WITH THE MUSIC"...
IT'S WEIRD...
WHEN I'M DOING RHYTHM TRAINING...
SOY COFFEE
...IT SOMEHOW MAKES ME THINK OF DRIBBLING A BASKETBALL.
SO...
WHAT DO I DO...?

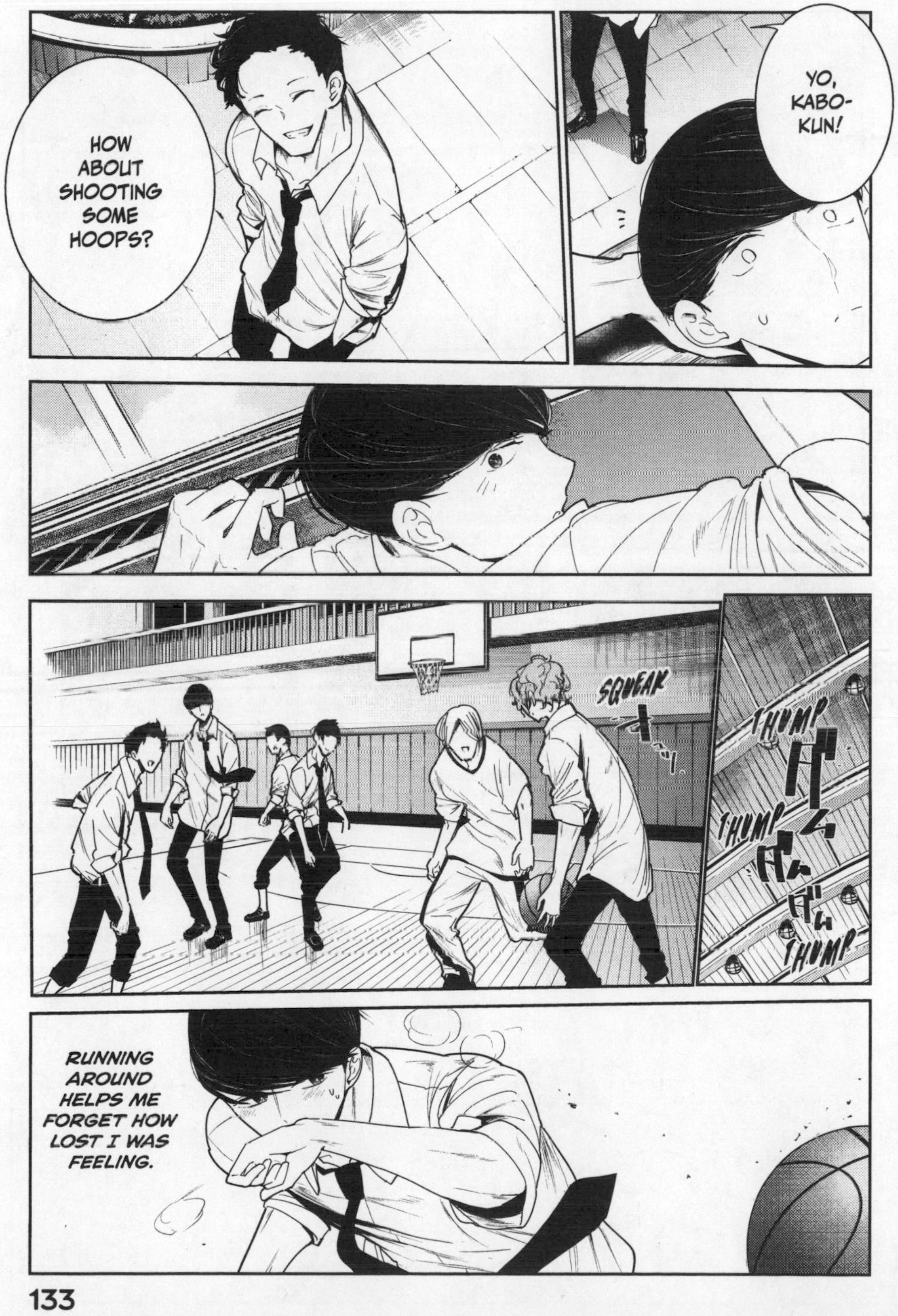
YO, KABO-KUN!
HOW ABOUT SHOOTING SOME HOOPS?
THUMP
THUMP
THUMP
SQUEAK
RUNNING AROUND HELPS ME FORGET HOW LOST I WAS FEELING.

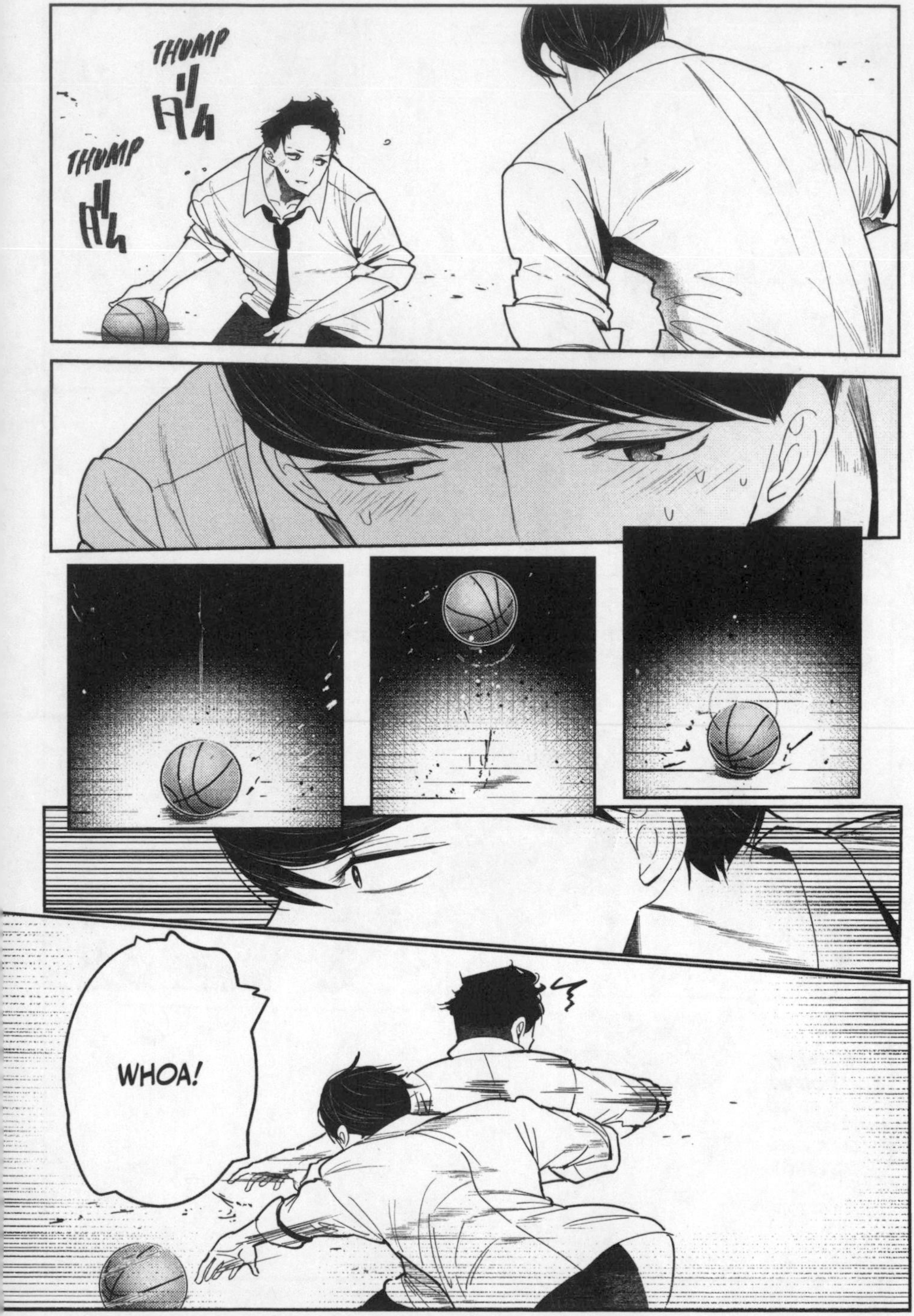
THUMP
THUMP
WHOA!

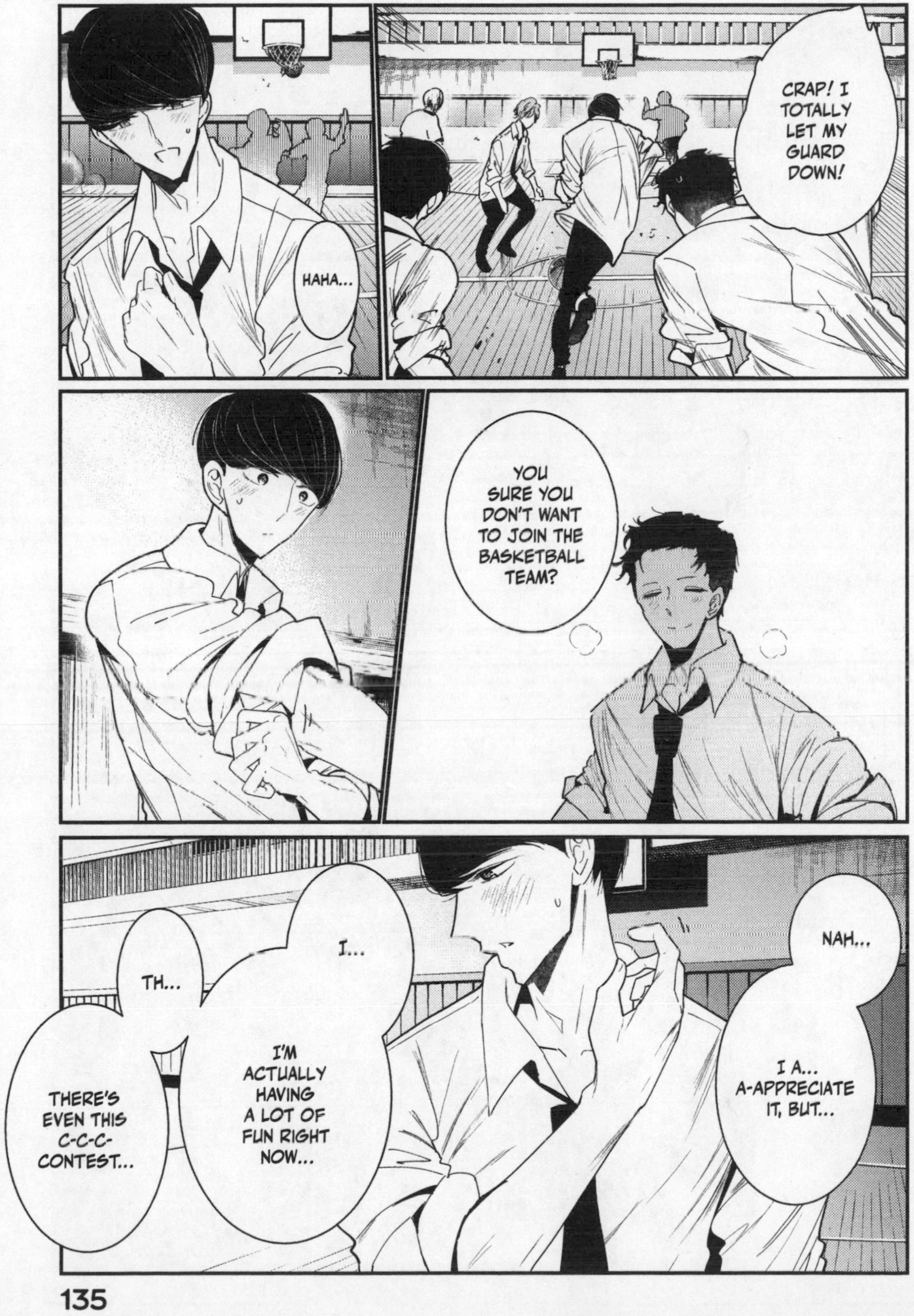
CRAP! I TOTALLY LET MY GUARD DOWN!
HAHA...
YOU SURE YOU DON'T WANT TO JOIN THE BASKETBALL TEAM?
NAH...
I A... A-APPRECIATE IT, BUT...
I...
I'M ACTUALLY HAVING A LOT OF FUN RIGHT NOW...
TH...
THERE'S EVEN THIS C-C-C-CONTEST...

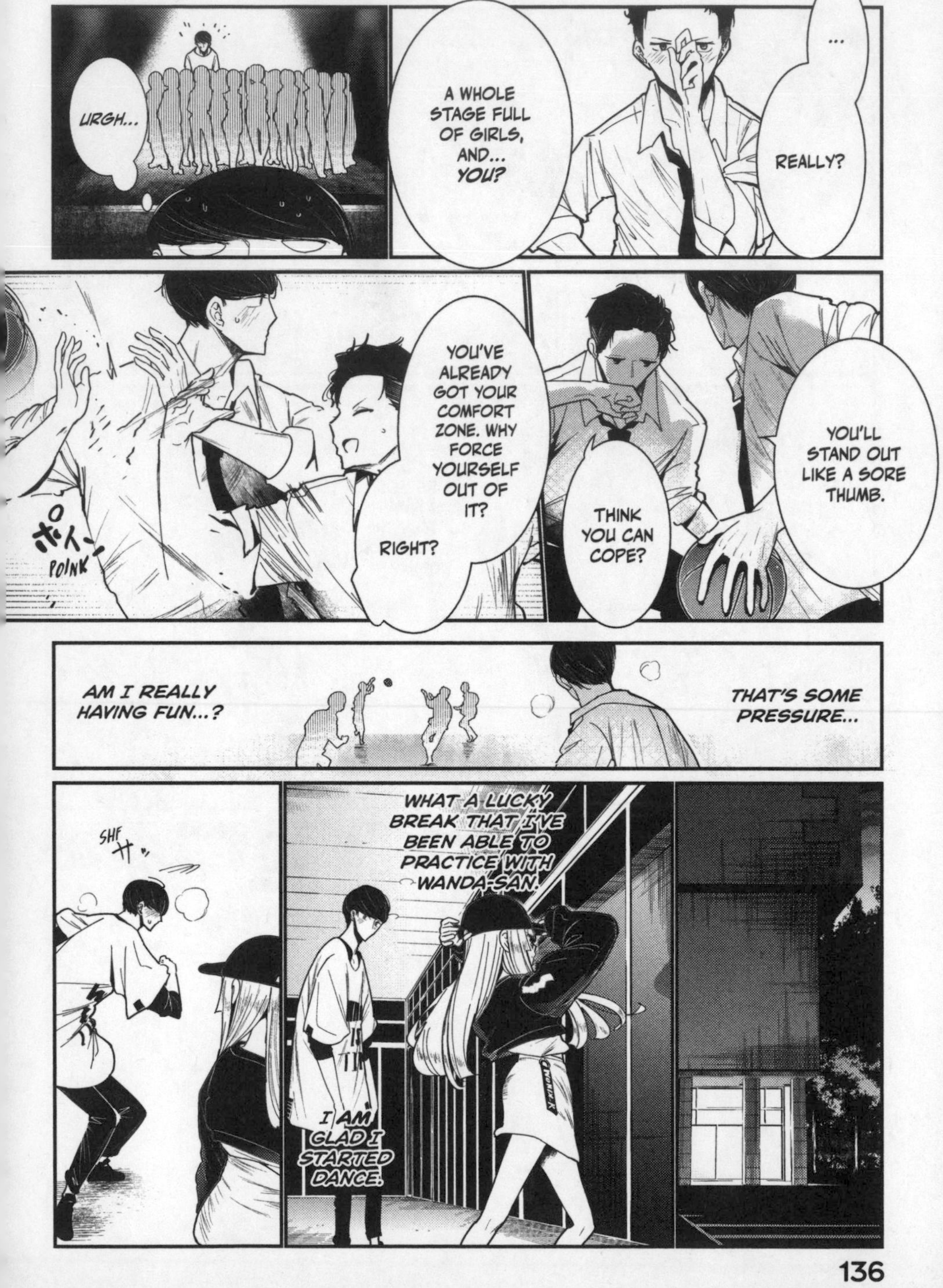

... REALLY?
A WHOLE STAGE FULL OF GIRLS, AND... YOU?
URGH...
YOU'LL STAND OUT LIKE A SORE THUMB.
THINK YOU CAN COPE?
YOU'VE ALREADY GOT YOUR COMFORT ZONE. WHY FORCE YOURSELF OUT OF IT?
RIGHT?
ポイン
POINK
THAT'S SOME PRESSURE...
AM I REALLY HAVING FUN...?
WHAT A LUCKY BREAK THAT I'VE BEEN ABLE TO PRACTICE WITH WANDA-SAN.
I AM GLAD I STARTED DANCE.
SHF
サッ

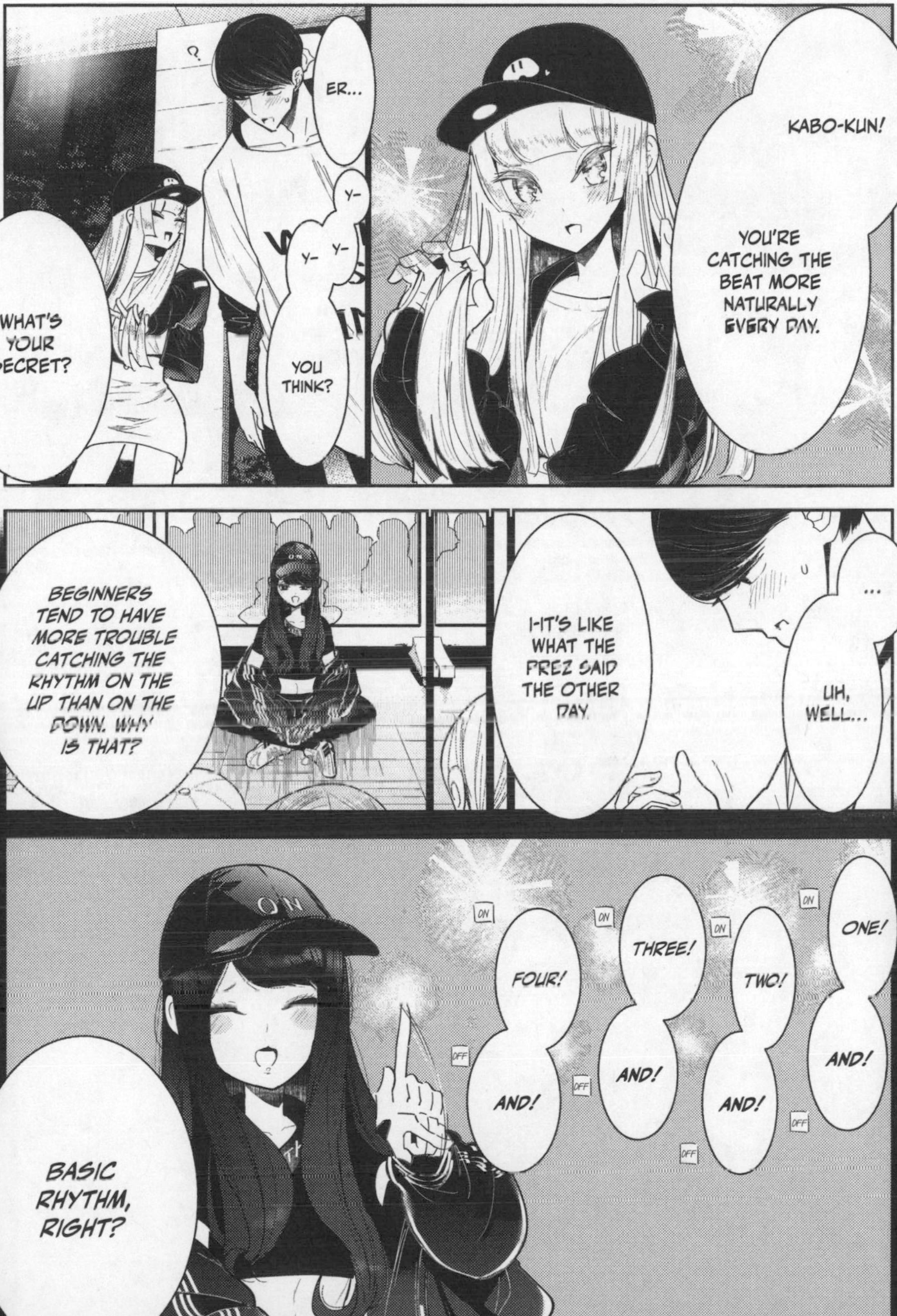
KABO-KUN!
YOU'RE CATCHING THE BEAT MORE NATURALLY EVERY DAY.
ER...
Y- Y- Y- YOU THINK?
WHAT'S YOUR SECRET?
...
UH, WELL...
I-IT'S LIKE WHAT THE PREZ SAID THE OTHER DAY.
BEGINNERS TEND TO HAVE MORE TROUBLE CATCHING THE RHYTHM ON THE UP THAN ON THE DOWN. WHY IS THAT?
ONE!
AND!
TWO!
AND!
THREE!
AND!
FOUR!
AND!
BASIC RHYTHM, RIGHT?

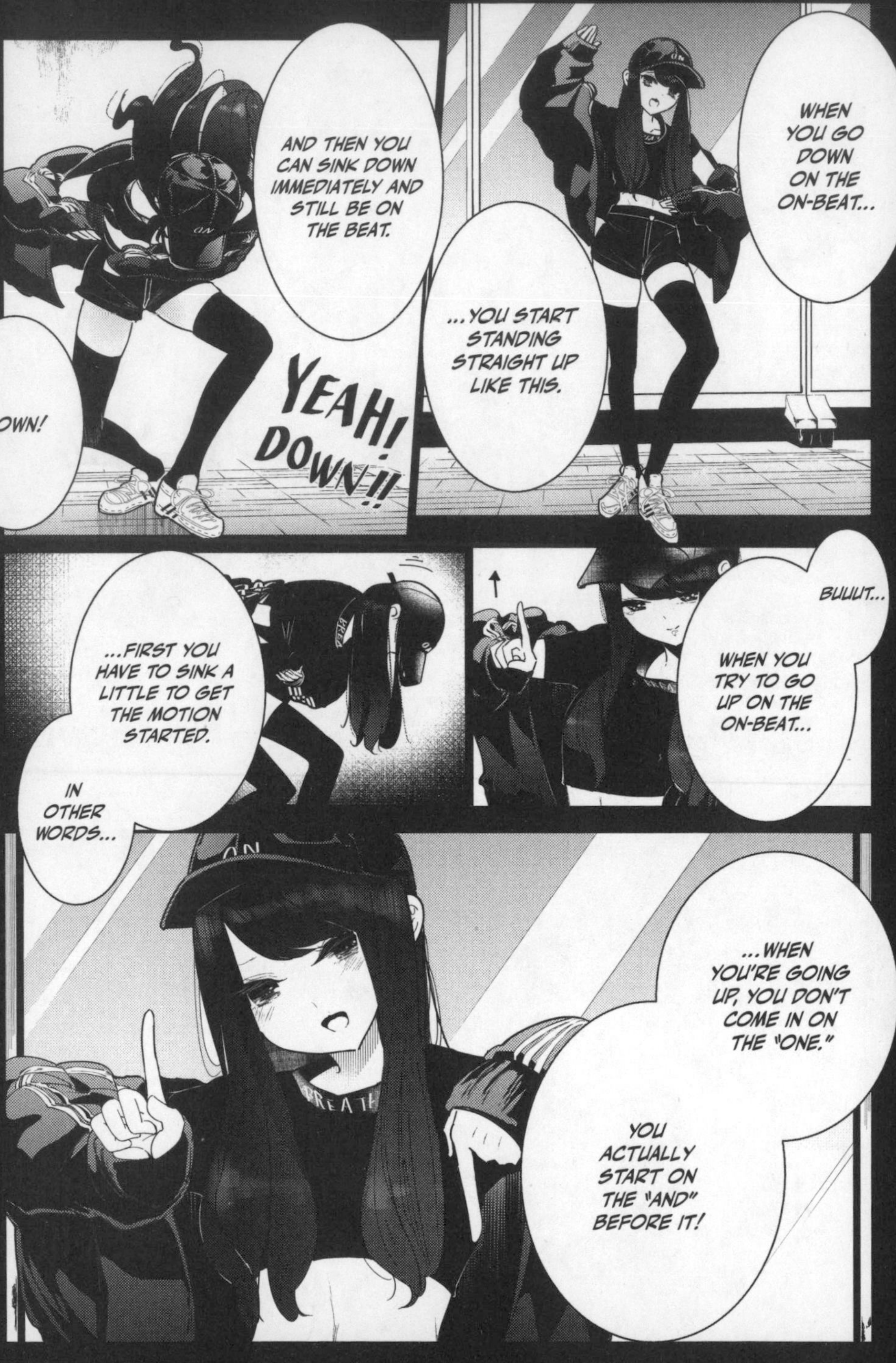
WHEN YOU GO DOWN ON THE ON-BEAT...
...YOU START STANDING STRAIGHT UP LIKE THIS.
AND THEN YOU CAN SINK DOWN IMMEDIATELY AND STILL BE ON THE BEAT.
YEAH! DOWN!!
DOWN!
BUUUT...
WHEN YOU TRY TO GO UP ON THE ON-BEAT...
...FIRST YOU HAVE TO SINK A LITTLE TO GET THE MOTION STARTED.
IN OTHER WORDS...
...WHEN YOU'RE GOING UP, YOU DON'T COME IN ON THE "ONE."
YOU ACTUALLY START ON THE "AND" BEFORE IT!

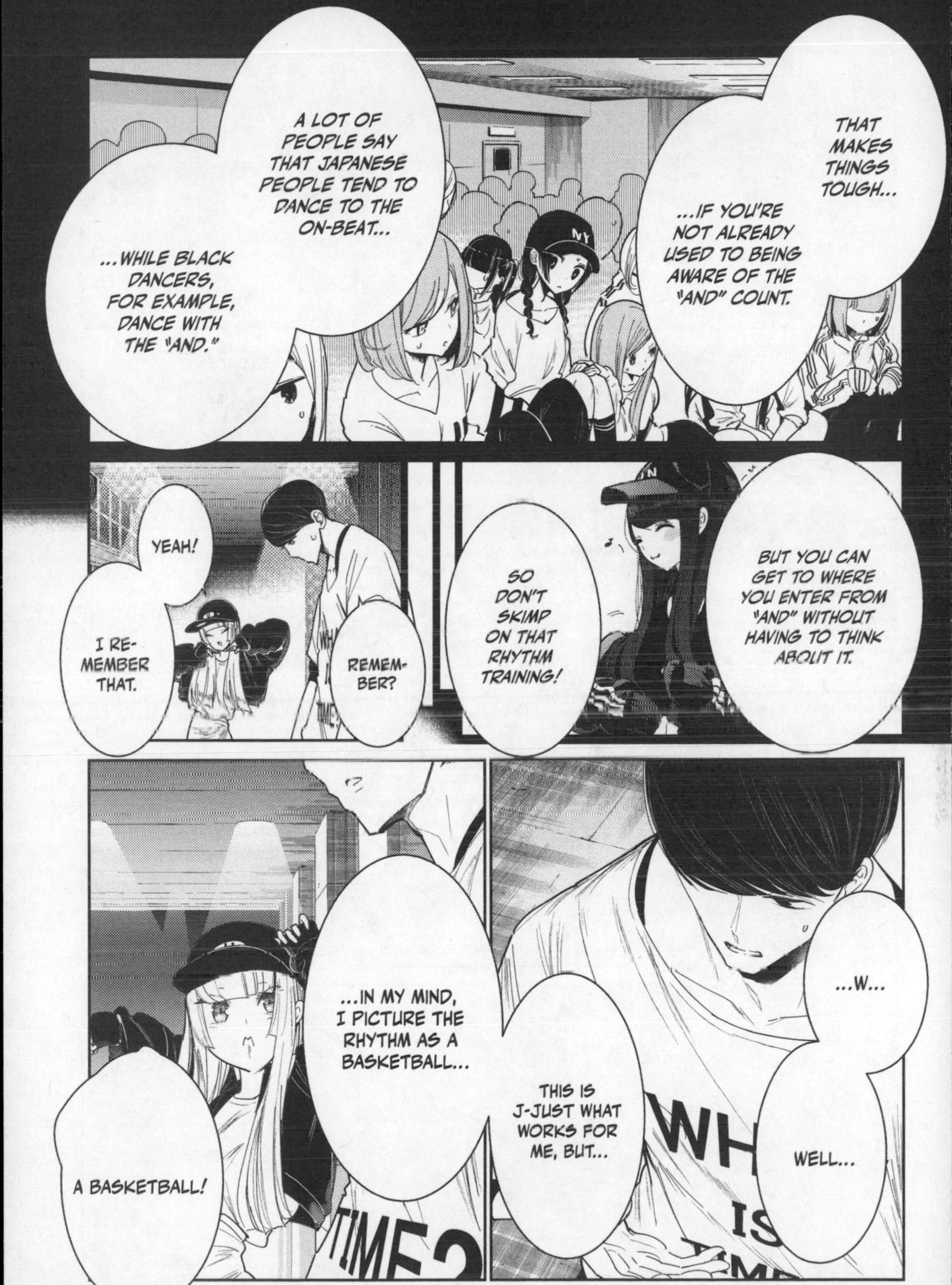
A LOT OF PEOPLE SAY THAT JAPANESE PEOPLE TEND TO DANCE TO THE ON-BEAT...
...WHILE BLACK DANCERS, FOR EXAMPLE, DANCE WITH THE "AND."
THAT MAKES THINGS TOUGH...
...IF YOU'RE NOT ALREADY USED TO BEING AWARE OF THE "AND" COUNT.
BUT YOU CAN GET TO WHERE YOU ENTER FROM "AND" WITHOUT HAVING TO THINK ABOUT IT.
SO DON'T SKIMP ON THAT RHYTHM TRAINING!
REMEM-BER?
YEAH!
I RE-MEMBER THAT.
...W...
WELL...
THIS IS J-JUST WHAT WORKS FOR ME, BUT...
...IN MY MIND, I PICTURE THE RHYTHM AS A BASKETBALL...
A BASKETBALL!

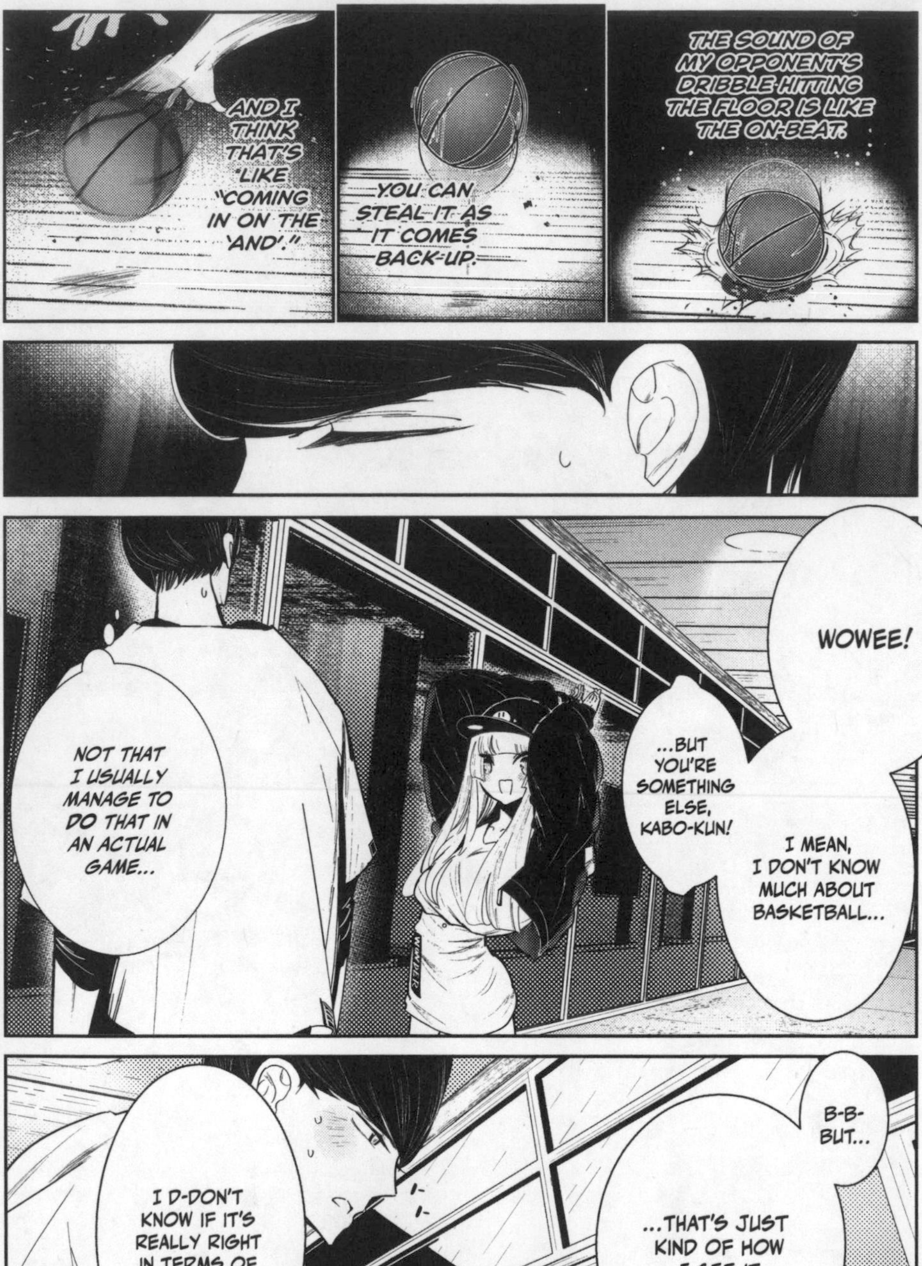
THE SOUND OF MY OPPONENT'S DRIBBLE HITTING THE FLOOR IS LIKE THE ON-BEAT.
YOU CAN STEAL IT AS IT COMES BACK UP.
AND I THINK THAT'S LIKE "COMING IN ON THE 'AND'."
WOWEE!
I MEAN, I DON'T KNOW MUCH ABOUT BASKETBALL...
...BUT YOU'RE SOMETHING ELSE, KABO-KUN!
NOT THAT I USUALLY MANAGE TO DO THAT IN AN ACTUAL GAME...
B-B-BUT...
...THAT'S JUST KIND OF HOW I SEE IT.
I D-DON'T KNOW IF IT'S REALLY RIGHT IN TERMS OF D-D-DANCE...

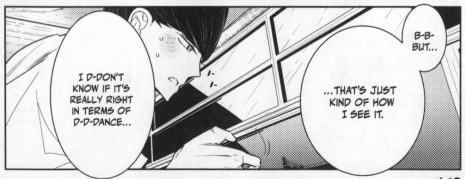

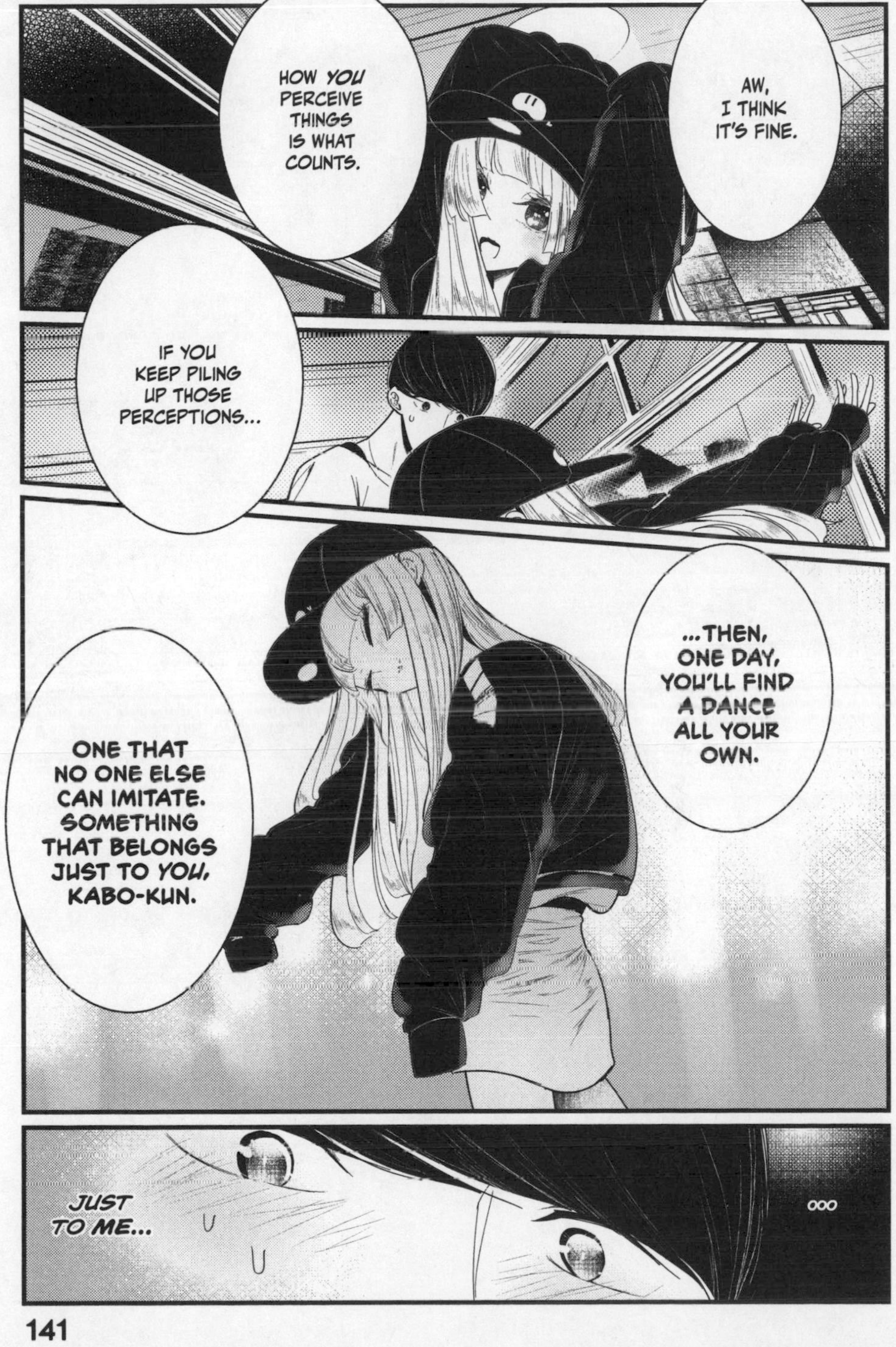
AW, I THINK IT'S FINE.
HOW *YOU* PERCEIVE THINGS IS WHAT COUNTS.
IF YOU KEEP PILING UP THOSE PERCEPTIONS...
...THEN, ONE DAY, YOU'LL FIND A DANCE ALL YOUR OWN.
ONE THAT NO ONE ELSE CAN IMITATE. SOMETHING THAT BELONGS JUST TO *YOU*, KABO-KUN.
ooo
JUST TO ME...

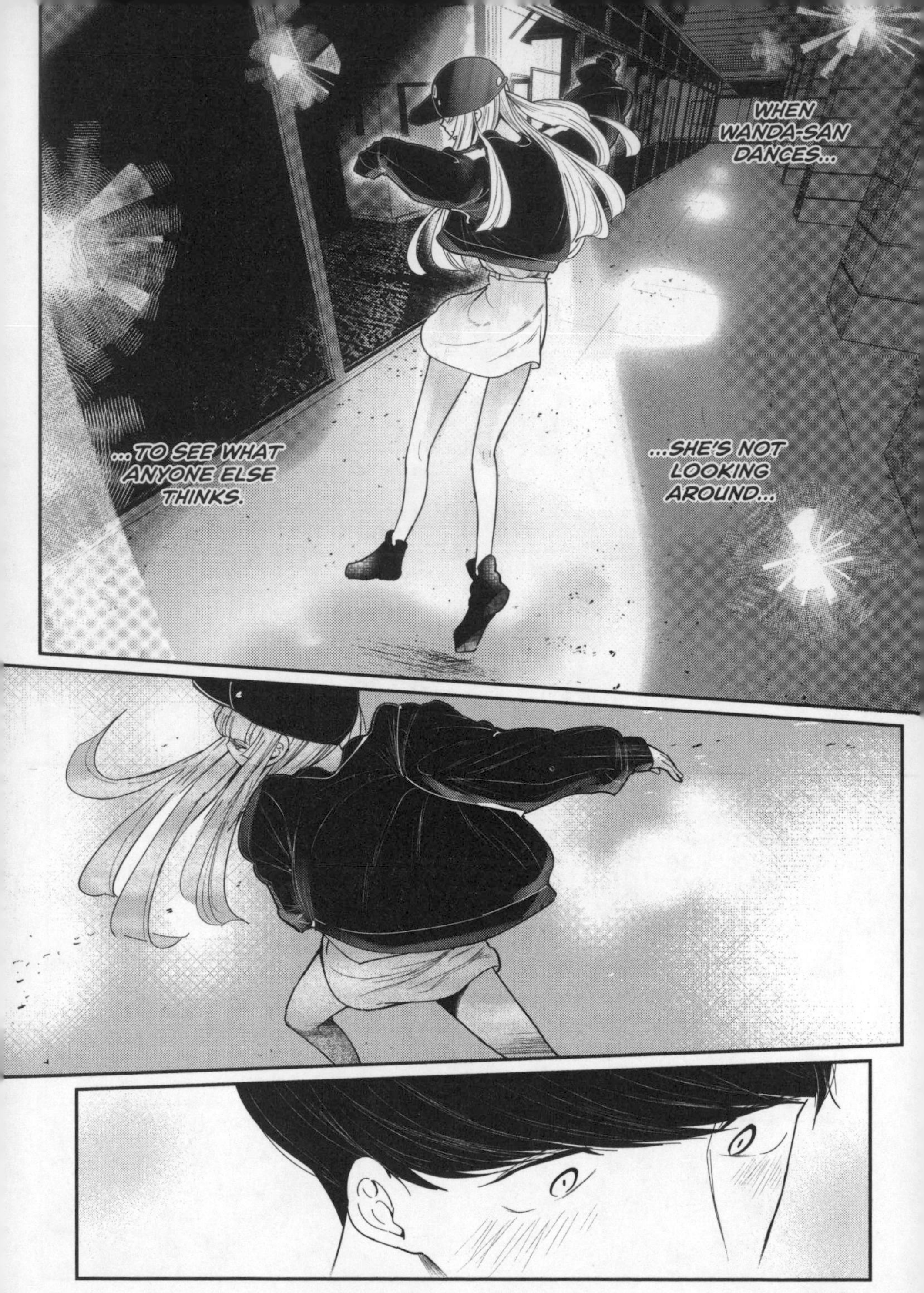
WHEN WANDA-SAN DANCES...
...SHE'S NOT LOOKING AROUND...
...TO SEE WHAT ANYONE ELSE THINKS.

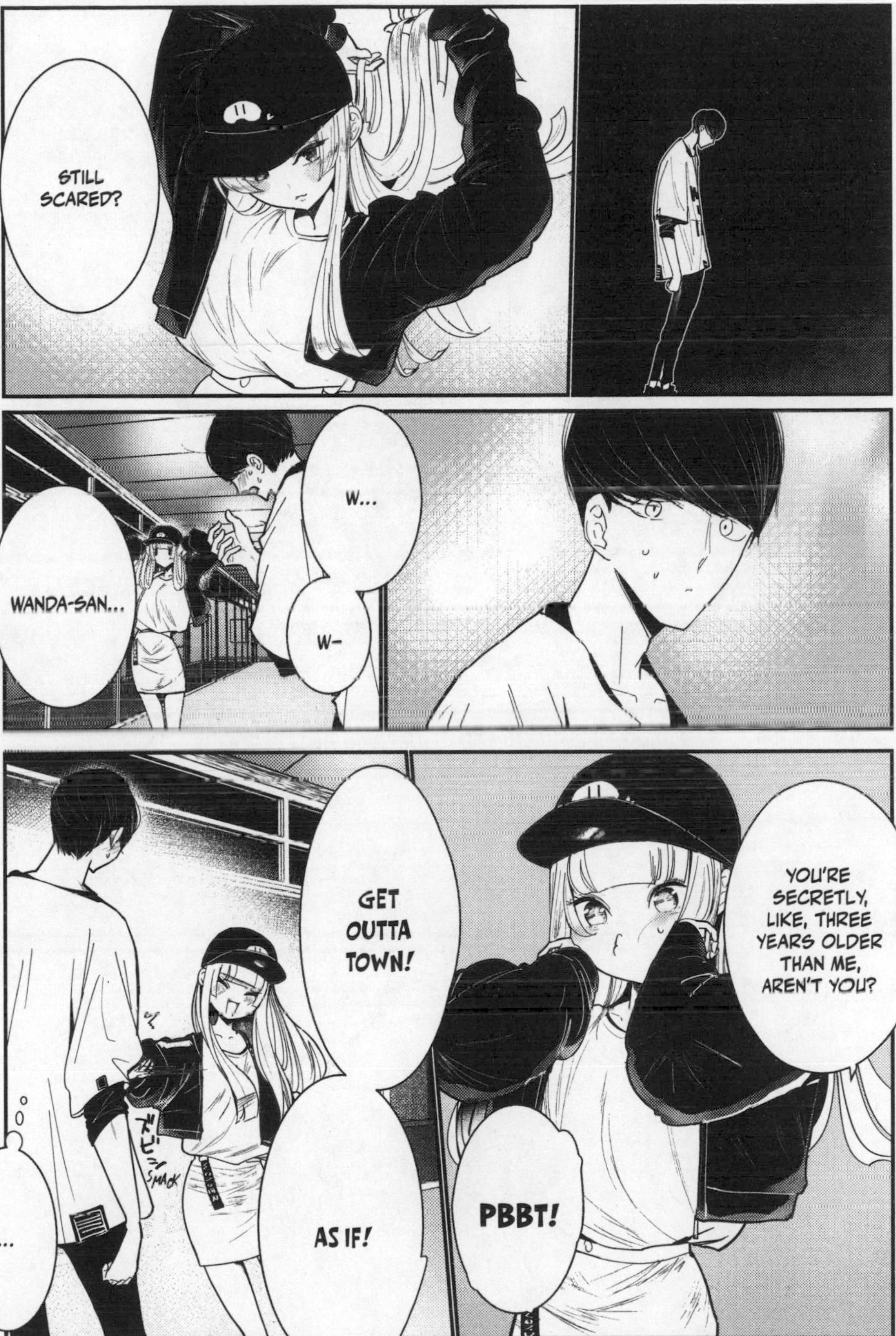
STILL SCARED?
W...
W-
WANDA-SAN...
YOU'RE SECRETLY, LIKE, THREE YEARS OLDER THAN ME, AREN'T YOU?
PBBT!
GET OUTTA TOWN!
SMACK
AS IF!
...

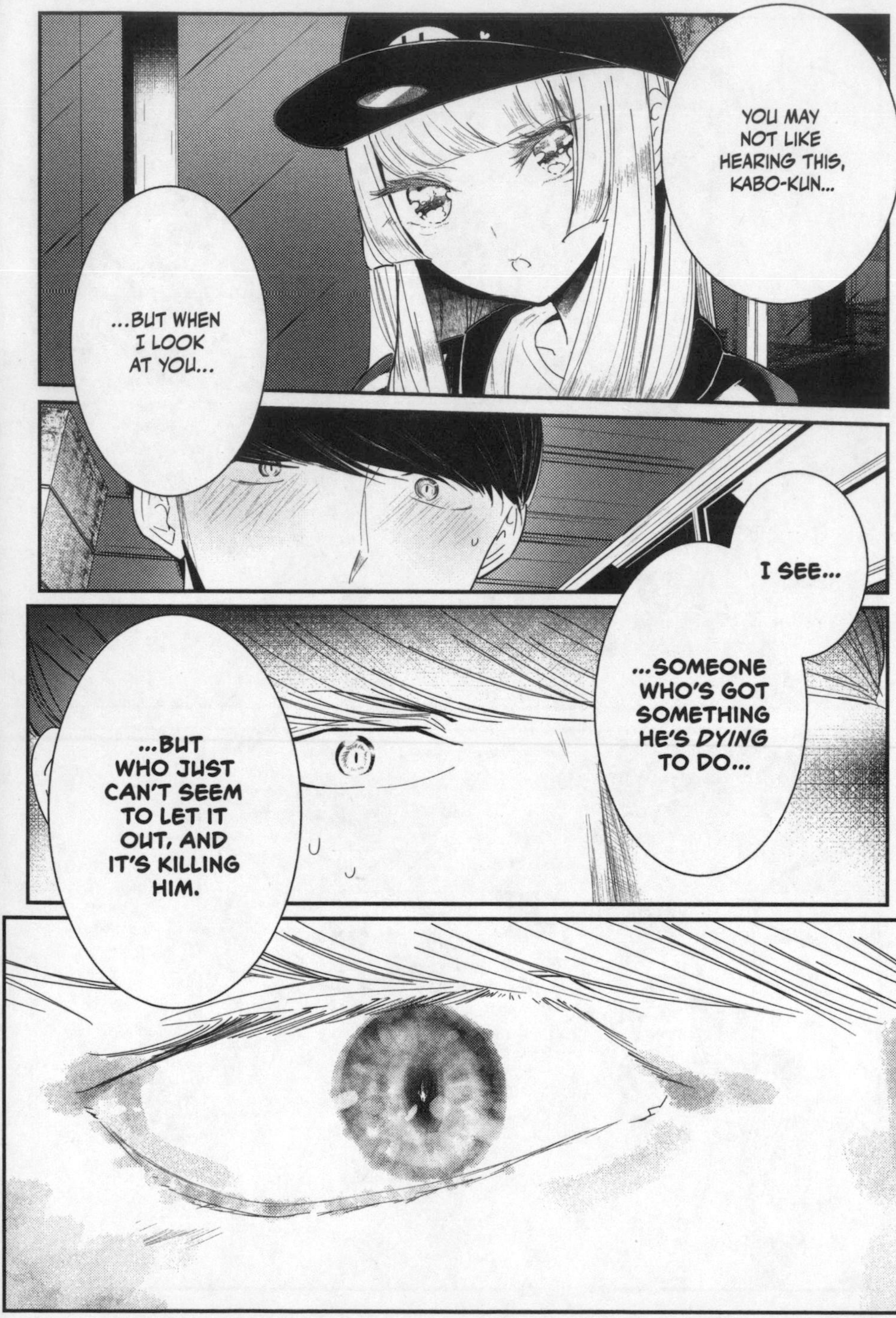
YOU MAY NOT LIKE HEARING THIS, KABO-KUN...
...BUT WHEN I LOOK AT YOU...
I SEE...
...SOMEONE WHO'S GOT SOMETHING HE'S *DYING* TO DO...
...BUT WHO JUST CAN'T SEEM TO LET IT OUT, AND IT'S KILLING HIM.

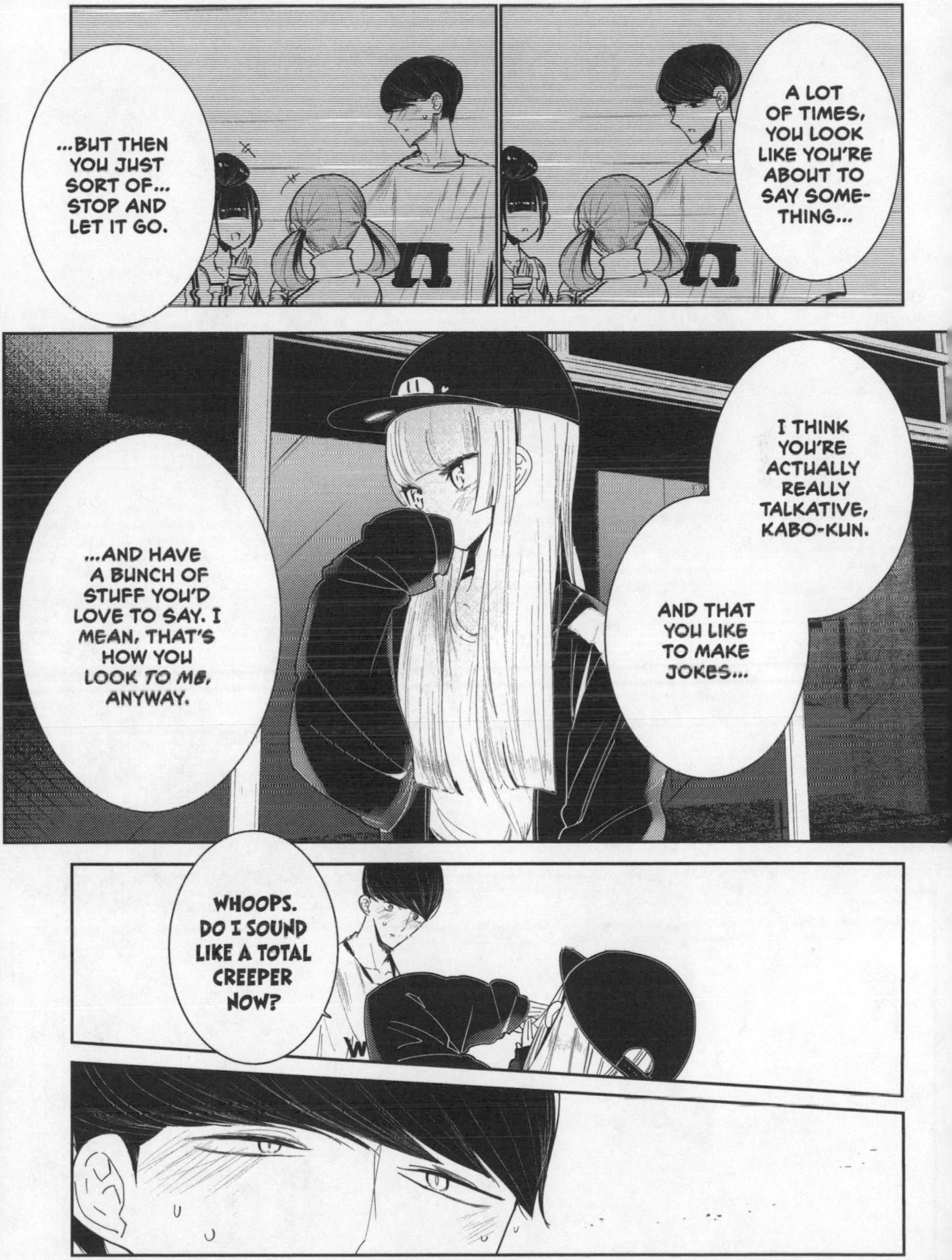
A LOT OF TIMES, YOU LOOK LIKE YOU'RE ABOUT TO SAY SOME-THING...
...BUT THEN YOU JUST SORT OF... STOP AND LET IT GO.
I THINK YOU'RE ACTUALLY REALLY TALKATIVE, KABO-KUN.
AND THAT YOU LIKE TO MAKE JOKES...
...AND HAVE A BUNCH OF STUFF YOU'D LOVE TO SAY. I MEAN, THAT'S HOW YOU LOOK TO ME, ANYWAY.
WHOOPS. DO I SOUND LIKE A TOTAL CREEPER NOW?

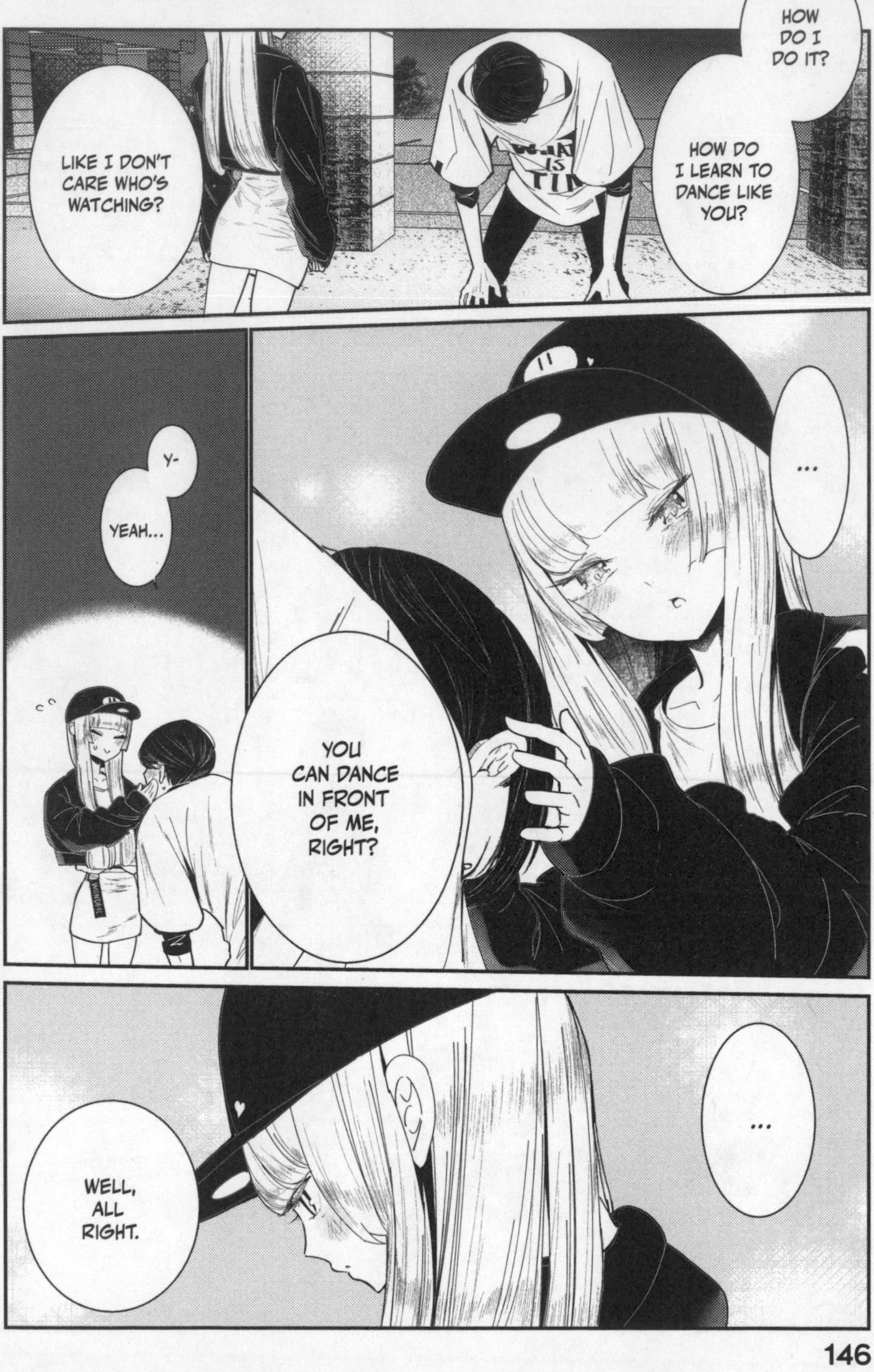
HOW DO I DO IT?
HOW DO I LEARN TO DANCE LIKE YOU?
LIKE I DON'T CARE WHO'S WATCHING?
...
YOU CAN DANCE IN FRONT OF ME, RIGHT?
Y-
YEAH...
...
WELL, ALL RIGHT.

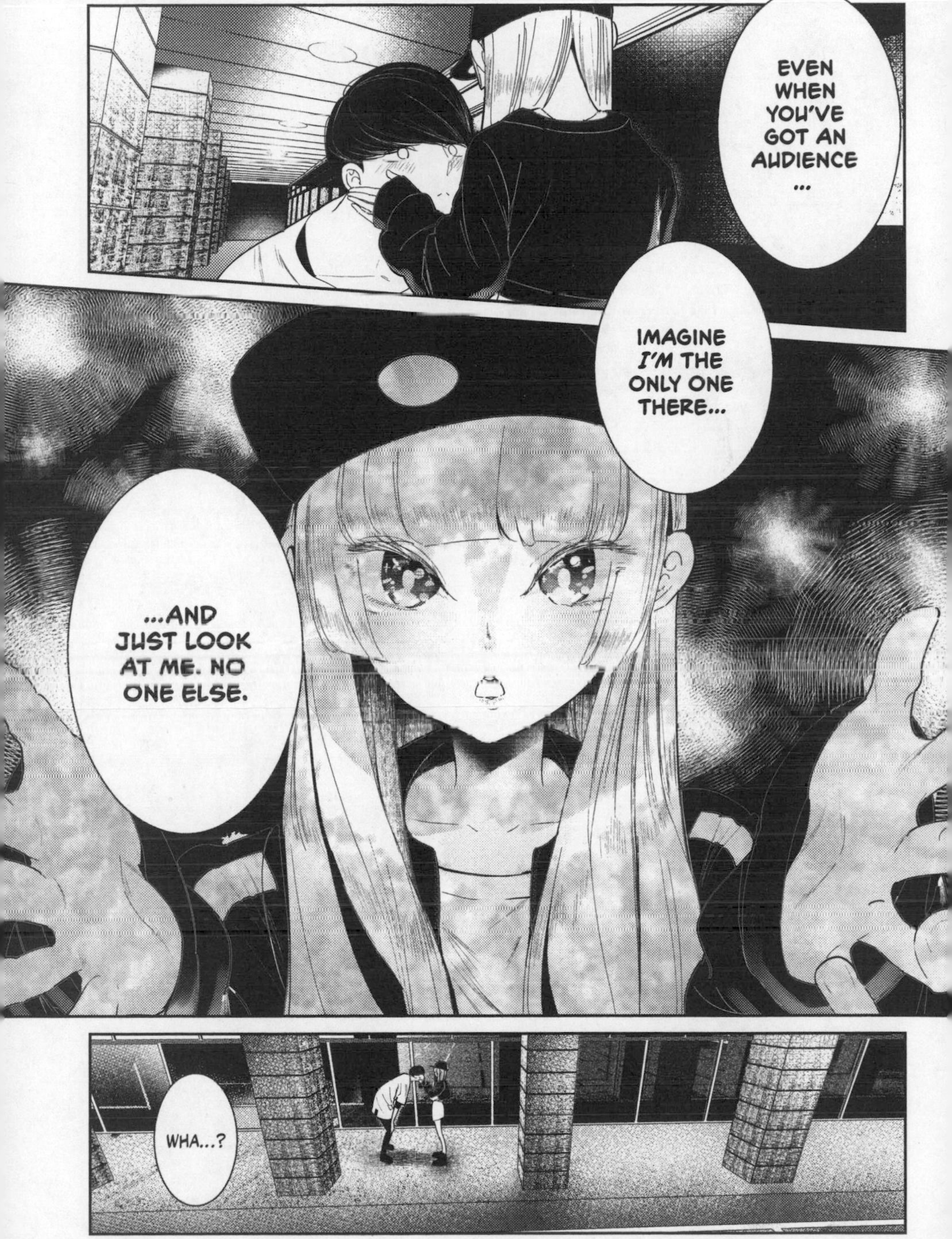
EVEN WHEN YOU'VE GOT AN AUDIENCE ...
IMAGINE *I'M* THE ONLY ONE THERE...
...AND JUST LOOK AT ME. NO ONE ELSE.
WHA...?

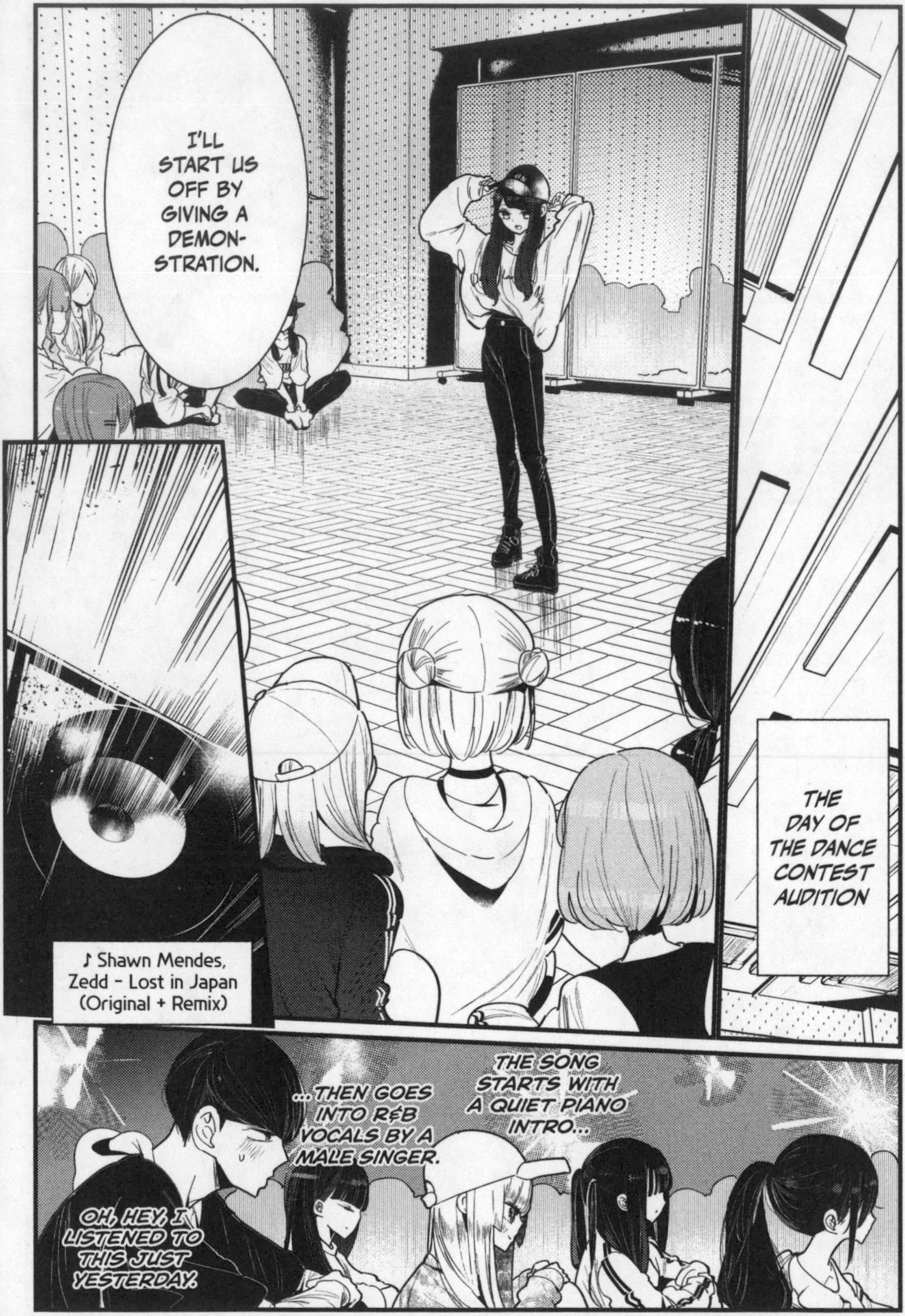
THE DAY OF THE DANCE CONTEST AUDITION
I'LL START US OFF BY GIVING A DEMON-STRATION.
♪ Shawn Mendes, Zedd - Lost in Japan (Original + Remix)
THE SONG STARTS WITH A QUIET PIANO INTRO...
...THEN GOES INTO R&B VOCALS BY A MALE SINGER.
OH, HEY, I LISTENED TO THIS JUST YESTERDAY.

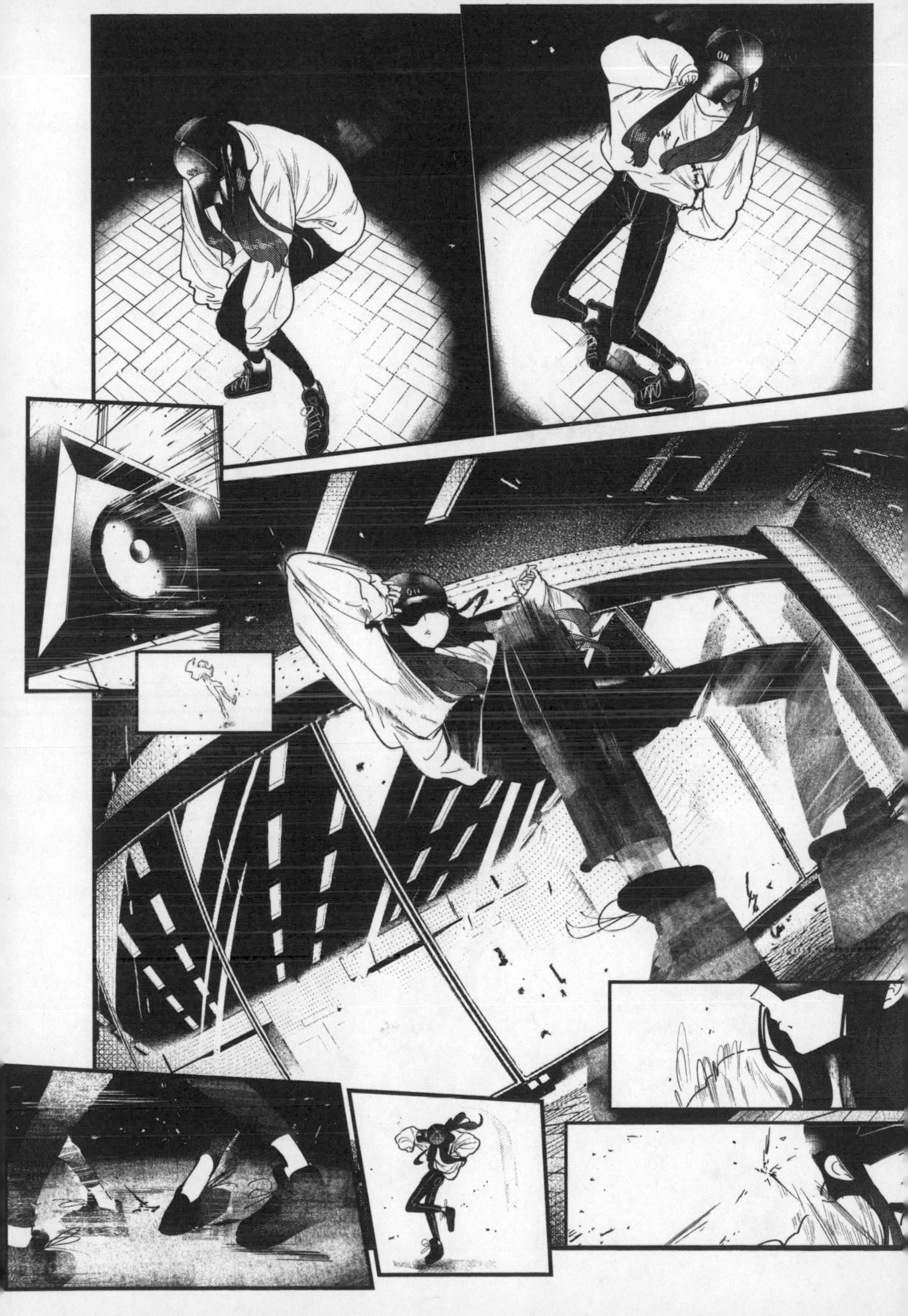
ON

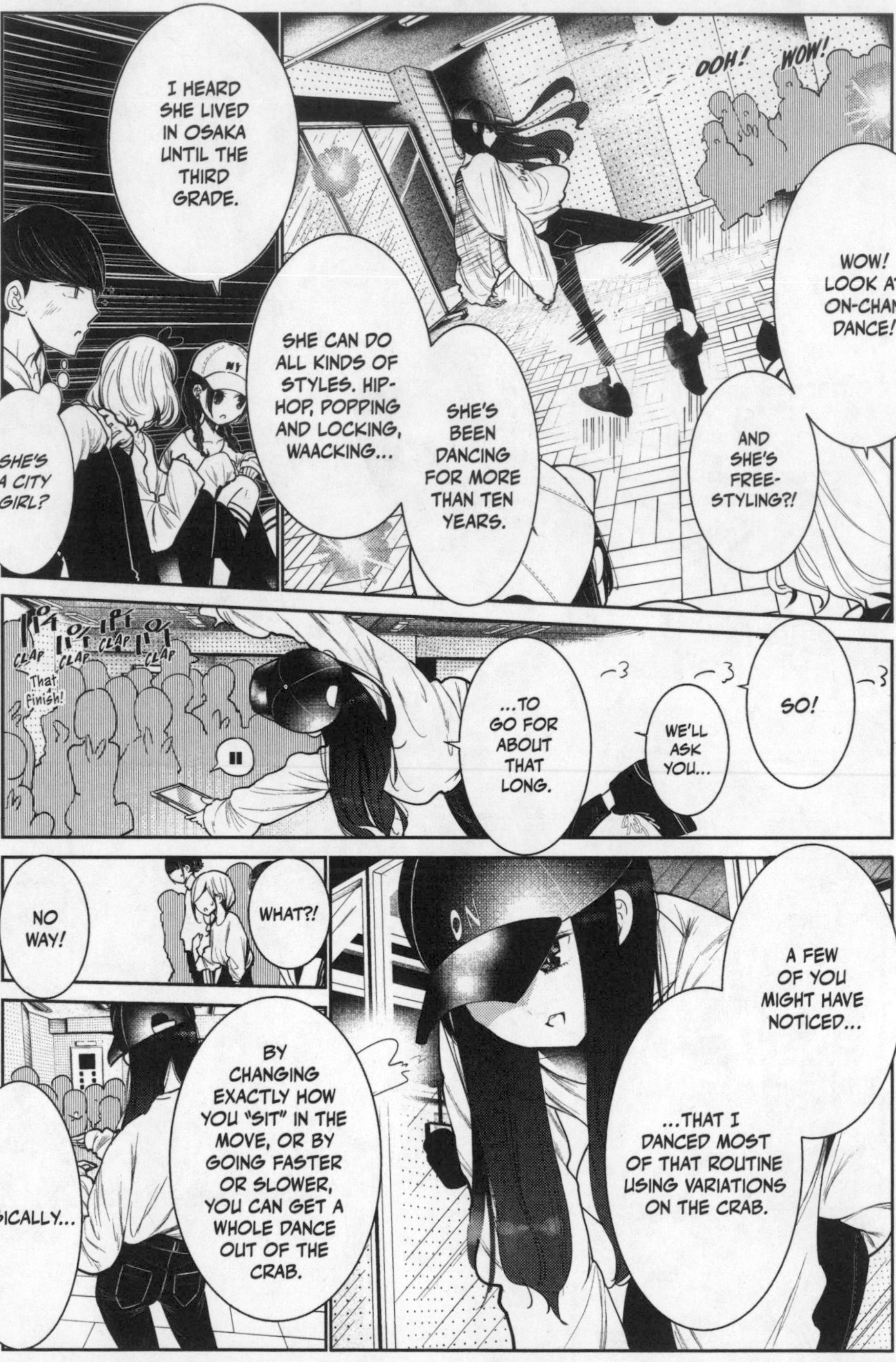
OOH!
WOW!
WOW! LOOK AT ON-CHAN DANCE!
AND SHE'S FREE-STYLING?!
SHE'S BEEN DANCING FOR MORE THAN TEN YEARS.
SHE CAN DO ALL KINDS OF STYLES. HIP-HOP, POPPING AND LOCKING, WAACKING...
I HEARD SHE LIVED IN OSAKA UNTIL THE THIRD GRADE.
SHE'S A CITY GIRL?
SO!
WE'LL ASK YOU...
...TO GO FOR ABOUT THAT LONG.
CLAP CLAP CLAP CLAP
That finish!
A FEW OF YOU MIGHT HAVE NOTICED...
...THAT I DANCED MOST OF THAT ROUTINE USING VARIATIONS ON THE CRAB.
WHAT?!
NO WAY!
BY CHANGING EXACTLY HOW YOU "SIT" IN THE MOVE, OR BY GOING FASTER OR SLOWER, YOU CAN GET A WHOLE DANCE OUT OF THE CRAB.
BASICALLY...

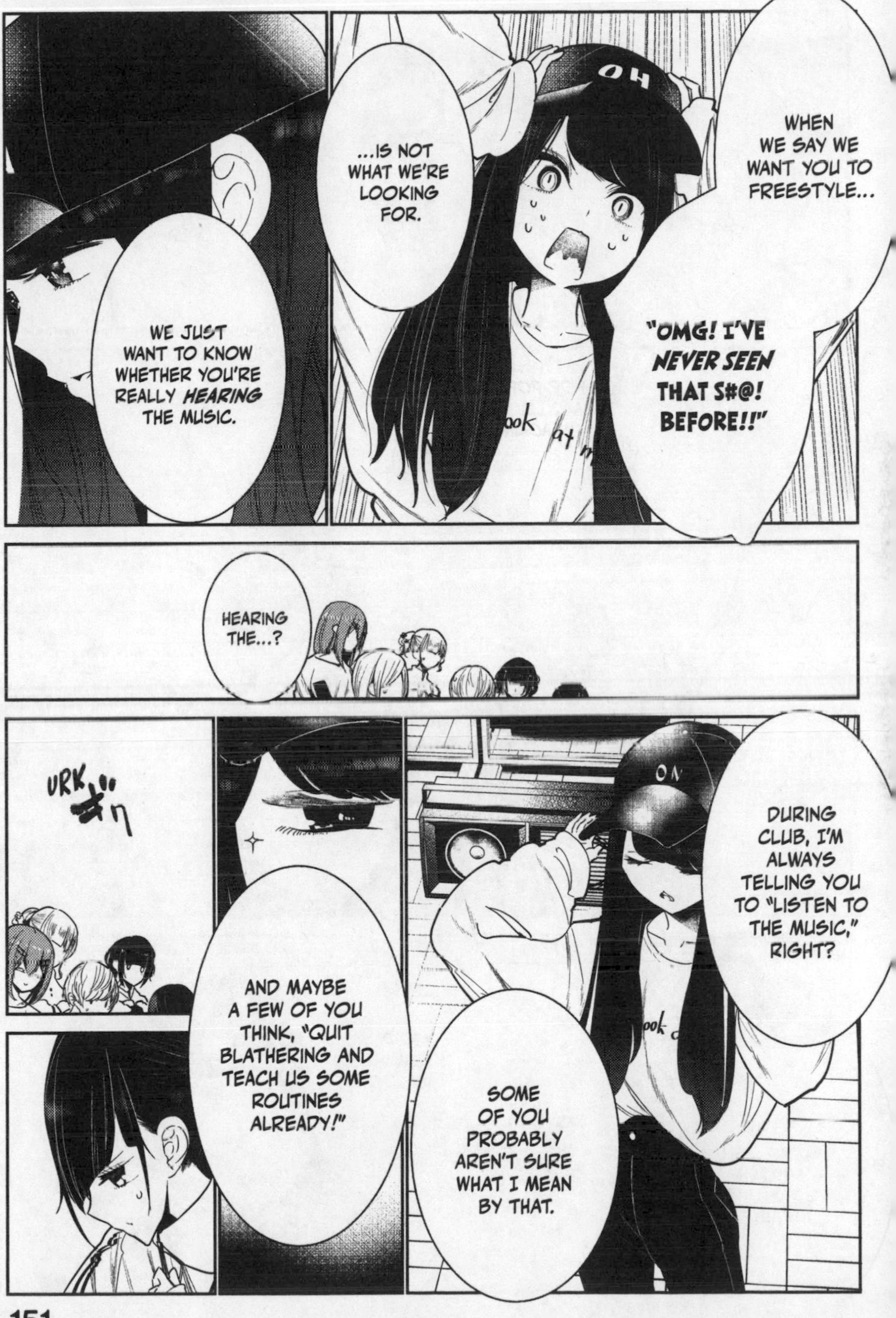
WHEN WE SAY WE WANT YOU TO FREESTYLE...
"OMG! I'VE *NEVER SEEN* THAT S#@! BEFORE!!"
...IS NOT WHAT WE'RE LOOKING FOR.
WE JUST WANT TO KNOW WHETHER YOU'RE REALLY *HEARING* THE MUSIC.
HEARING THE...?
DURING CLUB, I'M ALWAYS TELLING YOU TO "LISTEN TO THE MUSIC," RIGHT?
SOME OF YOU PROBABLY AREN'T SURE WHAT I MEAN BY THAT.
AND MAYBE A FEW OF YOU THINK, "QUIT BLATHERING AND TEACH US SOME ROUTINES ALREADY!"
URK

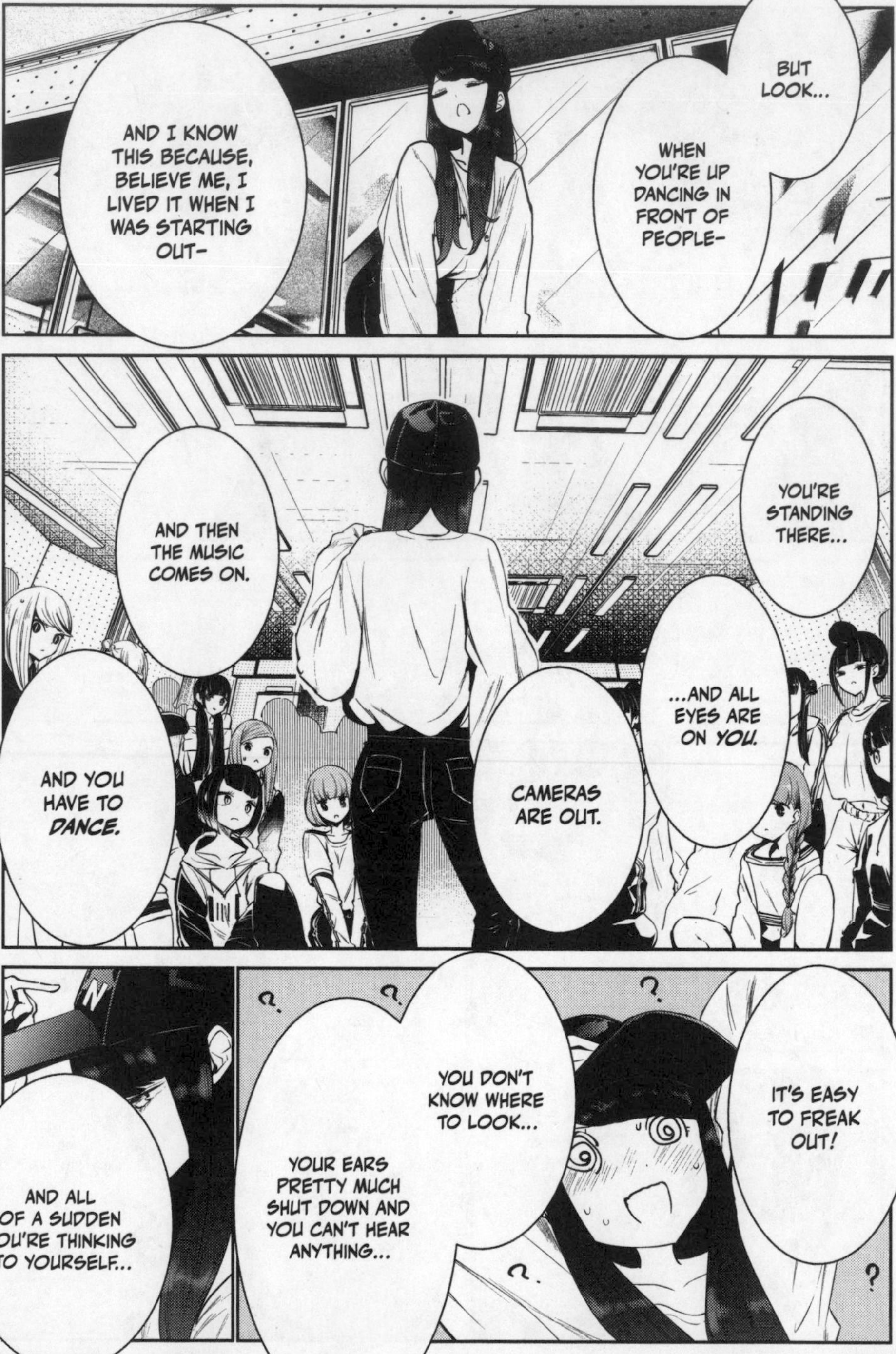
BUT LOOK...
WHEN YOU'RE UP DANCING IN FRONT OF PEOPLE-
AND I KNOW THIS BECAUSE, BELIEVE ME, I LIVED IT WHEN I WAS STARTING OUT-
YOU'RE STANDING THERE...
...AND ALL EYES ARE ON *YOU.*
CAMERAS ARE OUT.
AND THEN THE MUSIC COMES ON.
AND YOU HAVE TO *DANCE.*
IT'S EASY TO FREAK OUT!
YOU DON'T KNOW WHERE TO LOOK...
YOUR EARS PRETTY MUCH SHUT DOWN AND YOU CAN'T HEAR ANYTHING...
AND ALL OF A SUDDEN YOU'RE THINKING TO YOURSELF...

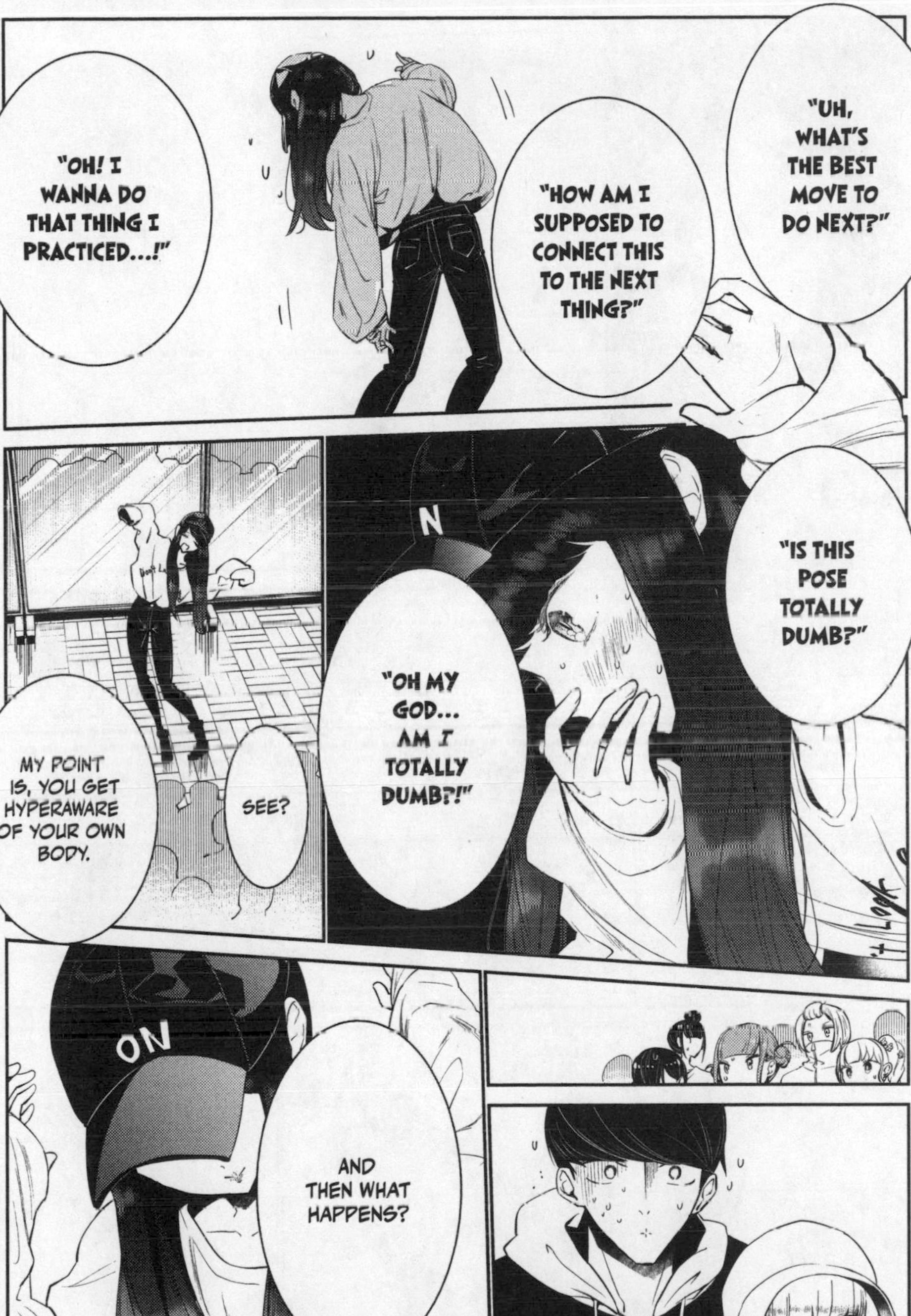
"UH, WHAT'S THE BEST MOVE TO DO NEXT?"
"HOW AM I SUPPOSED TO CONNECT THIS TO THE NEXT THING?"
"OH! I WANNA DO THAT THING I PRACTICED...!"
"IS THIS POSE TOTALLY DUMB?"
"OH MY GOD... AM *I* TOTALLY DUMB?!"
SEE?
MY POINT IS, YOU GET HYPERAWARE OF YOUR OWN BODY.
AND THEN WHAT HAPPENS?

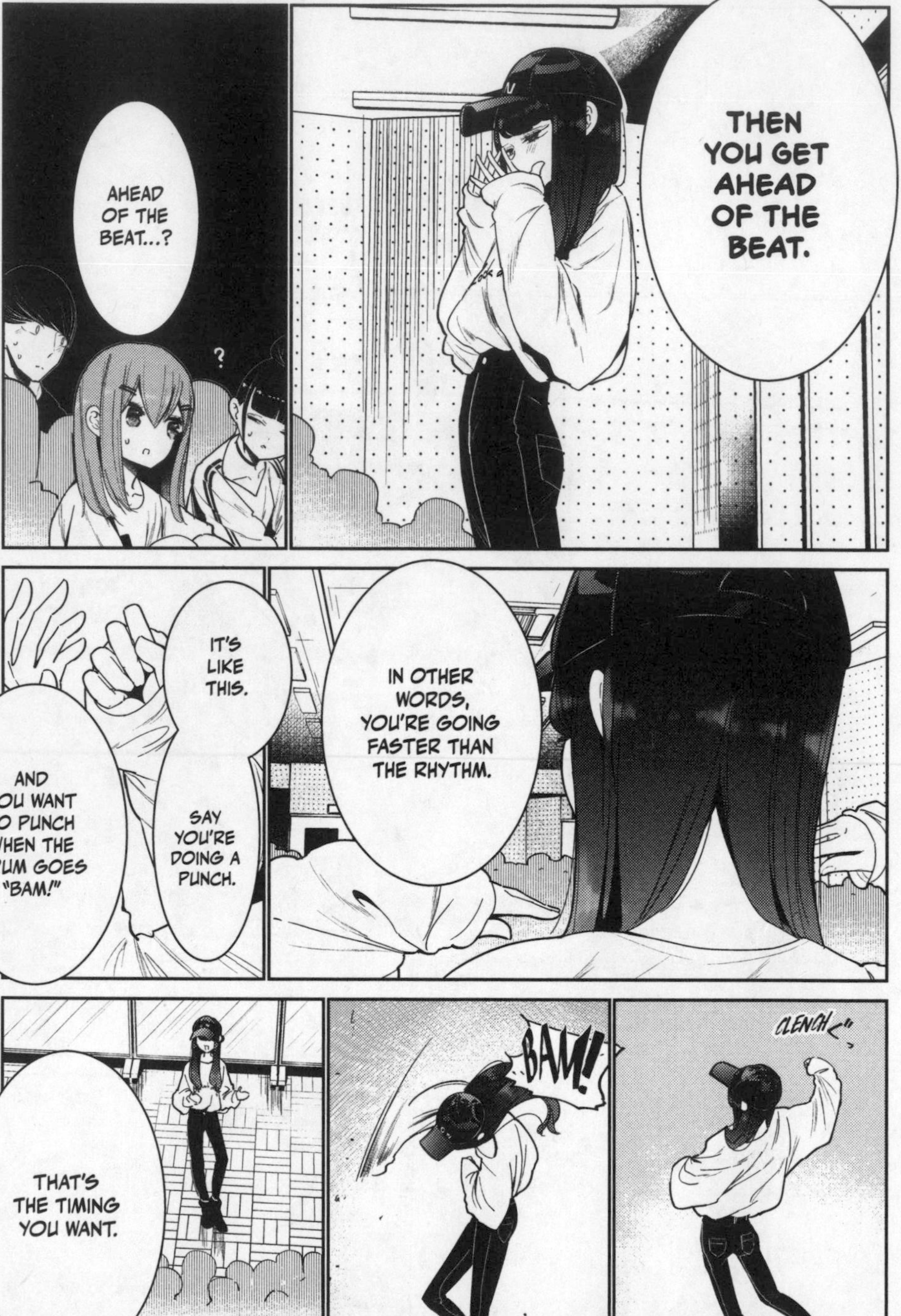
THEN YOU GET AHEAD OF THE BEAT.
AHEAD OF THE BEAT...?
IN OTHER WORDS, YOU'RE GOING FASTER THAN THE RHYTHM.
IT'S LIKE THIS.
SAY YOU'RE DOING A PUNCH.
AND YOU WANT TO PUNCH WHEN THE DRUM GOES "BAM!"
CLENCH
BAM!!
THAT'S THE TIMING YOU WANT.

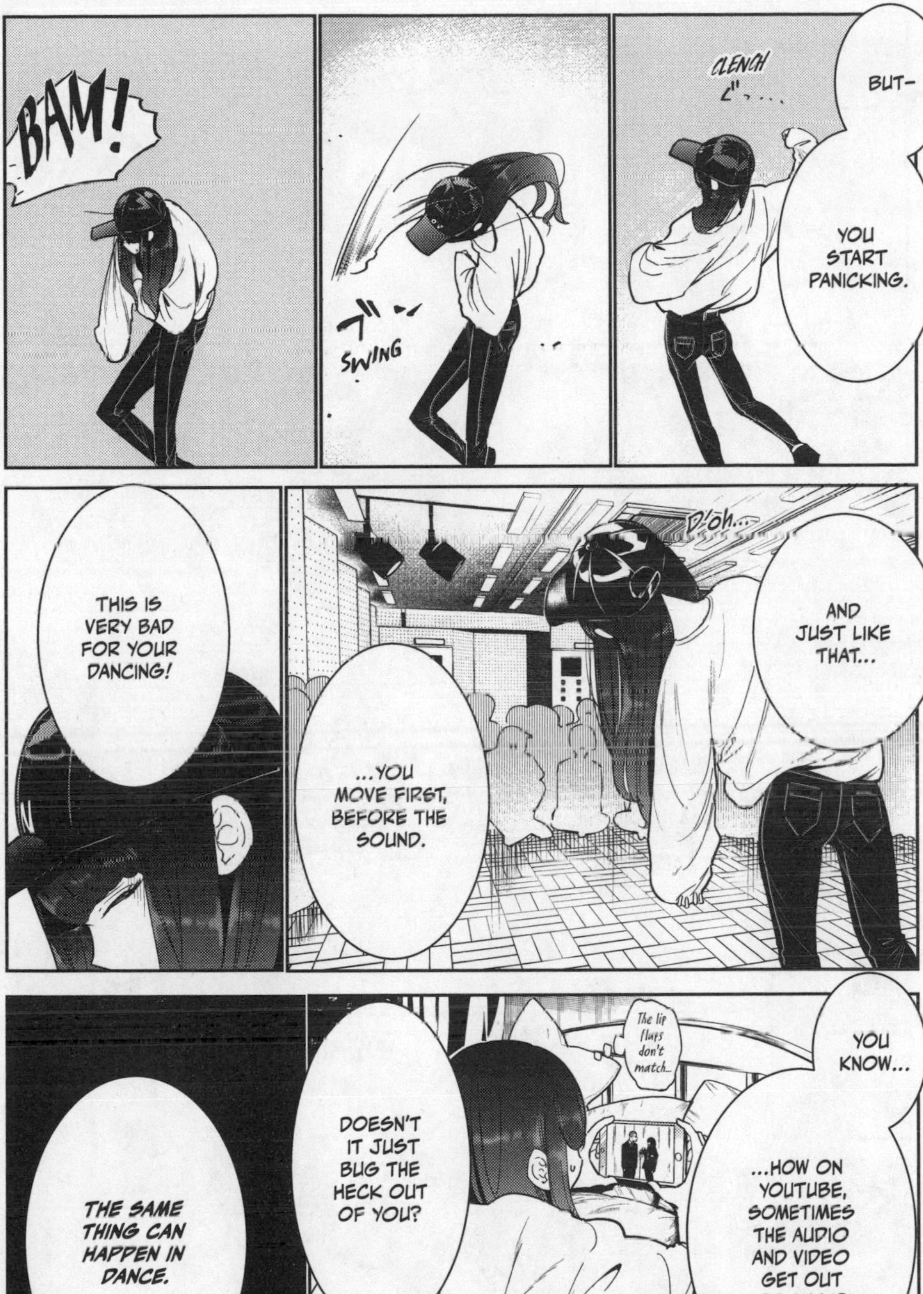
CLENCH
BUT–
YOU START PANICKING.
SWING
BAM!
D'oh...
AND JUST LIKE THAT...
...YOU MOVE FIRST, BEFORE THE SOUND.
THIS IS VERY BAD FOR YOUR DANCING!
YOU KNOW...
...HOW ON YOUTUBE, SOMETIMES THE AUDIO AND VIDEO GET OUT OF SYNC?
The lip flaps don't match...
DOESN'T IT JUST BUG THE HECK OUT OF YOU?
THE SAME THING CAN HAPPEN IN DANCE.

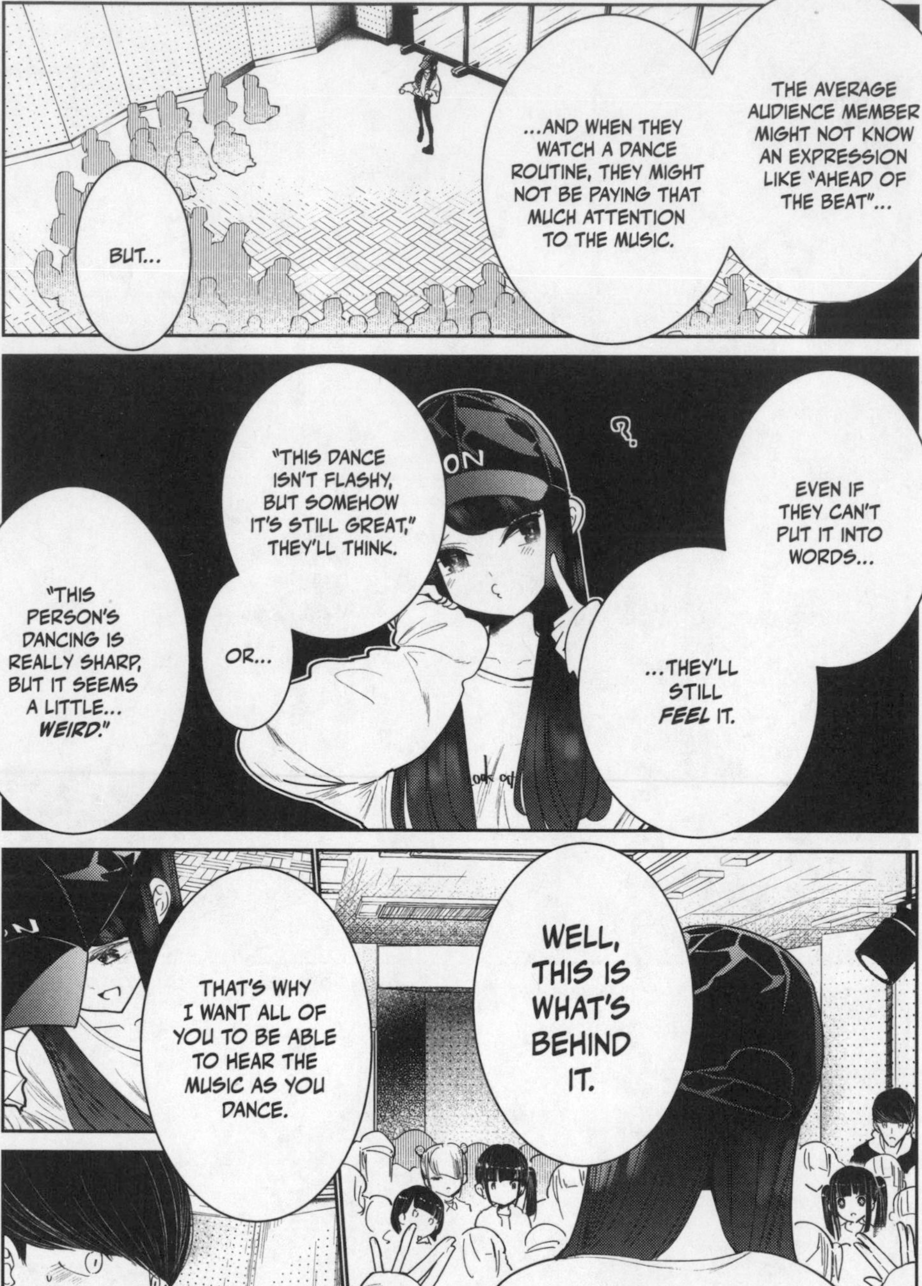
THE AVERAGE AUDIENCE MEMBER MIGHT NOT KNOW AN EXPRESSION LIKE "AHEAD OF THE BEAT"...
...AND WHEN THEY WATCH A DANCE ROUTINE, THEY MIGHT NOT BE PAYING THAT MUCH ATTENTION TO THE MUSIC.
BUT...
EVEN IF THEY CAN'T PUT IT INTO WORDS...
...THEY'LL STILL *FEEL* IT.
?
"THIS DANCE ISN'T FLASHY, BUT SOMEHOW IT'S STILL GREAT," THEY'LL THINK.
OR...
"THIS PERSON'S DANCING IS REALLY SHARP, BUT IT SEEMS A LITTLE... *WEIRD.*"
WELL, THIS IS WHAT'S BEHIND IT.
THAT'S WHY I WANT ALL OF YOU TO BE ABLE TO HEAR THE MUSIC AS YOU DANCE.

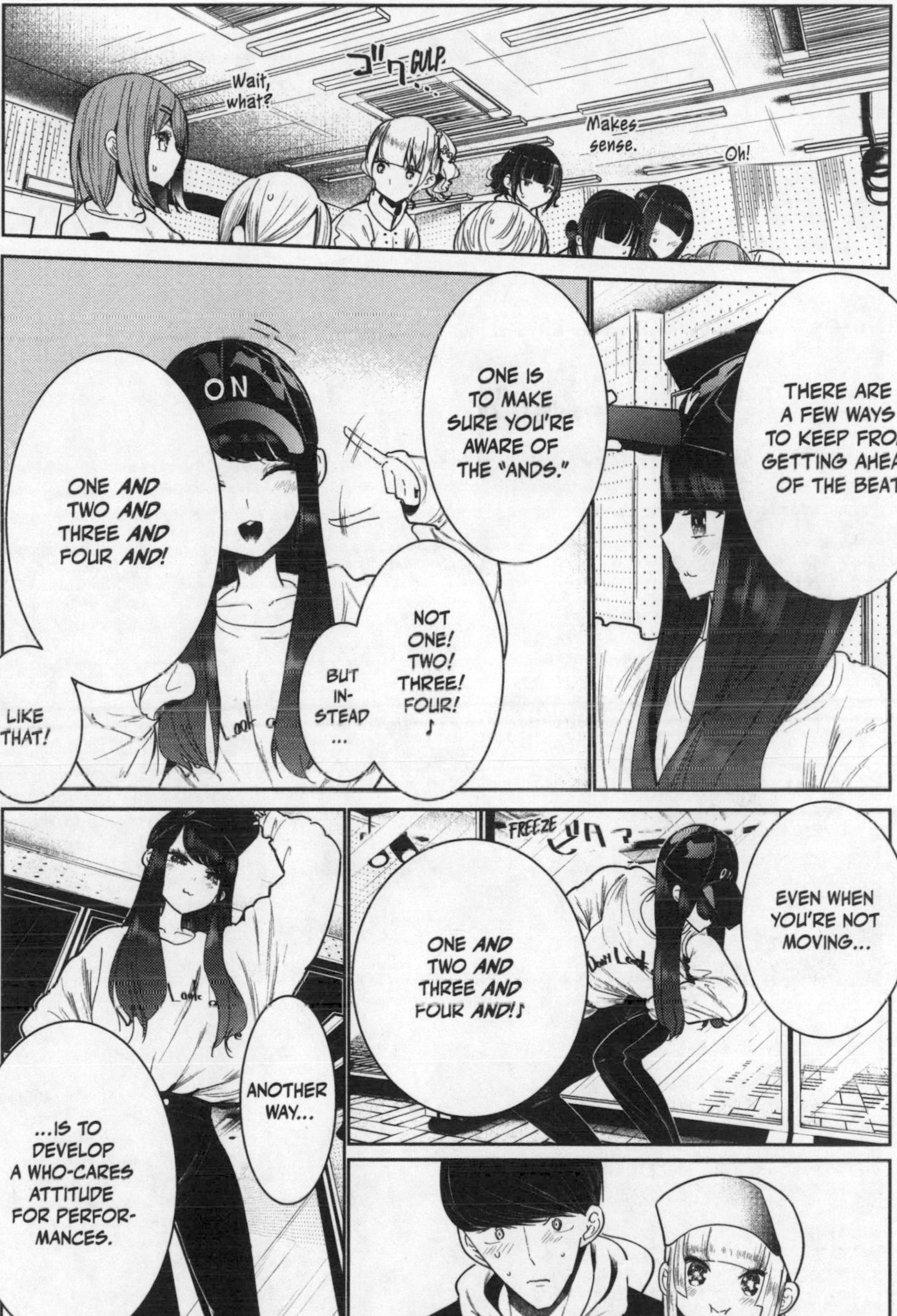
Oh!
Makes sense.
ゴクッ GULP
Wait, what?
THERE ARE A FEW WAYS TO KEEP FROM GETTING AHEAD OF THE BEAT.
ONE IS TO MAKE SURE YOU'RE AWARE OF THE "ANDS."
NOT ONE! TWO! THREE! FOUR! ♪
BUT IN-STEAD ...
ONE *AND* TWO *AND* THREE *AND* FOUR *AND*!
LIKE THAT!
FREEZE ピタッ
EVEN WHEN YOU'RE NOT MOVING...
ONE *AND* TWO *AND* THREE *AND* FOUR *AND*! ♪
ANOTHER WAY...
...IS TO DEVELOP A WHO-CARES ATTITUDE FOR PERFOR-MANCES.

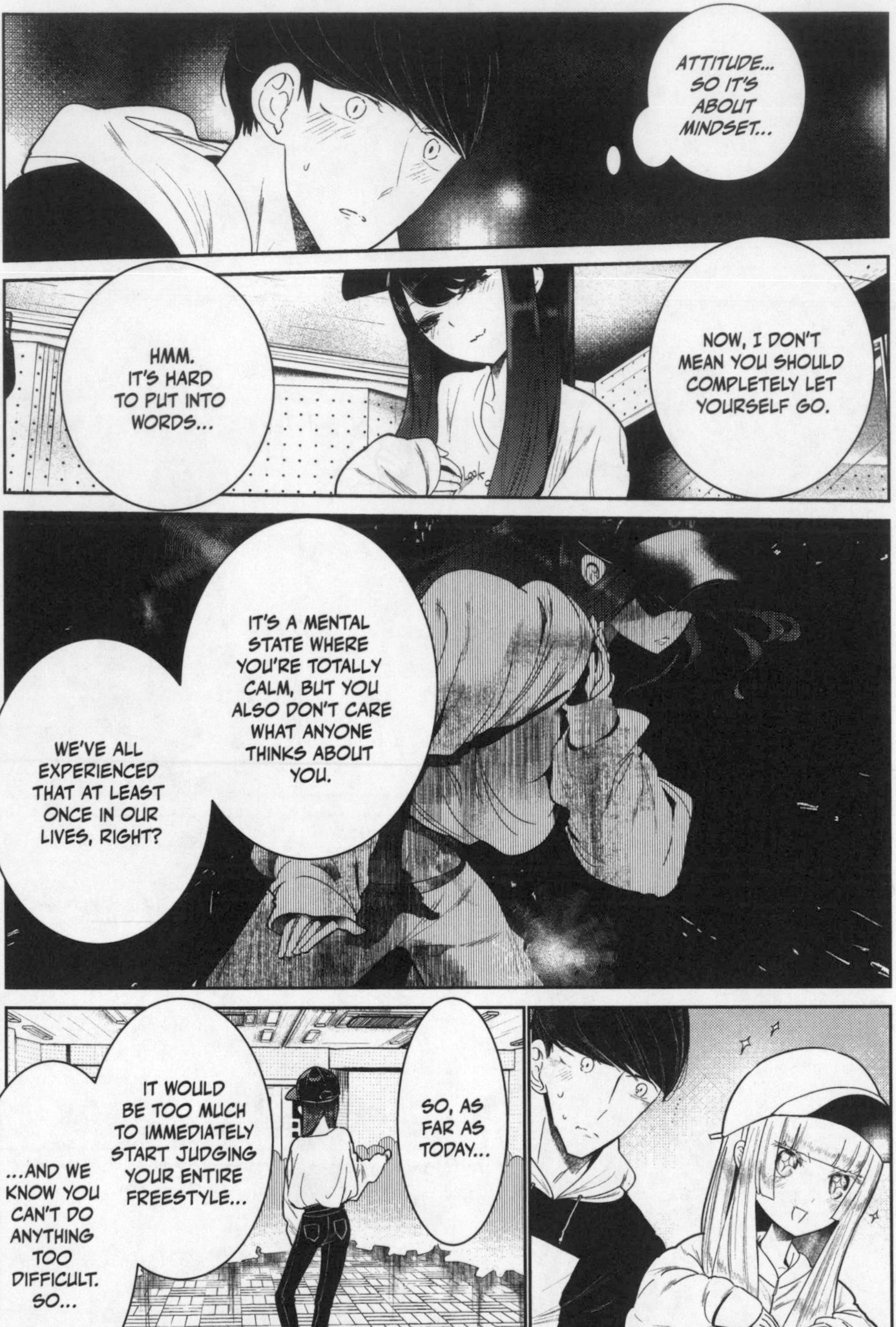
ATTITUDE... SO IT'S ABOUT MINDSET...
NOW, I DON'T MEAN YOU SHOULD COMPLETELY LET YOURSELF GO.
HMM. IT'S HARD TO PUT INTO WORDS...
IT'S A MENTAL STATE WHERE YOU'RE TOTALLY CALM, BUT YOU ALSO DON'T CARE WHAT ANYONE THINKS ABOUT YOU.
WE'VE ALL EXPERIENCED THAT AT LEAST ONCE IN OUR LIVES, RIGHT?
SO, AS FAR AS TODAY...
IT WOULD BE TOO MUCH TO IMMEDIATELY START JUDGING YOUR ENTIRE FREESTYLE...
...AND WE KNOW YOU CAN'T DO ANYTHING TOO DIFFICULT. SO...

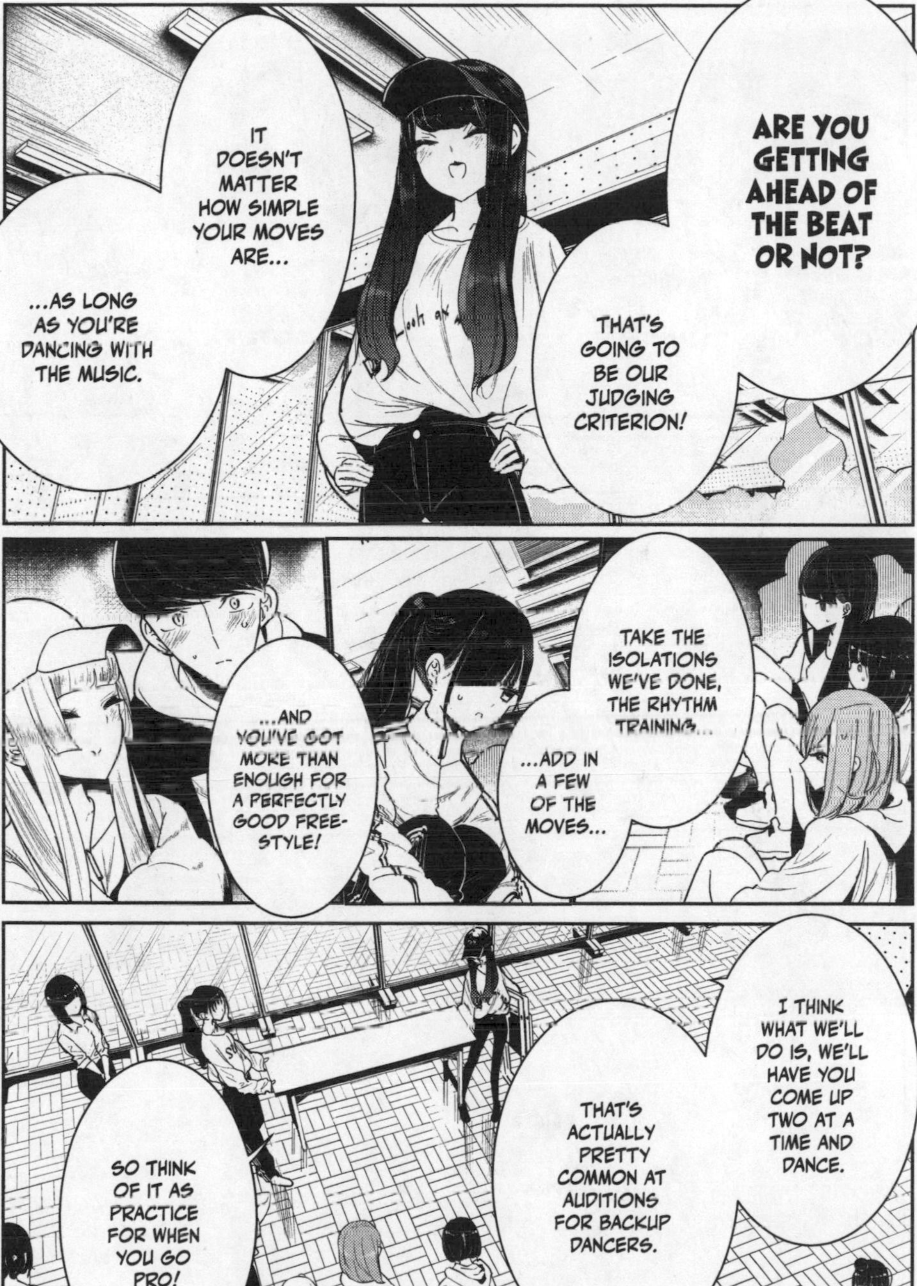
ARE YOU GETTING AHEAD OF THE BEAT OR NOT?
THAT'S GOING TO BE OUR JUDGING CRITERION!
IT DOESN'T MATTER HOW SIMPLE YOUR MOVES ARE...
...AS LONG AS YOU'RE DANCING WITH THE MUSIC.
TAKE THE ISOLATIONS WE'VE DONE, THE RHYTHM TRAINING...
...ADD IN A FEW OF THE MOVES...
...AND YOU'VE GOT MORE THAN ENOUGH FOR A PERFECTLY GOOD FREE-STYLE!
I THINK WHAT WE'LL DO IS, WE'LL HAVE YOU COME UP TWO AT A TIME AND DANCE.
THAT'S ACTUALLY PRETTY COMMON AT AUDITIONS FOR BACKUP DANCERS.
SO THINK OF IT AS PRACTICE FOR WHEN YOU GO PRO!

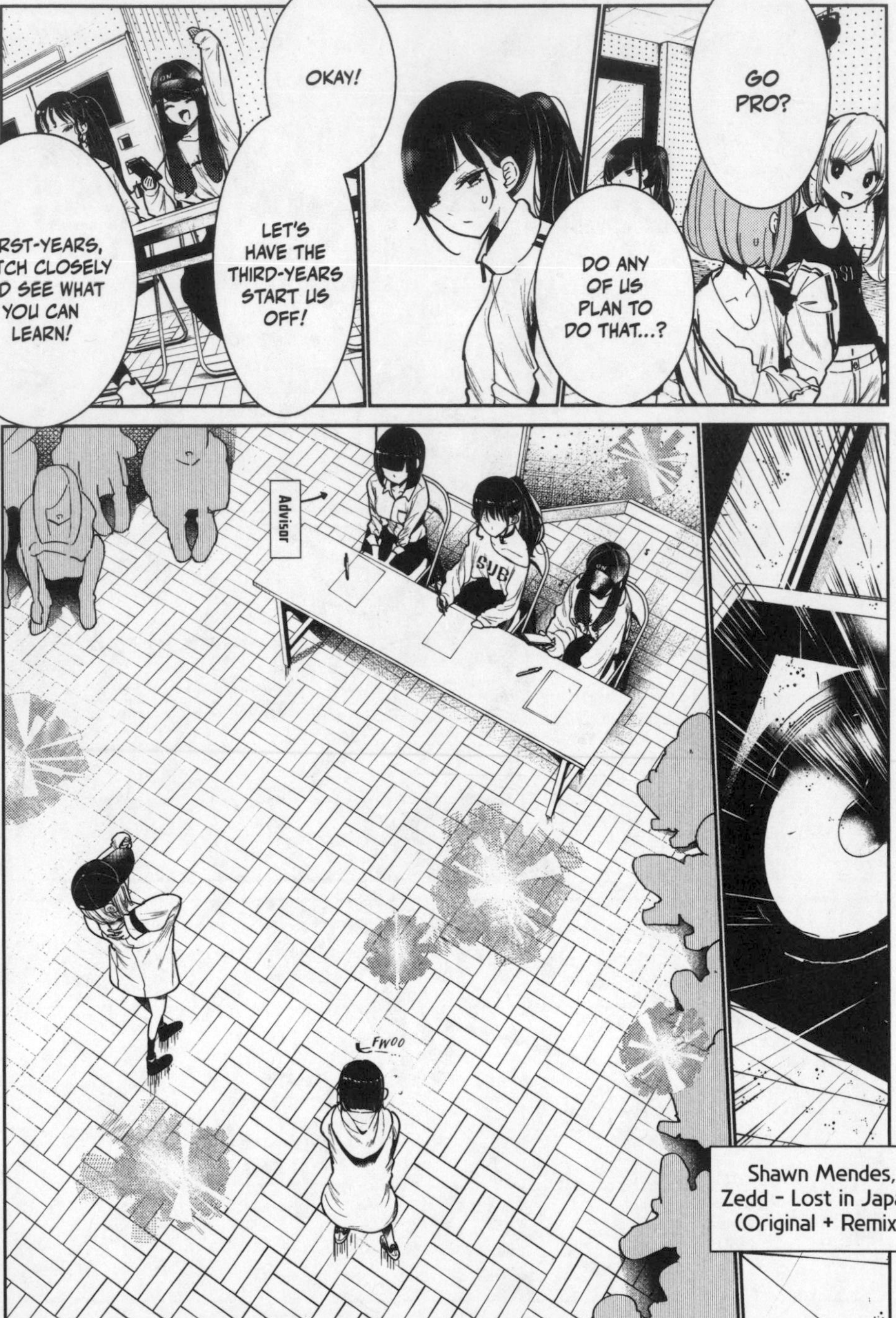
GO PRO?
DO ANY OF US PLAN TO DO THAT...?
OKAY!
LET'S HAVE THE THIRD-YEARS START US OFF!
FIRST-YEARS, WATCH CLOSELY AND SEE WHAT YOU CAN LEARN!
Shawn Mendes, Zedd - Lost in Japan (Original + Remix)
Advisor
FWOO

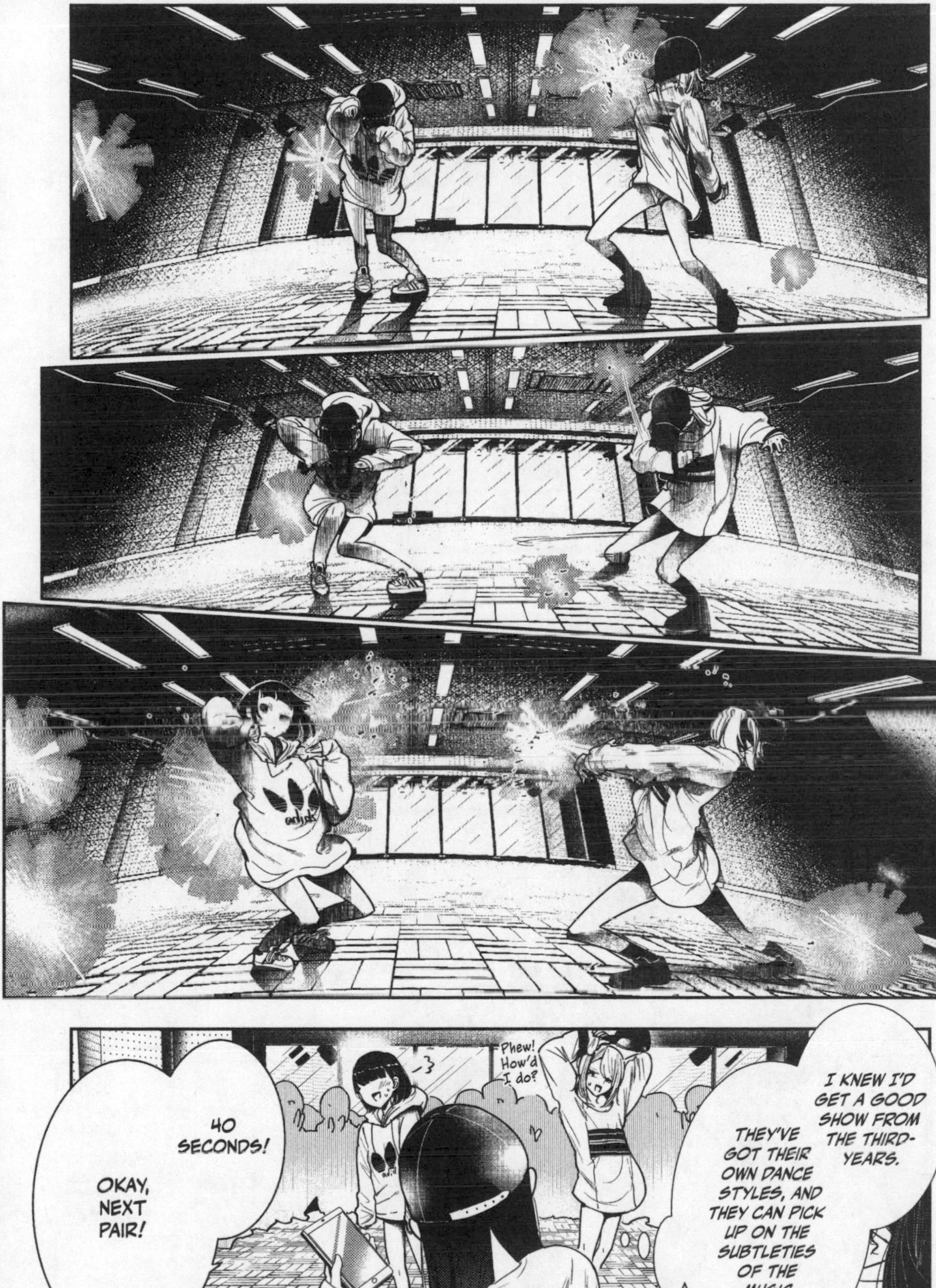
I KNEW I'D GET A GOOD SHOW FROM THE THIRD-YEARS.
THEY'VE GOT THEIR OWN DANCE STYLES, AND THEY CAN PICK UP ON THE SUBTLETIES OF THE MUSIC.
Phew! How'd I do?
40 SECONDS!
OKAY, NEXT PAIR!

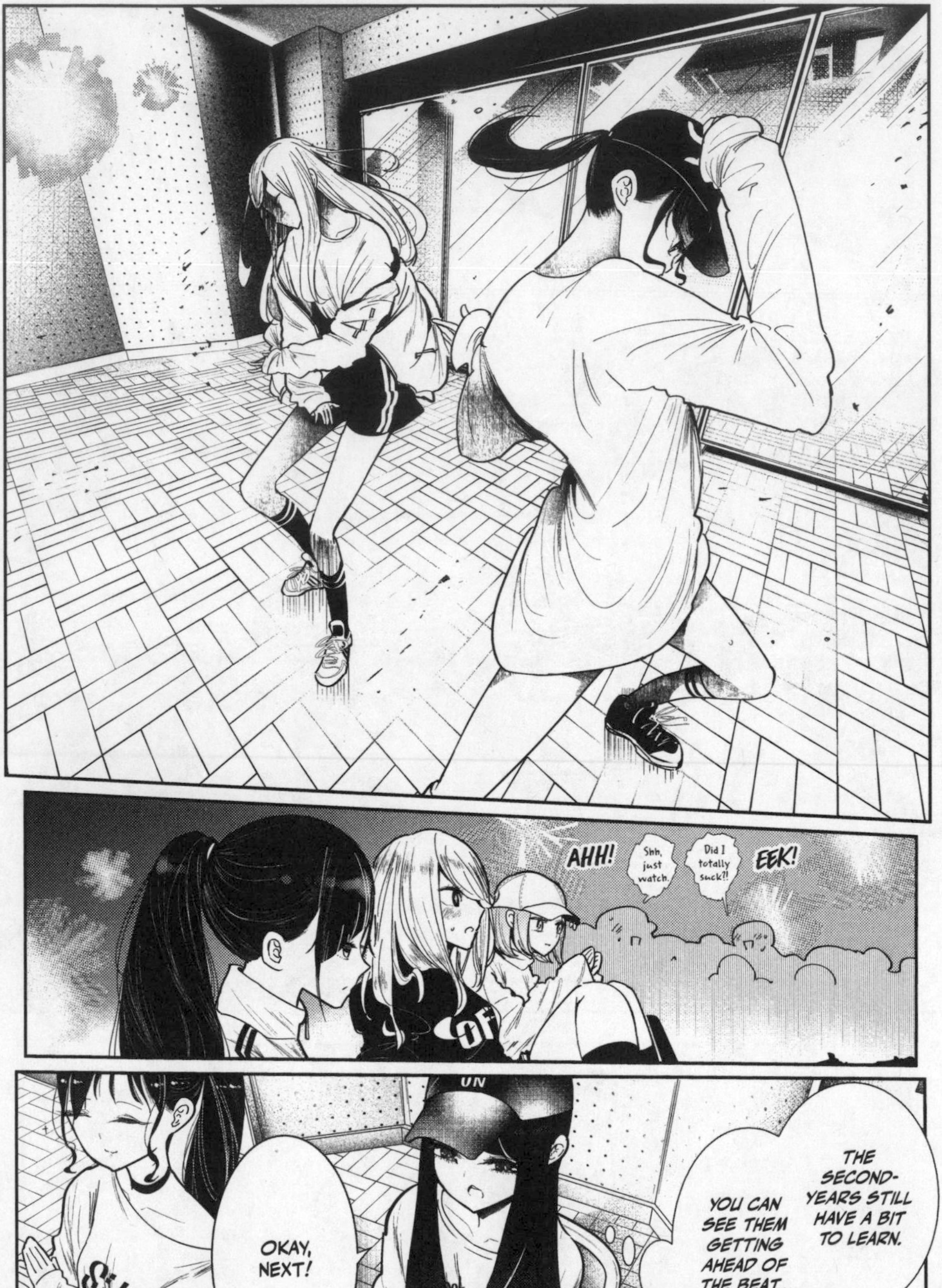
EEK!
Did I totally suck?!
Shh, just watch.
AHH!
THE SECOND-YEARS STILL HAVE A BIT TO LEARN.
YOU CAN SEE THEM GETTING AHEAD OF THE BEAT...
OKAY, NEXT!

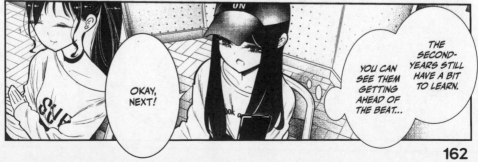

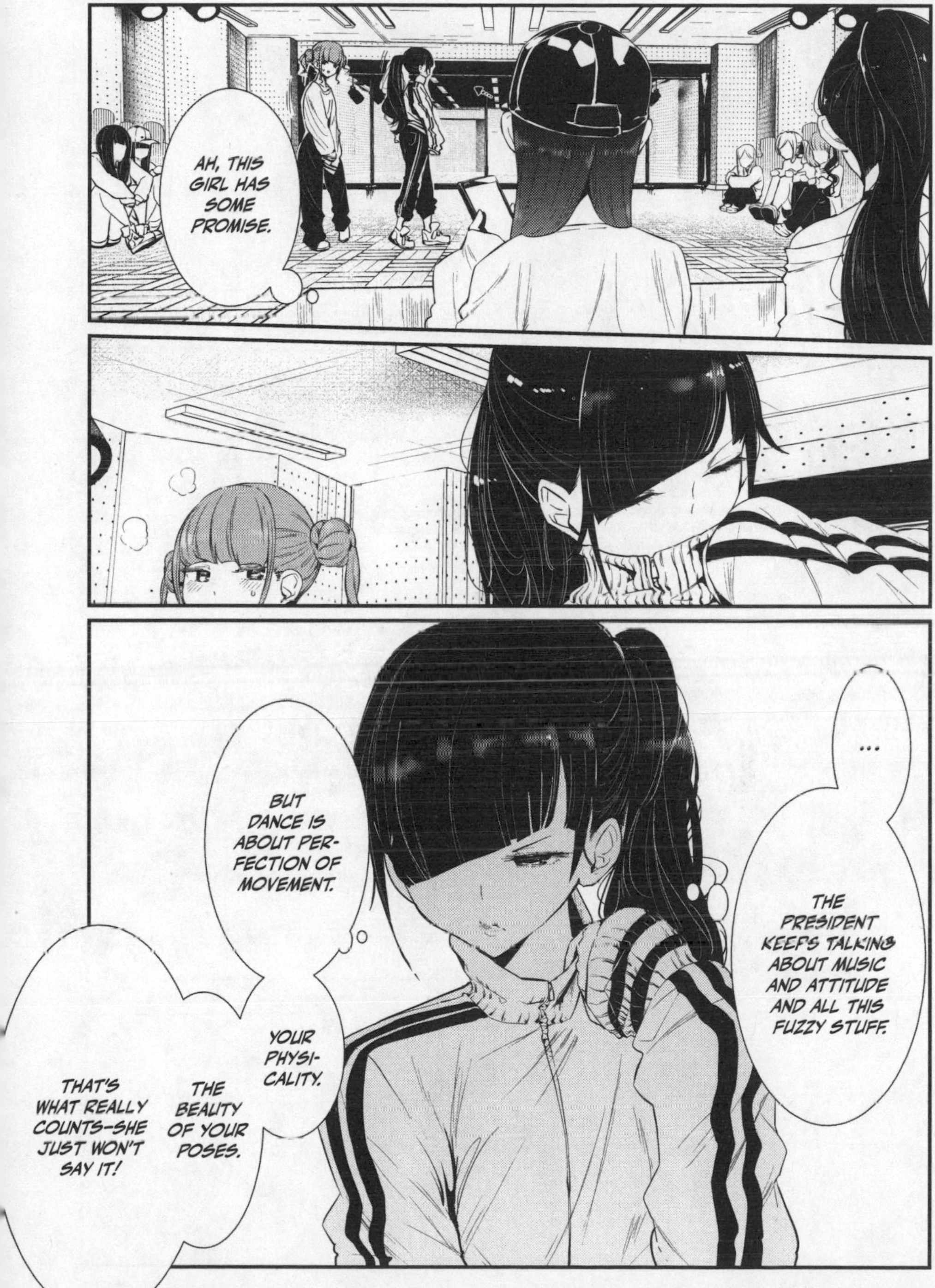
AH, THIS GIRL HAS SOME PROMISE.
... THE PRESIDENT KEEPS TALKING ABOUT MUSIC AND ATTITUDE AND ALL THIS FUZZY STUFF.
BUT DANCE IS ABOUT PERFECTION OF MOVEMENT.
YOUR PHYSICALITY.
THE BEAUTY OF YOUR POSES.
THAT'S WHAT REALLY COUNTS—SHE JUST WON'T SAY IT!

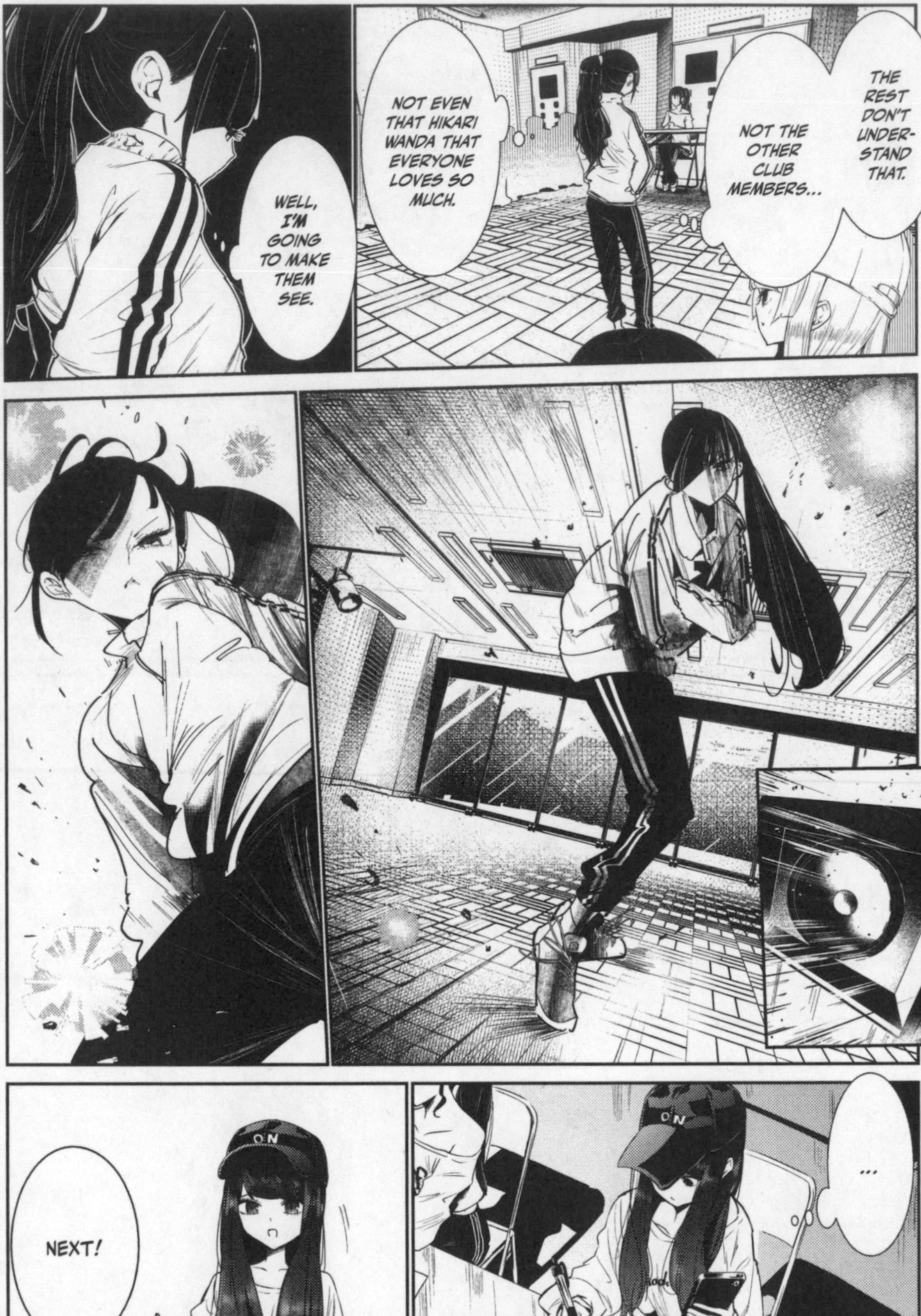
THE REST DON'T UNDER-STAND THAT.
NOT THE OTHER CLUB MEMBERS...
NOT EVEN THAT HIKARI WANDA THAT EVERYONE LOVES SO MUCH.
WELL, I'M GOING TO MAKE THEM SEE.
...
NEXT!

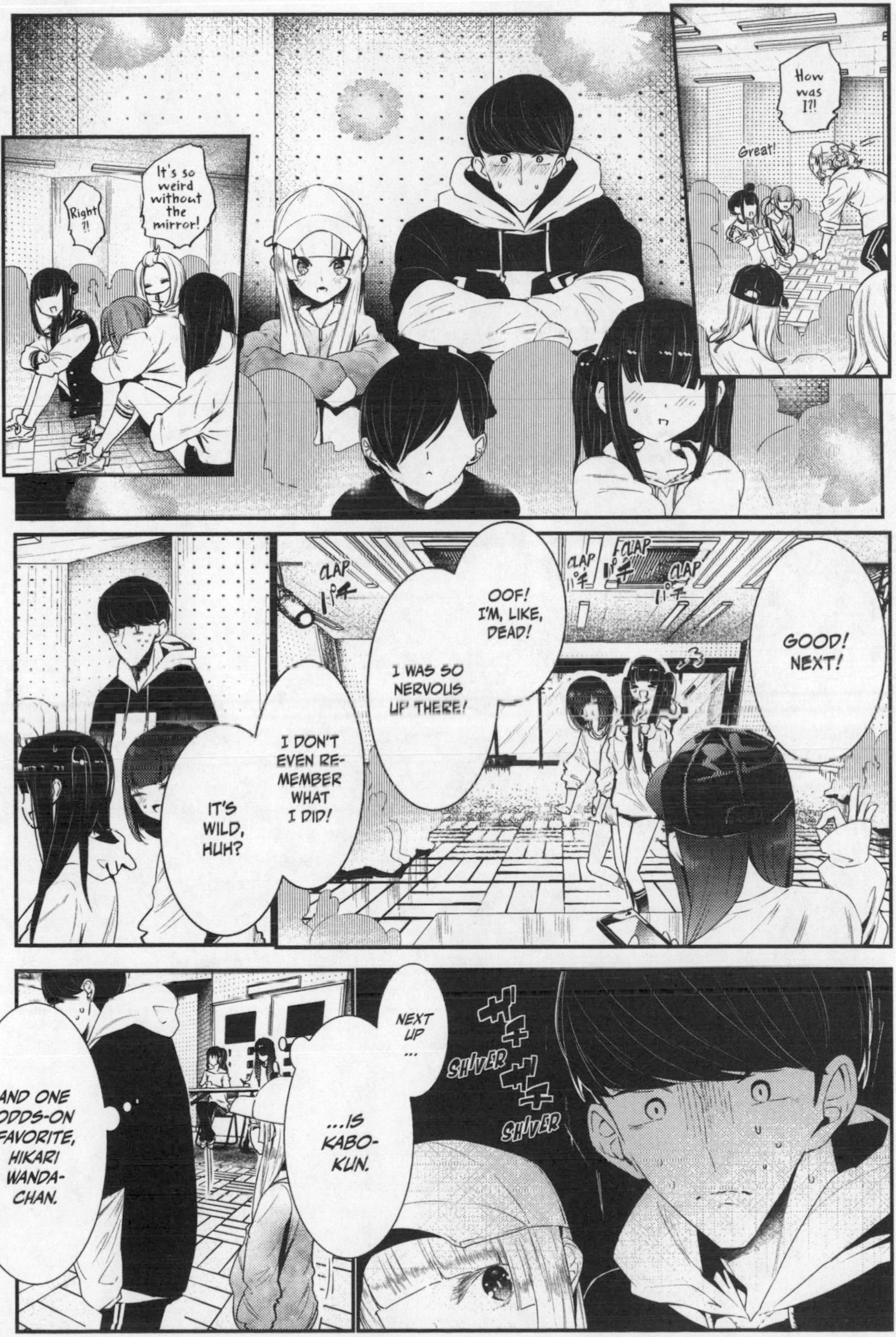
How was I?!
Great!
It's so weird without the mirror!
Right?!
GOOD! NEXT!
CLAP
CLAP
CLAP
CLAP
OOF! I'M, LIKE, DEAD!
I WAS SO NERVOUS UP THERE!
I DON'T EVEN RE-MEMBER WHAT I DID!
IT'S WILD, HUH?
SHIVER
SHIVER
NEXT UP ...
...IS KABO-KUN.
AND ONE ODDS-ON FAVORITE, HIKARI WANDA-CHAN.

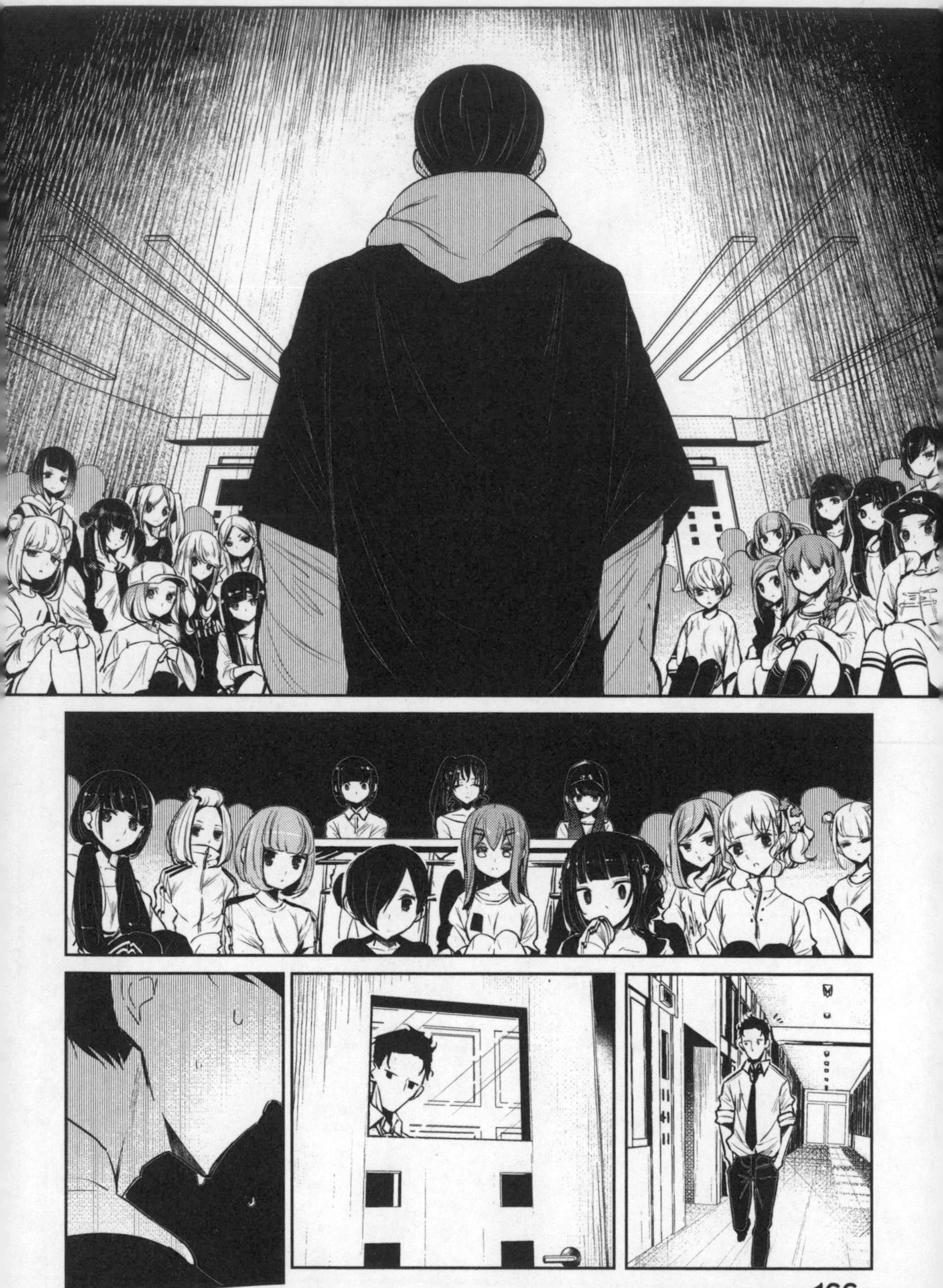

GLUB

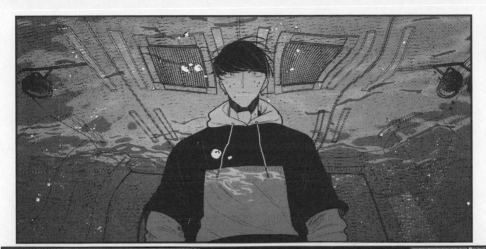

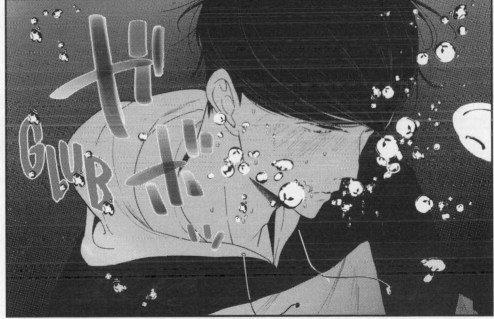

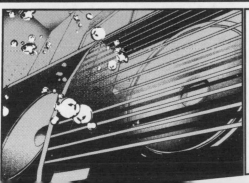

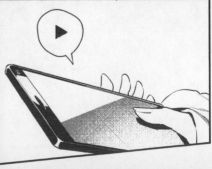

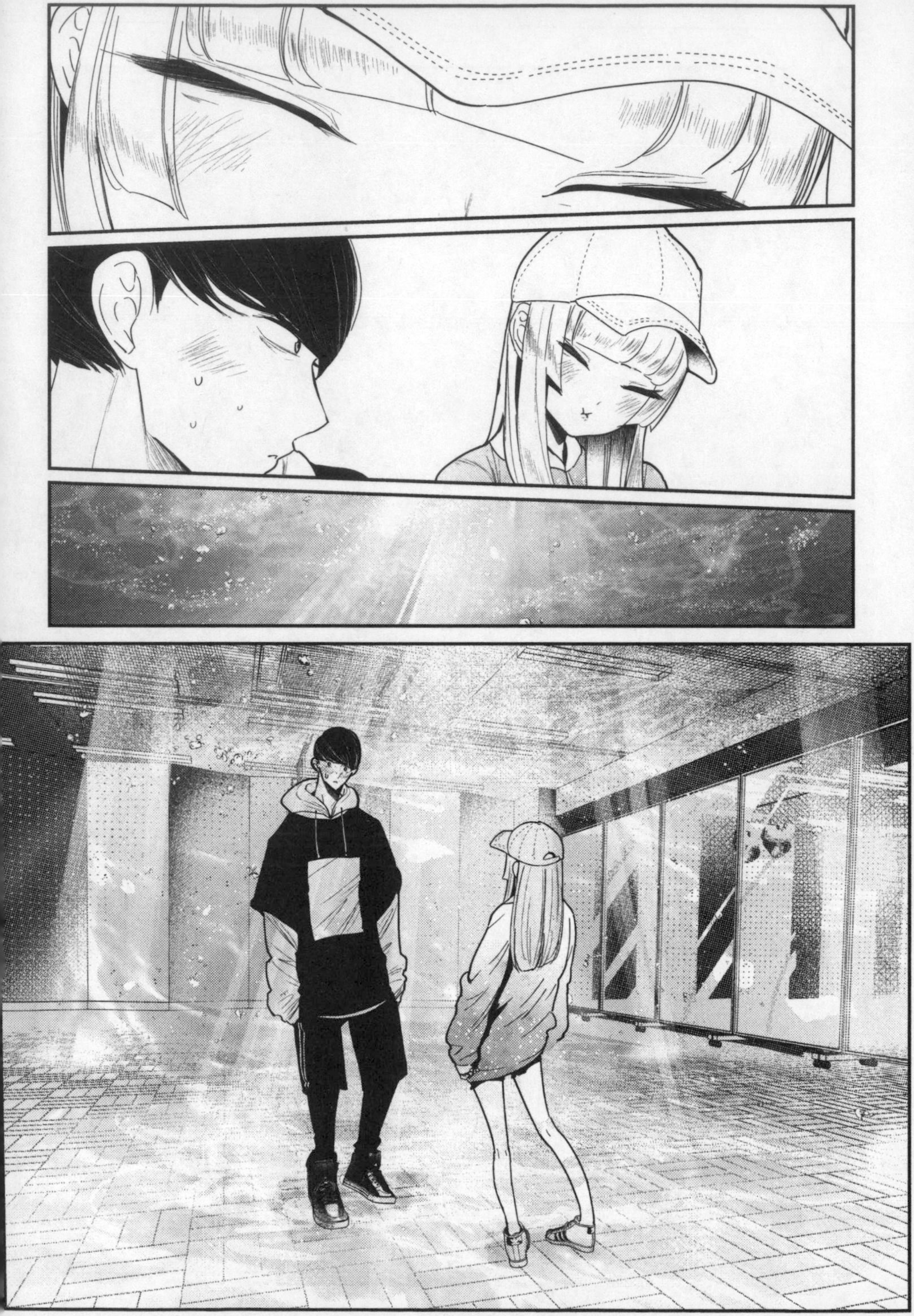

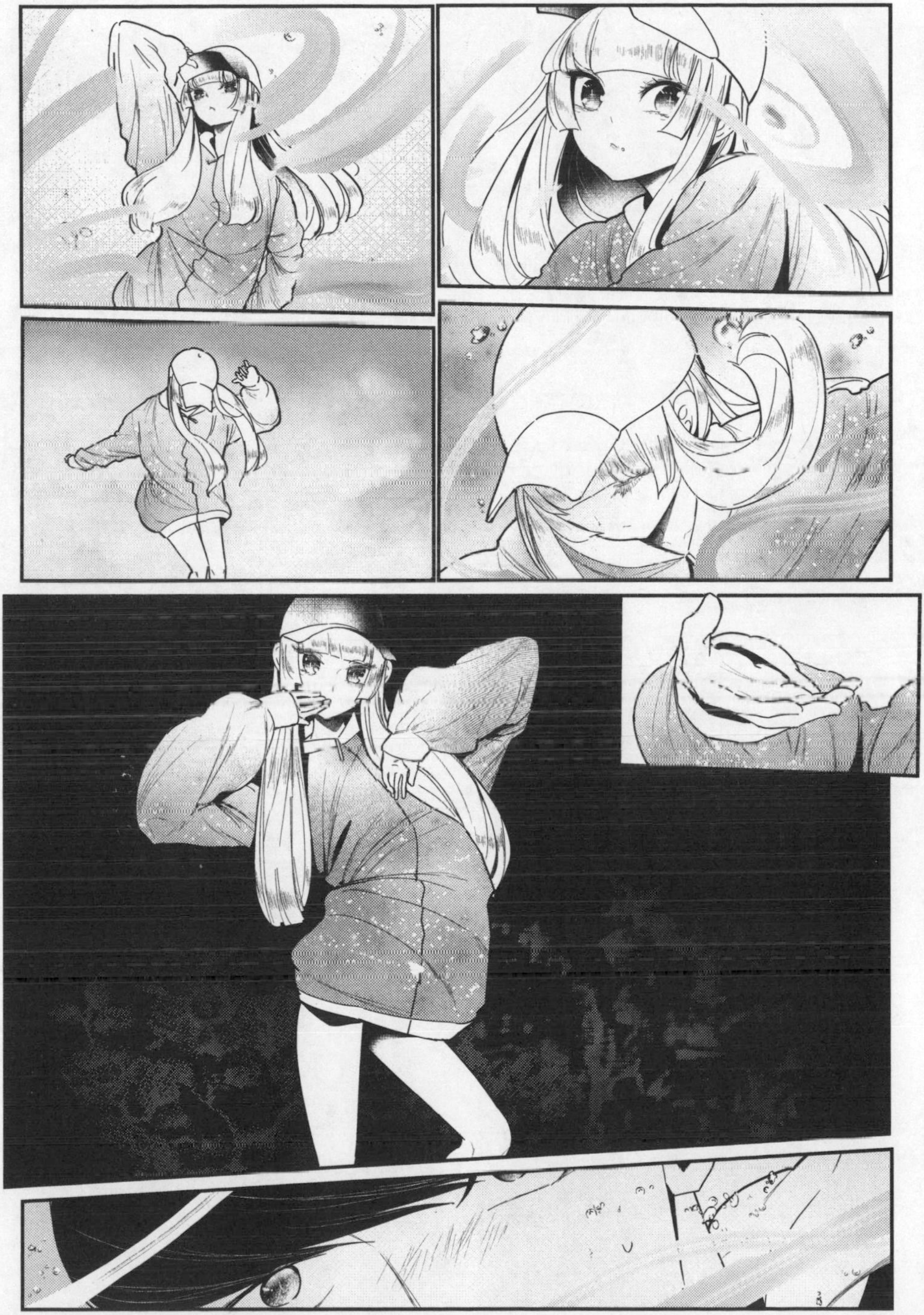

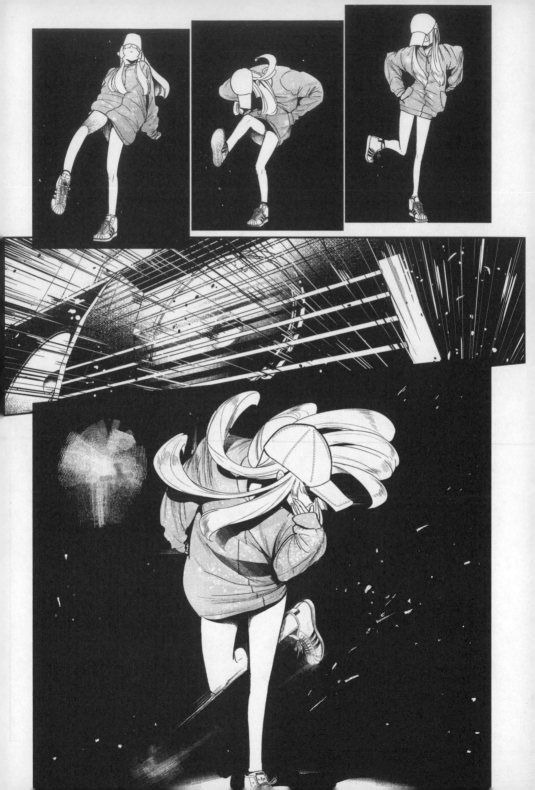

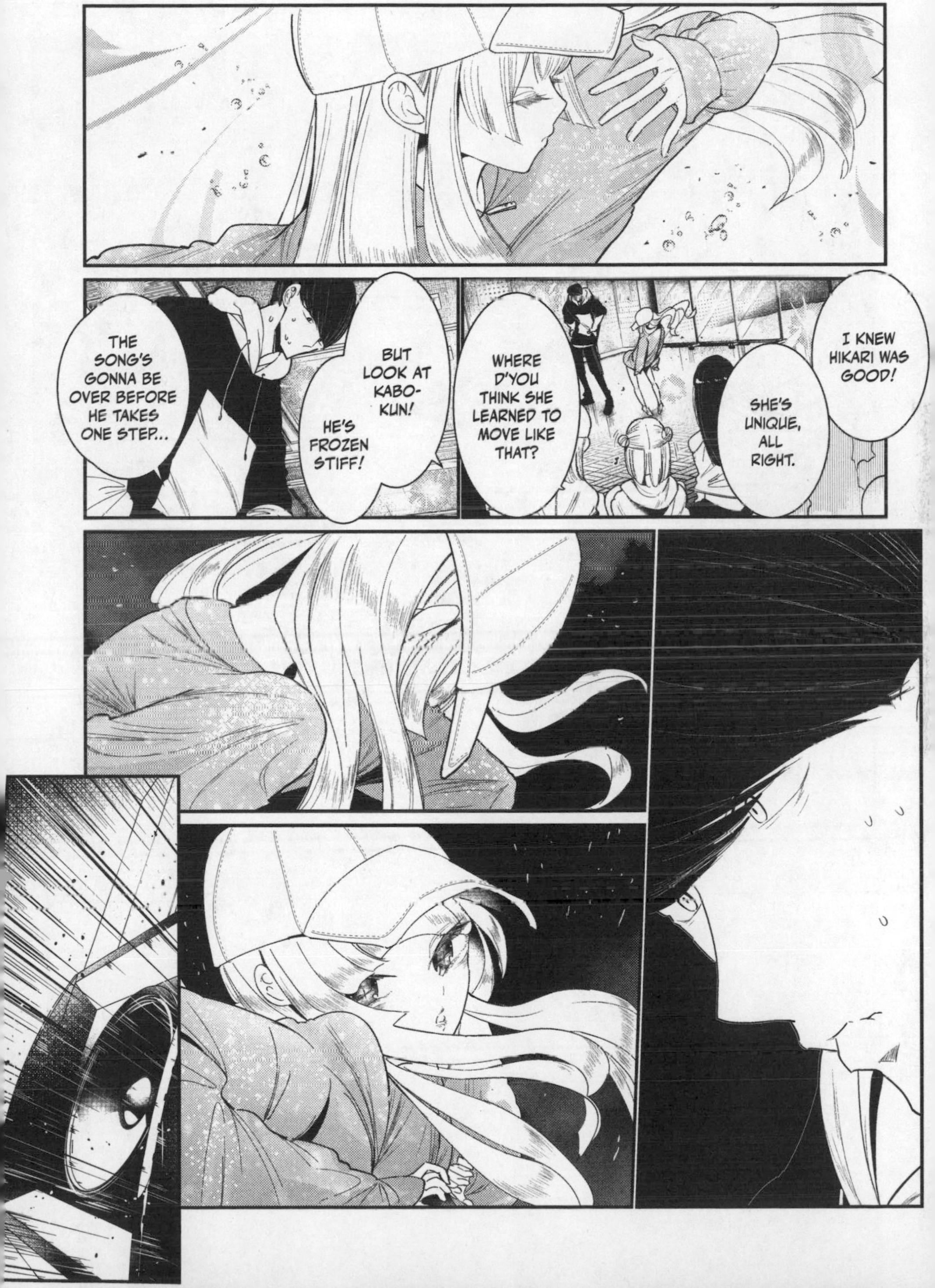
I KNEW HIKARI WAS GOOD!
SHE'S UNIQUE, ALL RIGHT.
WHERE D'YOU THINK SHE LEARNED TO MOVE LIKE THAT?
BUT LOOK AT KABO-KUN!
HE'S FROZEN STIFF!
THE SONG'S GONNA BE OVER BEFORE HE TAKES ONE STEP...

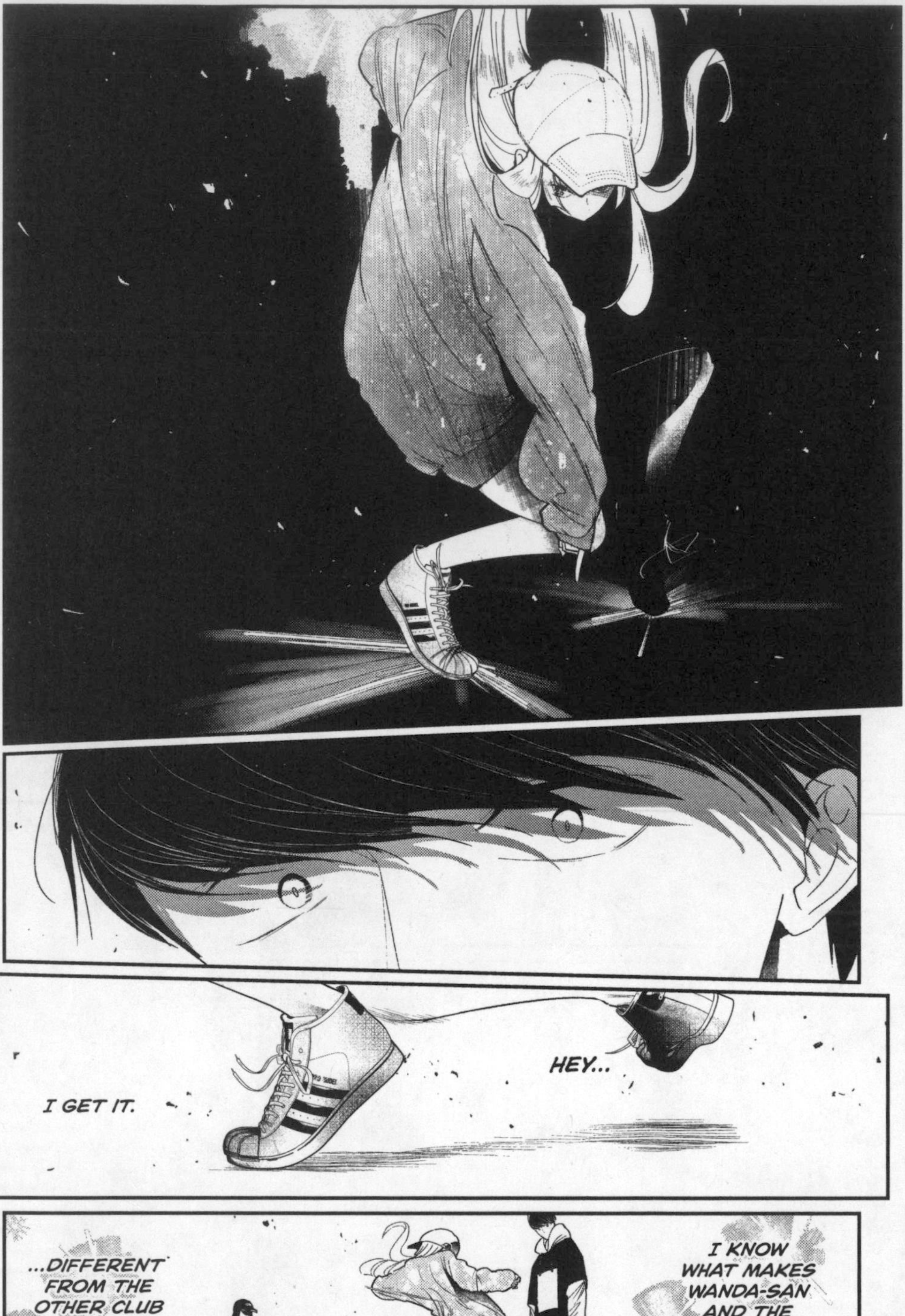
HEY...
I GET IT.
I KNOW WHAT MAKES WANDA-SAN AND THE PREZ...
...DIFFERENT FROM THE OTHER CLUB MEMBERS.

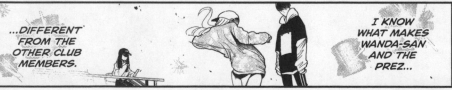

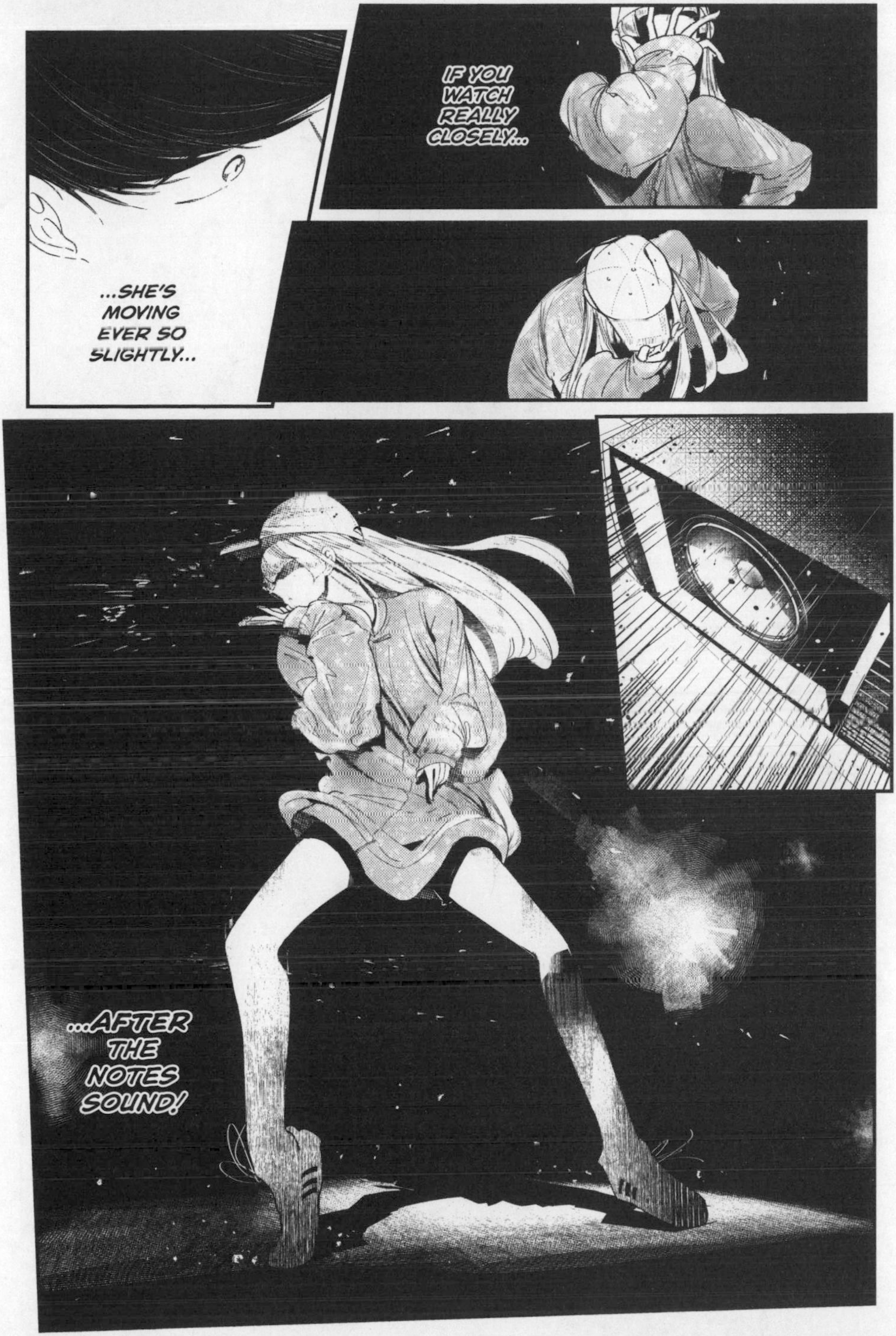
IF YOU WATCH REALLY CLOSELY...
...SHE'S MOVING EVER SO SLIGHTLY...
...AFTER THE NOTES SOUND!

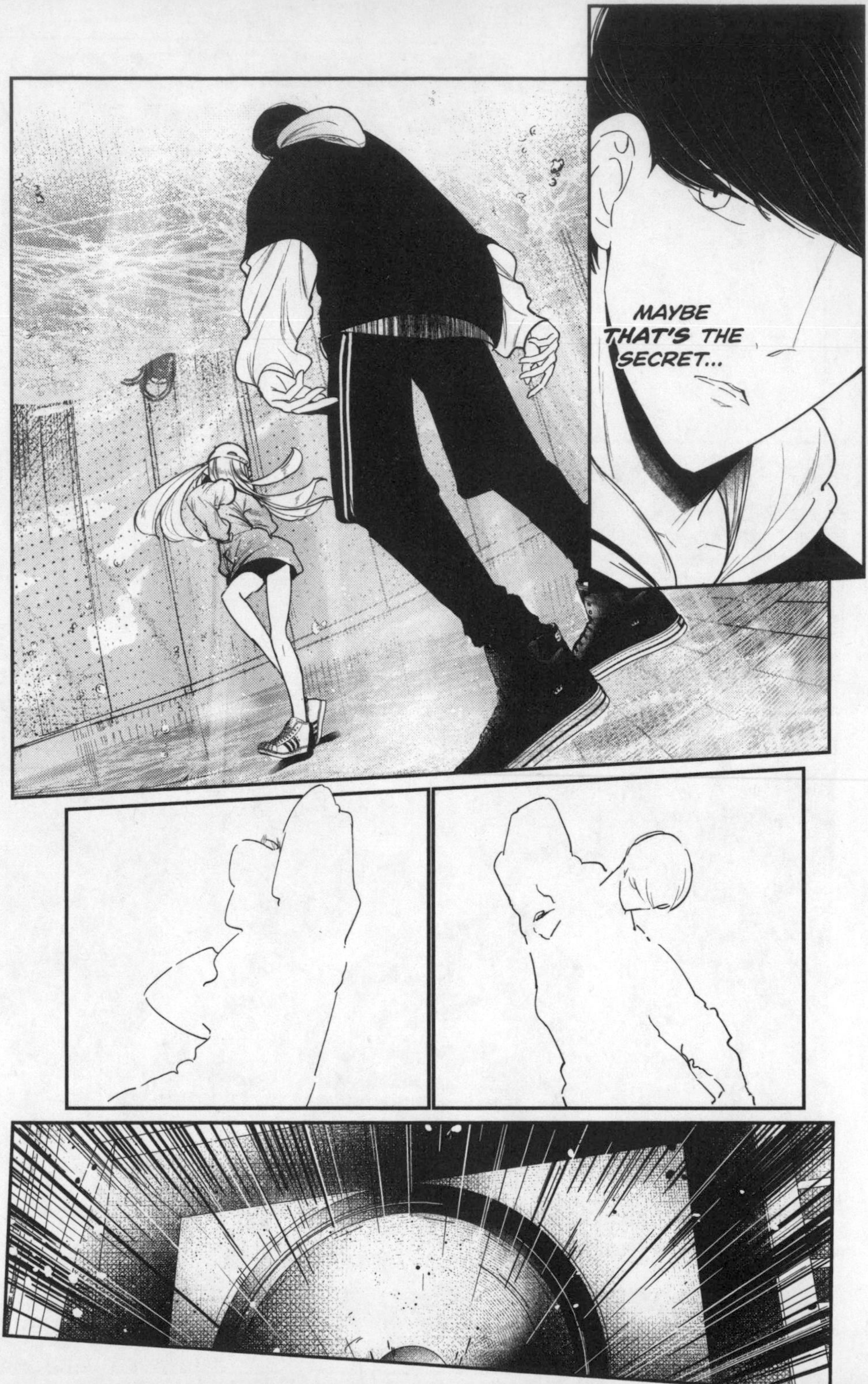
MAYBE THAT'S THE SECRET...

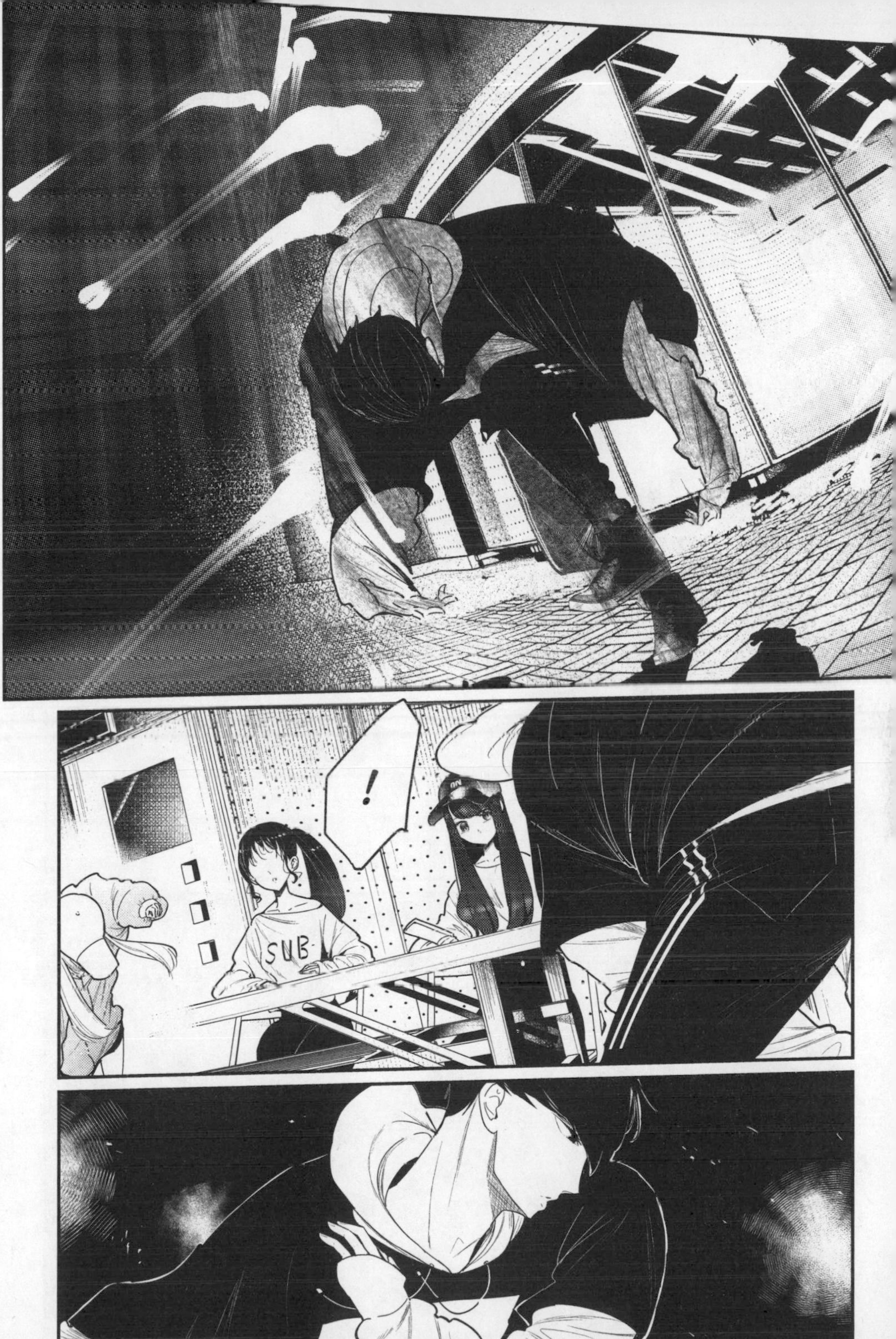
!
SUB

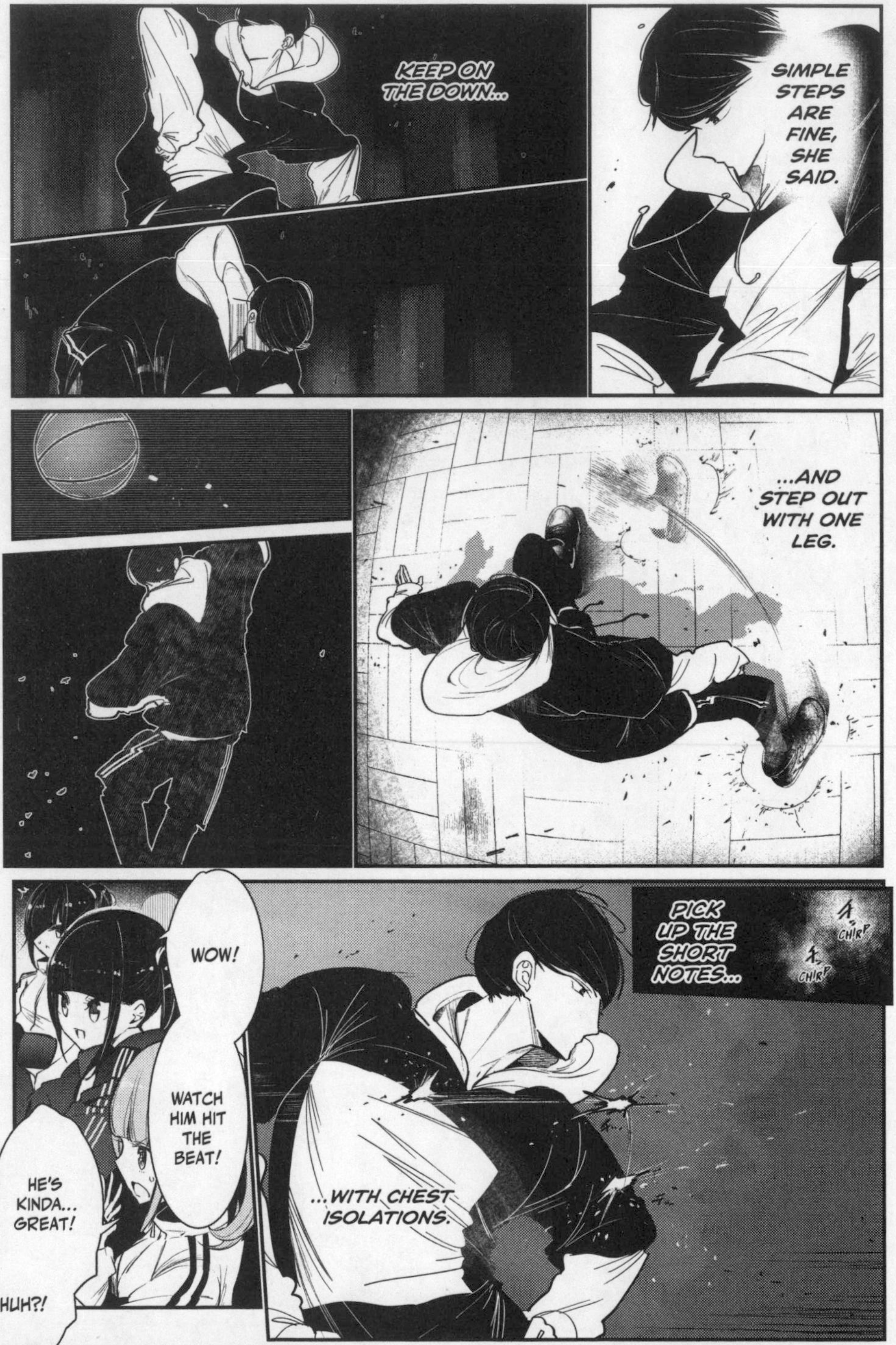
SIMPLE STEPS ARE FINE, SHE SAID.
KEEP ON THE DOWN...
...AND STEP OUT WITH ONE LEG.
PICK UP THE SHORT NOTES...
CHIRP
CHIRP
...WITH CHEST ISOLATIONS.
WOW!
WATCH HIM HIT THE BEAT!
HE'S KINDA... GREAT!
HUH?!

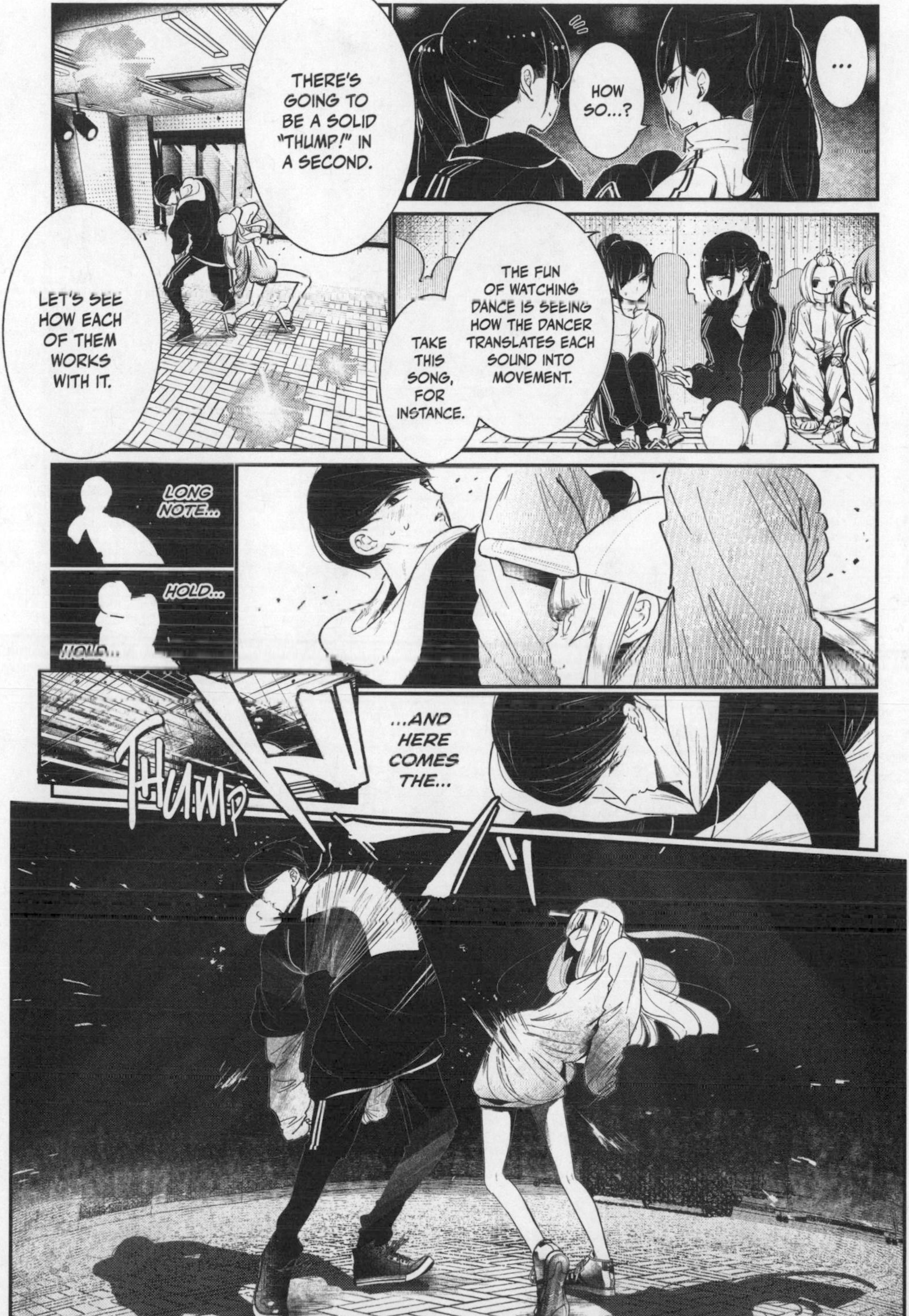
...
HOW SO...?
THE FUN OF WATCHING DANCE IS SEEING HOW THE DANCER TRANSLATES EACH SOUND INTO MOVEMENT.
TAKE THIS SONG, FOR INSTANCE.
THERE'S GOING TO BE A SOLID "THUMP!" IN A SECOND.
LET'S SEE HOW EACH OF THEM WORKS WITH IT.
LONG NOTE...
HOLD...
HOLD...
...AND HERE COMES THE...
THUMP

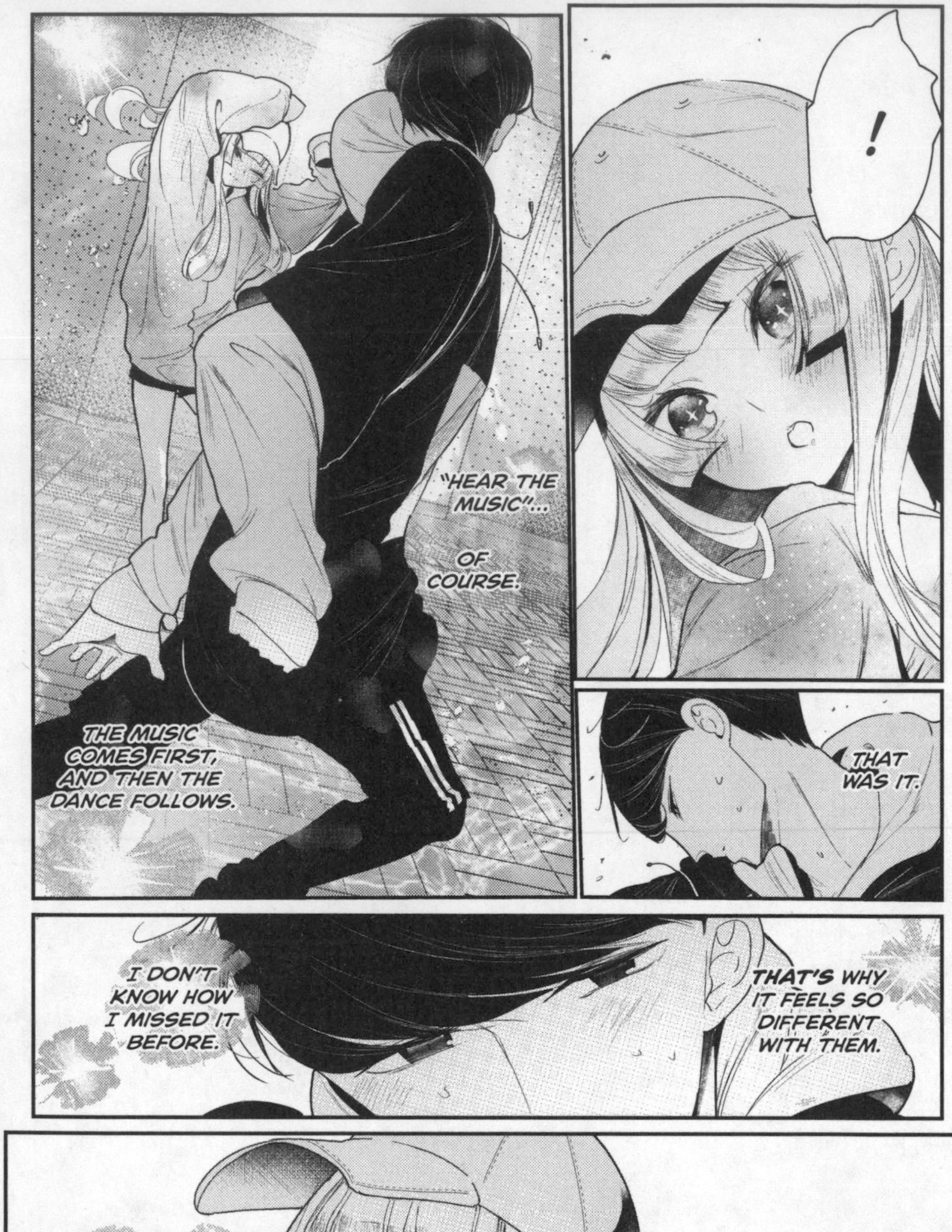
!
THAT WAS IT.
"HEAR THE MUSIC"...
OF COURSE.
THE MUSIC COMES FIRST, AND THEN THE DANCE FOLLOWS.
THAT'S WHY IT FEELS SO DIFFERENT WITH THEM.
I DON'T KNOW HOW I MISSED IT BEFORE.
BUT IT WAS WANDA-SAN WHO HELPED ME FIGURE IT OUT.

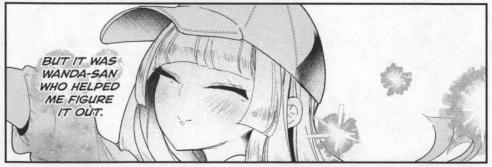

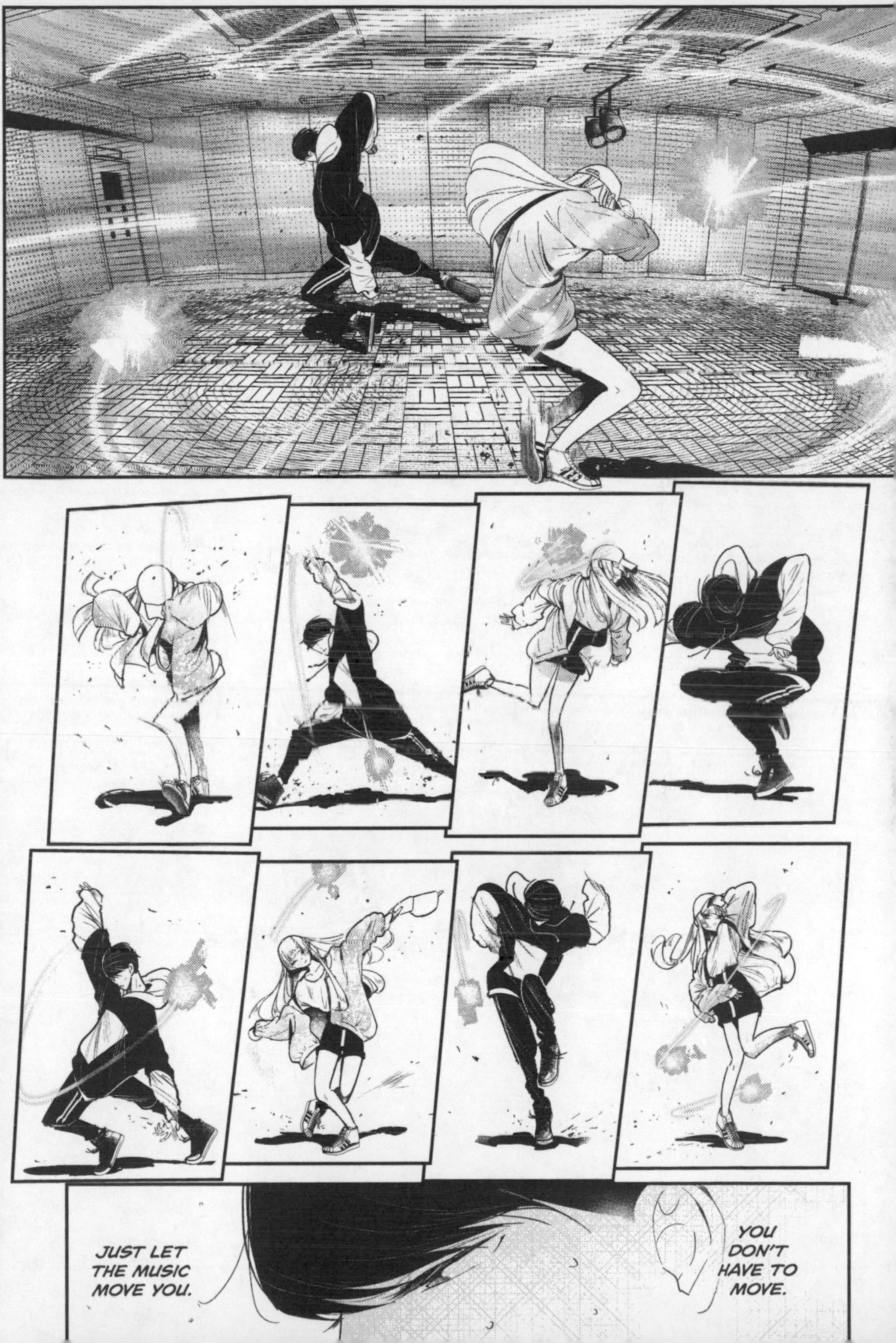
YOU DON'T HAVE TO MOVE.
JUST LET THE MUSIC MOVE YOU.

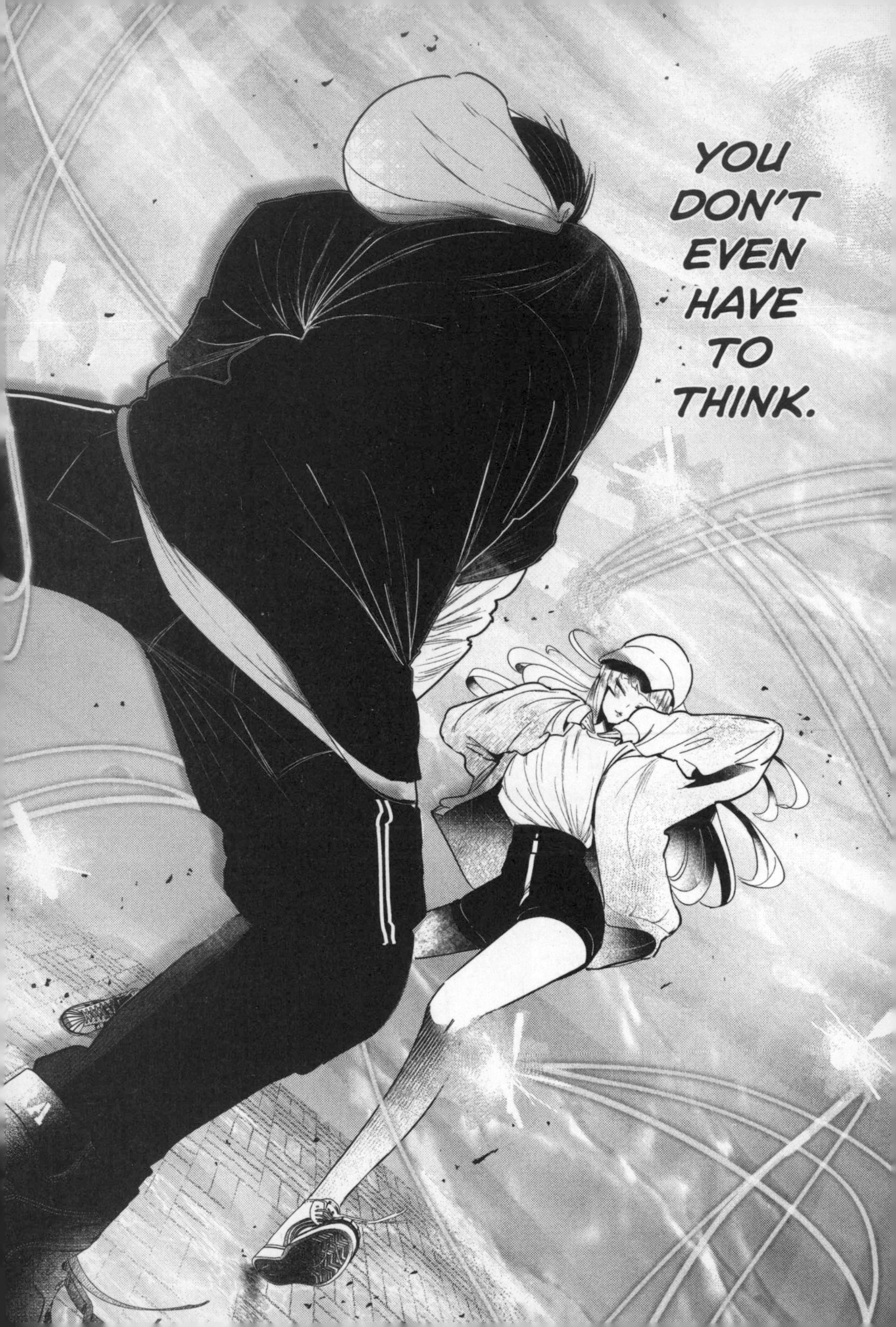
YOU DON'T EVEN HAVE TO THINK.

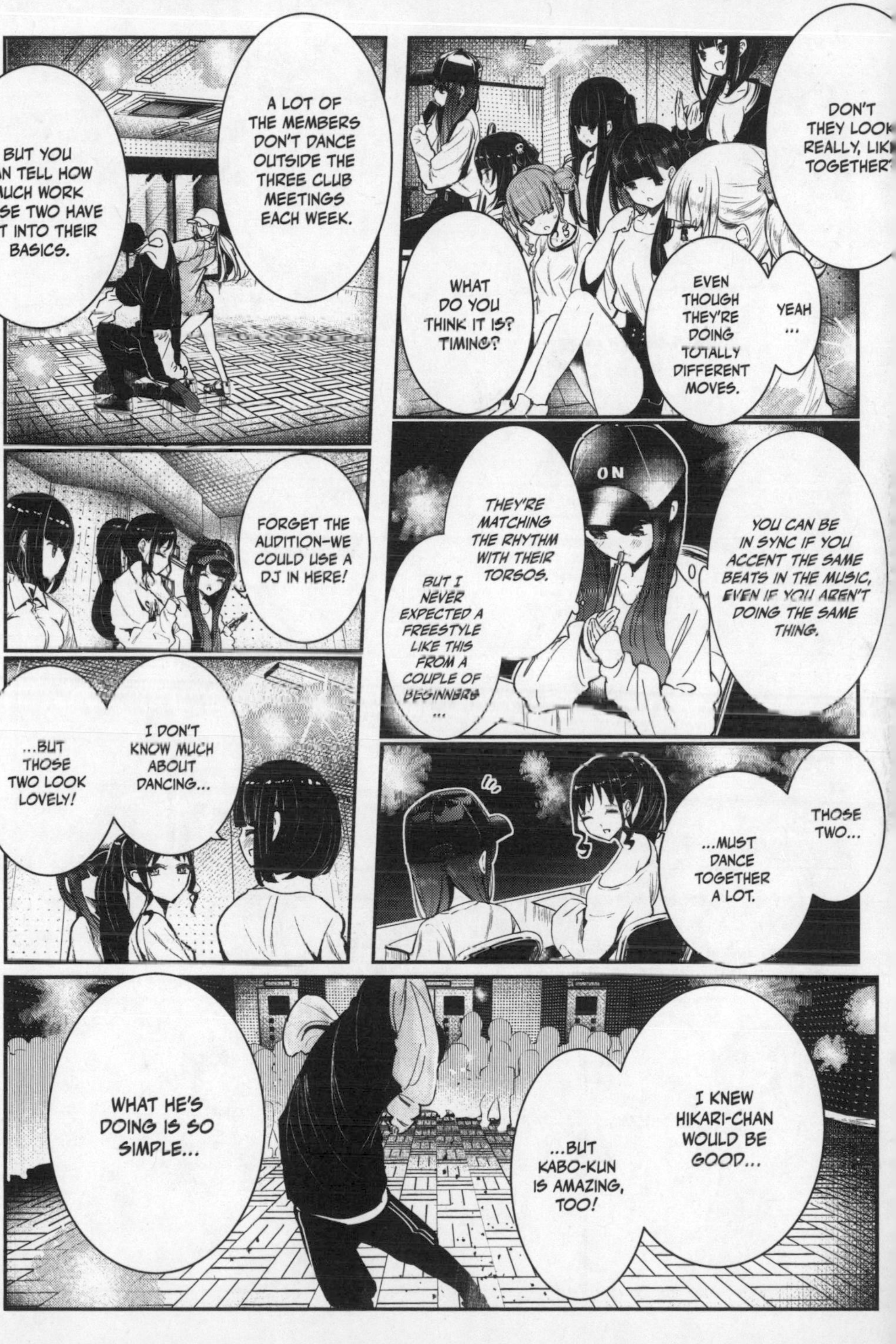
DON'T THEY LOOK REALLY, LIK TOGETHER
YEAH ...
EVEN THOUGH THEY'RE DOING TOTALLY DIFFERENT MOVES.
WHAT DO YOU THINK IT IS? TIMING?
A LOT OF THE MEMBERS DON'T DANCE OUTSIDE THE THREE CLUB MEETINGS EACH WEEK.
BUT YOU CAN TELL HOW MUCH WORK THESE TWO HAVE PUT INTO THEIR BASICS.
ON
YOU CAN BE IN SYNC IF YOU ACCENT THE SAME BEATS IN THE MUSIC, EVEN IF YOU AREN'T DOING THE SAME THING.
THEY'RE MATCHING THE RHYTHM WITH THEIR TORSOS.
BUT I NEVER EXPECTED A FREESTYLE LIKE THIS FROM A COUPLE OF BEGINNERS ...
THOSE TWO...
...MUST DANCE TOGETHER A LOT.
FORGET THE AUDITION—WE COULD USE A DJ IN HERE!
I DON'T KNOW MUCH ABOUT DANCING...
...BUT THOSE TWO LOOK LOVELY!
I KNEW HIKARI-CHAN WOULD BE GOOD...
...BUT KABO-KUN IS AMAZING, TOO!
WHAT HE'S DOING IS SO SIMPLE...

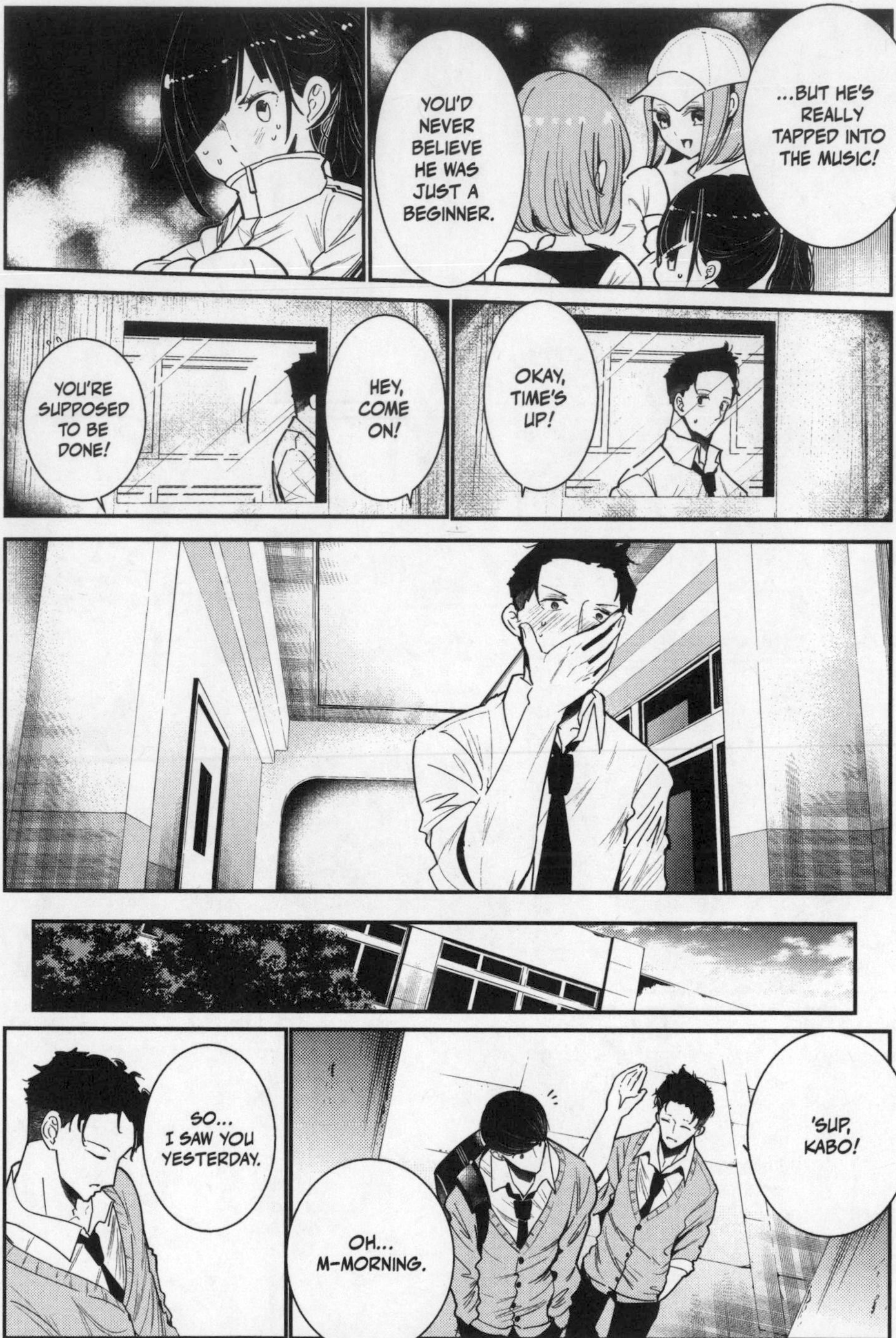
...BUT HE'S REALLY TAPPED INTO THE MUSIC!
YOU'D NEVER BELIEVE HE WAS JUST A BEGINNER.
OKAY, TIME'S UP!
HEY, COME ON!
YOU'RE SUPPOSED TO BE DONE!
'SUP, KABO!
OH... M-MORNING.
SO... I SAW YOU YESTERDAY.

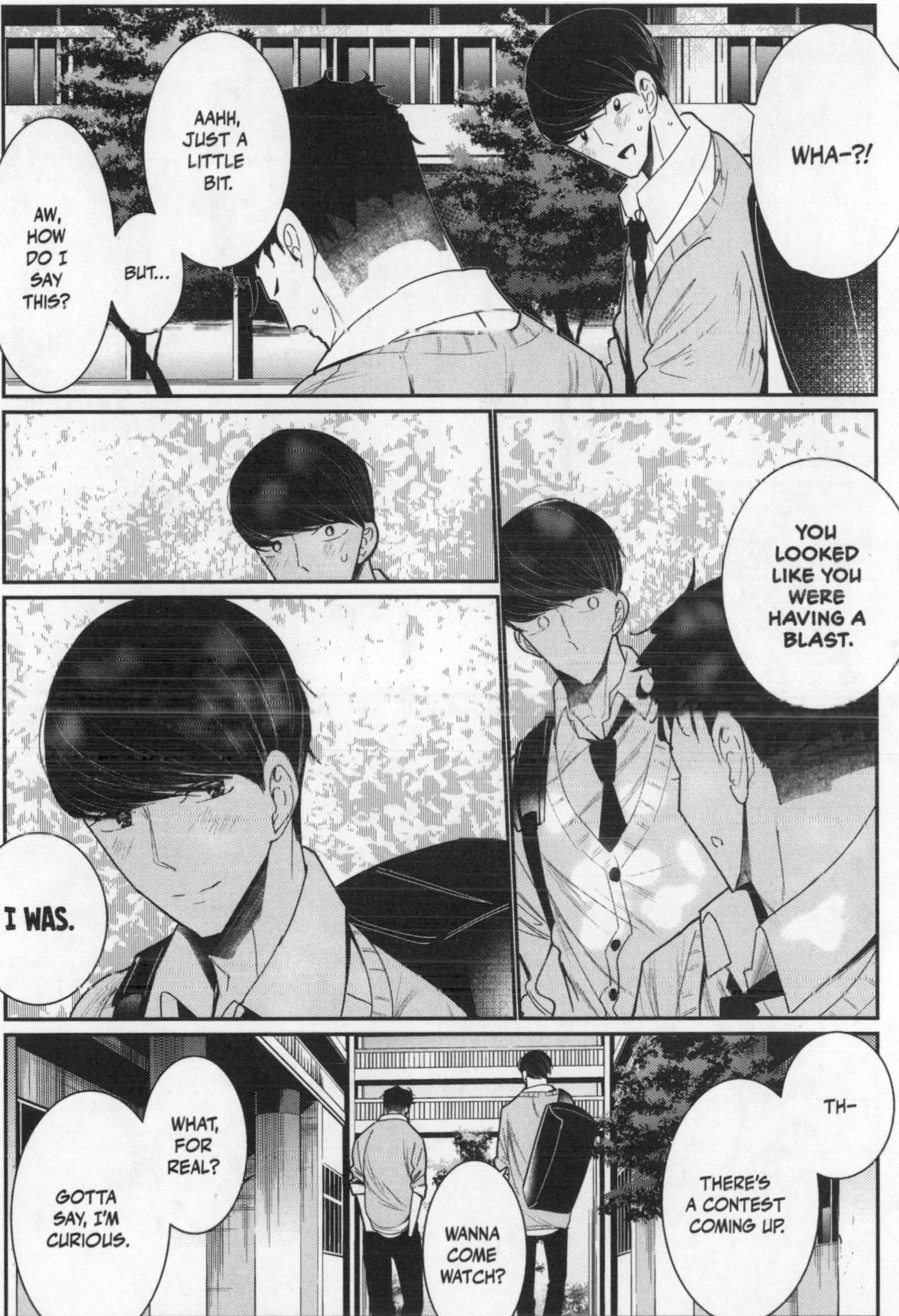
WHA-?!
AAHH, JUST A LITTLE BIT.
BUT...
AW, HOW DO I SAY THIS?
YOU LOOKED LIKE YOU WERE HAVING A BLAST.
I WAS.
TH-
THERE'S A CONTEST COMING UP.
WANNA COME WATCH?
WHAT, FOR REAL?
GOTTA SAY, I'M CURIOUS.

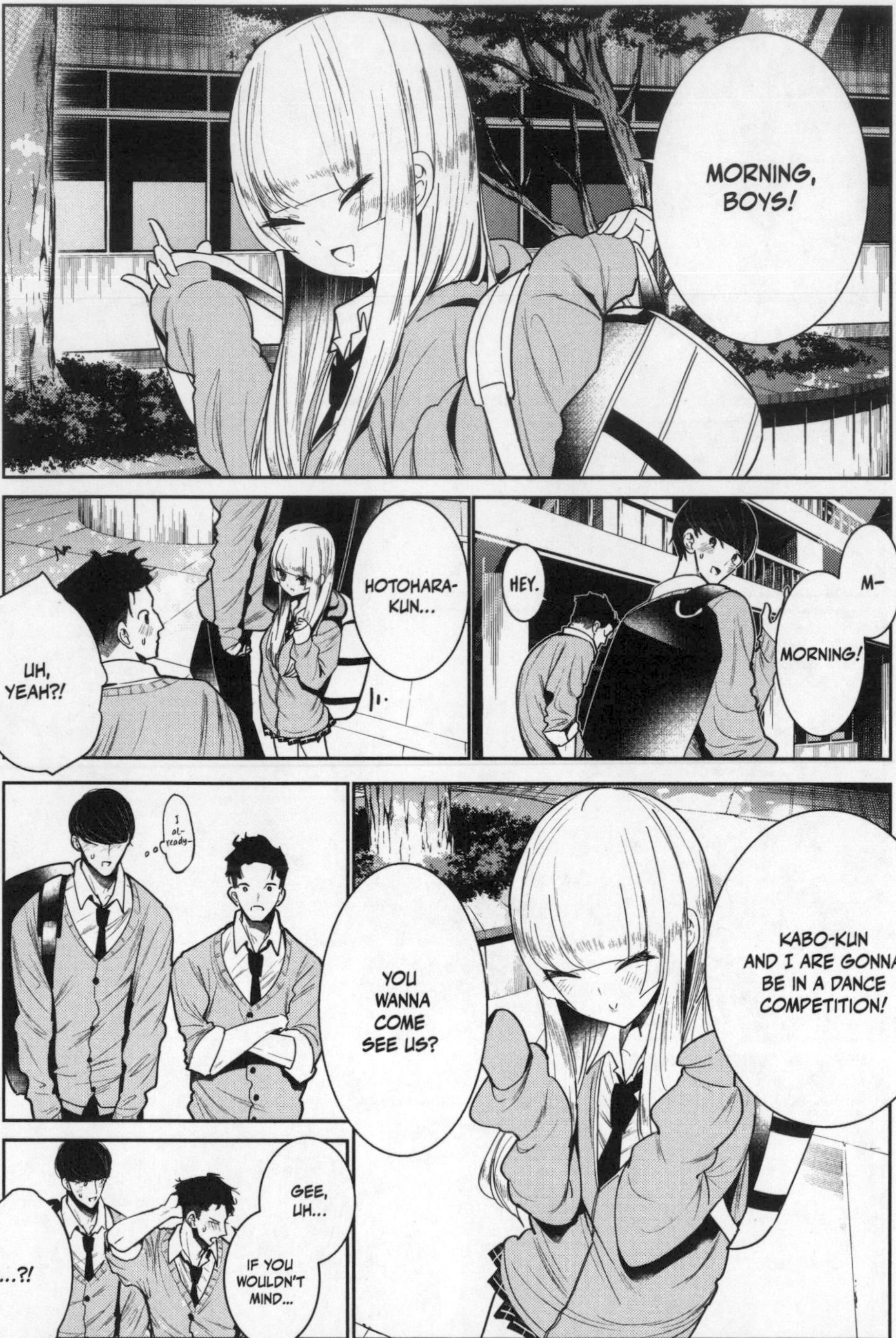
MORNING, BOYS!
M- MORNING!
HEY.
HOTOHARA-KUN...
UH, YEAH?!
KABO-KUN AND I ARE GONNA BE IN A DANCE COMPETITION!
YOU WANNA COME SEE US?
I al-ready-
GEE, UH...
IF YOU WOULDN'T MIND...
...?!

Ch. 3: END

Help with Materials
YUSUKE-SAMA (Arpeggio, SOUL TRIBE OSAKA, PLAYERS DANCE WORKS)
BEZI-SAMA (BUSTA JNKK BOOGIE)
YUKITOSHI SHIRASAKA-SAMA (The Dancing Math Teacher)
Uenomiya Senior High School Street Dance Club

Art Assistants
Bun'ya Kawaguchi-sama
Ayukan.-sama

WANDANCE

Bonus: Kotani-kun of the Dance Club Stutters

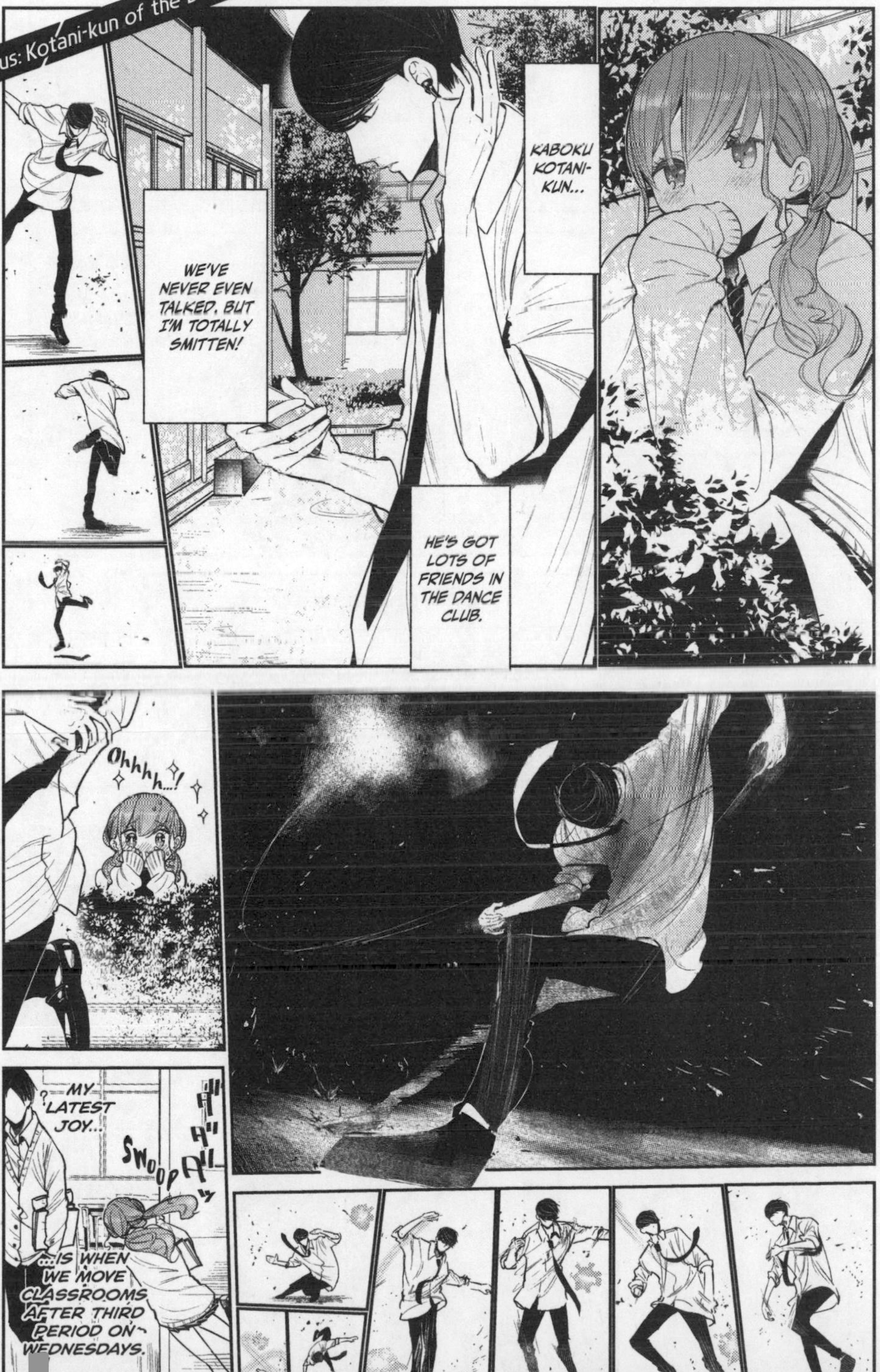
KABOKU KOTANI-KUN...
WE'VE NEVER EVEN TALKED. BUT I'M TOTALLY SMITTEN!
HE'S GOT LOTS OF FRIENDS IN THE DANCE CLUB.
Ohhhh...!
MY LATEST JOY...
SWOOP
...IS WHEN WE MOVE CLASSROOMS AFTER THIRD PERIOD ON WEDNESDAYS.

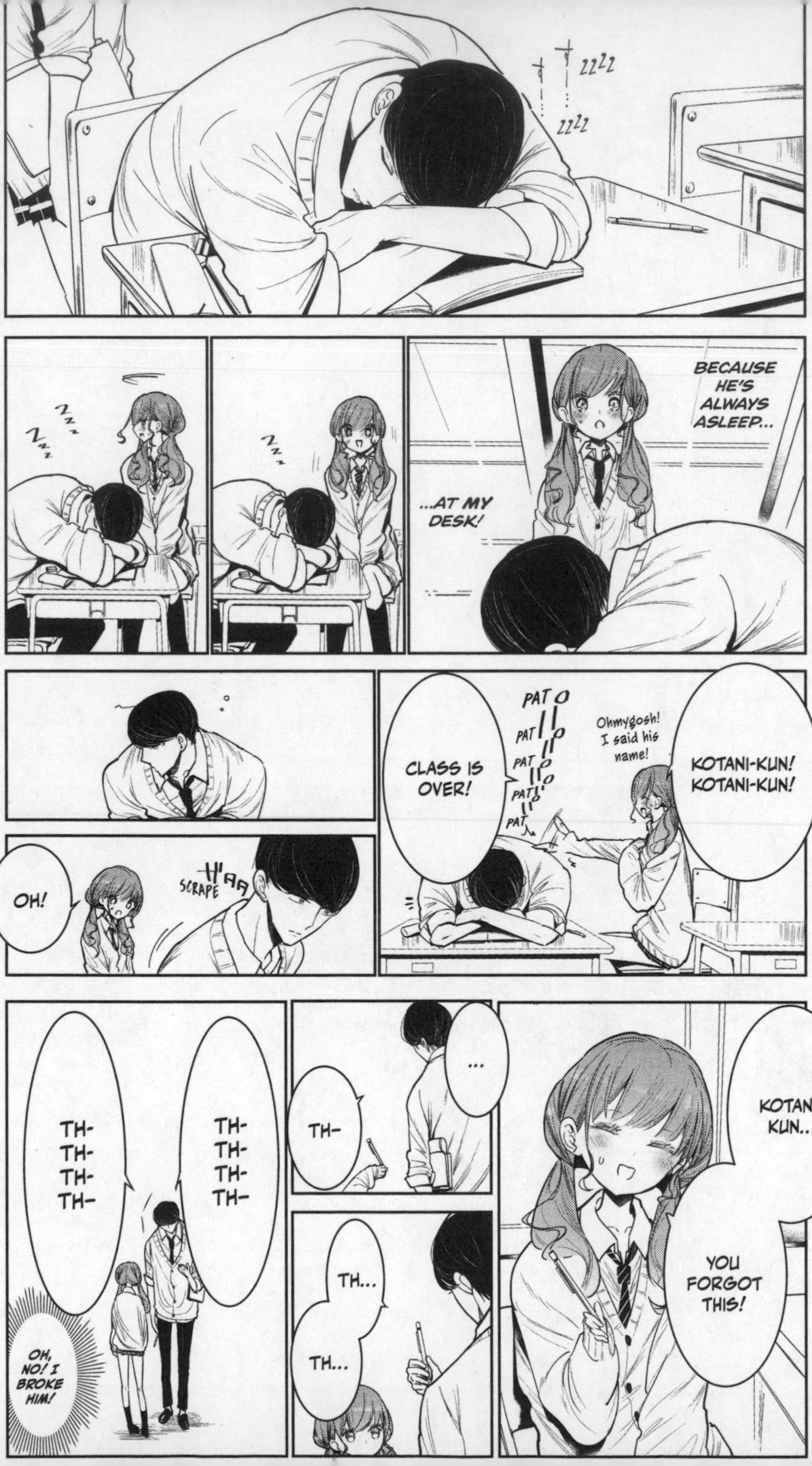
ZZZZ
ZZZZ
BECAUSE HE'S ALWAYS ASLEEP...
...AT MY DESK!
ZZZ
ZZZ
ZZZ
ZZZ
KOTANI-KUN! KOTANI-KUN!
Ohmygosh! I said his name!
PAT
PAT
PAT
PAT
PAT
CLASS IS OVER!
SCRAPE
OH!
KOTANI-KUN...
YOU FORGOT THIS!
...
TH-
TH...
TH...
TH- TH- TH- TH-
TH- TH- TH- TH-
OH, NO! I BROKE HIM!

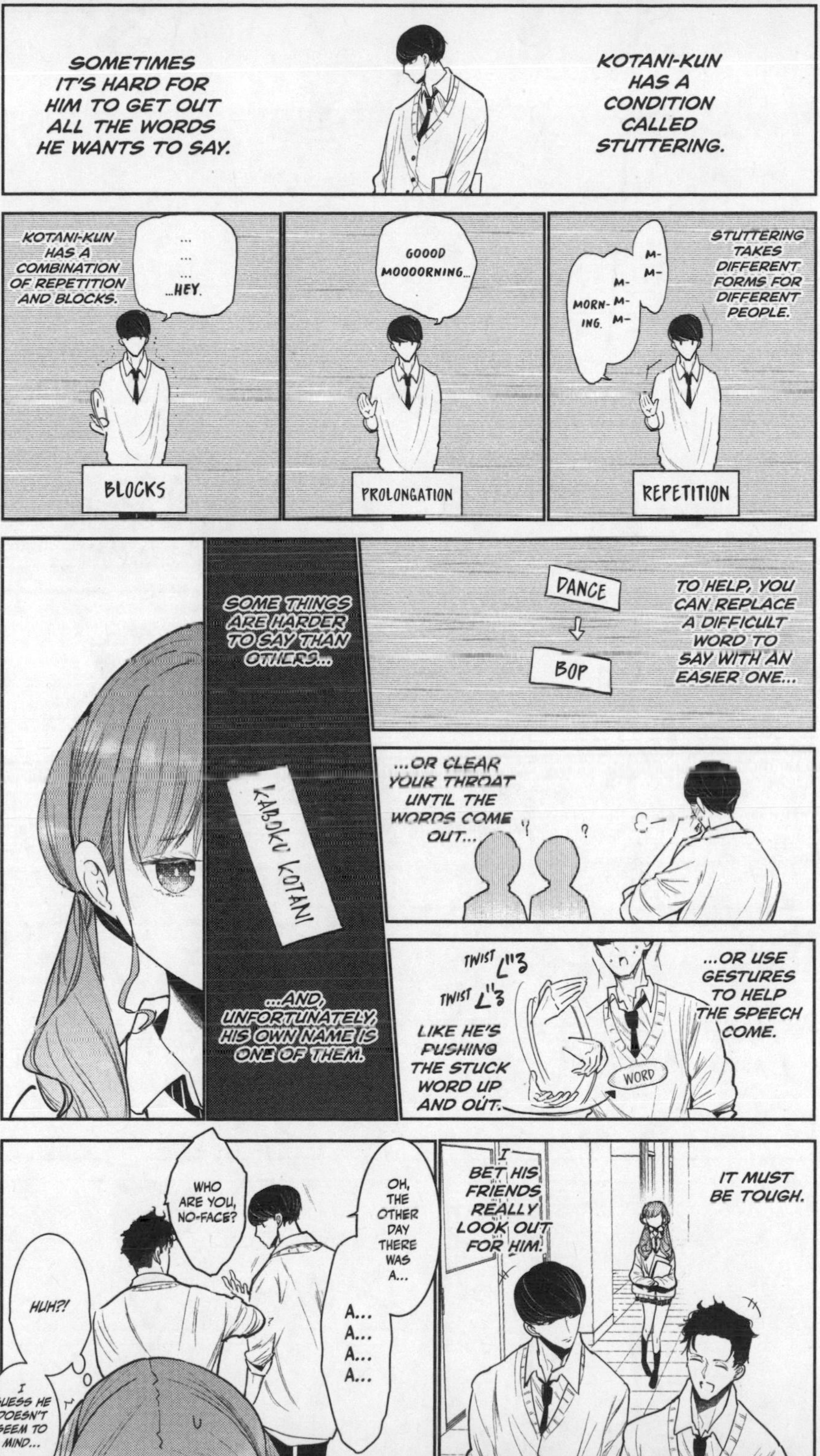
KOTANI-KUN HAS A CONDITION CALLED STUTTERING.
SOMETIMES IT'S HARD FOR HIM TO GET OUT ALL THE WORDS HE WANTS TO SAY.
STUTTERING TAKES DIFFERENT FORMS FOR DIFFERENT PEOPLE.
M- M- M- M- M- MORN- ING.
REPETITION
GOOOD MOOOORNING...
PROLONGATION
KOTANI-KUN HAS A COMBINATION OF REPETITION AND BLOCKS.
... ...HEY.
BLOCKS
TO HELP, YOU CAN REPLACE A DIFFICULT WORD TO SAY WITH AN EASIER ONE...
DANCE
BOP
...OR CLEAR YOUR THROAT UNTIL THE WORDS COME OUT...
...OR USE GESTURES TO HELP THE SPEECH COME.
TWIST ぐる
TWIST ぐる
LIKE HE'S PUSHING THE STUCK WORD UP AND OUT.
WORD
SOME THINGS ARE HARDER TO SAY THAN OTHERS...
KABOKU KOTANI
...AND, UNFORTUNATELY, HIS OWN NAME IS ONE OF THEM.
IT MUST BE TOUGH.
I BET HIS FRIENDS REALLY LOOK OUT FOR HIM.
OH, THE OTHER DAY THERE WAS A...
WHO ARE YOU, NO-FACE?
A... A... A... A...
HUH?!
I GUESS HE DOESN'T SEEM TO MIND...

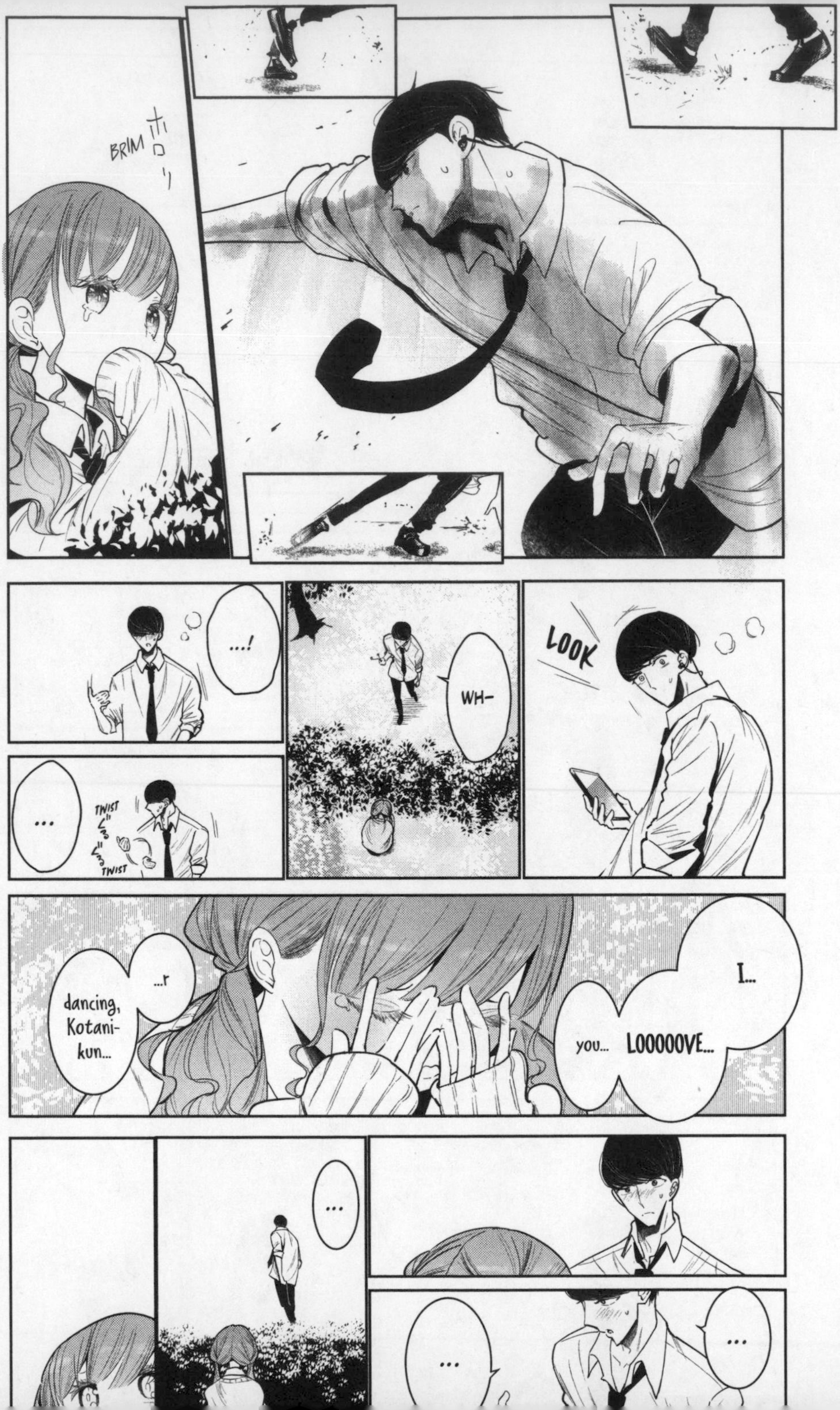
BRIM ポロリ
LOOK
WH-
...!
...
TWIST
TWIST
I... you... LOOOOOVE...
...r dancing, Kotani-kun...
...
...
...

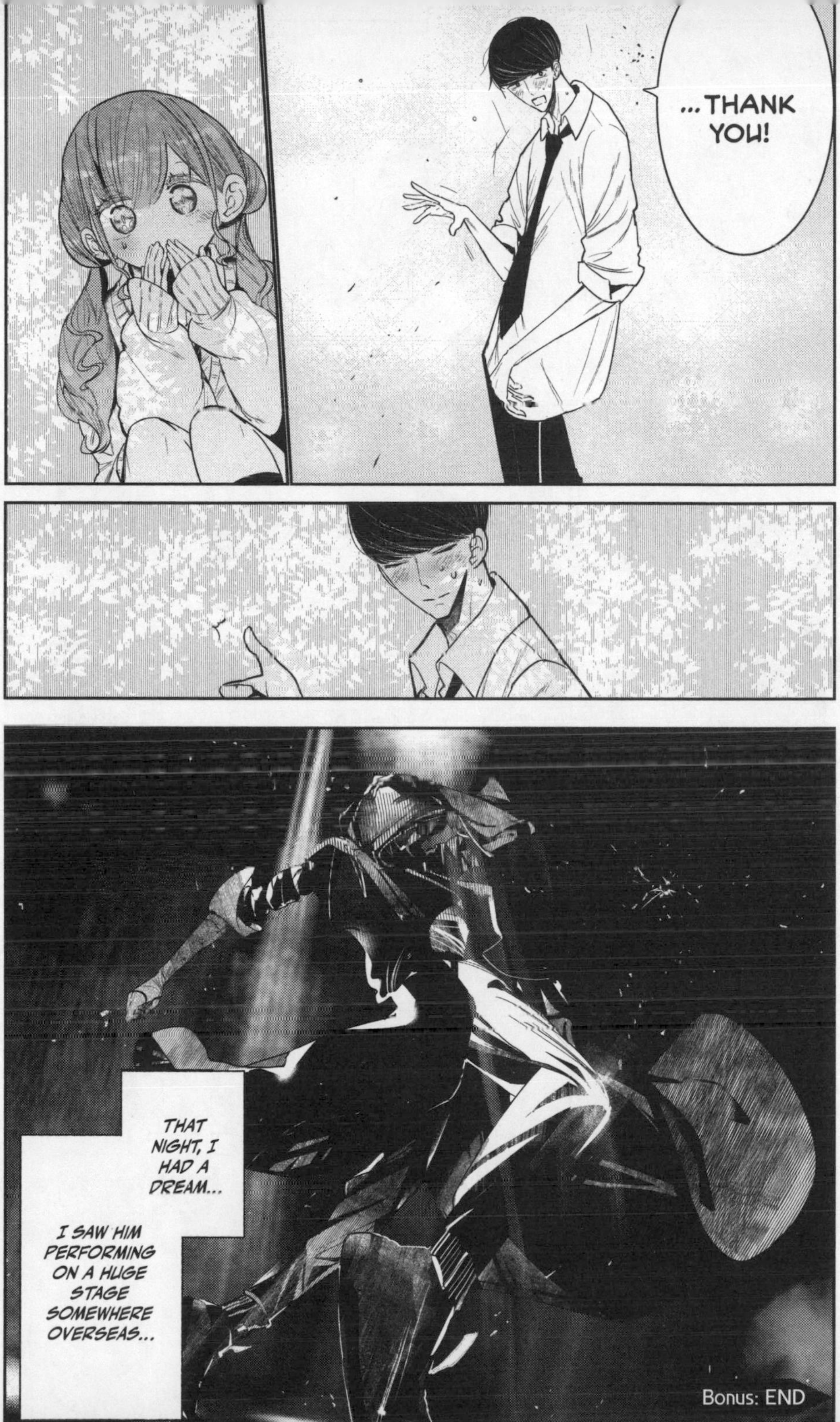
...THANK YOU!
THAT NIGHT, I HAD A DREAM...
I SAW HIM PERFORMING ON A HUGE STAGE SOMEWHERE OVERSEAS...
Bonus: END

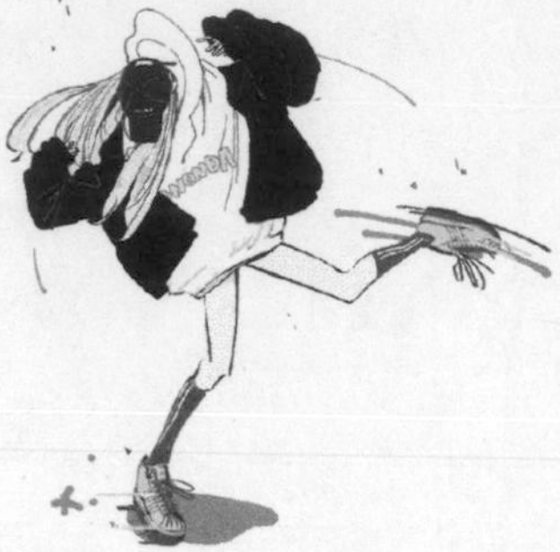
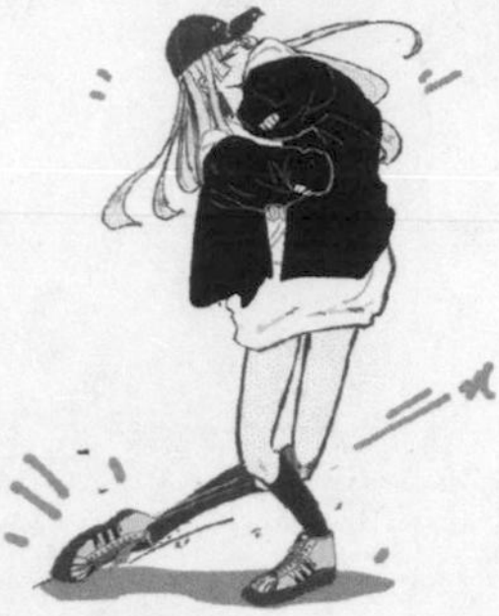
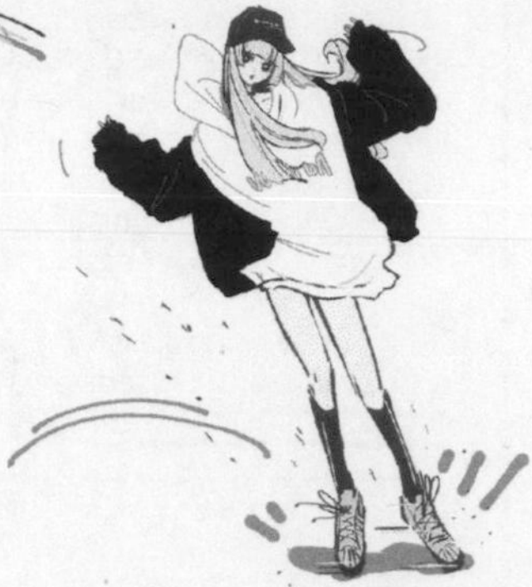
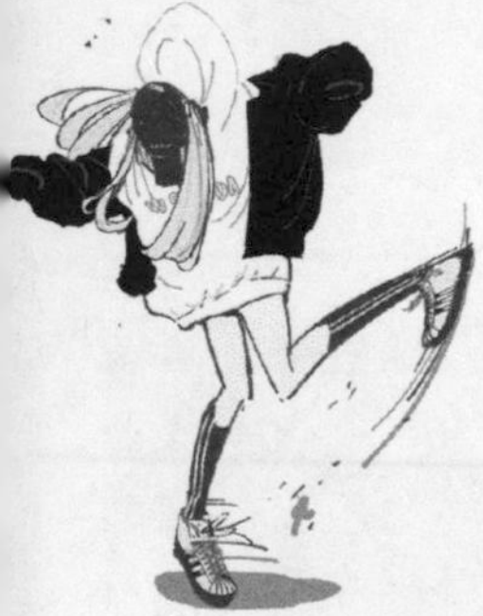
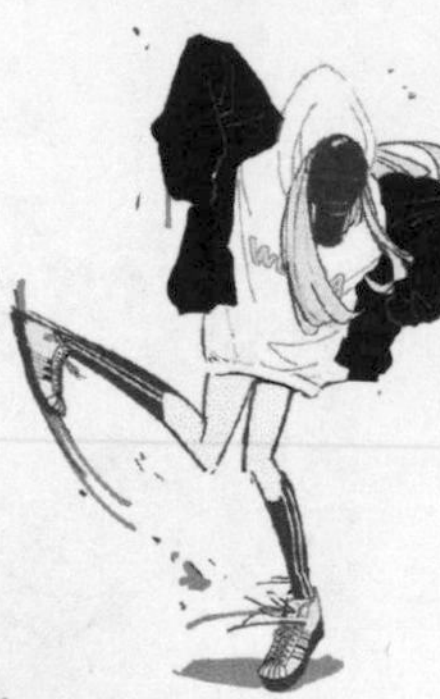

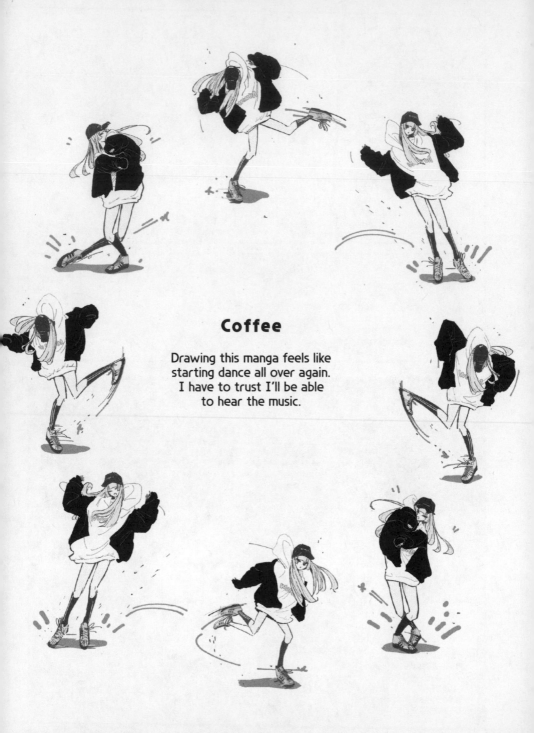

Coffee

Drawing this manga feels like
starting dance all over again.
I have to trust I'll be able
to hear the music.

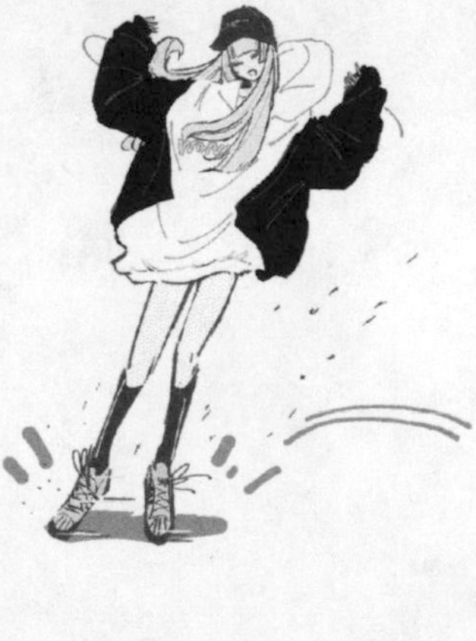
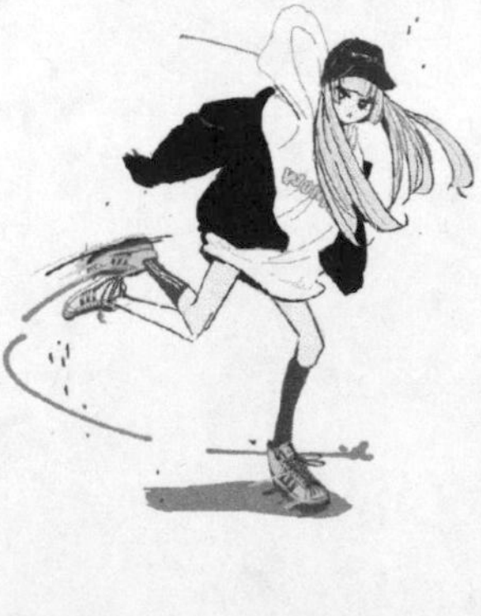
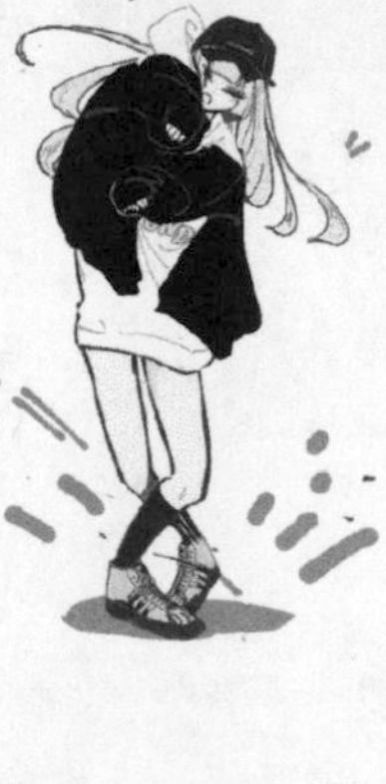

translation notes

Boy No. 14, page 9

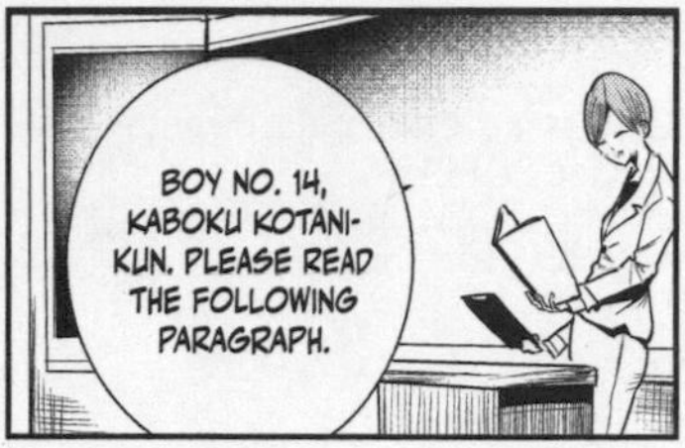
BOY NO. 14, KABOKU KOTANI-KUN. PLEASE READ THE FOLLOWING PARAGRAPH.

In some Japanese classrooms, students are assigned student numbers (*shusseki bangou*), which can be used to identify or call on them. Often, these numbers are assigned in alphabetical (or Japanese sound) order, and, in years past, all of the boys would come before any of the girls. Thus, even if a girl had a family name starting with "a" (which is at the beginning of the sound order in Japanese just as it's at the beginning of the alphabet in English), her student number would still come after that of any of the boys in the classroom. Increasingly, when student numbers are still used, they're assigned purely in name order, without regard to gender.

BOOSH, page 28

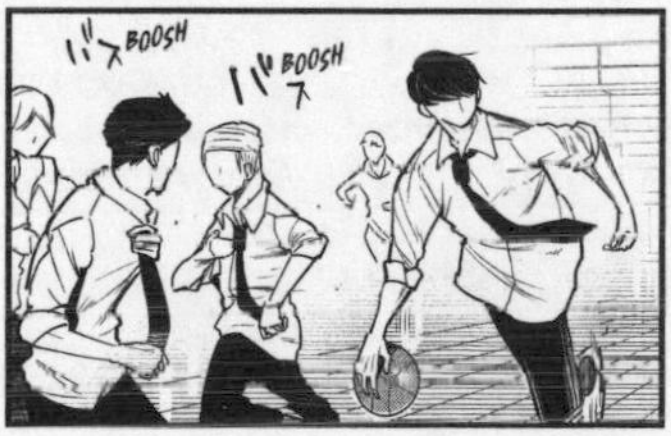
BOOSH
BOOSH

The sound effect here is the sound of the ball bouncing, but there's probably a bit of humor in the idea that the onomatopoeia for a bouncing basketball is *basu basu* ("basketball" being rendered as *basukettobooru* in Japanese).

Kaboku's Bookshelf, page 36

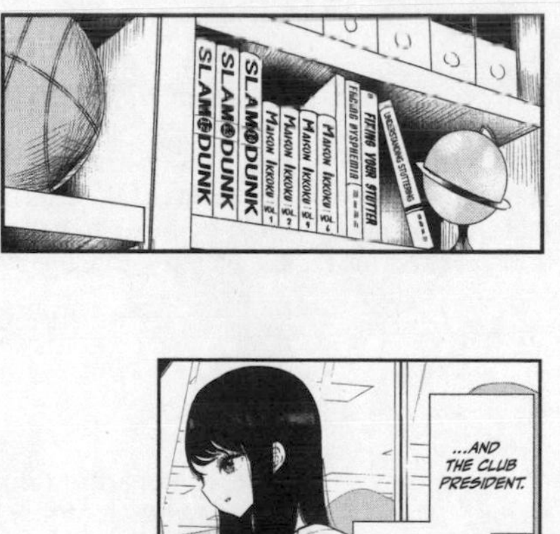
SLAM DUNK
SLAM DUNK
SLAM DUNK
MAISON IKKOKU VOL. 1
MAISON IKKOKU VOL. 2
MAISON IKKOKU VOL. 4
MAISON IKKOKU VOL. 6
FIXING YOUR STUTTER
UNDERSTANDING STUTTERING

In addition to his books on stuttering, Kaboku has several manga on his bookshelf. *Slam Dunk* is a famous basketball manga by Takehiko Inoue, while *Maison Ikkoku* is an early work by Rumiko Takahashi, who would go on to create *Ranma ½* and *Inuyasha*, among many other beloved series.

On Miyao, page 62

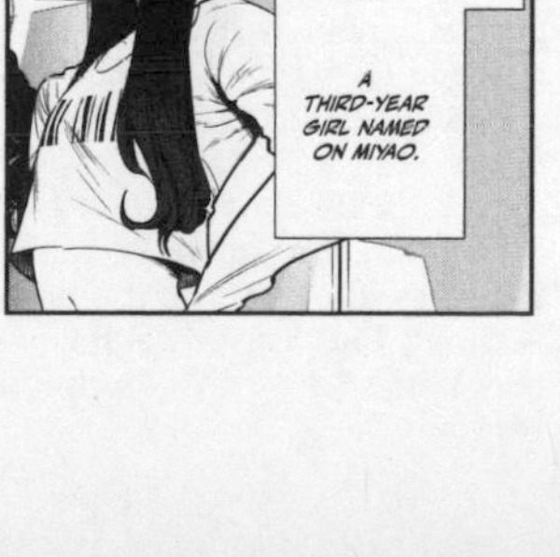
...AND THE CLUB PRESIDENT.
A THIRD-YEAR GIRL NAMED ON MIYAO.

The Dance Club president's given name uses the kanji for "favor" or "blessing." *Megumi* would probably be the more common reading of this character as a female name; however, the president's name uses the reading *on*, as in *ongaeshi* (to return a kindness). It's possible there's a pun here: the kanji 音, meaning "sound" or sometimes "music," can also be read as *on*.

translation notes

LINE, page 83

LINE is an extremely popular instant messaging app/service in Japan.

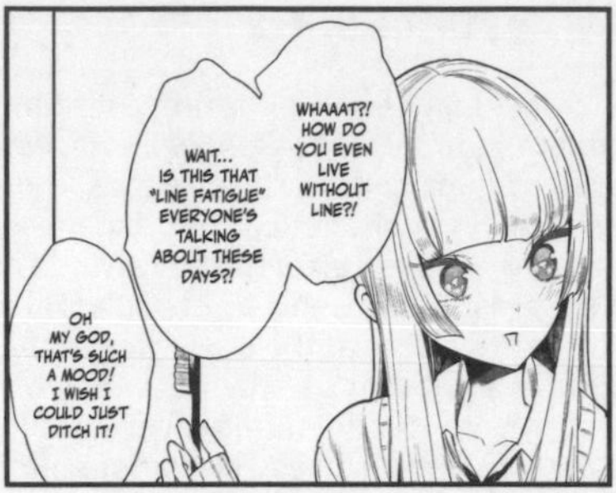
WHAAAT?! HOW DO YOU EVEN LIVE WITHOUT LINE?!
WAIT... IS THIS THAT "LINE FATIGUE" EVERYONE'S TALKING ABOUT THESE DAYS?!
OH MY GOD, THAT'S SUCH A MOOD! I WISH I COULD JUST DITCH IT!

Lockers, page 95

It's considered rude to wear outdoor footwear inside schools, homes, and some other buildings in Japan. Instead, at school, each student has a pair of slippers for indoor use. They're assigned a locker like the ones on this page where they put their outdoor shoes when they arrive in the morning (as Hikari is doing in the panel to the right), trading them for their slippers. (Every Japanese school also has a rack of slippers by the door for visitors' use.)

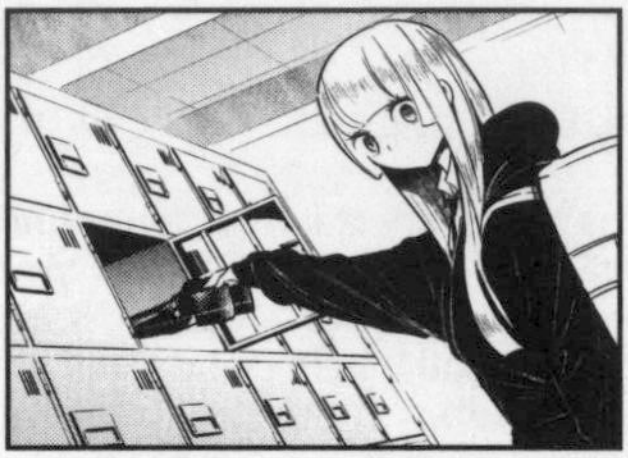

Greeting, page 116

When Kaboku greets the other members of the dance club in this panel, he actually says "good morning" (*ohayou gozaimasu*), even though it's the afternoon. This is common in many clubs and even a few office settings in Japan, but in terms of the translation (where a literal rendering would be likely to cause confusion), it makes the most sense simply to translate it as some form of "hello."

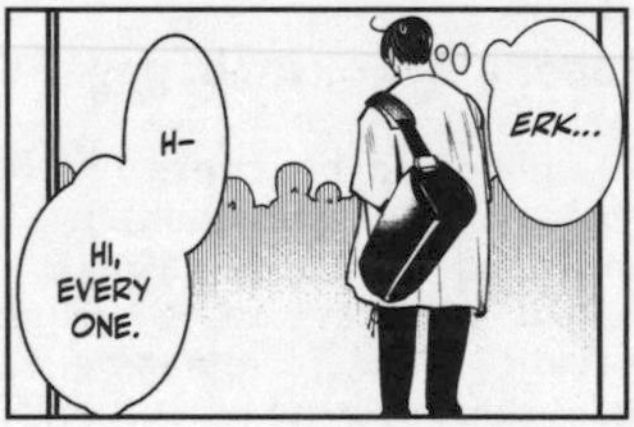
ERK...
H-
HI, EVERY ONE.

Mop Up, page 120

It's common in Japanese organizations, including school clubs, for the newest members—which, in practice, usually means the youngest members—to do cleaning and other necessary but tedious tasks. Partly this is because, hey, who doesn't want to have someone around to do the scut work? But it also helps the newest members become invested in the group, and means that when they move up in the hierarchy, they'll know what it's like to be at the bottom. (In some traditional settings, like a dojo, such work can also be considered part of the training or discipline.)

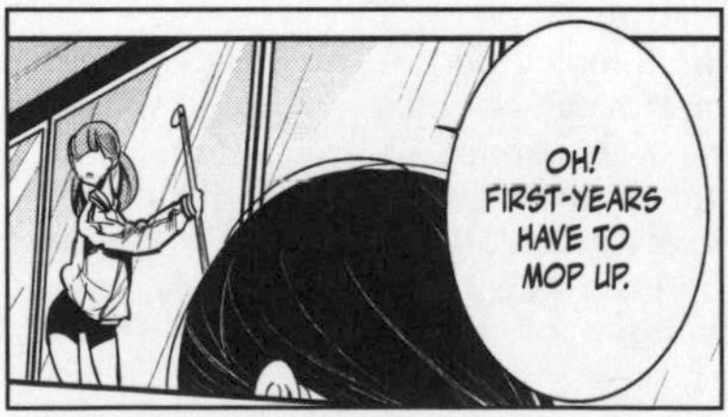
OH! FIRST-YEARS HAVE TO MOP UP.

translation notes

Faculty Advisors, page 160

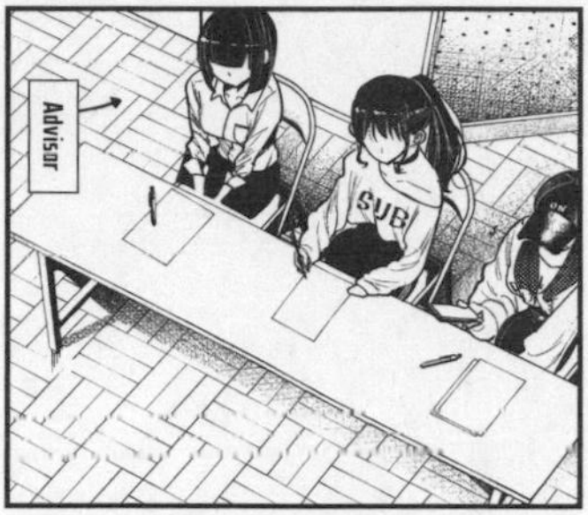
Advisor

All clubs at the high school level are required to have a faculty advisor, a member of the teaching staff associated with the club. This ensures that there's an adult available if the students need help with anything (like, say, renting a practice space), and, when the advisor has the relevant skills, they sometimes serve in a coaching capacity as well. Some advisors are heavily involved in their clubs, but others—whether because they lack the knowledge or because the students are highly capable of running the club themselves—keep their distance or aren't always present.

Move Classrooms, page 187

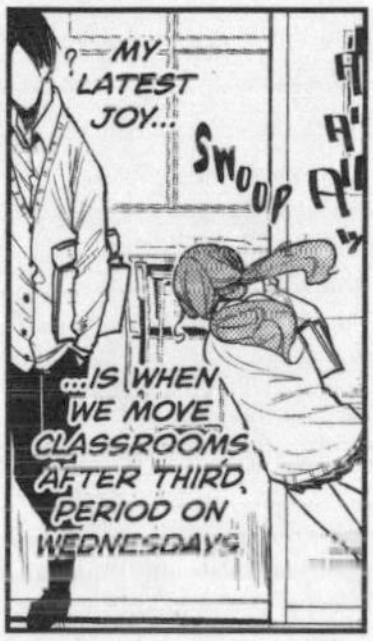
MY LATEST JOY...
SWOOP
...IS WHEN WE MOVE CLASSROOMS AFTER THIRD PERIOD ON WEDNESDAYS

Generally, Japanese high school students are assigned a single homeroom where they spend most or all of the day, and teachers, rather than students, switch rooms from period to period. However, sometimes students have to change rooms for particular subjects, especially if these require special equipment, like science or gym class. This is called *idou kyoushitsu* ("switching classrooms"). Exactly what class brings Kaboku into this young lady's classroom isn't entirely clear. (Occasionally, students move for electives, so it could just be some other class using the homeroom while its usual occupants are out.)

Dance/Bop, page 189

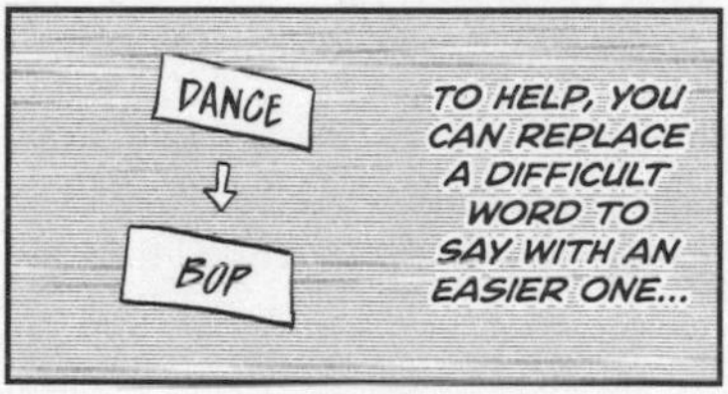
TO HELP, YOU CAN REPLACE A DIFFICULT WORD TO SAY WITH AN EASIER ONE...
DANCE
BOP

In the original Japanese, the example words Kaboku's crush lists here are *dansu*, "dance," which is written in katakana, and *odori*, the native Japanese term which is the verb for "to dance." Both are equally acceptable to use, (indeed, the characters in this manga favor the term *dansu*), but the *d* sound of *dansu* is tricky for Kaboku to produce, while the flowing vowels of *odori* are probably easier to say.

No-Face, page 189

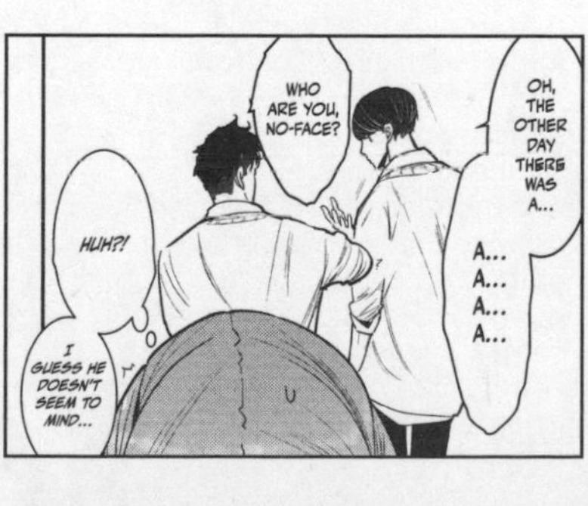
OH, THE OTHER DAY THERE WAS A...
WHO ARE YOU, NO-FACE?
HUH?!
A... A... A... A...
I GUESS HE DOESN'T SEEM TO MIND...

Here, Hotohara is making a reference to the character No-Face from Hayao Miyazaki's 2001 movie *Spirited Away*. Much of the character's dialogue consists of an insistent "Ah... Ah..." sound.

WANDANCE

Knight of the Ice

Yayoi Ogawa

Knight of the Ice ©Yayoi Ogawa/Kodansha Ltd.

SKATING THRILLS AND ICY CHILLS WITH THIS NEW TINGLY ROMANCE SERIES!

A rom-com on ice, perfect for fans of *Princess Jellyfish* and *Wotakoi*. Kokoro is the talk of the figure-skating world, winning trophies and hearts. But little do they know... he's actually a huge nerd! From the beloved creator of *You're My Pet* (*Tramps Like Us*).

Chitose is a serious young woman, working for the health magazine *SASSO*. Or at least, she would be, if she wasn't constantly getting distracted by her childhood friend, international figure skating star Kokoro Kijinami! In the public eye and on the ice, Kokoro is a gallant, flawless knight, but behind his glittery costumes and breathtaking spins lies a secret: He's actually a hopelessly romantic otaku, who can only land his quad jumps when Chitose is on hand to recite a spell from his favorite magical girl anime!

KC KODANSHA COMICS

A SMART, NEW ROMANTIC COMEDY FOR FANS OF *SHORTCAKE CAKE* AND *TERRACE HOUSE*!

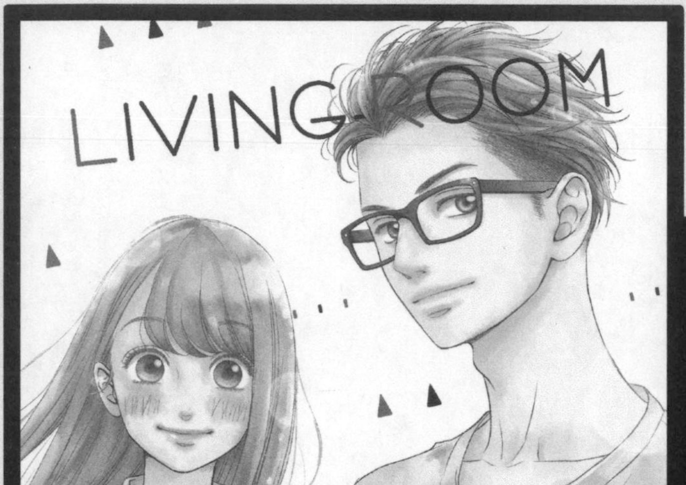
LIVING-ROOM
MATSUNAGA-SAN
1
Keiko Iwashita

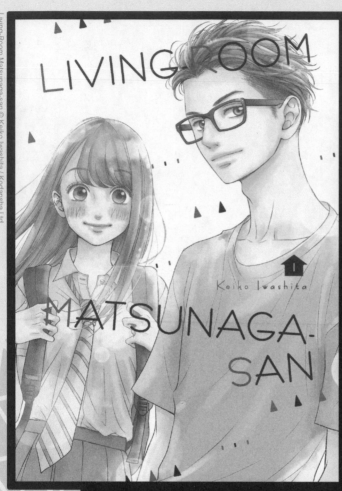

A romance manga starring high school girl Meeko, who learns to live on her own in a boarding house whose living room is home to the odd (but handsome) Matsunaga-san. She begins to adjust to her new life away from her parents, but Meeko soon learns that no matter how far away from home she is, she's still a young girl at heart — especially when she finds herself falling for Matsunaga-san.

PERFECT WORLD

Rie Aruga

A TOUCHING NEW SERIES ABOUT LOVE AND COPING WITH DISABILITY

An office party reunites Tsugumi with her high school crush Itsuki. He's realized his dream of becoming an architect, but along the way, he experienced a spinal injury that put him in a wheelchair. Now Tsugumi's rekindled feelings will butt up against prejudices she never considered — and Itsuki will have to decide if he's ready to let someone into his heart...

KC/ KODANSHA COMICS

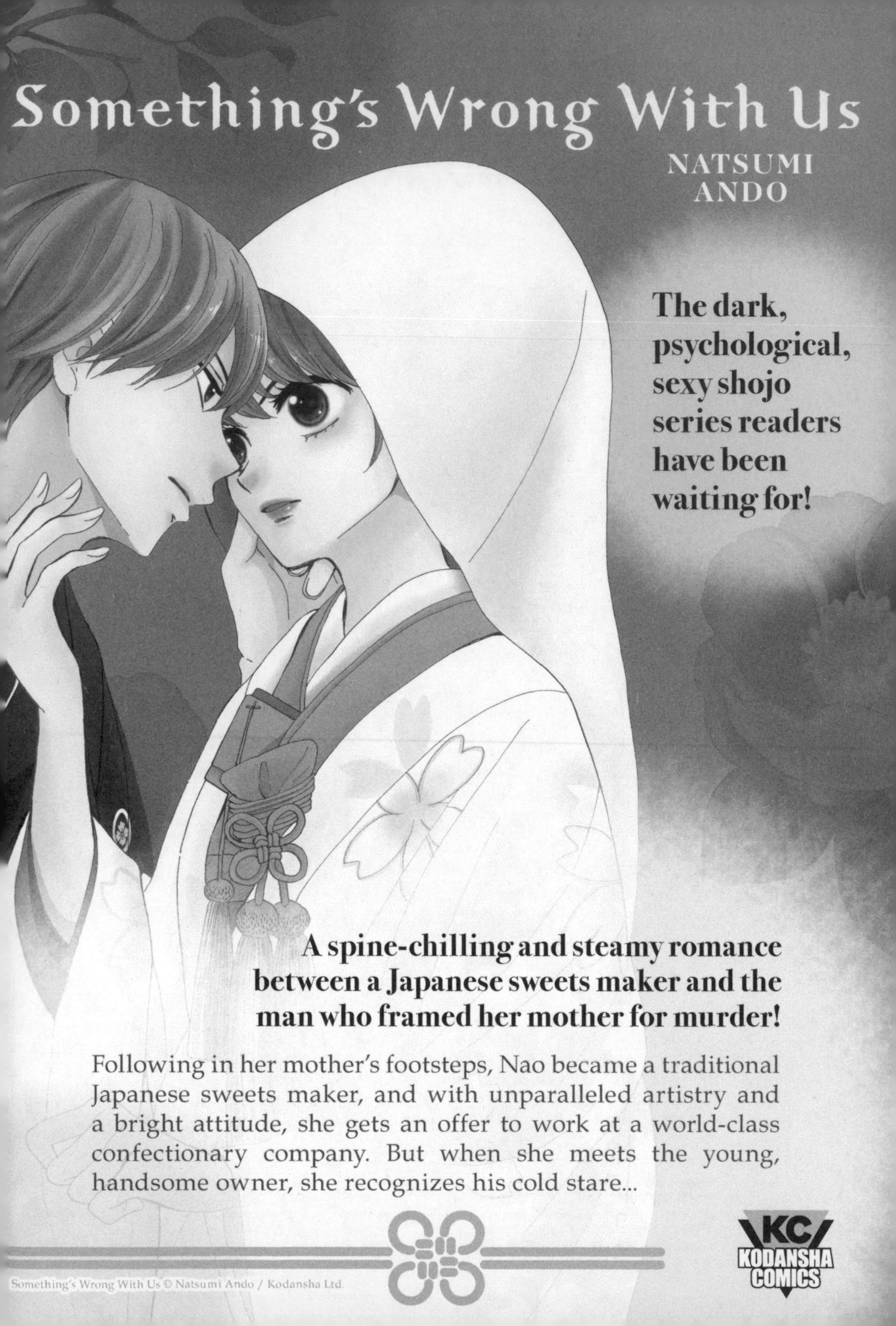
Something's Wrong With Us
NATSUMI ANDO
The dark, psychological, sexy shojo series readers have been waiting for!
A spine-chilling and steamy romance between a Japanese sweets maker and the man who framed her mother for murder!
Following in her mother's footsteps, Nao became a traditional Japanese sweets maker, and with unparalleled artistry and a bright attitude, she gets an offer to work at a world-class confectionary company. But when she meets the young, handsome owner, she recognizes his cold stare...
KC KODANSHA COMICS
Something's Wrong With Us © Natsumi Ando / Kodansha Ltd.

THE SWEET SCENT OF LOVE IS IN THE AIR! FOR FANS OF OFFBEAT ROMANCES LIKE *WOTAKOI*

Sweat and Soap © Kintetsu Yamada / Kodansha Ltd.

In an office romance, there's a fine line between sexy and awkward... and that line is where Asako — a woman who sweats copiously — meets Koutarou — a perfume developer who can't get enough of Asako's, er, scent. Don't miss a romcom manga like no other!

Young characters and steampunk setting, like *Howl's Moving Castle* and *Battle Angel Alita*

Beyond the Clouds © 2018 Nicke / Ki-oon

A boy with a talent for machines and a mysterious girl whose wings he's fixed will take you beyond the clouds! In the tradition of the high-flying, resonant adventure stories of Studio Ghibli comes a gorgeous tale about the longing of young hearts for adventure and friendship!

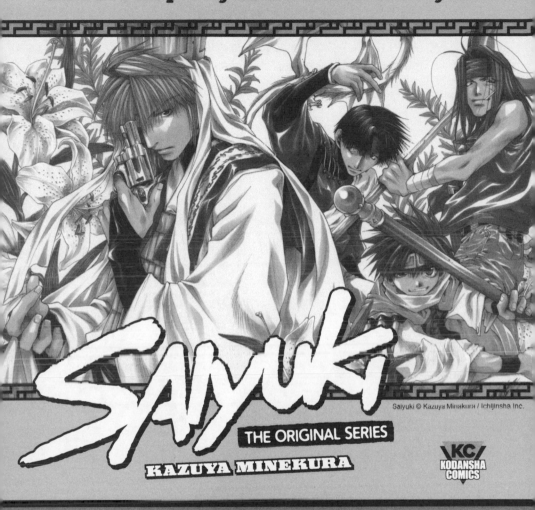

The art-deco cyberpunk classic from the creators of *xxxHOLiC* and *Cardcaptor Sakura*!

"Starred Review.
This experimental
sci-fi work from
CLAMP reads like a
romantic version of
AKIRA."
—Publishers Weekly

CLOVER © CLAMP-ShigatsuTsuitachi CO.,LTD./Kodansha Ltd.

Su was born into a bleak future, where the government keeps tight control over children with magical powers—codenamed "Clovers." With Su being the only "four-leaf" Clover in the world, she has been kept isolated nearly her whole life. Can ex-military agent Kazuhiko deliver her to the happiness she seeks? Experience the complete series in this hardcover edition, which also includes over twenty pages of ravishing color art!

MAGIC ● KNIGHT RAYEARTH
25TH ANNIVERSARY EDITION
CLAMP

A BELOVED CLASSIC MAKES ITS STUNNING RETURN IN THIS GORGEOUS, LIMITED EDITION BOX SET!

This tale of three Tokyo teenagers who cross through a magical portal and become the champions of another world is a modern manga classic. The box set includes three volumes of manga covering the entire first series of *Magic Knight Rayearth*, plus the series's super-rare full-color art book companion, all printed at a larger size than ever before on premium paper, featuring a newly-revised translation and lettering, and exquisite foil-stamped covers. A strictly limited edition, this will be gone in a flash!

The beloved characters from *Cardcaptor Sakura* return in a brand new, reimagined fantasy adventure!

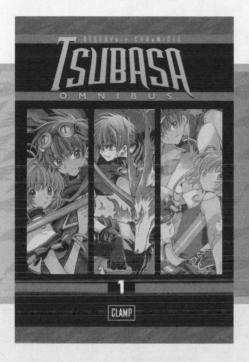

"[*Tsubasa*] takes readers on a fantastic ride that only gets more exhilarating with each successive chapter." —Anime News Network

In the Kingdom of Clow, an archaeological dig unleashes an incredible power, causing Princess Sakura to lose her memories. To save her, her childhood friend Syaoran must follow the orders of the Dimension Witch and travel alongside Kurogane, an unrivaled warrior; Fai, a powerful magician; and Mokona, a curiously strange creature, to retrieve Sakura's dispersed memories!

"Clever, sassy, and original....*xxxHOLiC* has the inherent hallmarks of a runaway hit."
—NewType magazine

Beautifully seductive artwork and uniquely Japanese depictions of the supernatural will hypnotize CLAMP fans!

Kimihiro Watanuki is haunted by visions of ghosts and spirits. He seeks help from a mysterious woman named Yuko, who claims she can help. However, Watanuki must work for Yuko in order to pay for her aid. Soon Watanuki finds himself employed in Yuko's shop, where he sees things and meets customers that are stranger than anything he could have ever imagined.

The adorable new odd-
couple cat comedy manga
from the creator of the
beloved *Chi's Sweet Home*,
in full color!

Praise for Chi's Sweet Home

"Nearly
impossible to
turn away... a true
all-ages title that
anyone, young or old,
cat lover or not, will
enjoy. The stories will
bring a smile to your
face and warm
your heart."

~School Library Journal

Sue & Tai-chan

Konami Kanata

Sue is an aging housecat who's looking forward to living out her life in
peace... but her plans change when the mischievous black tomcat Tai-
chan enters the picture! Hey! Sue never signed up to be a catsitter!
Sue & Tai-chan is the latest from the reigning meow-narch of cute kitty
comics, Konami Kanata.

THE MAGICAL GIRL CLASSIC THAT BROUGHT A GENERATION OF READERS TO MANGA, NOW BACK IN A DEFINITIVE, HARDCOVER COLLECTOR'S EDITION!

CARDCAPTOR SAKURA
COLLECTOR'S EDITION

CLAMP

KODANSHA COMICS
I
DELUXE • EDITION
Cardcaptor Sakura
CLAMP

Ten-year-old Sakura Kinomoto lives a pretty normal life with her older brother, Tōya, and widowed father, Fujitaka—until the day she discovers a strange book in her father's library, and her life takes a magical turn...

- A deluxe large-format hardcover edition of CLAMP's shojo manga classic
- All-new foil-stamped cover art on each volume
- Comes with exclusive collectible art card

KC KODANSHA COMICS

[redacted]

Wandance 1 is a work of fiction. Names, characters, places, and incidents are the products of the author's imagination or are used fictitiously. Any resemblance to actual events, locales, or persons, living or dead, is entirely coincidental.

A Kodansha Trade Paperback Original

Published in the United States by
Kodansha USA Publishing, LLC, New York.

Publication rights for this English edition arranged through
Kodansha Ltd., Tokyo.

First published in Japan in 2019 by Kodansha Ltd., Tokyo.

ISBN 978-1-64651-466-3

Printed in the United States of America.

9 8 7 6 5 4 3 2 1

Translation: Kevin Steinbach
Lettering: Nicole Roderick
Editing: Tiff Joshua TJ Ferentini
Kodansha USA Publishing edition cover design by Adam Del Re

Publisher: Kiichiro Sugawara

Director of Publishing Services: Ben Applegate
Director of Publishing Operations: Dave Barrett
Associate Director of Publishing Operations: Stephen Pakula
Publishing Services Managing Editors: Alanna Ruse, Madison Salters
Production Managers: Emi Lotto, Angela Zurlo

KODANSHA.US

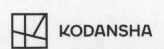

KODANSHA